3/95

AMERICAN WOMEN HUMORISTS

GARLAND STUDIES IN HUMOR
(VOL. 4)

GARLAND REFERENCE LIBRARY
OF THE HUMANITIES
(VOL. 1500)

GARLAND STUDIES IN HUMOR
Steven H. Gale, General Editor

AMERICAN WOMEN HUMORISTS
Critical Essays

Edited by
Linda A. Morris

Garland Publishing, Inc. • New York and London
1994

Library of Congress Cataloging-in-Publication Data

American women humorists : critical essays / [edited by] Linda A. Morris.
  p. cm. — (Garland studies in humor ; vol. 4) (Garland reference library of the humanities ; vol. 1500)
  Includes bibliographical references
  ISBN 0-8153-0622-9 (acid-free paper)
  1. American wit and humor—Women authors—History and criticism. 2. Women and literature—United States—history.
I. Morris, Linda. II. Series. III. Series: Garland reference library of the humanities ; vol. 1500.
  PS430.A49 1994
  817.009'9287—dc20   93-21788
                                                                       CIP

Printed on acid-free, 250-year-life paper
Manufactured in the United States of America

CONTENTS

Contents

GENERAL EDITOR'S NOTE

Linda A. Morris's *American Women Humorists: Critical Essays* is the fourth volume in Garland's Studies in Humor series. Each volume in the series is devoted to an assessment of the work of an individual major humorist or group of authors within a specified category and consists of collections of both previously published and original articles on subjects such as S.J. Perelman, Black Humor, Mark Twain, Geoffrey Chaucer, Classical Greek and Roman Humorists, and Woody Allen, among others.

The intent behind this series is to supply in a single volume a representative sample of the best critical reactions by the humorist's contemporaries (when available) and from subsequent scholarly assessments. Typically, the contents of each volume will include a chronology of the author's life and writing; the volume editor's introduction to the writer's canon; reviews (book, play, and/or film); interviews when appropriate; essays focusing on specific works (this section may contain both journal articles and parts of books); general essays treating particular aspects of the humorist's canon; a selected, annotated bibliography; and an index. This structure provides access to essential scholarship (some of which may no longer be easily obtainable) on the most important and best examples of the humorist's work, along with popular reactions to that work, and allows for comparisons to be made in critical and popular reactions over the course of the writer's career.

For her collection of articles on American women humorists, Morris has chosen pieces that approach their topics in a variety of ways. There are twenty-one selections by preeminent scholars in the field included; one, Jacqueline O'Connor's essay on Anna Cora Mowatt, was written expressly for this volume. In addition, Morris has included a comprehensive introduction, a bibliography, and an index.

Morris's objective in choosing the volume's contents was to provide a historical overview of both women's humor and the criticism of that humor that has been published from its beginnings through the twentieth century. She presents the essays in three categories: introductory essays to anthologies of American women's humor; articles devoted to exploring specific topics; and examinations of individual eighteenth-through twentieth-century humorists.

The elements of the critical discourse represented by these essays are brought together in *American Women Humorists: Critical Essays* in a way that makes the works clearer and more accessible as well as bringing readers a better understanding of the general subject and individual authors. It is especially valuable to be able to see how critical opinions and emphases have changed over the years, as is evident when the comments of the earliest published scholar of women humorists, Kate Sanborn, are compared with observations made in the late twentieth century by critics such as O'Connor and Morris herself. By looking at classic studies of American women's humor and new genres of that humor, the reader can determine the distinguishing qualities of the humor written by women in America.

Linda A. Morris is a senior lecturer and director of Women's Studies at the University of California at Davis. She is the author of *Women's Humor in the Age of Gentility: The Life and Works of Frances Miriam Whitcher* and *Women Vernacular Humorists in Nineteenth-Century America: Ann Stephens, Frances Whitcher, and Marietta Holley.*

Steven H. Gale
Kentucky State University

ACKNOWLEDGMENTS

In editing this collection of essays on women's humor in America, I have been assisted in every phase of the project by Tania Hammidi. Without her help, and her patience, this project simply would have been impossible; with her collaboration, however, the process has been (mainly) a pleasure. In preparing the final edited copy, I was also ably assisted by Peter Reichert. A faculty research grant from the University of California, Davis, supported the editing and bibliographic research for this collection.

The following publishers have generously given permission to use extended quotations from copyrighted works:

Martha Bensley Bruère and Mary Beard, "Introduction," *Laughing Their Way: Women's Humor in America*, New York: Macmillan, 1934. Reprinted with permission of Arlene Beard and Detlev Vagts.

Suzanne L. Bunkers, "'I am Outraged Womanhood': Dorothy Parker as Feminist and Social Critic," *Regionalism and the Female Imagination* (1978): 25–34. Reprinted with the permission of the author.

Jane Curry, "Introduction," *Samantha Rastles the Woman Question*, Urbana: University of Illinois Press, 1983, pp. 1–19. Reprinted with the permission of the author and the University of Illinois Press. Copyright 1983 by the Board of Trustees of the University of Illinois.

Zita Dresner, "Heterodite Humor: Alice Duer Miller and Florence Guy Seabury," *Journal of American Culture* 10.3 (1987): 33–38. Reprinted with the permission of the *Journal of American Culture*, American Culture Association, and Bowling Green State University Press.

Gloria Kaufman, "Introduction," in *Pulling Our Own Strings: Feminist Humor and Satire*, ed. by Gloria Kaufman and Mary K. Blakely. Bloomington: Indiana University Press,

1980, pp. 13–16. Reprinted with the permission of Gloria Kaufman.

Judy Little, "Humoring the Sentence: Women's Dialogic Comedy," in *Women's Comic Visions*, ed. by June Sochen, Detroit: Wayne State University Press, 1991, pp. 19–32. Reprinted by permission of the Wayne State University Press and June Sochen. Copyright 1991 by Wayne State University Press.

John Lowe, "Hurston, Humor, and the Harlem Renaissance," in *The Harlem Renaissance Re-examined*, ed. by Victor Kramer, New York: AMS Press, 1987, pp. 283–313. Reprinted with the permission of AMS Press, New York.

Lucinda H. MacKethan, "Mother Wit: Humor in Afro-American Women's Autobiography," *Studies in American Humor* 4:1+2 (Spring/Summer 1985): 51–61. Reprinted with the permission of *Studies in American Humor*.

Linda A. Morris, "Frances Miriam Whitcher: Social Satire in the Age of Gentility," in *Last Laughs: Perspectives on Women and Comedy*, ed. Regina Barreca. Originally published in *Women's Studies* 15, 1–3 (1988): 99–116. Copyright Gordon and Breach Science Publishers. Reproduced with permission.

Jacqueline O'Connor, "The Play's the Thing: Anna Cora Mowatt Catches the *Fashion* Conscience." Printed with the permission of the author. Copyright 1992 by Jacqueline O'Connor.

Thomas F. O'Donnell, "The Return of the Widow Bedott: Mrs. F. M. Whitcher of Whitesboro and Elmira," *New York History* 55 (January 1974): 5–35. Reprinted with permission of New York State Historical Association, Cooperstown, N.Y.

Linda Pershing, "There's a Joker in the Menstrual Hut: A Performance Analysis of Comedian Kate Clinton," in *Women's Comic Visions*, ed. by June Sochen, Detroit: Wayne State University Press, 1991, pp. 199–236. Reprinted by permission of the Wayne State University Press and June Sochen. Copyright 1991 by Wayne State University Press.

Alice Sheppard, "From Kate Sanborn to Feminist Psychology: The Social Context of Women's Humor, 1885–1985," *Psychology of Women Quarterly* 10 (1986): 155–69. Reprinted with the permission of the author and Cambridge University Press.

Peter Thorpe, "Sarah Kemble Knight and the Picaresque Tradition," *CLA Journal*, 10 (December 1966), 114–21. Reprinted by permission of the College Language Association.

Emily Toth, "A Laughter of Their Own: Women's Humor in the United States," in *Critical Essays on American Humor*, ed. by William Bedford Clark and W. Craig Turner, New York: G.K. Hall, 1984, pp. 199–215. Reprinted with permission of G. K. Hall and Co., an imprint of Macmillan Publishing Company. Copyright 1984 by William Bedford Clark and Willard Craig Turner.

Nancy Walker, "Wit, Sentimentality, and the Image of Women in the Nineteenth Century," *American Studies*, 22.2 (Fall 1981): 5–22. Reprinted with permission.

Nancy Walker and Zita Dresner, "Introduction," in *Redressing the Balance: American Women's Literary Humor from Colonial Times to the 1980s.* Jackson: University Press of Mississippi, 1988, pp. xv–xxxiv. Reprinted by permission of the University Press of Mississippi.

Naomi Weisstein, "Why We Aren't Laughing . . . Any More," *Ms.* 2.2 (Nov. 1973): 49–51+. Reprinted with the permission of the author.

Ann Douglas Wood, "The 'Scribbling Women' and Fanny Fern: Why Women Wrote," *American Quarterly* 23 (Spring 1971): 3–24. Reprinted with the permission of the author, *American Quarterly*, and the American Studies Association. Copyright 1971.

INTRODUCTION

W riting in 1885, Kate Sanborn, the earliest published scholar of American women's humor, attempted to put to rest the male contention that women have no sense of humor; nearly a century later, critics would still be addressing variations on the same theme, for until the last decade and a half, women's literary humor in America has remained virtually unexplored territory. By the mid-1970s, however, critics had the pleasure of rediscovering a host of forgotten writers and a long tradition of women's humor, and of extending their consideration to issues such as the distinguishing characteristics of women's humor. These early critics began also to explore the relationships between women's humor and the changing social, economic, and cultural circumstances of women's lives, and the relationships between humor and personal biography. Scholarship in the 1970s and early 1980s, focused, too, upon social and political dimensions of women's humor, and they exposed its subversive qualities, its challenges to the assumptions of the dominant culture.

As with other feminist scholars, the critics of women's humor worked across traditional disciplinary boundaries and found theoretical bases for their analyses wherever the ground seemed most productive—in literary theory, in psychology and anthropology, in the writings of Freud and Henri Bergson. Still, scholarship on women's humor was a fledgling art until only a few years ago when a flurry of publishing activities suggested that scholarly interest in women's humor was now "serious business." Wayne State University Press, for example, is developing an ongoing series of books on women's humor, and at least three collections of new essays on women's humor have appeared in the last several years.[1] In the popular arena, women comedians are no longer a rarity, a number of women cartoonists are now nationally syndicated in newspapers, and women's television and film humor is claiming a significant portion of the national audience. New studies of humor are emerging, by a new generation of scholars, to interpret and appreciate the humor that has virtually burst upon the American scene. It is time, then, to reflect upon the state of our art, to celebrate our past accomplishments, and to anticipate new directions in the scholarship on American women's humor.

The primary purpose of this work is to collect the "classic" essays on American women's humor, the essays that informed our initial thinking about women's humor, and the essays that are cited frequently by contemporary scholars of women's humor. Some of these early essays, because of the publication history of criticism on women's humor, are not always readily available to today's students and scholars. For example, in the late 1970s, the only journal to devote an issue exclusively to women's humor was a special double issue of *Regionalism and the Female Imagination*, edited by Emily Toth; this journal was printed on offset and distributed through the University of Pennsylvania English Department. Unless these ground-breaking essays have been revised and published elsewhere, they are almost impossible to find today. One essay from that issue is reprinted here—Suzanne Bunker's essay on Dorothy Parker, which remains one of the best single pieces devoted to Parker's humor.

Dorothy Parker herself is an interesting example of the fate of women's humor in critical circles. Any woman studying American women's humor is sure to be asked by her male colleagues if she is studying Dorothy Parker, for hers is the name best known to members of the literary establishment in the category "woman humorist." Even those wholly unfamiliar with her work may know that Parker had a reputation as a great wit and that she was a regular at the Algonquin Round Table, where no one dared be absent lest he or she become the object of the day's satiric barbs. Fewer know that many of her short stories and poems were undeniably humorous, many as wickedly barbed as her famous one-liners. Yet very little work has been done on Parker as a literary humorist; in fact, little serious scholarly writing has concentrated on Parker at all. One hope for this collection, then, is to stimulate new work on "old" writers, to encourage scholars to build upon the insights that have been established recently about the women's humor tradition in America by expanding our understanding and appreciation of the careers of writers who, like Dorothy Parker, were once well known and well read. As I hope this collection will make clear, much pioneering work already has been done to rediscover key nineteenth-century humorists such as Frances Miriam Whitcher and Marietta Holley whose work, for a substantial period in history, disappeared from public view.

In addition to the classic essays, some of the most recent "new" writing on women's humor is also collected here, in part to suggest the vast landscape of opportunities available to contemporary scholars. For example, an essay by John Lowe demonstrates how fruitful it can be to consider a widely popular writer, Zora Neale Hurston, from the point of view of her use of humor in both her personal life and her classic fiction and anthropology. At the other end of the spectrum, Linda Pershing's essay on the lesbian comedian Kate Clinton is included as much for the new directions it suggests for those interested in different genres of women's humor as for the sustained attention it gives to Clinton's energetic, boisterous stage routines.

Beyond considerations of "classic" essays and those that represent new genres of women's humor, the essays represented in this collection are divided into three categories: (1) introductory essays to key historical anthologies of women's humor, starting with Kate Sanborn's work in 1885 through to the present; (2) essays that examine issues related to the broader subject of women's humor, per se, and American women humorists in particular, or that examine a particular variety of women's humor, such as feminist humor or African American autobiographical humor; and (3) essays that focus on individual humorists. The humorists represented here span the range from Madam Sarah Kemble Knight in the eighteenth century to Kate Clinton, a contemporary comedian. With one exception, all of the essays included here originally appeared elsewhere and are hence part of our scholarly history. The chapter by Jacqueline O'Connor was written expressly for this volume. It represents ground-breaking work on a humorist who has yet to receive significant scholarly attention: Anna Cora Mowatt, whose play *Fashion* was the first popular American drama featured on the New York stage.

Anthologies of Women's Humor

Introductions to humor anthologies reveal especially interesting assumptions about the emerging field of women's humor when viewed across time. In addition, because so many contemporary critics cite passages from these introductions, some of which are now hard to locate, this seemed a particularly rich place to begin. As we will see, the changing nature of the introductions also reflects the changing nature of scholarship—the earliest anthologist, Kate Sanborn, made no apparent attempt to be representative and relied entirely upon personal anecdote and personal taste, while the most recent editors, Nancy Walker and Zita Dresner, include a wide range of writers.

In 1885, Kate Sanborn collected the first known anthology of American women's humor, *The Wit of Women,* in response to a challenge put forth by Alice Rollins in *The Critic* magazine: "Having heard so repeatedly that woman has no sense of humor, it would be refreshing to have a contrariety of opinion on that subject." Thus, the first anthology of women's humor in this country was born out of the same accusation that has haunted scholars to this day: the male assumption that women have no sense of humor. Citing the discouragement she received from men of her acquaintance for her undertaking, Sanborn sums up the "general" male opinion in the words of a peddler who came to her door: "You're gittin' up a book, I see, 'baout women's wit. 'Twon't be no great of an undertakin', will it?" Sanborn makes no attempt to explain why she thinks women were thought to have no wit or sense of humor—that task remains for scholars such as Alice Sheppard and Walker to take up one hundred years later; instead, she focuses on the dilemma that she faced in having too many witty women to include in her anthology. Rather than search widely for enough writers and wits to make up an anthology, as the men would presuppose, she had to exercise a principle of exclusion. What is presented here as the introduction to the anthology *The Wit of Women* is in fact the very brief preface that Sanborn wrote, and the first portion of the first substantive chapter of the collection, which more nearly resembles a familiar introduction. I cut off the chapter at the point when Sanborn moves, rather unceremoniously, into the substance of the chapter, women's puns.

A companion piece to Sanborn's introduction to *The Wit of Women* is an article that she wrote for *The New England Magazine* in 1906 entitled "New England Women Humorists." Lamenting (lightly) that a decade after the publication of her anthology men continued to believe that women had no sense of humor, Sanborn confirms that there were New England women writers who indeed lacked a sense of humor; she includes in this category writers such as Mercy Warren and Lydia Sigourney, whom Sanborn ironically says "was amusing, because so absolutely destitute of humor." She then begins to catalogue writers whom she finds undeniably witty, quoting short quips and lines from each to prove her point; characteristically, none of the women receives more than a fleeting look. Still, for modern readers Sanborn's piece is both instructive and delightful—it directs our attention to writers who may have escaped our attention, and it gives us one further example of the wit of Sanborn herself, who, as Sheppard reminds us in a later essay, was a humorist in her own right.

Thirty years after Sanborn published the first edition of her anthology, Martha Bruère and Mary Beard assembled *Laughing Their Way,* a second collection of American women's humor. Although they reveal less about their motivation for editing their anthology—their introduction is disappointingly brief—their selections, in contrast to Sanborn's, tend to be generous in length. Positioning themselves directly in relation to Sanborn, they rejoice in the notion that women's humor is well established in their day: "Instead therefore of having to emphasize the mere fact that American women have been merry as well as gloomy and righteous, we may move on to the larger issue: How do women disport themselves? At what have they been amused? What does their fun-making recorded by pen and pencil reveal as to the range and depth of their thinking? . . . may we learn something of the function of humor in civilization through the medium of their jests?" While these questions remain rhetorical questions, they suggest the direction that later scholars would take in considering the relationship of women's humor to the time and the circumstances of its origins. Implicit in these questions, too, is the notion that humor is both timeless and time-bound, and underlying this notion is the fact that tastes change.

The third introduction to a collection of women's humor included here is Gloria Kaufman's introduction to her 1978 work, *Pulling Our Own Strings,* an anthology of contemporary feminist humor that blew into the second wave of the American women's movement like a proverbial breath of fresh air. Kaufman is careful to distinguish between what she calls traditional "female" humor—the humor of hopelessness—and "feminist" humor—the humor of hope. Feminist humor, she says, tends to "avoid stereotypic characters," but not stereotypical actions. Significantly, Kaufman also argues that feminist humor is not simply the "obverse of male humor," but distinctively a humor of its own. She goes on to characterize the particular turn of feminist wit that she characterizes as "the pickup," an obvious reversal of "the putdown," and suggests, but does not elaborate upon, the notion that feminist humor serves to bring people together, to establish bonds between women rather than to create divisions and to exclude. Finally, in keeping with her underlying notion that feminist humor is a humor of hope, Kaufman concludes by proclaiming the healing power in humor: "By joking, we rehumanize, recivilize ourselves. By joking, we remake ourselves so that after each disappointment we become once again capable of living and loving."

The most recent and most comprehensive introduction included here is Walker and Dresner's extended introduction to *Redressing the Balance: American Women's Literary Humor from Colonial Times to the 1980s.* Walker and Dresner begin by accounting for the relative absence of women's humor from traditional studies of American humor, identifying a range of interconnected causes, but underscoring what is perhaps the most compelling historical argument: that traditional studies of American humor have literally equated American humor with male humor. This equation has been made by and large by male critics, who subsequently have found women's humor pale, even irrelevant, by comparison to men's, and hence of no concern.

Unlike Sanborn or Bruère and Beard, Walker and Dresner have behind them a relatively extensive body of scholarly work on humor upon which to draw in their introduction; they also have their own extensive experience writing about women's humor, which informs and shapes both their introduction and the collection itself. They use this body of scholarship to identify some of the distinguishing qualities of American women's humor, and they offer a fruitful overview of the historical development of women's humor from its beginnings to the current day. They end by tracing the changes in women's humor as it moved from the nineteenth century through the twentieth century, culminating in contemporary humor that, according to Walker and Dresner, challenges cultural taboos in an aggressive, non-apologetic way.

The Tradition of Women's Humor
in America, With Variations

While the introductions to the anthologies reflect changes in historical perspective over time, three essays included in this collection comment directly on a tradition of women's humor in America. Walker, one of the most distinguished and prolific scholars of American women's humor, explores the rich beginnings of a distinctive humor tradition in the nineteenth century. Emily Toth also looks back to the origins of a women's literary humor tradition in the nineteenth century, but she moves forward, as well, to the twentieth century and to contemporary writers. Her pioneering essay, the first to call attention to a women's tradition of humor in the larger context of American humor, establishes some of the salient characteristics of our humor across time. A third essay, by Sheppard, also looks at our humor tradition from a historical point of view, but Sheppard focuses on the central role played by Sanborn as the first anthologist/collector of women's humor; of further interest in Sheppard's approach to humor is her perspective as a psychologist interested in the social function of humor.

Approaching the tradition of women's humor from other points of view, three essayists explore variations within that tradition. The first of these, Naomi Weisstein, asks why women in the women's movement in the early 1970s were no longer laughing, then answers her own question by focusing on the inappropriate laughter of women within the context of the dominant culture. An essay by Lucinda MacKethan looks at "mother wit" and humor found in the autobiographies of three African-American writers—Harriet Jacobs, Hurston, and Maya Angelou, while a third essay, by Judy Little, explores the language of women's comedy—specifically "the sentences of women who write comedy [where] there is a double-voiced tension or 'dialogic imagination,' to use Mikhail Bakhtin's term, which immerses the piece in a subtle rebellious mockery."

In "Wit, Sentimentality, and the Image of Women in the Nineteenth Century," Walker concentrates on that period in American literature which is now widely recognized as the primary origin of women's literary humor: 1840–1870. Here, in one of her first of many essays on women's humor, Walker argues persuasively that the emergence of women's wit and humor in this era stands in a causal relationship to the simultaneous emergence of sentimental female authorship. "If sentimentality in literature is a result of powerlessness," Walker argues, "wit may be seen as its opposite: an expression of confidence and power." As Walker demonstrates, the principal humorists of this period all make sentimentality and the sentimental female author the targets of their humor. She begins her examination of individual authors with Sara Willis Parton (Fanny Fern), who was as given to sentimental moralizing in her work as she was to satiric attacks on contemporary "manners and values." Working out from Parton, Walker goes on to examine the careers of other key nineteenth-century figures: Caroline Kirkland, Whitcher (The Widow Bedott), Mary Abigail Dodge (Gail Hamilton), and Holley (Josiah Allen's Wife). Three of these writers, Fanny Fern, Whitcher, and Holley, receive more extended treatment later in this collection, but Walker's observations about their relationship to sentimental authorship remains germane to any evaluation of their place as writers in the women's humor tradition.

The first essay devoted exclusively to women's humor to appear in a collection of critical essays on American humor was Emily Toth's "A Laughter of Their Own: Women's Humor in the United States." Reflective of the way in which women's humor has been all but ignored in "mainstream," i.e., male, critiques of humor, Toth's essay was the only one in a collection purported to be about American humor that addresses women's humor and women's concerns, thus underscoring Walker and Dresner's observation that American humor has been treated as though it were synonymous with male humor.[2] Beginning by juxtaposing gender role reversal in the nineteenth-century humor of Holley with a similar technique employed by the modern writer Joanna Russ, Toth identifies a common target for women's humor: "the social roles which imprison us all." In an essay that moves across time and writers, Toth identifies a wide range of themes found in women's humor: domesticity, social hypocrisy, patriarchal norms, and sex roles. Toth also considers a host of women writers not known primarily as humorists, but for whom humor plays an important role nonetheless; these include Mary Wilkins Freeman, Sarah Orne Jewett, and Kate Chopin in the nineteenth century, and Edith Wharton, Toni Cade Bambara, and Alice Walker in the twentieth. By focusing on these writers as well as humorists per se, Toth establishes relatively early in the scholarship that looking at American humor from a woman's perspective is to redefine the whole field of American humor.

Two years after Toth's pioneering essay appeared in *Critical Essays*, Sheppard published an essay in *The Psychology of Women Quarterly* that looks at women's humor from the perspective of social psychology, considering especially the "intricate relationships between personality, gender roles, and historical time." Using Sanborn's *Wit of Women* as her touchstone, Sheppard explores a variety of issues related to women's humor, but none more persuasively than the nagging question why has women's humor been so persistently ignored. For Sheppard, the answer, while complex, resides in developing a sophisticated feminist theory of psychology: "Identifying a social group as oppressed or for whom certain actions are disallowed does not constitute a sufficient psychological interpretation of the group's experience and perceptions."

Naomi Weisstein's essay "Why We Aren't Laughing . . . Any More" originally appeared in *All She Needs*, a book of drawings by Ellen Levine, and was later revised for *Ms.* magazine, where it appeared in 1973 in the early days of the women's movement. While this essay is not in fact about literary humor at all, it is one of the classic essays on

American women's humor that is cited in nearly every scholarly article on the subject since its appearance. Weisstein, in her energetic and forthright style, comes squarely to terms with the difference between male and female humor, especially "the political or power-related uses of humor." Weisstein's point of view is unmistakable, as observations such as the following make clear: "Humor as a weapon in the social arsenal constructed to maintain caste, class, race, and sex inequalities is a very common thing. Much of this humor is pure slander." Before scholars such as Walker and Dresner had helped rediscover the tradition of women's humor in America, Weisstein writes that she knows of *no* tradition of women's humor "that recognizes a common oppression, notices its source and the roles it requires, identifies the agents of that oppression." Nonetheless, her main point remains fundamentally correct: women who define themselves as feminists are unwilling to laugh at humor directed against them, and feminists use humor to build a sense of community and to rebel against oppression.

In "Mother Wit: Humor in Afro-American Women's Autobiography," MacKethan begins by defining mother wit in the terms put forth by the folklorist Alan Dundes and then applies them to the autobiographies of three African American women writers. Mother wit as understood in this context "is the verbal weapon of survival that informs the experience in these works, and makes them, finally, celebrations . . . that simply being Black and a woman can affirm." MacKethan acknowledges that associating wit and humor with the autobiographies of Jacobs, Hurston, and Angelou may initially surprise her readers; nonetheless, she reminds us, for example, of passages in *Incidents in the Life of a Slave Girl* wherein Jacobs reduces her evil master, Dr. Flint, to a comic caricature of himself. She also shows how the term "mother wit" contains within it the notion of the importance of the mother figure who in all three texts is "a strong nurturing presence" who must rely on her wits. While according to MacKethan all three writers stress the importance of language as an enabling power, the specific terms of the three women's wit differs: Jacobs uses caricature and exaggeration to make her case for her northern audience, Hurston emphasizes the "comic sense of the disparity between desires and realities," and Angelou focuses on "a series of word-bringers" who empowered her as a child. MacKethan's essay, in the end, suggests that the term "mother" in "mother wit" is not accidental in African American culture, but a specific reference to a strong, empowering, older woman.

One final essay in this section addresses a more global issue of women's humor. Judy Little, in "Humoring the Sentence: Women's Dialogic Comedy," draws upon the insights of Bakhtin to explore the "double voiced tension" found "in the sentences of women who write comedy." Little's essay seems especially useful for critics of women's humor because it provides a language and a perspective from which to understand the tensions and play within the humor, encourages careful textual analysis, and helps explain the sometimes illusive, mocking tone of some comic writers. A "double voiced tension," according to Little, means in part that within the single voice of a humorist is also to be found "the parodied voice of (male) discourse." Once Little establishes this theoretical notion, she shows how it is played out in the works of Virginia Woolf and more recently in the works of Atwood, Plath, and Griffin whose discourse is marked by "collisions" of language and ideology. "When these writers humor the sentence, they make it unsay, or partly unsay, what it seems to say."

Essays on Individual Humorists

It is in the scholarly work on individual women's humor and humorous careers that the most nuanced readings take place, for it is here that relationships between social history, personal biography, and literary genius are explored. And it is here, ironically, that our scholarship is at once most advanced and most in need of additional sustained attention. Some rediscovered writers who speak to us most directly, such as Holley, have received considerable attention, while other writers such as Betty MacDonald (*The Egg and I*) have yet to be given their due. Even so, many high quality and instructive studies of individual writers have been published in the past two decades, so many so that my dilemma about inclusion and exclusion parallels Sanborn's in a different arena. Several principles govern the choices that I have made, especially with regard to essays on individual writers; they include, first and foremost, the question of quality and of influence, which necessarily gives a slight nod toward the earlier work that has made an impact on subsequent scholarship. I have also wanted to include a historical range of humorists, stretching back to the early eighteenth century and Sarah Kemble Knight; within a historical perspective, I have sought to represent a relatively broad spectrum of prose humorists, although many humorists are not represented here, especially more contemporary writers.

The first essay in this section is Peter Thorpe's 1966 piece on Sarah Kemble Knight, whose *Journal,* written in 1704, is one of the earliest pieces of American women's literary humor. Thorpe pays tribute to Knight's work by placing it firmly in the context of the European picaresque tradition, arguing not only that Knight's *Journal* can best be understood within this tradition but also that Knight made her own contributions to that honorable tradition. While Thorpe, writing in the mid-1960s, does not offer a gendered reading of Knight's journal, his essay calls Knight to our attention and alludes to a number of issues which we now recognize as distinguishing characteristics of women's humor; his essay paves the way for a new assessment of Madam Knight's pioneering humor.

Two essays on the New York satirist Frances Miriam Whitcher (aka The Widow Bedott) are included here. The first, by Thomas O'Donnell, is especially notable for the painstaking care that O'Donnell takes to reconstruct the social historical context in which Whitcher wrote her original Widow Bedott sketches, a pattern feminist scholars also pursued to understand how women used their humor to critique historical social norms and assumptions. Grounding his interpretation and appreciation for the Widow's dramatic monologue in Whitcher's Oneida County village of Whitesboro, New York, in the 1830s and 1840s, O'Donnell shows how Whitcher's finely tuned observations about human (especially female) nature reflect what he calls the "Yorker" village life of the period. He emphasizes especially the villagers' fondness for fads such as phrenology lectures and moral reform societies. In the pages that follow, O'Donnell traces the outlines of Whitcher's personal life and the parallel track that her writing takes; his reading of the humor captures its major themes, and his generous quotations from the text bring to life for contemporary readers Whitcher's voice.

I include also, as a companion piece to O'Donnell's, an essay of my own about Whitcher. While my initial reading of Whitcher is strongly indebted to O'Donnell, "Frances Miriam Whitcher: Social Satire in the Age of Gentility" places the writer firmly within an emerging tradition of women's humor and argues that although Whitcher was not an early feminist, our appreciation for the complexity of her social satire is greatly enriched when we read her work in the context of the Seneca Falls convention of 1848. That is, she is best understood from a feminist perspective. I further argue that her preoccupation with village women's social behavior reflects the same social and political ills taken up at the Seneca Falls convention. In addition, I base part of my argument on personal letters written by Whitcher that make explicit the connections between her social satires and her personal experience, especially her experience as a minister's wife in Elmira, New York.

In the mid-nineteenth century, Anna Cora Mowatt's play *Fashion* was performed in New York. A social satire on the *nouveau riche* of New York City who spoke with newly acquired French accents and otherwise tried to buy social status with their new wealth, *Fashion* has been recognized by some critics as one of the first truly American comedies and one of only a few popular dramas by a woman dramatist. Yet to date, *Fashion* has received very little critical attention in general, and no sustained treatment as women's humor. In an essay written expressly for this volume, Jacqueline O'Connor shows how by attending carefully to the humor of *Fashion* we can discover that even as Mowatt "attacks the fashionable pretentiousness of the *nouveau riche* overtly, with considerable subtlety she also undermines the home-spun values that counter the mores of fashion." O'Connor shows how *Fashion* seems to work within the male tradition of humor and does not fit the pattern of domestic humor usually identified with women authors yet appropriates male humorous types to identify significant gender inequalities that lie below both the common and genteel values of the period.

One of the most oft-quoted early works on a woman humorist is Ann Douglas Wood's essay, "The 'Scribbling Woman' and Fanny Fern: Why Women Wrote," an essay also of considerable interest to scholars of popular "serious" literature. In the first part of the essay Douglas situates Fanny Fern (Sara Willis Parton) in the conflict between the mid-nineteenth-century notion of "true feminine genius" (by which writers such as Grace Greenwood meant women who did not compete with men and who remained true to their domestic sphere) and writers with "masculine" energy. Hawthorne praised Parton by distinguishing her from "the damned mob of scribbling women"; indeed, according to Douglas, Hawthorne declared that Parton wrote "as if the Devil was in her; and that is the only condition under which a woman ever writes anything worth reading." The second half of her essay focuses specifically on Parton, detailing the difficult conditions of her life, "the repeated defection of the men in her life"—father, husbands, brother—and the split voice with which she wrote her famous columns for the New York *Ledger*, on the one hand sentimental and traditionally feminine, and on the other bitingly satirical. The latter voice, of course, is the one that gave rise to her reputation as an American humorist, but as

Douglas argues, to understand her career and success as a whole, we must understand both voices.

The Jane Curry essay that follows is the introduction to her book, *Samantha Rastles the Woman Question*, a collection of extended excerpts from the works of the nineteenth-century feminist humorist Holley. Before introducing modern readers to Holley's strong-minded protagonist, Samantha Allen, and Samantha's comic foil, her husband Josiah, Curry offers brief biographical information about this once-popular, prolific writer, who unlike her persona, Samantha, never married and basically lived a private life in upstate New York. In describing at some length the two characters who are at the center of all of Holley's twenty-one comic narratives, Curry identifies many of the comic techniques that allowed the humorist to advance the feminist cause through her humor: comic role reversals, debates over the woman question and its purported threat to traditional family values, Samantha's common-sense wisdom, and a healthy dose of wit and irony. As Curry points out, Holley's major appeal to contemporary readers ultimately rests on her life-long commitment to "the woman question," which is reflected in a wide array of subjects: "sketches on women's social position, suffrage, temperance, powerlessness before the law and the church, the double standard, female symbols in public life, and traditional roles."

Two feminist humorists from the early twentieth century are the subjects of Dresner's essay, "Heterodite Humor: Alice Duer Miller and Florence Guy Seabury." Both writers, Dresner points out, were members of the Greenwich Village club Heterodoxy, which between 1914 and 1940, was made up of "unorthodox" women. According to Dresner, the "two major characteristics of Heterodoxy—the expression of pro-woman sentiment and the exercise of woman's wit—are epitomized in the writing of two of the club's members who chose humor and satire as a medium of expression." Quoting generously from two volumes of Miller's verse, Dresner shows how the poet "reveals in her pro-suffrage satiric verse a penetrating perception of the ways in which gender stereotypes were (and have continued to be) manipulated to keep women in a subordinate place and men in positions of status and power." Like Holley, Miller used "humor as an instrument for change," but unlike Holley, she made women's purported lack of a sense of humor the subject of her own. Dresner's second subject, Florence Guy Seabury, used the essay form "to explore issues and questions concerning relations between the sexes in an era of changing ideas about sex roles, morals, and manners." Dresner demonstrates how Seabury used pseudo-science, incongruity, role reversal, reversals of stereotypes, and burlesque to promote an egalitarian society. Both writers, she argues, used their humor to undercut traditional social assumptions and to promote a shared vision of equality.

One of the most noted wits of the first half of the twentieth century—Dorothy Parker—also wrote some of her most memorable humor in the 1920s and 1930s. Unlike Seabury, her contemporary, Parker wrote biting satiric "poems and short stories [that] criticize the status quo rather than define new, three-dimensional female roles." In an essay that grew out of the author's own personal experience with Parker's famous short story, "The Waltz," Suzanne Bunkers explores the tensions "between the surface and subsurface of Parker's satire." By focusing on Parker's poems and short stories, and not on her famous wit as a member of the Algonquin Round Table, Bunkers re-establishes Parker as a skillful literary satirist and a serious critic of the gender roles of the 1920s and 1930s. Bunkers explores the dramatic tension in Parker's work, the anger that sometimes emerges in her biting sarcasm, and the use of stereotypes in the humor, and she offers extended analyses of several stories, including "Horsie" and "The Big Blond." Writing in 1978, Bunkers called for a re-examination of Parker's literary humor, but that call has been unheeded. Thus Bunkers' essay not only breaks new critical ground in considering Parker as a woman humorist but continues to stand as one of the few critical essays on her.

The longest, most sustained attention given to a single writer in this volume is John Lowe's 1987 essay entitled "Hurston, Humor, and the Harlem Renaissance." Celebrating the fact that "the world has finally rediscovered Zora Neale Hurston," Lowe asserts from the outset that Hurston was originally silenced "for her outrageous sense of humor." He places that sense of humor at the center of her life and the center of her works, whether literary or anthropological. Lowe begins his essay by locating Hurston in the Harlem Renaissance and exploring generally the source of Hurston's distinctive comic style through her personal and professional immersion in black folklore and folkculture. In Part II of the essay, Lowe focuses on Hurston's short fiction written between 1921 and 1933, fiction in which she establishes what he identifies as the hallmarks of her celebrated novels: joking relationships in oral culture, chilling irony, animal tales, a communal comic chorus, comic expressions, and laughter as a subject of the fiction. In the final section of the essay, Lowe shows how Hurston's "expanding use of humor and folklore in the early short stories . . . came to fruition in her novels."

Three works receive sustained attention in this part of Lowe's essay: *Jonah; Their Eyes Were Watching God;* and *Moses, Man of the Mountain.* His fullest attention, as one might expect, goes to *Their Eyes Were Watching God,* where laughter and play, wit and humor, personal laughter and communal laughter are key to Janie's story and our understanding of the novel. Lowe shows, too, how resistance to laughter is a significant theme in *Their Eyes*, and ends by arguing persuasively that in this novel, "Hurston indicates that to refuse one's heritage is cultural suicide, and the loss of laughter represents an early symptom. In a unique way, Zora Neale Hurston recognized and harnessed humor's powerful resources; using its magical ability to bring people together, she established the intimacy of democratic communion."

The final essay on an individual woman humorist represents a new genre of humor, the woman comedian. Linda Pershing's piece, "There's a Joker in the Menstrual Hut," analyzes two performances by the feminist, lesbian humorist Kate Clinton. Pershing articulates from the outset that in putting forth her analysis, she is using concepts from "performance theory as it has developed in folklore studies," then goes on to demonstrate how the theory proves to be well suited to the study of a verbal art form such as stand-up comedy. In identifying four categories of Clinton's jokes—"the Catholic church, men, bawdy sexual humor, and politics"— Pershing argues that Clinton "breaks the rules. The audience is incited to laughter because of repeated and unexpected shifting between the permitted and the taboo, the playful and the serious, fantasy and reality." Well-grounded in scholarship from the social sciences, Pershing cites anthropologists Richard Bauman, Mary Douglas, and Mahadev Apte, and psychologists David Zippin, Rose Laub Coser, and Alice Sheppard. But perhaps the richest source of citation in the essay is from Kate Clinton herself; her wit and unorthodox humor are the "text" upon which Pershing's analysis rests.

Notes

1. Regina Barreca, ed. *Last Laughs: Perspectives on Women and Comedy* (New York: Gordon and Breach, 1988); June Sochen, ed. *Women's Comic Visions* (Detroit: Wayne State University Press, 1991); Regina Barreca, Ed. *New Perspectives on Women and Comedy* (New York: Gordon and Breach, 1992).

2. William Bedford Clark and W. Craig Turner, eds. *Critical Essays on American Humor* (Boston: G. K. Hall, 1984).

CHRONOLOGY OF SELECTED WORKS OF WOMEN'S HUMOR IN AMERICA

1650	Anne Bradstreet, *The Tenth Muse Lately Sprung Up in America*
1704–5	Sarah Kemble Knight, *Journal* (written)
1790	Mercy Warren, *Poems Dramatic and Miscellaneous*
1825	Sarah Kemble Knight, *Journal*
1839	Caroline Kirkland, *A New Home, Who Will Follow?*
1845	Anna Cora Mowatt, *Fashion* (performed in New York)
1846	F. M. Whitcher, (first Widow Bedott sketch in Neal's *Saturday Gazette)*
1851	Fanny Fern (first article in New York *Ledger)*
1853	Fanny Fern, *Fern Leaves From Fanny's Portfolio*
1855	F. M. Whitcher, *The Widow Bedott Papers*
1873	Marietta Holley, *My Opinions and Betsey Bobbet's*
1885	Kate Sanborn, *The Wit of Women*
1910	Mary Roberts Rinehart (first Tish story in *Saturday Evening Post)*
1914	Alice Miller, "Are Women People?" (first column published in *The New York Times)*
1925	Anita Loos, *Gentlemen Prefer Blonds* (serialized in *Harper's)*
1926	Florence Seabury, *Delicatessen Husband*
1934	Bruère and Beard, *Laughing Their Way*
1937	Zora Neale Hurston, *Their Eyes Were Watching God*
1939	Dorothy Parker, *Here Lies*
1942	Cornelia Otis Skinner, *Our Hearts Were Young and Gay*
1942	Mary Lasswell, *Suds in Your Eye*
1945	Betty MacDonald, *The Egg and I*
1953	Shirley Jackson, *Life Among the Savages*

1956	Alice Childress, *Like One of the Family*
1960	Peg Bracken, *The I Hate to Cook Book*
1967	Erma Bombeck, *At Wit's End*
1972	Gloria Steinem, *Ms.* (first issue)
1973	Erica Jong, *Fear of Flying*
1980	Kaufman and Blakely, *Pulling Our Own Strings*
1988	Walker and Dresner, *Redressing the Balance*

I. Introductions to Anthologies of American Women's Humor

The Wit of Women

Kate Sanborn

Introduction

It is refreshing to find an unworked field all ready for harvesting.

While the wit of men, as a subject for admiration and discussion, is now threadbare, the wit of women has been almost utterly ignored and unrecognized.

With the joy and honest pride of a discoverer, I present the results of a summer's gleaning.

And I feel a cheerful and Colonel Sellers-y confidence in the success of the book, for every woman will want to own it, as a matter of pride and interest, and many men will buy it just to see what women think they can do in this line. In fact, I expect a call for a second volume!

— *Kate Sanborn*, Hanover, N.H., August, 1885.

Chapter I

The Melancholy Tone of Women's Poetry—Puns, Good and Bad—Epigrams and Laconics—Cynicism of French Women—Sentences Crisp and Sparkling.

To begin a deliberate search for wit seems almost like trying to be witty: a task quite certain to brush the bloom from even the most fruitful results. But the statement of Richard Grant White, that humor is the "rarest of qualities in woman," roused such a host of brilliant recollections that it was a temptation to try to materialize the ghosts that were haunting me; to lay to rest forever the suspicion that they did not exist. Two articles by Alice Wellington Rollins in the *Critic,* on "Woman's Sense of Humor" and "The Humor of Women," convince me that the deliberate task might not be impossible to carry out, although I felt, as she did, that the humor and wit of women are difficult to analyze, and select examples, precisely because they possess in the highest degree that almost essential quality of wit, the unpremeditated glow which exists only with the occasion that calls it forth. Even from the humor of women found in books it is hard to quote—not because there is so little, but because there is so much.

The encouragement to attempt this novel enterprise of proving ("by their fruits ye shall know them") that women are not deficient in either wit or humor has not been great. Wise librarians have, with a smile, regretted the paucity of proper material; literary men have predicted rather a thin volume; in short, the general opinion of men is condensed in the sly question of a peddler who comes to our door, summer and winter, his stock varying with the season: sage-cheese and home-made socks, suspenders and cheap note-paper, early-rose potatoes and the solid pearmain. This shrewd old fellow remarked roguishly: "You're gittin' up a book, I see, 'baout women's wit. 'Twon't be no great of an undertakin', will it?" The outlook at first was certainly discouraging. In Parton's "Collection of Humorous Poetry" there was not one woman's name, nor in Dodd's large volume of epigrams of all ages, nor in any of the humorous departments of volumes of selected poetry.

Griswold's "Female Poets of America" was next examined. The general air of gloom—hopeless gloom—was depressing. Such mawkish sentimentality and despair; such inane and mortifying confessions; such longing for a lover to come; such sighings over a lover departed; such cravings for "only"—"only" a *grave* in some dark, dank solitude. As Mrs. Dodge puts it, "Pegasus generally feels inclined to pace toward a graveyard the moment he feels a side-saddle on his back."

The subjects of their lucubrations suggest Lady Montagu's famous speech: "There was only one reason she was glad she was a woman: she should never have to *marry* one."

From the "Female Poets" I copy this "Song," representing the average woman's versifying as regards buoyancy and an optimistic view of this "Wale of Tears":

Ask not from me the sportive jest,
    The mirthful jibe, the gay reflection;
These social baubles fly the breast
    That owns the sway of pale Dejection.

Ask not from me the changing smile,
    Hope's sunny glow, Joy's glittery token;
It cannot now my griefs beguile—
    My soul is dark, my heart is broken!

Wit cannot cheat my heart of woe,
    Flattery wakes no exultation;
And Fancy's flash but serves to show
    The darkness of my desolation!

By me no more in masking guise
    Shall thoughtless repartee be spoken;
My mind a hopeless ruin lies—
    My soul is dark, my heart is broken!

In recalling the witty women of the world, I must surely go back, familiar as is the story, to the Grecian dame who, when given some choice old wine in a tiny glass by her miserly host, who boasted of the years since it had been bottled, inquired, "Isn't it very small of its age?"

This ancient story is too much in the style of the male story-monger—you all know him—who repeats with undiminished gusto for the forty-ninth time a story that was tottering in senile imbecility when Methuselah was teething, and is now in a sad condition of *anecdotage.*

It is affirmed that "Women seldom repeat an anecdote." That is well, and no proof of their lack of wit. The discipline of life would be largely increased if they did insist on being "reminded" constantly of anecdotes as familiar as the hand-organ repertoire of "Captain Jinks" and "Beautiful Spring." Their sense of humor is too keen to allow them to aid these aged wanderers in their endless migrations. It is sufficiently trying to their sense of the ludicrous to be obliged to listen with an admiring, rapt expression to some anecdote heard in childhood, and restrain the laugh until the oft-repeated crisis has been duly reached. Still, I know several women who, as brilliant *raconteurs,* have fully equalled the efforts of celebrated after-dinner wits.

It is also affirmed that "women cannot make a pun," which, if true, would be greatly to their honor. But, alas! their puns are almost as frequent and quite as execrable as are ever perpetrated. It was Queen Elizabeth who said: "Though ye be burly, my Lord Burleigh, ye make less stir than my Lord Leicester."

Lady Morgan, the Irish novelist, witty and captivating, who wrote "Kate Kearney" and the "Wild Irish Girl," made several good puns. Some one, speaking of the laxity of a certain bishop in regard to Lenten fasting, said: "I believe he would eat a horse on Ash Wednesday." "And very proper diet," said her ladyship, "if it were a *fast* horse."

Her special enemy, Croker, had declared that Wellington's success at Waterloo was only a fortunate accident, and intimated that he could have done better himself, under similar circumstances. "Oh, yes," exclaimed her ladyship, "he had his secret for winning the battle. He had only to put his notes on Boswell's Johnson in front of the British lines, and all the Bonapartes that ever existed could never *get through* them!"

"Grace Greenwood" has probably made more puns in print than any other woman, and her conversation is full of them. It was Grace Greenwood who, at a tea-drinking at the Woman's Club in Boston, was begged to tell one more story, but excused herself in this way: "No, I cannot get more than one story high on a cup of tea!"

You see puns are allowed at that rarely intellectual assemblage—indeed, they are sometimes *very* bad; as when the question was brought up whether better speeches could be made after simple tea and toast, or under the influence of champagne and oysters. Miss Mary Wadsworth replied that it would depend entirely upon whether the oysters were cooked or raw; and seeing all look blank, she explained: "Because, if raw, we should be sure to have a raw-oyster-ing time."

Louisa Alcott's puns deserve "honorable mention." I will quote one. "Query—If steamers are named the Asia, the Russia, and the Scotia, why not call one the *Nausea?*"

At a Chicago dinner-party a physician received a menu card with the device of a mushroom, and showing it to the lady next to him, said: "I hope nothing invidious is intended." "Oh, no," was the answer, "it only alludes to the fact that you spring up in the night."

A gentleman, noticeable on the porch of the sanctuary as the pretty girls came in on Sabbath morning, but *not* regarded as a devout attendant on the service within, declared that he was one of the "pillars of the church!" "Pillar-sham, I am inclined to think," was the retort of a lady friend.

To a lady who, in reply to a gentleman's assertion that women sometimes made a good pun, but required time to think about it, had said that *she* could make a pun as quickly as any man, the gentleman threw down this challenge: "Make a pun, then, on horse-shoe." "If you talk until you're horse-shoe can't convince me," was the instant answer.

New England Women Humorists

Kate Sanborn

Some time ago, I received a letter from a person entirely unknown to me asking that I send "at once, or it would be of no avail," a sketch of myself, latest photo, my most humorous passages, and "tell me the names of the New England women you consider humorists."

I was suffering from rheumatic gout at the time and didn't feel funny at all, and this series of demands of one who does not keep photos, autobiography, and humorous passages and lists of humorous women, on tap for male searchers for copy, wearied me. I replied, begging to be omitted from this valuable article. But of no avail! I was put in as professing to think humor was a sin and of course the date of my birth (39 B.C.) was prominently conspicuous.

And he made this extraordinary statement: "I do not recall many humorists among the literary women of New England."

No? Ah me! I see I'm in for it again! I have wasted quite a portion of my life answering and contradicting men who stubbornly insisted that women had no sense of humor. It was all of no use! They will not be convinced. I am sure that no man ever bought a copy of my large volume on "The Wit of Women." I have sent it to several as a gift but they never acknowledged its receipt. At last Mr. Higginson wrote me, "Do not waste any more of your time and your good brain on that silly topic. If any man who lives is such a fool as to say that woman does not often possess both wit and humor, then he is beneath your notice."

We all know that the first wife of Mr. Higginson was a brilliant wit, noted for her clever sayings, many of which he has preserved in his novel "Malbone."

I own Mr. Higginson gave me sensible advice but this latest male to dabble with the theme does not say New England women have not wit, but simply says he does not know of it.

So I must add a few names to his meagre list.

Oh, I forgot to confess that I am "gun shy" when approached by interviewers as to my own slender achievements ever since I did accede to a similar request from a youth in California and read later: "Unfortunately Miss Sanborn takes herself too seriously as a humorist." So if one avoids "Skilly" he runs into "Scarabogus," as someone put it.

Our literary Foremothers of New England were not witty; had no humor. They were tediously satirical; tried in a cumbersome way to be humorous but failed. Mercy Warren was a Satirist quite in the strain of Juvenal, only stilted and artificial. Hon. John Winthrop consulted her on the proposed suspension of trade with England in all but the necessaries of life, and she playfully gives a list of articles that would be included in that word.

> An inventory clear
> Of all she needs Lamira offers here:
> Nor does she fear a rigid Cato's frown,
> When she lays by the rich embroidered gown,
> And modestly compounds for just enough,
> Perhaps some dozens of mere flighty stuff:
> With lawns and lute strings, blonde and Mechlin laces,
> Fringes and jewels, fans and tweezer-cases;
> Gay cloaks and hat, of every shape and size.
> Scarfs, cardinals, and ribands, of all dyes.
> With ruffles stamped and aprons of tambour,
> Tippets and handkerchiefs, at least threescore;
> With finest muslins that fair India boasts,
> And the choice herbage from Chinesian coasts;
> Add feathers, furs, rich satins, and ducapes,
> And head-dresses in pyramidal shapes;
> Sideboards of plate and porcelain profuse,

With fifty dittoes that the ladies use.
So weak Lamira and her wants so few
Who can refuse? they're but the sex's due.

That's enough for the early dames.

Mrs. Sigourney was amusing, because so absolutely destitute of humor: as Howells says, a woman is only unconsciously humorous; that is when she is making a goose of herself. (The women he depicts illustrate his theory.) Mrs. Sigourney's style, a feminine Johnsonese, is absurdly strained and hifalutin. She thus alludes to green apples: "From the time of their first taking on orbicular shape, and when it might be supposed their hardness and acidity would repulse all save elephantine tusks and ostrich stomachs, they were the prey of roaming children."

She preserved, however, a long list of requests for poems for special occasions which shows she had a sense of humor. Here is a part of it:

"Some verses were desired as an elegy on a pet canary accidentally drowned in a barrel of swine's food.

An ode on the dog-star Sirius.

To punctuate a three-volume novel for an author who complained that the work of punctuating always brought on a pain in the small of his back.

An elegy on a young man, one of the nine children of a judge of probate."

Catherine Sedgwick [*sic*] showed in her letters a sense of humor as when speaking of a novel, she said: "There is too much force for the subject. As if a railroad should be built and a locomotive started to transport skeletons, specimens, and one bird of Paradise."

Mrs. Caroline Gilman, born in 1794, author of "Recollections of a Southern Matron," wrote several playful and humorous poems, "Joshua's Courtship" being comical enough to be copied entire.

11

"Fanny Fern," daughter of Richard Storrs Willis, and wife of James Parton, showed lots of sparkling wit as well as ginger in snappy, audacious, fearless articles in the Ledger.

The wit and humor of Mrs. Stowe needs no defence. I regard her "Canal Boat" as one of the most comical descriptions ever written of a night's horrors for travellers. It may be found in her volume of New England stories called "The Mayflower," little known now. And why isn't Sam Lawson fully as original and entertaining as Sam Weller?

Hannah F. Gould wrote many graceful and playful verses and some that would stand comparison with Saxe. Witness her epitaph on her friend, the active and aggressive Caleb Cushing.

> Lay aside, all ye dead,
> For in the next bed
> Reposes the body of Cushing;
> He has crowded his way
> Through the world, they say,
> And even though dead will be pushing.

Miss Sedgwick dealt somewhat in epigrams, as when she says: "He was not one of those convenient single people who are used, as we use straw and cotton in packing, to fill up vacant places."

Epigrams in verse are very rare; the kind I mean that deserve to live. Just here I would like to quote Eliza Leslie; the "Lady from Philadelphia," and Mrs. Whitcher, of "Widow Bedott" fame, who was a New Yorker. Many of our late literary women excel in the epigrammatic form in sentences crisp and laconic.

Gail Hamilton's books fairly scintilate with epigrams, and her conversation was sparkling with them as when she told a clergyman who was living with his fourth wife and was terribly severe on the Mormons: "The only difference I see is that the Mormon drives four abreast while you prefer a tandem team!"

Kate Field left many a witty thought in this condensed form, as, "Relations, like features are thrust upon us; companions, like clothes, are more or less of our own selection."

Miss Jewett's books are full of the most delicate yet irresistible humor. Speaking of a person who was always complaining, she says: "Nothing ever suits her. She ain' had no more troubles to bear than the rest of us, but you never see her that she didn't have a chapter to lay before ye. I've got's much feelin' as the next one, but when folks drives in their spiggits and wants to draw a bucketful o' compassion every day right straight along, there does come a time when it seems as if the bar'l was getting low."

"Emory Ann," a creation of the late Mrs. Whitney, often spoke in epigrams, as "Good looks are a snare: especially to them that haven't got 'em."

Mrs. Walker's creed, "I believe in the total depravity of inanimate things," is more than an epigram, it is an inspiration.

Charlotte Fiske Bates, who compiled the "Cambridge Book of Poetry," often gives an epigrammatic turn to a witty thought, as:

> Would you sketch in two words a coquette and deceiver?
> Name two Irish geniuses, Lover and Lever.

My dear friend, Mrs. Fannie Barrows, the beloved "Aunt Fanny," whose Saturday evenings in New York were renowned for the number of famous persons who crowded into her charming parlors, sure of a happy time, was always perpetrating delicious bons mots and jeux d'esprit and exquisite nonsense, which must have humor to be exquisite. She once sent a couple of peanut owls to Bryant and the aged poet was greatly amused with the accompanying doggerel:

> When great Minerva chose the Owl,
> That bird of solemn phiz,
> That truly awful-looking fowl,

To represent her wis-
Dom, little recked the goddess of
The time when she would howl
To see a Peanut set on end,
And called—Minerva's Owl.

Mrs. Phelps Ward is one of the wittiest women and her epigrams are as fine as they are plentiful.

"No men are so fussy about what they eat as those who think their brains the biggest part of them."

"As a rule, a man can't cultivate his moustache and his talents impartially."

"As happy as a kind hearted old lady with a funeral to go to."

Rose Terry Cooke was another perpetually witty woman. Listen to Lavinia, one of her sensible Yankee women: "Marryin' a man ain't like setting alongside of him nights and hearin' him talk pretty; that's the fust prayer. There's lots an lots o' meetin' after that."

"Land! if you want to know folks, just hire out to 'em. They take off their wigs afore their help, so to speak, seemingly."

I remember that when speaking to me of a lady who had seen better days, she said, "She's what they call a decayed gentlewoman," then added, "but not offensively so!"

Don't forget Louisa Alcott with her "Transcendental Wild Oats," or Mary Mapes Dodge, so long the Editor of St. Nicholas, with her essay on "The Insanity of Cain," and "Miss Molony on the Chinese Question."

Sarah Cowell had the honor of reading this before the Prince of Wales, who was fairly convulsed by its fun. (Dear! must cut her out; a New Yorker). And Dr. Hale's two witty sisters; Lucretia and Susan. Get out the "Peterkin" letters and reread them; also the "William Henry Letters," by Abby Morton Diaz. Sallie McLean with her Cape Cod pen pictures and Arabella Wilson's "Sextant." Marietta Holley and her Samantha; Sherwood Bonner's ill-bred but excruciatingly witty hit on "The Radical Club" of Boston.

Mrs. Ellen H. Rollins with "Her New England Bygones," was eminently gifted in humorous descriptions interwoven with simple pathos as the truest humor often is.

"Mrs. Meeker"! When I read of Roman matrons I always think of Mrs. Meeker. Her features were marked and her eyes of deepest blue. She wore her hair combed closely down over her ears, so that her forehead seemed to run up in a point high upon her head. Its color was of reddish-brown, and, I am sorry to say, so far as it was seen, it was not her own. It was called a scratch, and Betsey said Mrs. Meeker "would look enough sight better if she would leave it off."

"Whether any hair at all grew upon Mrs. Meeker's head was a great problem with the village children, and nothing could better illustrate the dignity of this woman than the fact that for more than thirty years the whole neighborhood tried in vain to find out."

Some of Mrs. Spofford's work shines with a silver thread of humor worked intimately into the whole warp and woof.

Anna Eichberg, daughter of the noted violinist of Boston, who is now Mrs. John Lane, wife of the publisher, is known on both continents as a woman richly blest with both wit and humor. Read her "Champagne Standard" if you doubt this.

Boston has had an uncommon number of witty women.

Mrs. Helen Bell, Rufus Choate's brilliant daughter, remarkable for her music and her wit, made that remark quoted without credit by Emerson, "To a woman, the consciousness of being well dressed gives a sense of tranquility which religion fails to bestow."

She told a friend how she was presented with a pig and did not really know what to do with it. But she said, "Afterward we found it most convenient to put things in."

By the way, Dr. Holmes wrote me that the phrase so often attributed to him describing a ladies' luncheon: "Giggle, Gabble, Gobble" was not his at all but belonged to a clever Boston woman.

Julia Ward Howe is undeniably witty. Her concurrence with a dilapidated bachelor, who retained little but his conceit, was excellent. He said: "It is time now for me to settle down as a married man, but I want so much; I want youth, health, wealth, of course, beauty, grace."

"Yes," she interrupted sympathetically, "you poor man, you do want them all."

When Sumner was a young man, he aired his disbelief at length, in a magazine article. She said, "Charles evidently thinks he has invented Atheism." And when in later years he declined a dinner invitation excusing himself by saying, "I have lost interest in the individual," she exclaimed:

"Why, Charles, God hasn't got as far as that yet!"

After dining with a Boston family, noted for their chilling manners and lofty exclusiveness, she hurried to the house of a jolly informal friend and seating herself before the glowing fire, sought to regain a natural warmth, explaining, "I have spent three hours with the Mer de Glace, the Tete Noir and the Jungfrau, and am nearly frozen."

It was Mrs. Oliver Wendell Holmes, Jr., who said that the Cunard steamer, Oregon, committed suicide to avoid being put on that company's Boston line.

There is much humor among the woman journalists of Boston, yet I'll wager that not one of them ever tried to be funny, like all newspaper men, about baked beans and brown bread.

In puns, parodies and repartee, the New England woman more than keeps up with her brothers. Louisa Alcott propounded this awful query: "If steamers are named the Asia, the Russia and the Scotia, why not call one the Nausea?"

Susan B. Anthony was witty to the last, as quick at reply as when years ago Horace Greeley said to her, "The ballot and the bullet go together. You women say you want to vote. And are you ready to fight too?"

"Yes, Mr. Greeley, we are ready to fight; at the point of the goose quill, the way you always have!"

I would dearly like to add the numerous witty women of New York, and the West: also to make a few feeble remarks about the so-called wit of some great men. May I do this later?

Laughing Their Way:
Women's Humor in America

Martha Bensley Bruère and
Mary Ritter Beard

Foreword

In discovering themselves, Americans have rediscovered many phases of their experience together—their political and economic, their military and social, their literary and aesthetic life. But their knowledge of their own humor lags. The few books on the subject have stuck rather faithfully to a traditional partial view; to a concept of American humor as beginning in the robust expression of frontiersmen and remaining in that gusto and temper while a new world was subdued to the plow, while an agricultural civilization swung toward an industrial one, while the nation was hammered into form by war and peace, by prosperity and depression. These earlier books, keeping to that fixed idea, have left a whole continent of humor to bide its time for revelation.

It may seem that in an hour of nation-wide depression, laughter is the last thing to ponder on. But wit and humor feed on failure as well as on success; their nutriment is absurdity, incongruity, and conflict, no less than satisfaction, security, and peace. The sharp edge of laughter can be devastatingly iconoclastic, showing up the mistakes of man from Moses to Mussolini. Is it a time to "wipe that silly grin away," to forego the weapon of ridicule and "quit fooling"? Dean Swift was not "fooling" when he poked fun at incompetence, selfishness, and bigotry; Lincoln used the power of laughter to strengthen the force of action. The English Cavaliers and Roundheads and

17

the Republicans of Holland fought part of their battles with caricature. Some of the best artists in Germany under the Wilhelminic régime, radical in their aims, resorted to the cartoon as their only weapon. During the struggle for enfranchisement American women were able through drawings to argue graphically about business and professional inequalities, and now through words and pictures women are laughing at themselves—the epitome of enlightened rationality. Under stress especially it is important to remember laughter, for it is more than a defense mechanism, a means of adjusting to circumstances, a safety-valve against tyranny—it is an agency in creative enterprise. From perceiving the blend of the tragic and comic which is life in its fulness and vitality, comes the kind of laughter indistinguishable from tears—springing from supreme philosophy.

This is a book about America. The temper of a people—its "humors," its cheerfulness, playfulness, buoyancy, stolidity, or bile—may not precisely lend itself to generalization, least of all along racial lines. National assumptions, however, are generally taken quite jovially, assuming pictorial form in the conventional figures of Johnny Bull, Uncle Sam, Michel, and Company whenever draughtsmen report international events, and apparently a rough justice is done through these established symbols. Before Babbitt was created as a personification of capitalist America in its post-war complacency, teasing had slowly evolved a personification of democratic America as a blend of independent farmer and sly Yankee trader, surviving in caricature as a kind of Sam Slick. But these symbols take scant account of feminine "humors," and of such is a nation also composed. Efforts to introduce woman into the national symbolism usually demonstrate merely the vigor of mythology, the persistence of the primitive. The "spirit of woman" amid the economic and political humors of men is distinctly matriarchal. Obviously if our national symbolism has "gone modern" and realistic in its depiction of man, it remains classical and mystical in its delineation of woman. The male type may be an amusing wag;

the female must be somber and suggest the superhuman. But think how relieved the tension among nations would be, and how much brighter their international discourse, if they could no longer fall back on the obscure divine mother for militant justification—if armored ladies symbolizing war, preparedness, and patriotism, or unarmed angels and Amazons leading on embattled hosts were removed from their minds!

However, it is the diverse "humors" within the nation, rather than national symbolism or international affairs which are the subject matter of this book—"humors" as reflected in the writings and drawings by American women through the past one hundred years. It would be possible to go behind that arbitrary boundary of time into the earlier century when Sarah Knight jotted down her observations of America-in-the-making as she journeyed from Massachusetts into Connecticut; and when Mercy Warren, during the Revolution, undertook to laugh the Tories out of countenance—Minerva in a merry mood armed only with her wit. But the adventure of democracy and the rounding out of a continent forms a unit in itself.

Within the century now closing many races with all sorts of tempers have opened up and settled a vast area under the aegis of a single government innovative in design and individualistic in philosophy. And as these peoples have advanced indomitably from coast to coast over the thousands of intervening miles, they have guffawed, wise-cracked, joked, giggled, and written about the absurdities connected with the undertaking, giving a stamp to the national personality complex. Even when the Pacific waters halted that westward migration and the older problems of the older civilizations began to bear down upon a population finally thwarted from escape by movement alone, the mocking at things, at one another, and at one's self continues to meet the urge to self-expression and the pubic demand for entertainment, and by so doing brought permanent values into review.

During the first half of this century of love and strife and experimentation, men appear to have assumed that they alone enjoyed a sense of humor; that even theirs was principally derived from the frontier spring, and that that was all the humor possible. Consequently in 1885 Katherine Abbot Sanborn, popularly known as Kate Sanborn, finding not a single woman represented in Parton's *Collection of Humorous Poetry* or in other humorous poetry anthologies, published a collection of women's witty observations on the American scene. It now seems a long, long way from 1885, when such a corrective for ill-conceived assumptions was necessary!

No one today can pick up a newspaper, read a magazine, or work in a library without meeting face to face laughing women who peer through the printed pages. Instead therefore of having to emphasize the mere fact that American women have been merry as well as gloomy and righteous, we may move on to the larger issue: How do women disport themselves? At what have they been amused? What does their fun-making recorded by pen and pencil reveal as to the range and depth of their thinking? Have their jests been simply "brain fleas among slumbering ideas," as Heine described joking? Or may we learn something of the function of humor in civilization through the medium of their jests? Humor has been called "the most philosophic of all the emotions, making our impulses elastic." What kind of impulses has it made elastic in America?

In spite of differences of time and condition, women's humor always bears their proprietary brand. The sexes have their own directions for toleration. Naturally men's derision has centered about biological occupational peculiarities. And among women, the flowers of their humor are as varied as their lives. Would that austere saint, Elizabeth Fry, break into ripples of joy over Beatrice Lillie? Would Harriet Beecher Stowe lose herself delightedly in *The New Yorker?* Yet the angle of vision from which women see a lack of balance, wrong proportions, disharmonies, and incongruities in life is a thing of their world as it must be—a world always a little apart.

We have tried to show how American women for a century have laughed their way through life by the help of their needles and their scissors, their brushes and their chisels and their pens. Not by any means have we covered the whole ground. Some of the best wit and humor is withheld from us by copyright restrictions. All we could do is what the government inspector does when he grades wheat—take a sample here and there and let its quality stand for that of a carload.

Pulling Our Own Strings: Feminist Humor and Satire

Gloria Kaufman

It is easy to identify overtly political humor as feminist ("Rock the boat, not the cradle" or "A woman's place is in the White House"). We need, however, a definition that encompasses indirect and subtle feminist humor as well as the obvious kinds.

Feminist humor is based on the perception that societies have generally been organized as systems of oppression and exploitation, and that the largest (but not the only) oppressed group has been the female. It is also based on the conviction that such oppression is undesirable and unnecessary. It is a humor based on visions of change.

The persistent attitude that underlies feminist humor is the attitude of social revolution—that is, we are ridiculing a social system that can be, that must be changed. *Female* humor may ridicule a person or a system from an accepting point of view ("that's life"), while the *nonacceptance* of oppression characterizes feminist humor and satire. The following anecdote exemplifies feminist humor:

It was New Year's Eve of 1961. At a lively party in Watertown, Massachusetts, a psychiatrist was conversing with an attractive divorced woman.

"So you have only one child?"

"Yes," she said, "a four-year-old."

"That means," he said, magnanimously sharing his expertise, "that you don't yet know what it means to be a mother."

"Well, then," she returned, "when you have a child, I'm sure you'll tell me."

The professional man is playing an authority role, but the woman does not accept the authority he assumes for himself. Her remark, which exhibits an amused awareness of his intellectual limitation, clearly demonstrates the feminist stance of nonacceptance. In contrast, the Lithuanian joke that follows is an example of female (nonfeminist humor):

A farmer loudly asserted to his wife that she did not enjoy the same rights in the house as he. She was a mere woman, not a member of mankind. The next day, when he was putting on his boots, she heard him curse.

"What's the matter, dear?"
"There's shit in my boot, God damn it!"
"Was it the cat, dear?"
"No—it's not cat stuff."
"Perhaps the dog?"
"No, no, no! It's human."
"Human, is it? Then it was I."

The farmer's wife *accepts* her bad marriage as a norm. She is powerless to change things, and she can only express her resentment in a destructive, sarcastic way. The bitterness and the antimale feelings of the wife are frequently seen in female humor but occur far less often in feminist humor. Perhaps that is because the entrapped female regards her husband as the inevitable oppressor, whereas the feminist perceives him ultimately as a person who can or who will change (or as a person she can leave). Feminist humor tends to be a humor of hope, female humor of hopelessness. (This is not to contend that bitterness is absent from feminist humor, merely that, compared to female humor, it occurs much less regularly.)

It will not be clear to most readers without an explanation why some humor is feminist. Why, for example, isn't the menstruation humor in "Rhythm Reds" female (rather than feminist) humor? It might have been. If the humor were created with the idea that menses are dirty, smelly, ugly, and shameful (the traditional attitude that society has inculcated), it would have been female humor. Since, however, the underlying attitude is that menses are normally and naturally female; since, moreover, the attitude is that menses are not to be hidden (as shameful) but to be joked about (as normal) or even celebrated (as naturally female), the humor is deeply feminist. Not by explicit statement but by implicit posture, the expression of such humor attacks the unhealthy and oppressing idea cultivated for thousands of years that women's bodies are foul. There is, of course, a great deal of menstruation humor that is female or male rather than feminist, but such humor has been excluded from our collection.

Feminist satire, like other satire, is didactic and often overtly so. No matter how pessimistic it sounds, it seeks to improve us by demonstrating—through devices of irony, of exaggeration, of sarcasm, and of wit—our human folly. It exposes realities not merely out of love for truth but also out of desire for reform. Whether or not reforms are achieved, they are implicit ideals. In this sense, feminist satire, like feminist humor, is founded on hope and predicated on a stance of nonacceptance.

Stereotypes are accepted norms upon which a great deal of mainstream humor is built. Mother-in-law jokes, for example, are understood when the stereotype—that of an interfering and intrusive relative—is conceded. Feminist humor does not respond by creating father-in-law jokes. Since it arises from a subculture that has no patience with stereotyping, especially in relation to sex roles, we should not be surprised at the tendency of feminist humor to avoid stereotyped characters. *Actions,* however, do become stereotyped in feminist humor. There is much material based on typical limitations of the male. Masculine illogic, for example, is a favorite target. In such humor the man may be a doctor or a check-out boy, old or young, educated or not—but his penchant for illogic is not automatically linked to other identifying traits in the way that "interfering" and "overbearing" are linked to mother-in-law.

The particular human behavior might be regarded as *typed* behavior, but the character who commits the behavior is not a stereotyped character.

In the early 1970s, it did look as if one feminist stereotype might emerge—the male chauvinist pig (MCP). His existence, however, was relatively short-lived. And he was not universally accepted in feminist circles. (A sizeable minority objected to the "reduction" of man to four-legged animal. Another minority saw no reason to insult the pig.) Characterizations of that brief stereotype can be seen in "The Male Chauvinist Pig Calendar" (1974) by Betty Swords. Most of the references to the MCP that I came across were, curiously, not from feminists but from men—especially from men in the media. The journalistic practice of reducing feminist issues to slogans and catch-words has done much to trivialize complex issues raised by the women's movement. MCP served that purpose. It appealed to the imagination of males in the media: "I used to be an MCP," or (on interview shows with a feminist guest), "Do *you* think I'm an MCP?" Readers will find only a few MCP references in our collection. The male chauvinist pig actually derives from the protest rhetoric of the 1960s. The "pig," the visible oppressor, frequently a policeman, became MCP when rebelling feminists tried to show their fellow male protestors that oppression of women was a fact of life in everyday radical politics. The MCP is definitely a derived stereotype rather than an original creation. We note his demise with no sorrow.

An unwarranted expectation of stereotypes accounts, I believe, for the nervous response of many men to the term "feminist humor." They have assimilated the misogyny of male humor, and with some guilt they expect that feminist humor will return their treatment in kind. Let us be clear about how the female is treated in mainstream (male) humor. It has taken many centuries to produce the stereotypical female of male comedy. By A.D. 101, in Juvenal's "Sixth Satire," the female stereotype is firmly defined as nasty, lying, vicious, pretentious, emasculating, garrulous, aggressive, vulgar, nymphomaniacal, gluttonous, dishonest, shameless, greedy, selfish, quarrelsome, impertinent, and disgusting. Notably absent in Juvenal is the idea of woman as stupid and ineffectual. Instead, she is offensively intelligent—the legitimate castrating bitch. When we add stupidity and ineffectuality to the Juvenalian list, we have a fairly complete picture of the stereotypical woman targeted by male humorists.

Many men assume incorrectly that feminists have created, as a counter or opposing stereotype, a nasty and oppressive male as repulsive and disgusting as their stereotypic female. That assumption is perhaps founded on an unacknowledged belief on men's part that women are, after all, just like men and that we will act exactly as they do when we attain positions of power. But we do not have historical precedent for determining how women in power will act. The exceptional women who have "ruled" (Elizabeth I of England, Catherine the Great, Golda Meir) nonetheless functioned in traditionally patriarchal worlds. They dealt not with an assortment of men and women, they dealt not with other women, but they dealt mostly or even exclusively with men committed to established hierarchical power systems. The idea that a single woman can ignore or change the entire partriarchal social order is ludicrous, but it is an argument that antifeminists are quick to offer. It is, therefore, interesting to see that given the freedom to go in our own direction, women do so. Feminist humor is NOT the obverse of male humor. If it is true that people are revealed through their humor, our collection is an important document that testifies to a difference, if not between female and male, at least between feminist female and mainstream male. Feminist humor and satire demonstrate that *culturally* we have not been doing what the male does. It may be that politically our ways will also be our own.

Even more than humor, satire tends to rely heavily on stereotypical characters. In "New Discoveries Hailed as Birth Control Breakthroughs," Jane Field satirizes behavior, not an individual. Virginia Woolf in *Three Guineas* (perhaps the most sustained and elegant piece of sarcasm in the English language) does not approach the terrain of stereotype. In Una Stannard's sophisticated burlesque, "Why Little Girls Are Sugar and Spice and When They Grow Up Become Cheesecake," a parody of the entire process of history and of scholarship, the stereotyping so natural to burlesque (compare Dostoevski's "The Crocodile") is not even a factor. In each of these feminist works behavior is satirized and stereotypical men are not invented to commit the objectionable behaviors. Quite to the contrary. Virginia Woolf wittily examines the statements of British philosopher C.E.M. Joad, a real figure rather than a contrived stereotype. Una Stannard quotes the poet Byron rather than invent a foolish statement to put into the mouth of an available stereotype.

Feminist humor and satire are not new. Perhaps the best-known example of both dates from the 5th century B.C. In Aristophanes' *Lysistrata,* the women of Athens and Sparta force the men to make peace by withdrawing sexual favors from their husbands, whose desires for sexual activity ultimately overpower their desires to make war. The play presents men as incompetent in their roles as leaders of state and reveals women as having a more valid social perspective. Women are not idealized. They also have their pugnacious side, and they are ready physically to do battle with men. When the Chorus of Old Men attempts to smoke the striking women out of the Acropolis, a counter-Chorus of Old Women appears, and there is a fight between the men with the burning torches and the women with pitchers of water. When the men's torches are extinguished, they complain to the magistrate: "Besides their other violent acts, they threw water all over us, and we have to shake out our clothes just as if we'd leaked in them."[1]

In the comic tradition, women battle with household supplies, no one gets hurt, and responsible social action follows. Mother Jones's labor-organizing activity comes from that tradition. In "How the Women Mopped Up Coaldale," a chapter of her autobiography, she recounts how she organized a female force armed with mops and brooms. The women faced a militia whose colonel threatened to charge with bayonets. The scene was worthy of Aristophanes, but the union struggle was no prewritten play with a guaranteed safe outcome. Mother Jones used humor to defuse a situation in which danger was terribly real. In the Coaldale battle (which she described as "a great fight"), she led her army to the militia's headquarters and had them eat the soldiers' breakfasts. Like Aristophanes, she was a master of comic irony—he the writer, she the practitioner.

Mai Zetterling, in her film *The Girls* (1968), again focuses feminist attention on Aristophanes' *Lysistrata*. Not only does she invoke and reinforce Aristophanes' themes, but she also addresses contemporary feminist issues satirically. The film presents an acting group on tour with Aristophanes' play. Zetterling shows the twentieth-century audience (at the time of the Vietnam war) to be still unreceptive to the antiwar sentiment of *Lysistrata*. Turning to modern issues, she treats contemporary sexual relations with dry wit. In a hotel bedroom, for example, a touring actress asks her businessman-husband about his mistress, who is physically present as a mannikin. As the husband stuffs the mistress-mannikin into a large trunk (with the wife watching), he insists there is no other woman. The trunk-stuffing involves much physical contact between husband and mistress (compared to no contact with the wife). The sequence, which is well executed, is funny as plain slapstick. But it also implies that he regards the mistress entirely as object (in *that* sense, there really is no other woman). The visual treatment of woman-as-object has never been done more imaginatively. With subtlety Zetterling also suggests that the wife and the mistress share similar problems (vis-à-vis men) as well as a common humanity. There is a magical sympathy between them. We see the wife as a person of civilized complexity, the husband as superficial and farcical. To treat farce, which is based on crudely obvious exaggeration, with such complex subtlety is fine and rare art.

Between Aristophanes and Zetterling there is a space of more than two millennia. It is not an empty space. A history of feminist humor is in order, but that is far beyond the space and the scope of my introductory remarks. It will require a volume of its own. To comment only on the recent past in the United States, we note that the suffrage movement created its share of platform wits—Anna Howard Shaw, Sojourner Truth, Susan B. Anthony, Lucretia Mott, Harriot Stanton Blatch, and Elizabeth Cady Stanton, to mention a few. Marietta Holley (who is not in our collection) and Fanny Fern (who is included) wrote as declared feminist humorists. Their issues are today's issues. Although the tradition of feminist humor continued into the twentieth century, the current movement, which emerged in the '60s and has produced so much humor and satire of its own, seems to have lost touch with the earlier feminist humor tradition. We are largely unaware of the wit of the early suffragists as well as the "new suffragists" of our own century. We don't remember the feminist wit that flourished in the flapper age, and much of the work of the '30s and '40s, such as Ruth Herschberger's "Josie Takes the Stand" (1948), Dorothy Sayers' "The Human-Not-Quite-Human" (1947), and even Virginia Woolf's *Three Guineas* (1938), is not widely known. Although our collection is a highly selected sampler, not an anthology that can be used to reconstruct a history of feminist humor, perhaps it will inspire such an effort.

Feminist humor is richly various, but a dominant undercurrent is the pickup, an obvious reversal of the putdown. In some cases pickups happen in response to putdowns ("A woman's place is in the home" generates "A woman's place is *every*place"). Some pickups are extended. The last sentence of Gabrielle Burton's "No One Has a Corner on Depression But Housewives Are Working on It" is a calculated pickup. Naomi Weisstein closes her long standup-comic routine, "The Saturday Night Special: Rape and Other Big Jokes," with a deliberate pickup. Such humor is a healthy contrast to mainstream humor, most of which seems to knock people down—or to laugh at people who are already down.

Laughs come from a perceived superiority of the hearer or reader to the character ridiculed. Pickup humor, however, is based on equity. Through it, we do not laugh *at* people, we bond *with* them.

One of the best and most popular pickups of the movement is Flo Kennedy's remark, "A woman without a man is like a fish without a bicycle." Our society has asserted and reinforced the idea that no woman is complete until she finds her "other half" and unites in heterosexual marriage. Society says, "You are half." Kennedy says, "You are whole." It is interesting (but not surprising) that many men take this powerful and clever pickup of women to be an indictment of men as both unnecessary and worthless. Rather, it defies a system that tells woman she is singly incomplete; in a larger sense it is a revolutionary celebration of woman alone. It ignores rather than attacks men.

The selections in *Pulling Our Own Strings* were made chiefly on the basis of quality, but there were other major criteria. We were unable to get permission for all of the material we wanted to use. Limitations of space forced us to reject other good material, including some of our favorite pieces. Although we did try to give a sense of the variety of forms, of approaches, and of subject-matters, we cannot offer a comprehensive sampler that fairly represents the rich variety of both feminist humor and feminist satire. Our selections have been deliberately weighted toward the humor at the expense of the satire—not because feminist satire is less interesting or less distinguished, but because we feel that at this moment in its history, the feminist movement needs to share its humor even more than its satire, which has already found an audience through print.

Feminists are not simply angry women. As persons, we are complex: we are as likely to explode with laughter as with anger; we are as likely to write satirical essays as to circulate petitions; and we value all aspects of our feminism—our street actions and our scholarship, our poetry and our doggerel, our anger and our laughter.

31

The world is always humor-poor. There is never enough of it. Yet, without humor we cannot survive. Our world is too relentlessly cruel, too callous, too uncivilized, and feminists who contemplate it will die of depression or lapse into cynicism and inaction without our humor. By joking, we rehumanize, recivilize ourselves. By joking, we remake ourselves so that after each disappointment we become once again capable of living and loving.

Notes

1. Tr. Charles T. Murphy, *Ten Greek Plays,* ed. L.R. Lind, Cambridge, Mass.: Riverside Press, 1957, p. 381.

Redressing the Balance: American Women's Literary Humor from Colonial Times to the 1980s

Nancy Walker and Zita Dresner

I

Until recently, women's literary humor, like the other genres and subgenres of women's writing in America, was relatively unexplored by critics and scholars. Students of American literature and even those who study American humor have been largely unaware of the rich tradition of women's humor that has flourished ever since women began writing and publishing in the New World in the seventeenth century. Such a critical lapse might, on the surface, seem to stem partly from the fact that humor is an ephemeral art, often depending upon the fleeting interests and events of a particular time and place for its appeal to the reader, and partly from the notion that humor, in general, is less significant as a record of human aspirations and experience than is "serious" literature. As E. B. White wrote in 1941, "The world likes humor, but treats it patronizingly. It decorates its serious artists with laurel, and its wags with Brussels sprouts."[1] More recently, in his introduction to *American Humor,* editor Arthur P. Dudden again acknowledges this bias: "American humor, in spite of the genius of many of its practitioners, has received little serious attention from critics or historians."[2]

Yet, beginning in the 1930s, a series of studies of American humor has attempted to demonstrate how closely tied are humorous expression and cultural values, as the humorist exposes and mocks the absurdities and incongruities of society.[3] None of these studies, however, gives significant consideration to women's contributions to the humorous exploration of American values. Many reasons have been advanced to account for this omission, ranging from masculine attacks on the quality of women's humor to feminist assertions that women's humor threatens men and has therefore been derogated by them. Despite disagreement about causes, however, the uncontestable result is that women writers have been consistently underrepresented in or excluded from anthologies of humor and also underrated or relegated to the footnotes in scholarly studies of American humor.

Clearly, the subordinate position of women in American society—legally, economically, socially, politically, and culturally—from the Puritan era through the twentieth century, has been responsible in large part for women's secondary status as both writers and humorists.[4] In addition, the antifemale bias of humor written by men—for example, the assortment of stereotypical gossips, nags, gold diggers, and harridans that populate such humor—has helped to perpetuate the assumption that men are devoid of humor.[5] Perhaps more important, the established tendency of male critics to define American humor in terms of traditionally male (rather than female) concerns, language, and style has set a standard of humor based on what men have promoted as funny and, consequently, has demoted women's humorous writing to a lesser, minor class of literature when it has been considered at all. Finally, the social perception of humor as a masculine prerogative and as an aggressive, unfeminine mode not "proper" for women has further contributed to what Mahadev L. Apte calls the social unacceptability of women's humor, which he finds worldwide and which he attributes to two basic factors:

> First, women's humor reflects the existing inequality between the sexes, not so much in its substance as in the constraints imposed on its occurrence, on the techniques

used, on the social setting in which it occurs, and on the kind of audience that appreciates it. Second, these constraints generally, but not necessarily universally, stem from the prevalent cultural values that emphasize male superiority and dominance together with female passivity and create role models for women in keeping with such values and attitudes. . . . men's capacity for humor is not superior to women's. Rather, both the prevalent cultural values and the resultant constraints prevent women from fully utilizing their talents.[6]

Apte's conclusions only echo those that have been advanced by American women in arguments about women's humor since the nineteenth century—arguments that inform the four anthologies of women's humor that have appeared in this country to date.

Inspired by a debate in two 1884 issues of the *Critic* concerning women's sense of humor, Kate Sanborn, in her 1885 anthology *The Wit of Women,* intended to prove that women did indeed possess a capacity for humor and wit. Including chiefly, though not exclusively, the humor of American women, Sanborn's anthology ranges widely over various forms of humor, from the dinner-party bon mot and children's stories to satire and literary parody. Although Sanborn's tendency to use brief quotations from individuals and works (rather than longer excerpts or entire selections) makes the collection more useful as a starting point for research than as a compendium of women's humor for the modern reader, she demonstrates that women writers in the nineteenth century were not merely the sentimentalists that critics have traditionally labeled them. In addition, the selections testify to women's active interest in political and social, as well as domestic, concerns.

In 1934 Martha Bensley Bruère and Mary Ritter Beard edited *Laughing Their Way: Women's Humor in America* with a motive somewhat different from Sanborn's. Citing *The Wit of Women* in their introduction, Bruère and Beard consider "a corrective for ill-conceived notions" about female humorlessness no longer necessary, but they do see a need to correct

America's "partial view"—i.e., masculine view—of its tradition of humor. They declare their intent to provide that corrective by presenting women's works that have been ignored by those who equated "native" American humor with men's humor. At the same time, they take pains to show that women have created their own tradition in humor—a tradition, however, that the editors do not analyze other than to assert that it reflects the different world of women, "a world always a little apart."[7]

Despite Bruère and Beard's rather optimistic assessment of the acceptance of women as humorists in the 1930s, some forty years later Deanne Stillman and Anne Beatts, in apparent ignorance of Sanborn's and Bruère and Beard's collections, subtitled their own anthology *The First Collection of Humor by Women*. Stillman and Beatts's assumption that they were breaking new ground belies their predecessors' optimism about women's humor; because both earlier anthologies had long been out of print by the 1970s, the word *first* in their title is not surprising. Mark Twain and James Thurber had endured and were household names to many Americans, but the authors collected by Sanborn, Bruère, and Beard—Frances Whitcher, Josephine Daskam, Cornelia Otis Skinner, and many others—were by this time almost lost to history.

What *is* surprising is that, despite the success of female stand-up comedians and comedy writers in the 1960s and 1970s, Beatts and Stillman begin their introduction to *Titters* by stating: "Nobody will admit to not having a sense of humor. . . . Nobody, that is, except women. . . . Women aren't supposed to be funny, particularly. It's not part of the feminine role-model, the set of stereotypes that got dished out to us along with our pablum. . . . Just because women really *are* funny doesn't change the prevailing attitude. And the prevailing attitude has been, and to some extent continues to be, 'Chicks just aren't funny.'"[8] The editors' comments echo those of Sanborn almost a hundred years before, and the purpose of *Titters,* like that of *The Wit of Women,* was to demonstrate once again that women *are* funny—at least to other women. However, unlike their predecessors, who attempted to be comprehensive, Stillman and Beatts limited their selections to contributions from their contemporaries, friends, and colleagues. Similarly, Gloria Kaufman and Mary Kay Blakely, editors of *Pulling Our Own Strings: Feminist Humor and Satire* (1980), collected examples, almost exclusively from the 1970s, of what they define as "feminist" humor, including cartoons, jokes, verse, comic routines, articles, and excerpts from larger works. While the editors' primary motive seems to have been the preservation of humor that, because of its feminist orientation, they assumed would be ignored by male and nonfeminist female anthologies, the introductory segments of the book also suggest other intentions: to rebut the popular attacks on the women's movement and on feminists for being humorless and to scuttle the notion (an aim also of the editors of *Titters*) that women who purport to be humorists have to limit themselves to what have been considered "feminine" tools of expression: self-deprecation, ladylike language, and negative female stereotypes.

These earlier anthologies, though they have been important sources for this one, have certain limitations this anthology seeks to address. In Sanborn's and Bruère and Beard's work, for example, the selections are fragmentary (and in Sanborn's book sometimes even unidentified by author). The two later anthologies focus, by design, on a particular type of humor from a fairly narrow time period. Moreover, none of the previous collections provides the biographical, bibliographical, and critical source material so necessary to the scholar and so useful to the student or the general reader who wishes to find additional work by or about an author. The present anthology is intended in part to supply this information by providing reference material to document and selections to illustrate, comprehensively and over time, the varied threads that make up the tapestry of American women's literary humor.

Some of the authors who appear in this volume will be familiar to most readers. For example, Erma Bombeck is a household word today, even more so than was Dorothy Parker in the 1920s; Jean Kerr's *Please Don't Eat the Daisies* (1957) inspired a movie and a television series, and Anita Loos's *Gentlemen Prefer Blondes* (1925) inspired film and stage versions spanning five decades; Judith Viorst's verse appeared first in *New York* magazine; Ellen Goodman's column appears in newspapers nationwide. Other authors, now unfamiliar but often as well known in their own time as these are today, have been retrieved from out-of-print sources to be restored to their rightful place in the history of American women's humor. Frances Whitcher's mid-nineteenth-century dialect sketches, Caroline Kirkland's depictions of frontier characters and ways of life, Florence Guy Seabury's comments on the difficulties of dual-career marriage, and Helen Rowland's delightful satires on male-female relationships are just some of the many works that retain a sparkle and freshness while evoking the particular circumstances of women's lives in different periods of our history.

Not all the authors represented here are primarily humorists. For example, Anne Bradstreet, the first published poet in America, was a serious writer of meditative poetry, and "Fanny Fern" was known in the nineteenth century and again today for her sentimental prose as well as her realistic 1885 novel *Ruth Hall.* Judith Sargent Murray, Charlotte Perkins Gilman, and Gloria Steinem are thought of as social critics; "Gail Hamilton" and Nora Ephron, as columnists. Mary Roberts Rinehart achieved fame as a mystery writer, and Edna St. Vincent Millay and Paula Gunn Allen as serious poets. However, all the pieces in this collection display the sense of irony and awareness of absurdity that underlie humorous expression. Further, they all reflect perhaps the major function of humor: redressing the balance. Our hope is that the selections in this volume not only entertain and enlighten the reader but also stimulate further study of women's humor, a task that has begun only within the past ten years.

II

Despite the relative recency of American humor studies, a considerable body of literature has accumulated over the past century concerning the nature and functions of humor. Within the past two decades in particular, psychologists, sociologists, and cultural anthropologists have conducted research into humor motivations and responses and, emphasizing the social uses of humor, have analyzed the roles of the humorist and the humor preferences of different groups within cultures. Looking at the samples of women's humor presented in this volume in light of humor research and theory, as well as in relation to the critical studies of literary humor and feminist analyses of women's literature that have appeared in recent decades, we can draw some preliminary conclusions about the themes, techniques, and purposes that distinguish American women's literary humor.

First, while America's female humorists have often written in the same modes as their male counterparts, used many of the same devices, and followed similar trends in humor, their work has been neither imitative nor derivative. As a popular art that must appeal to large numbers of readers, humorous writing by both genders is as subject to changes in fashion as are clothing styles and television programming. Public taste and current fads are in part responsible for the subject matter and style of the newspaper column, the book of light verse, and the humorous sketch or novel. But while responding to the pressure to conform to the expectations of the marketplace, American female writers have created a distinctive body of humor with common subjects and themes that set it apart from the male tradition of American humor. Reflecting, by necessity, their roles and positions as women in the culture, female writers have focused largely on the domestic sphere of wife and mother and on the social sphere that, differently in different eras, has been defined as women's work and activities. In short, they have written about "things which women in general find interesting," as Stillman and Beatts note in explaining why their collection, *Titters,* does not contain jokes about "jock straps, beer, trains, mothers-in-law, dumb blondes, cars, boxing, the Navy, chemistry, physics, stamp catalogues, spelunking, pud-pulling or poker" (4).

Second, as Mahadev Apte argues convincingly, because of "the behavioral, expressive, and other sociocultural constraints imposed on women . . . many common attributes of men's humor seem to be much less evident or even absent in women's humor" (69). In particular, Apte notes, cross-cultural research has shown that "women's humor generally lacks the aggressive and hostile quality of men's humor. The use of humor to compete with or to belittle others, thereby enhancing a person's own status, or to humiliate others either psychologically or physically, seems generally absent among women. Thus the most commonly institutionalized ways of engaging in such humor, namely, verbal duels, ritual insults, and practical jokes and pranks, are rarely reported for women" (70). Consequently, the degree to which aggression and hostility are overt in a particular woman's humorous expression depends on the degree of gender equality permitted in her society, as well as on her audience and on those who control the dissemination of her humor. For example, as Apte's research confirms, women are generally more free to ridicule men and make sexual jokes when the audience is exclusively female than they are when it is mixed.

Because of the constraints on women's expression, which in most cultures have included taboos against women's appropriation of sexual subject matter and language, women's humor has been described as more gentle and genteel than men's, more concerned with wit than derision, more interested in sympathy than ridicule, more focused on private than on public issues. These attributes, along with women's greater reliance on verbal devices of understatement, irony, and self-depreciation, have enabled women to mask or defuse the aggressive component of humor making, thereby minimizing the risks involved in challenging the status quo.

Third, because of women's unequal social, political, and economic status in most cultures, and the fact that they are regarded by men as "other" (factors compounded for women belonging to racial or ethnic minorities), women's and men's humor have been directed to different ends and/or realized in different ways. For example, most humor theorists consider the venting of aggression to be a major function of humor.[9] Freud was the first to suggest that humor is a socially acceptable way of releasing repressed antisocial or hostile impulses, and recent proponents of the aggression theory maintain that humorous pleasure drives from the derision, ridicule, deprecation, deflation, degradation, humiliation, and general mockery of individuals, groups, institutions, values, or ideas that threaten one's sense of security or well-being. As has already been suggested, however, most cultures harbor prohibitions against women's expression of aggression and hostility, especially in public and in mixed audiences. Moreover, women have been traditionally conditioned to assume passive, subordinate roles, and as Naomi Weisstein asserts in "Why We Aren't Laughing . . . Any More," the role of "a funny, nasty clown doesn't go along with the definition of WOMAN that gets us our provider."[10] These factors have not eliminated aggression as a motivation of women's humor, but they have compelled women to exercise it in more covert and indirect ways than men do.

In addition to the release of aggression or hostility, the exposure of incongruity is generally accepted by theorists as a major, universal function of humor. Proponents of the incongruity theory believe that humor operates primarily through surprise, shock, dislocation, or sudden reversal of expectations. However, because the perception of incongruity is based on shared values, beliefs, customs, habits, and experiences, the degree to which the genders (and races or ethnic groups) are differentiated by their cultures into separate classes of people will determine the degree to which they can share and enjoy each other's perceptions of the incongruities that make up their humorous visions. At the same time, whereas all groups in a society are aware of the values, beliefs, and behaviors that are promoted by the dominant culture, those belonging to the dominant culture do not generally have the same awareness of the attitudes, habits, and experiences of those excluded from or oppressed by it. Thus, as Bruère and Beard contend, "the angle of vision from which women see a lack of balance, wrong proportions, disharmonies, and incongruities in life is a thing of their world as it must be—a world always a little apart" (viii).

To the extent that woman's world is differentiated from man's, the incongruities revealed in women's humor reflect a world at odds with, and potentially threatening to, that of men. Because in women's humor, frustration and anger at gender-based inequities have had to be expressed obliquely, incongruity has been a major device for decoding the myths of the patriarchy. By exposing the discrepancies between the realities of women's lives and the images of women promoted by the culture, between the inequities to which women have been subjected and the egalitarian ideals upon which the nation was founded, American women humorists have targeted the patriarchal social system. For women of racial or ethnic minorities, of course, the conditions to be attacked and discrepancies to be exposed have been at least doubled.

Finally, the aggression and incongruity theories of humor have been further refined by social theorists who agree with Henri Bergson's position in *Laughter* that humor, in all of its manifestations, has primary social functions; they have argued that both the expression of hostility and the disclosure of discordance through humor depend upon social factors. Analysts have proposed, for example, that humor works in a number of ways as an agent of group enhancement and social control.[11] If the humor expressed in one group (the ingroup) disparages another group (the outgroup), it boosts the morale of and solidifies the ingroup as well as promoting hostility against the outgroup. If the ingroup is culturally dominant (in America, the white middle-class men), humor not only reinforces its sense of superiority but, at the same time, controls the behavior of the disparaged group (e.g., women, minorities) by creating or fostering conflict in or the demoralization of the disparaged group. In other words, humor is used by those in power, whether consciously or not, to preserve the status quo.

On the other hand, humor initiated in a group lacking status in the culture may bolster the members' self-esteem by disparaging the bases of the dominant group's claim to superiority. However, researchers have found that individuals and groups at the top of a social hierarchy use humor more often than those at the bottom, and generally direct it downward, while those at the lower level (e.g., women, minorities), when they use humor, direct it more frequently at themselves or at those below them than at those above them.

The use of self-deprecating humor by women could be a defensive reaction of those who feel themselves too weak or vulnerable to attack with impunity the forces that oppress them, but the seemingly defensive weapons of humor can also become offensive in the hands of women and other outgroups. For example, as psychologists have observed, laughing at one's shortcomings is not only a way of diminishing their importance and potentially overcoming them but is also a technique for cleansing them of pejorative connotations imposed by the dominant culture and, thereby, turning them into strengths. Similarly, the use of incongruity in humor by women as a means of targeting attributes and behaviors prescribed for them by the dominant culture is an act of rebellion. Finally, the use of humor by women against women, when it is used to advance ideas that might conflict with those of the male establishment about women's roles and prerogatives, represents a step toward empowerment rather than capitulation.

III

These various ideas about the nature, functions, and concerns of women's humor, which account for the different "angle of vision," the "world always a little apart," of American women's literary humor, can be seen in women's writing from the colonial era to the contemporary period. Two types of early American humor, usually identified with male writers, have been described by literary critics and historians: the formal, or "high," literary style of the British satirical mode and the informal, seemingly unconscious ironic style of such personal literary forms as diaries, journals, and travel books. The poetry of Anne Bradstreet (1612–1672), for example, uses devices of wit associated with male Elizabethan and Metaphysical poets, but Bradstreet uses these devices to express a woman's thoughts on marriage, motherhood, creativity, and religion at a time and in a place, Puritan New England, especially hostile to any public role or voice for women. In a poem such as "The Author to Her Book," therefore, Bradstreet adopts an overtly deferential tone about her work to appease her potential critics, but at the same time, the irony with which she presents her anomalous position as a woman poet serves to undermine both the seriousness of her apology and the logic of the patriarchal attitudes that would deny women minds, voices, and talents in anything other than domestic work. Similar uses of such double-edged irony can be found in the "apologies" of succeeding humorists, from Judith Sargent Murray in the eighteenth century to Jean Kerr in the twentieth, especially in what has been called "domestic" or "housewife" humor. As Neil Schmitz writes in reference to Gertrude Stein's work, "What aggression lurks in the deferential tone of the humorous woman, the ironist knows."[12]

The second strain of early American humor appears in Sarah Kemble Knight's diary, which records her five-month journey in 1704 from Boston to New York City and back. While the journal contains many of the elements of humor found in the travel accounts of such early American male writers as William Byrd II, its satiric treatment of regional manners, customs, and dialects reflects Knight's particular concern, as a Puritan woman, with ideas of proper "house-wifery." This emphasis on women's roles, as well as the realistic details that make up her humorous depictions of people and places, continues to inform the humor of regional writers, from Caroline Kirkland in the nineteenth century to Betty MacDonald and Cyra McFadden in the twentieth.

During the Revolutionary era, both Mercy Otis Warren and Judith Sargent Murray, like their male contemporaries, used satire to promote the cause of the American Patriots, but unlike the men, Warren and Murray were also concerned with women's rights and status in the new republic. Warren's patriotic play *The Group,* for example, closes with a female Patriot speaking about the connections between the Patriots' fight for freedom, women's desire for equality, and nature's revolt against the corruptions of Britain's tyranny. Similarly, while her political poetry has been compared to that of the "Connecticut Wits," other poems reveal that Warren's irony and wit, like Bradstreet's, served to present views that opposed the prevailing masculine view of religion, rationality, and relationship between the sexes.

While Warren's interest in women's rights tended to be voiced covertly in her poetry and plays, Judith Sargent Murray addressed questions of women's place in the new nation more openly. In essays, articles, comedies, and fiction, she directed her wit against those male assumptions about woman's physical, mental, and moral weakness that were used to preclude women's political participation in the Republic. Following Mary Wollstonecraft's position in *A Vindication of the Rights of Women* (1792), Murray protested restrictions on women's training, education, and political activity. In addition, in connecting women's moral behavior with civic virtue and in positing a social order based on marital equity and a balance between domestic and political activity, she not only represented what Nancy Cott calls "the equalitarian feminist view" of the late eighteenth century[13] but also anticipated the position of subsequent women writers who employed the devices of humor to deal with similar issues of women's rights in the nineteenth and twentieth centuries.

By advocating education and training for women that would promote their self-sufficiency and informed civic involvement, Murray sought, at least in part, to counter the prevailing sentimentalism of late-eighteenth-century popular literature. As the sentimental novel proliferated in the nineteenth century, later humorists attempted to do the same by painting satirical portraits of women suffering from the disease of sentimentality. The earliest of these, Tabitha Tenney's satirical novel, *Female Quixotism* (1801), recounts the lifelong romantic delusions that leave the heroine, Dorcasina Sheldon, in old age, with a wasted life, for which she blames her addiction to sentimental novels. Similarly, Caroline Kirkland's depiction of the "poet" Miss Eloise Fidler, in *A New Home—Who'll Follow?* (1839), ridicules both the claptrap of sentimental poetry and the pretensions of Miss Fidler herself, whose behavior and dress, modeled on sentimental literature, are particularly absurd in the backwoods Michigan environment that Kirkland describes. Continued satirical treatment of sentimental women in the work of Frances Whitcher and Marietta Holley prefigure the portraits in twentieth-century humor, from Betty MacDonald in the 1940s to Erma Bombeck in the 1970s, of women who accept and promote romanticized fantasies of female attributes and roles.

In Kirkland's work, the portrait of Miss Fidler is just one example of the "strong antiromance sentiment"[14] that, as in the work of later male frontier humorists, served to counterbalance increasingly romanticized accounts of life in the American West. But what differentiates Kirkland's work from that of the male humorists/realists is her emphasis on the problems and hardships faced by women living on the fringes of civilization. In addition, Kirkland's antiromanticism; descriptions of regional characteristics, language, and customs; and emphasis on depicting the realities of women's lives place her work in a line of women's humorous writing that began with Sarah Kemble Knight and extends to the work of journalist Mary Abigail Dodge (pseud. Gail Hamilton) and the local color realists of the latter part of the nineteenth century, as well as to twentieth-century writers who have used irony and satire to challenge prevailing myths about women's roles and about the communities in which they live.

As the cult of domesticity and the notion of separate spheres for men and women gained adherents in the nineteenth century, the contrasts between Kirkland's perspective and that of male humorists expanded to include other differences in men's and women's humorous literature. While men were developing a brand of American humor that began, as Bruère and Beard wrote, "in the robust expression of frontiersmen and [remained] in that gusto and temper while a new world was subdued to the plow, while an agricultural civilization swung toward an industrial one, while the nation was hammered into form by war and peace, prosperity and depression" (v), women were increasingly restricted to roles and admonished to cultivate qualities that were at odds with these changes and developments. Consequently, in the work of nineteenth-century female humorists, from Caroline Kirkland to Marietta Holley, there is a concern with the discrepancies between the opportunities opening up for men and the constraints closing in on women.

This concern appears most obviously in the locale of women's humorous stories: the kitchen or the sewing circle, the parlor or the dress shop, rather than the mining camp, the riverboat, the business or political office, or the saloon. The world perceived to be comically askew is the world of children and neighbors and teakettles, of relationships between men and women in the family and in society, of all that constituted what has traditionally been designated women's "proper sphere." Throughout the nineteenth century, most female humorists took as their subjects the domestic environment that formed a large part of their acquaintance with the world: the home, courtship and marriage, and those community activities assumed to be the special province of women—shopping, volunteer work, church and school groups. Ann Warner's "Susan Clegg" stories, for example, published at the turn of the twentieth century, show the garrulous and unconsciously funny Susan enmeshed in housework and the care of her invalid father, having postponed thoughts of marriage in order to fill the role of housekeeper and nurse. Even Emily Dickinson, who did not participate directly in most community activities, comments ironically on woman's "sphere" and the social perception of her role, and the imagery of domestic life permeates both her comic and serious poetry.

Along with this common subject matter, women who have written humor have pursued several common themes. The most pervasive of these has been a concern with the incongruities between the realities of women's lives and the sentimental or idealized images fostered by the culture; between women's awareness of their abilities and ambitions, and their perception of the laws and conventions that have restricted them to a limited sphere of activity. In pointing out these incongruities, female humorists have encouraged an enlargement of woman's sphere and protested the restrictions that, in barring women from utilizing their talents and abilities in the public arena, have countenanced their dissipating their energies in the pursuit of husbands, social status, fashion, spotless floors, perfect bodies, and super momism. Their techniques have included realistic portrayals of women's lives; contrasts between what the authors believe to be strong, positive images of women and weak, negative stereotypes; and deflation of masculine notions of male superiority.

These themes and techniques were first evident in nineteenth-century works, from Anna Cora Mowatt's popular comedy *Fashion* (1850) to Marietta Holley's "Samantha Allen" series, published between 1873 and 1914. While Mowatt satirizes the genteel pretensions and frivolous behavior of middle-class urban women through the characters of Mrs.

Tiffany and her daughter, she also shows, through the contrasting character of Gertrude Truelove, that women become virtuous and self-reliant when they are raised with traditional rural values and taught the skills with which to support themselves. Frances Whitcher's work also ridicules the excesses of gentility by using women as both subjects and objects of her humor. The Widow Bedott, the narrator of her most popular work, is a garrulous, middle-aged widow obsessed with finding a second husband. In lampooning Bedott and her circle for self-righteousness and malicious gossiping, however, Whitcher did not intend, as did her male counterparts, merely to perpetuate negative stereotypes of women. Rather, as her "Aunt Maguire" letters and her novel *Mary Elmer* illustrate, she hoped to motivate change by depicting the ways in which women betray their nature, themselves, and each other by adopting the cold, commercial values of the male world. Marietta Holley, whose books rivaled Mark Twain's in sales at the turn of the twentieth century, followed Whitcher's Aunt Maguire in creating as her spokesperson Samantha Allen, an unsophisticated farm wife who combines commonsense practicality with the simple logic born of experience. Through Samantha's discussions of her domestic responsibilities with Betsey Bobbet—another caricature of a sentimental spinster given to perorations about women as ivy needing man as oak to cling to—Holley exposes the contradictions between the illusions and the realities of married life. In the twentieth century, the tradition of using contrasting characters to explore the conflict between the real and ideal is continued in the juxtaposition of the compulsive Mrs. Hicks to the slovenly Mrs. Kettle in Betty MacDonald's *Egg and I,* and of black domestic servant and white employer in Alice Childress's *Like One of the Family.*

This conflict between real and ideal serves to point up another theme in women's humor: the need to be taken seriously. Sara Willis Parton, for example, a newspaper columnist who published two volumes of articles titled *Fern Leaves from Fanny's Port-Folio* (1853 and 1854) using the pseudonym Fanny Fern, is in the tradition of those, from Bradstreet to Beatts, who have attacked male attitudes toward women writers, as well as exposed the difficulties of trying to combine a literary career with housework and child rearing. As a social commentator, she used satire to expose, in particular, the ways in which an obsession with power and money corrupts. As an advocate of education and independence for women, she challenged the idea that married women were happy, or at least happier than single women, echoing Judith Sargent Murray in attributing much of the unhappiness in marriage to imbalances of power and calling for greater equality for women. Harriet Beecher Stowe's "The Minister's Housekeeper" similarly urges a re-vision of women's talent and worth, as represented by the efficiency and common sense of Huldy. And Marietta Holley, in her twenty-one humorous books, used Samantha Allen in part to illustrate that although "women's work" has been presumed to be trivial, it is, in fact, important and should be taken seriously. As Samantha avows in Holley's first book, *My Opinions and Betsey Bobbet's* (1873), "Why jest the idee of paradin' out the table and teakettle 3 times 3 hundred and 65 times every year is enough to make a woman sweat."[15] Women's work was also vehemently defended by Phyllis McGinley for several decades of the twentieth century and, slyly, by Shirley Jackson, who remarks in *Life Among the Savages* (1953) after a flurry of housework and child care, "I don't care what *anyone* says, that's a morning's work."[16]

Taking women seriously, for Marietta Holley, also meant granting them equal rights, and by focusing on the issues that most concerned women's rights proponents of the late nineteenth century—suffrage, temperance, entry into the professions, equal pay for equal work—Holley introduced a feminist theme that sharply distinguishes women's humor from men's. As Jane Curry notes in her introduction to *Samantha Rastles the Woman Question,* a selection of excerpts from Holley's books, "When one reads the Samantha books, she begins to view the 19th century not as 'then' so much as it was the beginning of 'now.'"[17] Like Jonathan Slick, the "wise fool" figure of Ann Stephens's work, and the popular personae of early nineteenth-century "Down East" humor, Samantha exposes pretentiousness and hypocrisy through her ability to see and call a spade a spade. Throughout the many Samantha books, Holley's implacable logic contrasts with other people's illogicality of sentiment or prejudice. In her first book, for example, Holley reverses the traditional images of the genders, depicting Josiah, Samantha's husband, as physically smaller and weaker than she, less rational, more susceptible to fads and fashions, and more dependent. Consequently, the arguments advanced by Josiah against women's rights—based on popular notions of woman's weakness, fickleness, and irrationality—are reduced to absurdity. Holley's use of ironic role reversal and her concern with social issues, particularly political equality for women, anticipate the suffrage work of Alice Duer Miller and Josephine Daskam in the early twentieth century, as well as the more recent feminist humor of the 1970s and 1980s. Similar techniques have been used by ethnic humorists to undermine the cultural assumptions of inferiority that have been used to deny them equal rights.

By the turn of the century, some of the characteristics that had distinguished women's humor through the nineteenth century began to change as American humor in general began to reflect the shift in population from rural areas to the cities and as new magazines emerged to appeal to the values and tastes of an increasingly urbane, cosmopolitan audience for humor. Providing outlets for cartoons, light verse, and humorous sketches that emphasized sophisticated wordplay rather than dialect humor, these new publications also reflected the new interest of an urban cultural elite in technological advances, in the social sciences and psychology, and in the images of the "new woman" and "little man" that were transforming American life.

The increased freedom that women achieved in the decades just before and after the passage of the suffrage amendment in 1920, at the same time that men were experiencing what Norris Yates describes as a diminution of their status and influence,[18] contributed to the "war between the sexes" that American humorists of both genders waged in their work during the first three decades of the twentieth century. At the same time, the new freedoms for women increased the opportunities for social mingling of men and women, while the growth of the media promoted a popular culture of interests and activities, fads and fashions that cut across gender and even class lines. In Bruère and Beard's selection of humor by women after 1900, these shifts are apparent both in the subject matter and in the publications in which the humor originally appeared. Working as journalists, columnists, and cartoonists for major newspapers in New York and Chicago and for magazines such as *Harper's,* the *New Yorker, Vanity Fair,* the *Saturday Evening Post,* and even political organs such as the *New Leader,* these early twentieth-century female humorists had a less restricted audience than did many of their nineteenth-century counterparts. Consequently, their humor reflects greater diversity of subject matter, as well as concern with gender roles and relationships in a rapidly changing society.

One indication of these changes is that the prevalent nineteenth-century notions of separate spheres for men and women and of distinct masculine and feminine natures and functions do not serve as a basic premise for this later humor. For example, in the political satire of Alice Duer Miller and Charlotte Perkins Gilman, it is not women's special, feminine contributions that are emphasized to justify their gaining the vote so much as their simple right as human beings in a democratic society to legal and political equality with men. Similarly, tacit assumptions about woman's moral superiority, nurturing qualities, and instinctive sensitivity to others are challenged by writers such as Josephine Daskam, Helen Rowland, and Florence Guy Seabury, who work both with and against established stereotypes of men and women to give the genders "realistic" advice about, and images of, each other.

Moreover, in the work of such writers as Dorothy Parker and Anita Loos, who deal with the "war between the sexes," women characters are portrayed as being just as morally and psychologically confused, self-absorbed, and manipulative as their male counterparts. Finally, the expansion of women's options is reflected in Mary Roberts Rinehart's "Tish" stories, published between 1910 and 1937, which present an embodiment of "new woman" in the attitudes and behavior of Letitia "Tish" Carberry, an independent spinster who, content with her single status, engages herself and two spinster friends in a variety of activities and adventures, from automobile racing, flying, and camping to catching crooks and even liberating a town from the Germans in World War I.

Despite the proliferation in the early decades of the twentieth century of female humorists exhibiting a wide diversity in style, form, and subject matter, the main thread that continued to run through women's humor of the 1930s and 1940s was the "little woman," the counter of the "little man" of male humorists such as Thurber and Benchley. Whether urban, suburban, or rural, the young housewives and new mothers depicted first by Parker and later by Cornelia Otis Skinner and Betty MacDonald are as bewildered by the conflicting demands of other people, as controlled by the technology and bureaucracy of modern life, and as intimidated by their own fear of failure as the "little men."

By the fifties and sixties, the "little woman" had become the housewife heroine of the "domestic" humor that dominated the period. Inspired by the post-World War II campaign to return the American woman to the home, this humor concerns the trials and tribulations of middle-class housewives who, in increasing numbers, inhabited suburban communities featuring commuting husbands, children, and other frantic women. Disseminated primarily in magazines and sections of newspapers addressed to women, this humor spoke to an audience that could be characterized by the title of Phyllis McGinley's poem "Occupation: Housewife." Like their nineteenth-century forebears, these women were cut off from the public world of business and enterprise that their husbands inhabited and restricted to a routine of domestic chores and child rearing. Domestic humor provided a way for both writer and audience to minimize through laughter and, thereby, better cope with the frustrations and demands of their lives.

Betty Friedan's 1963 analysis of the housewife's discontent, *The Feminine Mystique,* not only helped to spark the rebirth of a movement for female equality but also abetted the emergence in the late sixties and early seventies of a feminist humor more overt and aggressive than the political humor of the suffrage era. The women who created this humor were influenced by the iconoclastic style and irreverent tone of a new generation of black and white male comics, beginning with Lenny Bruce, whose political and social satire appealed to increasing numbers of college students and young adults who were in rebellion against the competitive and conformist values of the fifties and inspired by the civil rights and peace movements of the sixties.

Selecting specific agents of oppression as targets, women humorists of the seventies and eighties have attacked the greater privilege and freedom of men, derided patriarchal institutions, and ridiculed social, sexual, and racial stereotyping. Influenced by the new wave of male comics, women humorists have appropriated subject matter once considered taboo for women, accepting the totality of female experience—including sexual relationships, menstruation, lesbianism, anxieties about one's attractiveness, and the ineptitude of men—as material for humor. Moreover, humorists such as Erica Jong have addressed these topics with a bawdy tone and in graphic sexual and scatological terms that, because they come from a woman, still shock or offend segments of the population. Although domestic humor has maintained its popularity alongside feminist and new wave humor, women's humor of the past two decades has generally become more confrontational on social and political issues, rather than sly or cute.

IV

A careful reading of the humor of American women from the seventeenth century to the 1980s, then, makes it clear that we must revise our notions of "traditional" American humor. Most twentieth-century analysts have assumed that the large subjects of this nation's humor have been the frontier experience, democracy, and the growth of bureaucracy and technology. They have seen humor as an index to national identity, a guide to changes in values. There is no doubt that its humor provides important clues about the character of the nation, but considering as relevant the humor of only half the population, as most scholars have done, leads to a partial and distorted picture. The humor of the American male has posited a world of energy, mobility, and privilege—a world from which women have been systematically excluded.

The humor in this anthology shows us a different world, one in which the minutiae of the private, daily existence loom larger than the political misdeed or the corporate maneuver, but one which can have an impact, for good or ill, on the public sphere. The important developments of American society, according to this separate tradition, have been those that have affected woman's place in the culture: changes in clothing styles and etiquette manuals; successive child-raising theories; moves to the frontier or to the city; industrial and technical advancements that have changed women's work; social movements that have influenced society's conceptions of women's nature and roles; cultural theories that have altered women's images of themselves and relationships to others; and periods of political or economic agitation, especially about women's rights, that have enlarged women's options for participation in the world.

Consequently, an anthology of women's humor is an important and necessary first step in demonstrating the range and complexity of the "other half" of America's humorous tradition. A second, equally important reason for such a collection is to make available some nearly forgotten, out-of-print examples of women's humor from various periods in American literary history. At the end of each headnote is a list of sources consulted and a selected list of humorous works by the author.

The choice of selections, as in all such anthologies, is limited to some extent by space and reprint restrictions, as well as by the fact that humor is a matter of taste as much as of aesthetic judgment. Nonetheless, we have attempted to present a fair representation of authors, eras, genres, and styles, in choosing pieces that seek, through the devices of humor, to mirror and to motivate changes in the experiences, character, and aspirations of American women.

Notes

1. E.B. White and Katharine S. White, eds., *A Subtreasury of American Humor* (New York: Modern Library, 1948), xviii.

2. Arthur Power Dudden, ed., *American Humor* (New York: Oxford Univ. Press, 1987), xi–xii.

3. This series includes Constance Rourke, *American Humor: A Study of the National Character* (New York: Harcourt, 1931); Walter Blair, *Native American Humor* (1800–1900) (Hartford: American Book, 1937); Norris Yates, *The American Humorist: Conscience of the Twentieth Century* (Ames: Iowa State Univ. Press, 1964); Jesse Bier, *The Rise and Fall of American Humor* (New York: Holt, 1968); Louis D. Rubin, Jr., *The Comic Imagination in American Literature* (New Brunswick, N.J.: Rutgers Univ. Press, 1973); Walter Blair and Hamlin Hill, *America's Humor: From Poor Richard to Doonesbury* (New York: Oxford Univ. Press, 1978); Neil Schmitz, *Of Huck and Alice: Humorous Writing in American Literature* (Minneapolis: Univ. of Minnesota Press, 1983).

4. See Judith Fetterly's discussion of the treatment of nineteenth-century women writers in her introduction to *Provisions: A Reader from 19th Century American Women* (Bloomington: Indiana Univ. Press, 1985), 16–31.

5. See Jesse Bier's discussion of misogyny in *The Rise and Fall of American Humor*, 22.

6. Mahadev L. Apte, *Humor and Laughter: An Anthropological Approach* (Ithaca, N.Y.: Cornell Univ. Press, 1985), 69.

7. Martha Bensley Bruère and Mary Ritter Beard, eds., *Laughing Their Way: Women's Humor in America* (New York: Macmillan, 1934), v–viii.

8. Deanne Stillman and Anne Beatts, eds., *Titters: The First Collection of Humor by Women* (New York: Collier, 1976), 3.

9. This discussion of the aggression theory and the following discussion of the incongruity theory of humor is based on papers in Antony J. Chapman and Hugh C. Foot, eds., *Humor and Laughter: Theory, Research, and Applications* (New York: Wiley, 1976), and *It's A Funny Thing, Humour* (New York: Pergamon, 1977); Jeffrey H. Goldstein and Paul E. McGhee, eds., *The Psychology of Humor* (New York: Academic Press, 1972).

10. Naomi Weisstein, "Why We Aren't Laughing . . . Any More," *Ms.* (November 1973): 89.

11. See, for example, William H. Martineau, "A Model of the Social Functions of Humour," in *The Psychology of Humor;* Charles Winick, "The Social Contexts of Humour," *Journal of Communication 26* (Summer 1976): 124–28; Joseph Boskin, *Humor and Social Change in Twentieth-Century America,* Lectures delivered for the NEH Boston Public Library Learning Library Program (Boston: Trustees of the Public Library of the City of Boston, 1979).

12. Schmitz, *Of Huck and Alice,* 210.

13. Nancy Cott, *The Bonds of Womanhood: "Woman's Sphere" in New England, 1780–1875* (New Haven: Yale Univ. Press, 1977), 202.

14. Josephine Donovan, *New England Local Color Literature* (New York: Frederick Ungar, 1982), 26.

15. Marietta Holley, *My Opinions and Betsey Bobbet's* (Hartford: American Publishing Co., 1873), 59.

16. Shirley Jackson, *Life Among the Savages* (New York: Farrar, Straus and Young, 1953), 2.

17. Jane Curry, Introduction to *Samantha Rastles the Woman Question* (Urbana: Univ. of Illinois Press, 1983), 1.

18. Yates, *The American Humorist,* 38.

II. The Tradition of Women's Humor in America

Wit, Sentimentality, and the Image of Women in the Nineteenth Century

Nancy Walker

I
n two articles in *The Critic* in 1884, Alice Wellington Rollins attempted to counter the conventional notion that a sense of humor was "that rarest of qualities in woman," as Richard Grant White had written earlier in the same publication. Though she acknowledged that "as we have had no feminine Artemus Ward, so we have had no woman novelist in whose work humor has even so prominent a part as it has in Dickens," she insisted that in conversation as well as in writing women had great talent for humor.[1] But Twain's portrait of Emmeline Grangerford in *Huck Finn* the following year seems to have solidified the image of the nineteenth-century female writer as a wan poet obsessed with morbidity. However, in the same year that *Huck Finn* was published, Kate Sanborn followed Alice Rollins' lead and published an anthology called *The Wit of Women*.[2] Sanborn did not adhere to a rigid definition of "wit" in her comments or in her selections, which range from an eighteenth-century poem by Mercy Warren (whom Sanborn calls "a satirist quite in the strain of Juvenal") to the dialect humor of Harriet Beecher Stowe and "Grace Greenwood," and include parodies, poems for children and bits of witty conversation overheard at dinner parties. Frances Whicher's *Widow Bedott Papers* she deems too popular to require a selection—"every one who enjoys that style of humor knows them by heart"—but she did include excerpts from Caroline Kirkland, Rose Terry Cooke, Sarah Orne Jewett and many others.

Despite the grab-bag nature of her anthology, Sanborn was both acknowledging and participating in a trend which ran counter to the prevailing sentimentality of women's literature in the nineteenth century. At the same time as the image of the literary woman, as well as that of the educated, middle-class woman in general, increasingly partook of the characteristics which Twain ascribed to Emmeline—frailty, emotionalism, a consummate uselessness—the female humorists of the century waged a little-recognized but persistent war against that figure. In their own work, the "witty women"—"Fanny Fern," Caroline Kirkland, Frances Whicher, "Gail Hamilton" and Marietta Holley—consistently satirized the woman who wrote pious, sentimental prose and poetry. Their efforts to demote this figure from the high status accorded her by genteel society were part of their rebellion against widely-held notions of woman's "proper" role in American culture.

In *The Feminization of American Culture,* Ann Douglas argues persuasively that an unstructured but potent coalition of Protestant ministers and middle-class, Northern women led to the sentimentalization of American popular literature between 1820 and 1880. Douglas asserts that just as liberal Protestant clergymen lost authority through the disestablishment of religion in the early nineteenth century and the concurrent rise to prominence of more evangelical sects such as the Methodists and the Baptists, so women lost status by virtue of the shift from a home-based to a factory-based economy. The home, "formerly an important part of a communal productive process under her direction, . . . had become a place where her children stayed before they began to work and where her husband rested after the strain of labor."[3] The woman became "influence" rather than producer, and the nature of her influence was defined by the conventions of Christianity. Both ministers and women turned to literature as a means of promoting their own, strikingly similar values. "They inevitably confused theology with religiosity, religiosity with literature, and literature with self-justification."[4] A sentimental literature, according to Douglas, was the inevitable result. "Sentimentalism is a complex phenomenon. It asserts that the values a society's activity denies are precisely the ones it cherishes; it attempts to deal with the phenomenon of cultural bifurcation by the manipulation of nostalgia. Sentimentalism provides a way to protest a power to which one has already in part capitulated."[5]

If sentimentality in literature is a result of powerlessness, wit may be seen as its opposite: an expression of confidence and power. The word remains closely associated with its Old English origin in *wita,* "one who knows." Long before it acquired the connotation of amusement, wit was connected with knowledge, understanding, perception. Sentimentality exerts a passive, often subversive power; wit, on the other hand, is a direct and open expression of perceptions, taking for granted a position of strength and insight. It was this confident stance which both Alice Rollins and Kate Sanborn admired in the women humorists they praised in the 1880's. Humor functioned as an antidote to the pious religiosity of the sentimental novel and poem.

Among major authors of the nineteenth century, the foremost "witty woman," as Constance Rourke pointed out long ago, is Emily Dickinson, who "contrived to see a changing universe within that acceptant view which is comic in its profoundest sense, which is part reconciliation, part knowledge of eternal disparity."[6] It is ironic that Dickinson's reclusiveness and eccentricity have caused her to remain, at least in the popular imagination, an embodiment of conventional femininity, a retiring New England spinster with her eyes fixed on the next world. In sharp contrast to this image, Dickinson's humor emerges from her lyrics precisely as moments of insight; she is the "one who knows," and her wit denies sentimentality, even—or especially—when the subject is death, that favorite subject of Emmeline Grangerford and other satiric representations of the female writer. For Emily Dickinson, wit was a natural mode; but for the more popular women writers of the nineteenth century, sentimentality was a constant temptation and had to be dealt with in satire.

The recurrent satire on the sentimental female author in nineteenth-century women's humor may therefore be seen as having a different and more pointed motive than does Twain's portrait of Emmeline. Twain's description is part of his more comprehensive attack, in *Huck Finn* and elsewhere, on Victorian tastelessness and lack of refinement, is of a piece with his depiction of the vulgarities of household adornment and the behavior of the crowds who witness the debased versions of Shakespearean plays presented by the Duke and the Dauphin. The systematic attack on the sentimental female author—her person as well as her product—in the works in Kirkland, Whicher, Holley and other nineteenth-century female humorists, however, is an attempt to deny the image of woman as a weak, frail vessel of Christian piety, and to posit instead an image of the "witty" woman: one who sees through sham and stereotype, for whom courage and strength of mind are positive virtues.

"Fanny Fern" (Sara Willis Parton) must figure prominently in any discussion of both witty and sentimental women writers in the nineteenth century because of her mastery of both styles. F. L. Pattee calls her "the most tearful and convulsingly 'female' moralizer of the whole modern blue-stocking school,"[7] and Sanborn refers to her "talent for humorous composition," and says her style "was thought very amusing."[8] Both are correct.

Sara Willis Parton was born in 1811 and grew up in the Calvinistic atmosphere which also influenced Harriet Beecher Stowe (her father was a friend of Lyman Beecher, and she attended Catharine Beecher's Female Seminary). After two marriages, one ending in death and the other in divorce, she turned to writing to support herself. When her sketches were rejected by her brother, Nathaniel Parker Willis, editor of *The Home Journal,* her career was championed by James Parton who became her third husband. The first series of *Fern Leaves from Fanny's Portfolio* (1853) consists of both extremely sentimental and sharply satiric pieces, and the contemporary reviewer for *Putnam's Magazine* described them quite accurately:

> They are acute, crisp, sprightly, knowing, and, though sometimes rude, evince much genuine and original talent, a keen power of observation, lively fancy, and humorous as well as pathetic sensibilities.[9]

In Parton's own preface to the book, she announces that "some of the articles are sad, some are gay,"[10] and the first three-quarters of the book consists chiefly of the former, with titles such as "The Widow's Trial," "A Night-Watch with a Dead Infant," and "The Invalid Wife." Death and loss are the major themes, and the style is pious and overblown in the manner of the sentimental novel. Even in this section, however, Parton's wit and her objective distance from such sentimentality are apparent. The selection "A Chapter on Literary Women" consists of a dialogue between Colonel Van Zandt, who has a "perfect horror of satirical women," and Minnie, who introduces him to the woman he marries—who turns out to be a writer. The Colonel is finally forced to acknowledge that "a woman may be literary, and yet feminine and lovable."[11]

Parton's awareness that she is merely following fashion by writing sentimental sketches is amply demonstrated in the brief essay "Borrowed Light," in which she sarcastically advises beginning authors to imitate the work of popular writers:

> Borrow whole sentences, if you like, taking care to transpose the words a little. Baptize all your heroes and heroines at the same font;—be facetious, sentimental, pathetic, terse, or diffuse, just like your leader.

And she mocks her own choice of a pseudonym when she advises:

> In choosing your signature, bear in mind that nothing goes down, now-a-days, but *alliteration*. For instance, Delia Daisy, Fanny Foxglove, Harriet Honeysuckle, Lily Laburnam,

Paulena Poppy, Minnie Mignonette, Julia Jonquil, Seraphina Sunflower, etc., etc.[12]

The selections in Part II of *Fern Leaves,* in which this essay appears, are as satiric as those in Part I are sentimental. Using a tone of ironic sarcasm, Parton comments on the vanity of women, the helplessness of men, the problems of ministers and the hypocrisy of editors. The sane, sprightly satire and the curt, pithy style are the direct opposite of the sentimental prose in the first part of the book. In "The Model Widow" she presents a husband-hunter who anticipates the Widow Bedott, and in "Bachelor Housekeeping" she satirizes the helplessness of men as Florence Guy Seabury would many years later in "The Delicatessen Husband." After quoting a scene in which a man, in answer to his servant's announcement that there is no bread for his breakfast, says, "No bread! then bring me some toast," Parton begins:

> I think I see him! Ragged dressing-gown; beard two days old; depressed dickey; scowling face; out at elbow, out of sorts, and—out of "toast!" Poor thing! Don't the sight make my heart ache? How should he be expected to know that bread was the forerunner of toast, without a wife to tell him?[13]

The humor of this and other pieces, such as "Aunt Hetty on Matrimony," bespeaks a sincerity completely lacking in the sentimental sketches and stories. This is the real "Fanny Fern"—or rather, this is Sara Willis Parton—following no stereotypical pattern of "feminine" writing, but taking a brisk, analytical look at manners and values.

"Borrowed Light" is the closest Parton came to satirizing the sentimental female writer, but the tradition of such satire had begun some years before in Caroline Kirkland's *A New Home—Who'll Follow!* (1839). A native of New York City, Kirkland spent seven years in frontier Michigan with her husband William, a schoolteacher turned town-builder, and wrote about this experience with candor and much satiric humor in *A New Home* and the later *Forest Life* (1842). The chapter epigraphs—quotations from Rochefoucalt, Bacon, Pope, Byron and Shakespeare—testify to Kirkland's education, but are oddly at variance with her straightforward, somewhat understated style, which purports to be that of her *persona*, Mary Clavers. Mary Clavers is from the civilized East, but she is not a snob; instead she seems honestly bewildered by the actual crudeness of frontier life, and copes as well as she can with the privations of western settlement.[14]

Into this frontier community comes the female poet, Miss Eloise Fidler, for a visit of some months, and Kirkland uses the occasion for some of her most delicate yet most barbed wit. Here, as in other female humorists' portraits of this figure, the satire is directed as much to the personality of the sentimental writer as to the quality of her writing. In fact, one of the evidences of her uselessness in society is that she produces very little. In comparison with Marietta Holley's Betsey Bobbet, later in the century, Miss Fidler is young, but "at least at mateable years; neither married, nor particularly likely to be married":

> Her age was at a stand; but I could never discover exactly where, for this point proved an exception to the general communicativeness of her disposition. I guessed it at eight-and-twenty; but perhaps she would have judged this uncharitable, so I will not insist.

Miss Fidler has an album in which she encourages her friends to write verses; Kirkland admits to having kept the book for three months without being able to think of anything to write which will match the overblown style of the entries already there. One assumes that Miss Fidler's own poetry resembles that of her friends; Kirkland is more concerned to present a picture of the artist at work:

> It was unfortunate that she could not walk out much on account of her shoes. She was obliged to make out with diluted inspiration. The nearest approach she usually made to the study of Nature, was to sit on the woodpile, under a

girdled tree, and there, with her gold pencil in hand, and her "eyne, grey as glas," rolled upwards, poefy by the hour.

Miss Fidler's desire to marry comes not so much from romantic notions of marriage as from the fact that she hates her maiden name, and "the grand study of her life had been to sink this hated cognomen in one more congenial to her taste." She fixes her attention on a store clerk whose name she supposes to be Edward Dacre; when she discovers that it is actually the less euphonious "Edkins Daker," she is temporarily disenchanted, but ultimately marries him despite this fault.

It is worth noting that the occasion of Daker's entrance into the story is a debate regarding the "comparative mental capacity of the sexes," at the conclusion of which the young clerk prevails with the opinion that:

> if the natural and social disadvantages under which women labored and must ever continue to labor, could be removed; if their education could be entirely different, and their position in society the reverse of what it is at present, they would be very nearly, if not quite, equal to the nobler sex, in all but strength of mind, in which very useful quality it was his opinion that men would still have the advantage.[15]

The "strength of mind" which Kirkland mentions here is a concomitant of wit, and a quality which Emily Dickinson possessed in abundance. The fact that Miss Fidler has neither is what qualifies her as the object of Kirkland's satire.

Shortly after Kirkland's first book was published, Frances M. Whicher[16] began writing in the dialect of rural New York State in the "Widow Bedott" sketches and other work, published in the Albany *Argus, Neal's Saturday Gazette* and *Godey's Lady's Book.* None of her work was collected in book form until after her death in 1852. In 1856 Alice B. Neal, widow of the editor of *Neal's Saturday Gazette,* published a collection of the "Widow Bedott" and "Aunt Maguire" pieces, and in 1867 Whicher's earlier pieces were published in a volume titled *Widow Spriggins, Mary Elmer and Other*

Sketches. Extremely publicity-shy, Whicher refused for a time to reveal her identity even to editor Neal, and replied to a request for information about herself with a flippant poem in which she described herself as having:

> Hands and feet
> of respectable size
> *Mud-colored* hair,
> And dubious eyes.[17]

Part of her desire for anonymity seems to have come from a genuine retiring nature and a lack of confidence in her own abilities. Soon after she began writing the "Widow Bedott" sketches for Neal, she apparently considered giving up the series, which prompted a letter from Neal that testifies to the popularity of the sketches:

> All the world is full of Bedott. Our readers talk of nothing else and almost despise "Neal" if the Widow be not there. An excellent critic in these matters, said to me the other day, that he regarded them as the best Yankee papers yet written, and such is indeed the general sentiment. I know for instance, of a lady who for several days after reading one of them, was continually, and often, at moments the most inopportune, bursting forth into fits of violent laughter, and believe me that you, gifted with such power, ought not to speak disparagingly of the gift which thus brings wholesome satire home to every reader.[18]

Though Whicher continued to write for *Neal's* and later for *Godey's,* her shunning of the public eye was no doubt due in part to what Neal calls her "wholesome satire," but which was not so kindly regarded by some of her targets. In a letter to Alice Neal, Whicher testifies that her satiric talent was a mixed blessing from the beginning:

> I received, at my birth, the undesirable gift of a remarkably strong sense of the ridiculous. I can scarcely remember the time when the neighbors were not afraid that I would "make fun of them." I was scolded at home, and wept over and

prayed with, by certain well-meaning old maids in the
neighborhood; but all to no purpose.[19]

As the wife of a clergyman, Whicher ran particular risks as a
satirist, and her husband's congregation in Elmira, New York,
finally decided that they could do without his services after
one parishioner threatened a lawsuit, claiming he recognized
his wife in one of Whicher's comic portraits. It is probably not
necessary to speculate on this gentleman's opinion of his own
wife; suffice it to say that most of Whicher's portraits of
women are far less than flattering.

The humor in Whicher's sketches arises in part from stock
comic devices of the 1840's: humorous names for people and
places (the "Rev. Sniffles," "Wiggletown," "Scrabble Hill,"
etc.), broadly phonetic spelling and ludicrous situations. But
underlying this humorous surface is telling satire on human
characteristics—in particular, vanity, foolishness and false
pride. The Widow Bedott, who became a popular stage
character in the 1880's, embodies several of the characteristics
which are most commonly found in satiric sketches of women
in the nineteenth century. She is a gossip, a man-chaser and a
"scribbling woman." But Whicher goes a step further than the
usual satiric portrait. In Kirkland's descriptions of Miss Fidler,
as well as in Holley's later characterization of Betsey Bobbet,
the *persona* of the sensible, reasonable narrator provides
contrast and distance to the humorous character. The
character, in other words, is at two removes from the reader,
eliciting laughter but little sympathy. Whicher, however, uses
the technique of Josh Billings and Artemus Ward: the Widow
Bedott tells her own story in her own dialect, and thus
seemingly unwittingly reveals her flaws as she earnestly
pursues her interests. Whicher increases the humorous
potential by having the Widow criticize the very
characteristics which she herself embodies. Having set her cap
for Mr. Crane the instant she hears he has been widowed, she
immediately assesses the competition for his interest, one
Polly Bingham Jenkins:

> Now I shouldn't wonder if she should set tew and try tew
> ketch Mr. Crane when he comes back, should you? I'll bet
> forty great apples she'll dew it, she's been ravin' distracted
> to git married ever since she was a widder, but I ruther guess
> Timothy Crane ain't a man to be took in by such a great fat,
> humbly, slanderin' old butter tub. She's as gray as a rat, tew,
> that are hair o' hern's false . . . . I think 't would be a good
> idear for some friendly person to warn Mr. Crane against
> Poll Jinkins as soon as he gits here, don't you?[20]

The "friendly person" is, of course, the Widow herself, who
writes a poem for Mr. Crane in which she purports to describe
his feelings upon losing his wife. Like most of the Widow's
poetry, it is a spoof of the sentimental poem, with contrived
rhymes, awkward grammar, and ludicrous emotional excess.
Titled "Mr. Crane's Lamentations on the Death of His
Companion," the poem reads in part:

> I used to fraquently grumble at my fate
>   And be afeered I was a gwine to suffer sorrer—
> But since you died my trouble is so great
>   I hain't got no occasion for to borrer.[21]

Perhaps the best example of Whicher's satire on the
sentimental poem itself is the one which the Widow writes to
Rev. Sniffles during her ultimately successful pursuit of his
hand in marriage. Not only does the Widow manage to rhyme
"frenzy" and "influenzy," but the poem also contains the
following bit of self-serving "comfort" for the widower:

> Then mourn not for yer pardner's death,
>   But to submit endevver;
> For s'posen she hadent a died so soon,
>   She couldent a lived forever.[22]

The most direct satire on the sentimental female writer in *The
Widow Bedott Papers* occurs as the Widow and Aunt Maguire
discuss Sally Hugle, who writes poetry for the "Scrabble Hill
Luminary," a local newspaper. Sally Hugle, a spinster, also

pursues the Rev. Sniffles, and thus is a double rival of the Widow. Aunt Maguire describes her poetry:

> She generally calls 'em *"sunnets"*—Jeff [Aunt Maguire's son] says they ought to be called *moonets,* cause they're always full o' stuff about the moon and stars, and so on. She's always groanin' away about her *inward griefs,* and *unknown mysteries.* I don't know what to make on't. Sally Hugle never had no partickler trouble as I know on—without 't was her not bein able to ketch a husband.

Aunt Maguire recites several stanzas of one of Sally Hugle's poems, which is almost identical to the Widow's efforts, but the Widow asserts that she could "make better poitry 'n that by throwin' an inkstand at a sheet o' paper."[23] The composite picture of the single female—widow or spinster—who writes poetry for the local paper is one which involves extremes of vanity, petty competition and an appalling lack of sophistication. The satire, in fact, seems directed as much to low editorial standards for "literature" as to the individual perpetrators of execrable verse.

Though the Widow's nickname is "Silly" (short for "Priscilla"), she can hardly compete in silliness with her predecessor, the Widow Spriggins. Whicher wrote the Widow Spriggins letters for the Albany *Argus,* and they were later collected in the 1867 volume of her work. The humor lacks the depth and complexity of the Widow Bedott and Aunt Maguire sketches, but the Widow Spriggins letters are interesting as a different sort of satire on the "scribbling women." Sprinkled with malapropisms, the Spriggins letters tell of the courtship of Permilly Ruggles and Jabez Spriggins from the point of view of Permilly, whose romantic notions of behavior are derived from the sentimental novel.[24] In anticipation of Tom Sawyer following the dictates of romantic fiction for setting Jim free at the end of *Huck Finn,* Permilly imitates her fictional heroine Amanda at every turn, and insists that her suitor does likewise, to the extent of requiring that he draw a small sketch of himself that she can pretend is a daguerrotype to keep when they are parted. A brief exchange between two of Permilly's sisters captures the essence of the satire. Permilly has uttered a long, derivative lament, ending by calling herself "the most onfortinate of creturs":

> "How much she talks like a book," says Ketury.
> "How much she talks like a fool," says Mirtilly, and off she went to bed.[25]

The Widow Spriggins is even more a figure of ridicule than is the Widow Bedott, but she was undoubtedly a model for Whicher's later creation. At the conclusion of the Spriggins letters is a note to the "eddyter" saying that these sketches have been written during her widowhood after fifteen years of marriage to Spriggins, and she would be happy to tell the story of her second marriage:

> So if you ever git run ashore for stuff to put in yer paper, jest let me know, and if I ain't too much occerpied with my domestic abberations, Ile be happy to giv ye sum account of my "second love."[26]

Despite the sincerity one detects in Whicher's satire, it seems clear that she wrote humor because of the ready market for it rather than from a commitment to the mode. Near the end of her short life she wrote to Alice Neal: "I am heartily sick of Bedotting and Maguiring, and only wish I could be as well paid for more sensible matter." She was at this point at work on *Mary Elmer,* a novel which was incomplete at the time of her death. Though serious, *Mary Elmer* lacks the flowery sentimentality of some of "Fanny Fern's" work. Whicher was afraid the writing was "too plain and homely," and in a letter to her publisher she explains both her style in the work and her attitude toward the sentimental female writer:

> I have been so anxious to avoid the grandiloquent style of many of our female story writers, that I may have gone too far the other way. I have become so entirely disgusted with that sort of composition, applied to the commonest and most

trifling subjects, as well as to those more important, that I never have patience to get through an article of that description.[27]

It is fortunate for today's readers that economic necessity forced Whicher to devote herself to humor. *Mary Elmer* is conventional; but the Widow Spriggins, the Widow Bedott and Aunt Maguire are unforgettable characters in American humor, ranking with Jack Downing and Colonel Sellers. *The Widow Bedott Papers* was a very popular book; the first edition sold more than 100,000 copies,[28] and it remains livelier and less dated than much of the dialect humor of its era.

Far removed from the rural New York of Frances Whicher was the work of "Gail Hamilton" (Mary Abigail Dodge), whose career as a journalist and social commentator began about the time of Whicher's death and lasted until her own death in 1896. Though not a humorist in the popular mold of Whicher and Holley, Gail Hamilton was a witty observer of the political and social scenes, writing columns for the *National Era* and essays and stories for *The Atlantic Monthly*. Kate Sanborn mentions Gail Hamilton in *The Wit of Women,* though she does not include a selection from her work, and Hamilton is one of Alice Wellington Rollins' proofs that women have a sense of humor:

> In the lighter department of descriptive writing, we may fairly match against Charles Dudley Warner's "Summer in a Garden" Gail Hamilton's experience with Halicarnassus in taking a country place for the summer; and if it is objected that we have only one Gail Hamilton, we may remark that the world is not overburdened with Charles Dudley Warners.[29]

The comparison with Warner is an apt one. Both authors use a subtle humor which sneaks out of apparently serious passages. Gail Hamilton's writing ranged over a variety of subjects, including three books on the role and status of women.[30] Though she was sometimes equivocal about women's participation in the "male" world of politics, she ultimately rejected female suffrage on the grounds that voting would make women "aggressive, pugnacious, self-centered";[31] but she argued strongly that women should be self-reliant and powerful, and her writing testifies to the intellectual self-assurance which is basic to wit.

Hamilton's book *Wool-Gathering* (1867), about her travels to various parts of the country, is quite similar in style and approach to Caroline Kirkland's *A New Home,* as well as reminiscent of the journals of Sarah Kemble Knight. Hamilton writes, as do Kirkland and Knight, as an outsider who is alternately perplexed and delighted by what she encounters. Her descriptions of Minnesota recall Kirkland's more extensive ones of Michigan; but Hamilton is a traveler, not a settler, and she declares that "the worst thing about Minnesota is, that it is fifteen hundred miles from Boston!"[32] Like Kirkland, she does not romanticize the West nor the journey to get there. There are mice in hotel rooms, unpleasant traveling companions and sometimes actual dangers. Although she holds the unusually enlightened view for her day that the violence of the Indians was the result of white injustice in dealing with them, she asserts that "the last place in the world to be sentimental over Indians is Minnesota":

> In a country where, until lately, a woman might stand frying doughnuts at her kitchen fire, and look up to see a dark, dreadful face in the gathering twilight pressed against the window-pane, watching the process, and receive for her ostensibly hospitable, but really affrighted greeting, only a noncommittal grunt, it is just as well not to rhapsodize over the noble savage. When, in addition to this, the noble savage yells out a war-whoop, whips out his tomahawk, and takes off your scalp, it is all over with the poetry of the thing.[33]

Gail Hamilton was equally unsentimental about the writing of fiction. In the middle of an otherwise straightforward and serious story published in *The Atlantic Monthly,* she pauses to comment on the romantic novel. Noting that her reader will have guessed that the couple she has introduced will eventually get married, she says, "Of course they will. Is there any reason why they should not? . . . Scoff as you may, love is the one vital principle in romance." She then protests that in comparison to the novels the "professional novel-reader" may be accustomed to, her story may seem "threadbare." However:

> Please to remember that I am not writing about a princess of the blood, nor of the days of the bold barons, but only the life of a quiet little girl in a quiet little town in the eastern part of Massachusetts; and so far as my experience and observation go, men and women in the eastern part of Massachusetts are not given to thrilling adventures, hairbreadth escapes, wonderful concatenations of circumstances, and blood and thunder generally,—but pursue the even tenor of their way, and of their love, with a sober and delightful equanimity.[34]

In the early 1870's Marietta Holley launched the most comprehensive satire on the sentimental female poet in *My Opinions and Betsey Bobbet's* (1873) with a preface in which she declares herself unqualified to write a book:

> I don't know no underground dungeons. I haint acquainted with no haunted houses, I never see a hero suspended over a abyss by his gallusses, I never beheld a heroine swoon away, I never see a Injun tommy hawked, nor a ghost, I never had any of these advantages; I cant write a book.

In other words, she cannot write a romantic novel. But a "voice" inside her mind keeps telling her to write a book about "the great subject of Wimmin's Rites," and she has a "cast iron resolution" to do just that.[35] The "voice" was in reality the American Publishing Company which had published several of Twain's books and which had commissioned Holley's first book after seeing a dialect piece she had written for *Peterson's Magazine.* [36]

My Opinions and Betsey Bobbet's, like the twenty "Samantha" books which followed it, is dialect humor of the "Widow Bedott" variety. Holley's *persona,* Samantha, makes it plain that she "never went to school much and don't know nothin' about grammer, and I never could spell worth a cent,"[37] and Holley, like Whicher, was from rural New York State, which was the basic setting for her works. By the time her last books were published on the eve of the women's suffrage amendment, the rustic style and settings were out of fashion, but her books consistently sold well, and at the turn of the century her name was as well known, some say, as that of Mark Twain. Since the vogue of dialect humor had begun to wane at this point, we must seek other reasons for her continued popularity. For some, the appeal lay in Samantha's championing of women's equality while she remained a devoted wife and homemaker; the marriage of the conventional role and the liberal philosophy would have made her views palatable to those who were threatened by more radical feminist positions. For others, the attraction was the travel format she frequently used, that of Twain's *Innocents Abroad* and Margaret Halsey's later *With Malice Toward Some;* the "wise innocent" had its greatest durability as an observer of notable places. Holley's Samantha traveled to Saratoga, the World's Fair, the St. Louis Exposition and Europe,[38] and her commentary served to reinforce middle America's belief in traditional values of moderation and common sense (one of Samantha's favorite words is "megum" [medium]).

More importantly, Holley's work is delightfully comic. The mixture of broad caricature and delicate, ironic wit remains lively even though some of its targets have an old-fashioned ring.[39] Like Whicher, Holley exposed human failings traditionally associated with women—vanity, nosiness, sentimentality—but her range of subjects was much wider, including racial conflict, political and social ethics and especially sexual equality. Samantha's implacable logic is the source of much of the humor, contrasted as it is with the illogicality of sentiment or prejudice, and the homely metaphor serves here, as in much of Emily Dickinson's poetry, to reinforce common sense. In *Samantha on the Race Problem* (1892), Samantha visits her son and his family in Georgia and

runs head-on into a racial prejudice which rural New York has
not prepared her for:

> The colored men and wimmen they [white Southerners]
> seemed to look upon about as Josiah and me looked onto our
> dairy, though mebby not quite so favorably, for there wuz
> one young yearlin' heifer and one three-year-old Jersey that I
> always said knew enough to vote.[40]

In London she and Josiah compare the crowded conditions in
the House of Commons to those in their hen-house back home,
and Samantha concludes that "there both on em kep' in too
clost quarters to do well."[41] Tied to their rural domesticity,
Samantha and Josiah are to some extent stock comic
characters: the nagging wife with tongue or rolling pin always
at the ready, and the stubborn, somewhat lazy henpecked
husband who fears neither her bark nor her bite.

But Holley's humor is more complex and delicate than
this stereotypical portrait would suggest. Samantha Allen is—
underneath her dialectical locutions—a woman of intelligence
and wit, and this is nowhere more apparent than in her
arguments about "wimmen's rites." As a committed feminist,
Holley was well aware of the major arguments against female
suffrage. On the one hand, women were too fragile to endure
the demands of the political process; on the other, they were
destined—biologically and socially—to fulfill the "higher
calling" of wife and motherhood, which presumably did not
place such a strain on their delicate minds and bodies. The
contradiction inherent in this stance does not escape
Samantha, who is capable of launching into irate, sarcastic
monologues when provoked—usually by Josiah, who, after
fourteen years of marriage, continues to trot out the same
arguments, as when he says:

> "If wimmin know when they are well off, they will let poles
> and 'lections boxes alone, it is too wearin for the fair sect."
> "Josiah Allen," says I, "you think that for a woman to
> stand up straight on her feet, under a blazin' sun, and lift
> both her arms above her head, and pick seven bushels of

hops, mingled with worms and spiders into a gigantic box, day in, and day out, is awful healthy, so strenthenin' and stimulatin' to women, but when it comes to droppin' a little slip of clean paper into a small seven by nine box, once a year in a shady room, you are afraid it is goin' to break down a woman's constitution to once."[42]

And when Samantha's friend Betsey Bobbet insists that it is woman's "greatest privilege" to be "a sort of poultice to the noble, manly breast when it is torn with the cares of life," Samantha snaps, "Am I a poultice, Betsey Bobbet, do I look like one?"[43]

From her alliterative name—reminiscent of "Fanny Fern" and others—to her desire to be a "clinging vine," Betsey Bobbet is a fullblown caricature of the sentimental spinster who writes mournful verse. Samantha comments that "of all the sentimental creeters I ever did see Betsey Bobbet is the sentimentalist, you couldn't squeeze a laugh out of her with a cheeze press."[44] Betsey is pretentious about her grammar, which is often incorrect: she says "I have saw" instead of "I have seen," and thinks it vulgar to pronounce final "r" sounds, saying deah for "dear." As Samantha observes, "I don't know much about grammer, but common sense goes a ways."

But Betsey Bobbet is not merely a set-piece borrowed from other nineteenth-century humorists. *My Opinions and Betsey Bobbet's* is an extended allegory, putting common sense against sentiment, with Samantha Allen as the primary representative of the former (one of her favorite statements is "I love to see folks use reason") and Betsey as one of the embodiments of the latter. In this allegorical framework, marriage as "woman's sphere" (or "spear," as Samantha spells it, fully conscious of the pun) is part of the anti-suffrage argument, and singlehood is as unnatural as voting. Samantha several times attacks the illogicality of this stance. One of her arguments is that it takes two to make a marriage: "As our laws are at present no woman can marry unless she has a man to marry to," she says to Elder Minkly, and then challenges him:

> Which had you rather do, Elder, let Betsey Bobbet vote, or
> cling to you? She is fairly achin' to make a runnin' vine of
> herself, and says I, in slow, deep, awful tones, are you
> willin' to be a tree?

Elder Minkly, like other men to whom Samantha puts the
same question, cannot answer, and takes the first opportunity
to change the subject.[45] If the situation provokes Samantha to
logical argument, it provokes Betsey to poetry, the composition of a "song" for the "glorious cause of wimmen's only
true speah," one stanza of which reads:

> Oh, do not be discouraged, when
> You find your hopes brought down;
> And when you meet unwilling men,
> Heed not their gloomy frown;
> Yield not to wild despaih;
> Press on and give no quartah,
> In battle all is faih;
> We'll win for we had orteh.[46]

And Betsey does "win," in the sense that she eventually gets
married. But it is a hollow victory, for Holley's final thrust is
to have her marry a lazy drunkard with several children, and
our final view of Betsey shows a woman worn with care and
hard work. Her "clinging vine" has found a spindly tree which
will not bear its weight, and Betsey is left defending a position
which has become as pathetic as it once was ludicrous.

Marietta Holley went further than most of her fellow
humorists in demolishing the image of the sentimental female
writer, but the fact that so many female humorists in the
nineteenth century satirized sentimentality argues persuasively that the popular image of the woman writer as soggy
sentimentalist was considered as an insult by women of wit.
The figure of the sentimental female poet was much more than
a stock comic character. In the work of women humorists, it
became the embodiment of all that these women knew
themselves *not* to be: weak, dependent, illogical. With varying
degrees of acidity, they mocked the notion that women were

humorless creatures, incapable of the insight and perspective which underlay the witty utterance. Almost every nineteenth-century female humorist felt the need to create and demolish this image as if exorcising a demon which would have prevented her from writing humor.

Pointing to a deeper reality in women's humor of the nineteenth century is the fact that in the works of these humorists the sentimental female writer is inevitably single, and just as inevitably would rather be married. In the popular imagination the witty woman was not attractive, not feminine; she was considered too strong, too threatening, too "masculine." It is accurate, though somehow too pat, to point out that Mary Abigail Dodge ("Gail Hamilton") and Marietta Holley never married, and that Frances Whicher spoke with regret of her gift for satire. There is no necessary and simple correlation between a writer's life and her subject matter. What is clear is that these writers caricatured the sentimental female writer not on the sole basis of her style of writing, but also because of her habits and personality—her unwillingness or inability to be strong and self-reliant. They laughed at her because she was unable to laugh at herself. The issue was not that she preferred marriage to "single blessedness," but that she equated femininity with weak-minded dependence and sentimentality. For humor, as Dorothy Parker said, "There must be courage."[47]

Notes

1. "Woman's Sense of Humor," *The Critic and Good Literature*, 1 (new series), no. 13 (29 March 1884), 145–46. This was followed by "The Humor of Women," 1, no. 26 (28 June 1884), 301–302.

2. 2nd edition (New York, 1885). The second and third "editions" of this book are actually reprintings.

3. Ann Douglas, *The Feminization of American Culture* (New York, 1977), 48.

4. *Ibid.*, 9.

5. *Ibid.*, 12.

6. Constance Rourke, *American Humor: A Study of the National Character* (Garden City, New York, 1931), 211.

7. Fred Lewis Pattee, *The Feminine Fifties* (New York, 1940), 110.

8. *The Wit of Women,* 54–55.

9. Quoted in Pattee, *The Feminine Fifties* (New York, 1940), 110.

10. "Fanny Fern" [Sara Willis Parton], *Fern Leaves from Fanny's Portfolio* (n.p., [1853]), vi.

11. *Ibid.,* 175–79.

12. *Ibid.,* 231–32.

13. *Ibid.,* 329.

14. One wonders what Pattee was thinking of when he wrote that Kirkland "romanticized the new Western settlements" (*Feminine Fifties,* 63).

15. Mrs. Mary Clavers [Caroline Matilda Kirkland], *A New Home— Who'll Follow? Glimpses of Western Life,* ed. William S. Osborne (1839; rpt. New Haven, Conn., 1965), 87, 109, 139–44.

16. This is the spelling on the title page of the 1856 edition of *The Widow Bedott Papers,* but the name is spelled Whitcher in the 1867 *Widow Spriggins, Mary Elmer and Other Sketches.* I have used the earlier spelling.

17. Alice B. Neal, "Introductory," *The Widow Bedott Papers* (New York, 1856), xv.

18. *Ibid.,* x.

19. Mrs. M. L. Ward Whitcher, "Biographical Introduction," *Widow Spriggins, Mary Elmer and Other Sketches* (New York, 1867), 15.

20. *Widow Bedott Papers,* 38.

21. *Ibid.,* 45.

22. *Ibid.,* 137.

23. *Ibid.,* 130–31.

24. Whicher refers to an actual novel here: *The Children of the Abbey,* by Regina Maria Roche (1798), which was a best-seller according to Frank Luther Mott's formula. See Mott's *Golden Multitudes: The Story of Best Sellers in the United States* (New York, 1947), 64. This is also the novel to which "Gail Hamilton" refers in "The Pursuit of Knowledge Under Difficulties."

25. *Widow Spriggins,* 44.

26. *Ibid.,* 140.

27. "Biographical Introduction," *Widow Spriggins,* 32, 34.

28. See Walter Blair, *Native American Humor,* 44, and F. L. Pattee, *The Feminine Fifties,* 232–38.

29. "Woman's Sense of Humor," 146.

30. *A New Atmosphere* (Boston, 1865); *Woman's Wrongs: A Counter-Irritant* (Boston, 1868); *Woman's Worth and Worthlessness* (New York, 1872).

31. *Woman's Worth and Worthlessness,* 275.

32. "Gail Hamilton" [Mary Abigail Dodge], *Wool-Gathering* (Boston, 1867), 96.

33. *Ibid.,* 158–59.

34. "The Pursuit of Knowledge Under Difficulties," *Atlantic Tales: A Collection of Stories from The Atlantic Monthly,* 5th ed. (Boston, 1869), 111–13.

35. Josiah Allen's Wife [Marietta Holley], *My Opinions and Betsey Bobbet's* (Hartford, 1874), v–vii.

36. May Lamberton Becker, ed. *The Home Book of Laughter* (New York, 1948), 225.

37. *My Opinions and Betsey Bobbet's,* v.

38. Much of this travel, however, was imaginary. Holley often worked from guidebooks and other materials without stirring from her home in New York. This mild duplicity seems not to have disturbed her readers, who apparently remained unaware of it.

39. Not all critics agree. In explaining his selections for a 1947 anthology of American humor, James Aswell says that Holley "most particularly . . . didn't amuse me." (*Native American Humor* [New York, 1947], xiii). C. Carroll Hollis describes some of her work as "of interest to historians, not citizens" ("Rural Humor of the Late Nineteenth Century," *The Comic Imagination in American Literature,* ed. Louis D. Rubin [New Brunswick, N.J., 1973], 174). Most recently, Walter Blair and Hamlin Hill say that Holley "could never have become as popular today as she did during her lifetime." (*America's Humor: From Poor Richard to Doonesbury* [New York, 1978], 496). However, the rediscovery of America's women writers and the current woman's movement have caused many to find her work both amusing and relevant. See especially Jane Curry, "Samantha 'Rastles' the Woman Question," *Journal of Popular Culture,* 8, no. 4. (Spring 1975), 805–24.

40. Josiah Allen's Wife [Marietta Holley], *Samantha on the Race Problem* (New York, 1892), 259.

41. Josiah Allen's Wife [Marietta Holley], *Samantha in Europe* (New York, 1896), 417.

42. *My Opinions and Betsey Bobbet's,* 92.

43. *Ibid.,* 62.

44. *Ibid.,* 27.

45. *Ibid.,* 135.

46. *Ibid.,* 185.

47. Introduction to *The Most of S. J. Perelman* (New York, 1958), xii.

A Laughter of Their Own: Women's Humor in the United States

Emily Toth

Nelt Chawgo, a handsome bachelor, thinks himself invulnerable—until the day he is deceived by dashing Angerose Wilds. She promises marriage, then abandons him. Nelt, heartbroken, is also condemned by nearly everyone: he is a "ruined feller"—a "young he-hussy."[1] After all, "young wimmen must sow their wild oats," while young men must see to their own "manly modesty" (p. 306). But Samantha Allen, Marietta Holley's mouthpiece in "A Male Magdalene" (1906), defends Nelt. Could a "he-belle" help it, she asks, if Angerose turned his weak mind with flatteries? (p. 315) The seducer should bear the blame—and finally Angerose does confess to ruining the innocent youth. She will marry Nelt after all, she decides, and make an honest man of him.

Marietta Holley makes her comic points through role reversal—the same technique Joanna Russ uses in 1972, listing heroic plots for female characters:

> Two strong women battle for supremacy in the early West. A young woman in Minnesota finds her womanhood by killing a bear.

As Russ wittily points out, these plots do not work. They are historically improbable, culturally implausible, or both.[2] But Russ' targets, like Holley's, are not her own hapless characters. Nor, like so many satirists, do Holley and Russ attack their readers. Rather, their target is the target of most humorous writing by women: the social roles which imprison us all.

Women humorists, like other women writers, have not yet been given their due. In Marietta Holley's day, for instance, a *Critic* reviewer wrote that Holley "has entertained as large an audience, I should say, as has been entertained by the humor of Mark Twain."[3] Over an unusually long career (1873–1914), Holley published twenty-one very popular novels, many of them about the most pressing social issue in post-Civil War America: women's rights. She even outlived Twain. Still, literary historians, as Susan Koppelman will show in a forthcoming study, routinely leave out virtually all women (and minority) writers of the past,[4] and tend to give fuller coverage only to women of their own era—so that American women's humor appears to begin with Dorothy Parker.[5] In fact, American women's humor begins with the "first" American poet in English: Anne Bradstreet.

Like most women writers, Bradstreet chose women's subjects: home, children. Her humor is gentle—except on one subject. Anne Bradstreet knew, over three centuries before Joanna Russ, that women writers would not be taken seriously by the dominant sex. Either the women would be told to return to their proper domestic role:

> I am obnoxious to each carping tongue
> That says my hand a needle better fits.

Or women's cleverness would be disparaged in no uncertain terms:

> If what I do prove well, it won't advance,
> They'll say it's stolen, or else it was by chance.[6]

Perhaps because she desperately wanted to be judged fairly, Anne Bradstreet followed the humane humor rule—one of the distinguishing characteristics of most women's humor. Unlike such satirists as Swift and Juvenal, who build their humor on attacking women for their physical imperfections, Bradstreet and her successors do not satirize what cannot be helped.[7]

Women writers have not produced savage criticisms of male bodies—but they have criticized the *choices* both sexes make: affectations, hypocrisies, irrationalities. Often, in fact, what women writers really criticize are traditional social norms themselves—and the foolish choices made by those who do not think or criticize their own society.[8]

Sarah Kemble Knight's diary (1704–1705), for instance, is a compendium of social criticism. Knight laughs at men who show less sense than their horses, or who support public punishment for a man who kisses his wife where others might see them. She enjoys describing guests at an inn who argue all night about the origin of the word "Narragansett," until the rum they are drinking makes further speech impossible.[9] Similarly, during the American Revolution, Mercy Otis Warren laughed at enemy Tories in poems and plays full of gory incidents. In 1776, she even poked fun at General Gage's army of occupation in Boston—and she called her play *The Blockheads.*

But female humorists have rarely ventured, as Knight and Warren did, into the public (male) world of commerce, politics, and diplomacy. Rather, they have directed their satire toward the irrationalities of life at home. In *A New Home— Who'll Follow?* (1839), for instance, Caroline Kirkland suggests that *no one* should. The rigors of backwoods Michigan life, she says, are made far worse by the sticky fingers of her neighbors, who borrow her broom, thread, and scissors—and, ultimately, even her cat and her husband's pantaloons.[10] Likewise, Frances Berry Whitcher, who wrote as "The Widow Bedott," satirized her neighbors in western New York State for their peculiar dialect and their habit of talking much and saying little. But somehow the neighbors discovered she was "The Widow"—and forced her out of town. She died two years later, in 1852, having remarked that it is "a very serious thing to be a funny woman."[11] Kirkland, Whitcher, and "Fanny Fern" (Sara Willis Parton, who criticized the deplorable smoking habits of men in "Tabitha Tompkins' Soliloquy") all follow the humane humor rule: they mock people for their choices.[12] They support better living standards, sensible conversation, clean air—in short, all that makes a home livable, especially for women.

Marietta Holley, born in upstate New York, was twelve years old when Elizabeth Cady Stanton, Susan B. Anthony, Lucretia Mott, and the others met in Seneca Falls in 1848 and wrote their "Declaration of Principles" ("We hold these truths to be self-evident: that all men and women are created equal . . . "). Between 1848 and 1920, the year women's suffrage was finally ratified, women and sympathetic men kept up an unceasing battle for the vote. Throughout her career, Marietta Holley used her wit to support The Cause— and to ask pointed questions about marriage, women's rights, and the real differences between the sexes. In 1873, she published her first Samantha book: *My Opinions and Betsey Bobbet's,* "by Josiah Allen's wife." In all the books, Samantha Allen is the crackerbox philosopher, the wise innocent, the supporter of "megumness" (mediumness, or moderation). In the first book, Samantha's dialogues with her neighbor Betsey, who opposes women's rights, show the gap between high-minded descriptions of women's "calling"—"to soothe lacerations, to be a sort of poultice to the noble manly breast when it is torn with the cares of life"—and the reality. "Am I a poultice, Betsy Bobbet, do I look like one?" Samantha asks—as she irons, stirs preserves, makes maple sugar, bakes, and worries. "What has my sect done, that they have got to be lacerator soothers, when they have got everything else under the sun to do?" Samantha wonders.[13]

Women, Holley notes in other books, are indeed the protected sex—"protected" from having a say in church, in the ballot box, and even over their own clothing, which legally belongs to their husbands. Samantha wonders about the wives of Old Testament prophets ("Miss Daniel, Miss Zekiel, Miss Hosey")—who most likely had to work twice as hard, while their men wandered around in goatskins and took off on "prophesying trips."[14] Holley shows that the rules are made by men—but that it is actually women who do the work of the world, especially its most down-to-earth, practical work. Samantha insists on calling the Meeting House "she" and referring to "our Revolutionary foremothers"—and she asks her husband Josiah to explain something: when do terms like "men" include women, and when don't they? *Laymen,* Josiah says without any apparent opinion, always means women "when it is used in a punishin' and condemnatory sense, or in the case of work." But what about power and salaries? Well, in that case, "or anything else difficult," the word *laymen* "always means men."

Marietta Holley was too shy to speak at suffrage meetings; she was a storyteller rather than an activist. But her sly questions—are men the most logical beings? are women really ladies?—form the core of some of the greatest examples of comic irony produced by the suffrage movement. Alice Duer Miller, for instance, took on the contention that voting would destroy women's mental and moral health, because of the brutal creatures they might meet at the polls (the "men-are-incorrigible-brutes" argument still used by right-wingers today). In "A Consistent Anti to Her Son" (1915), Miller writes:

> You must not go to the polls, Willie,
> Never go to the polls,
> They're dark and dreadful places
> Where many lose their souls;
> They smirch, degrade and coarsen
> Terrible things they do
> To quiet, elderly women—
> What would they do to you?[15]

What is really being criticized, of course, is the double standard that one sex is to be sheltered, and judged, and kept from power—while the other, regardless of its behavior, runs the world.

The value of being a "lady" was also satirized by suffragists—notably by Sojourner Truth, a former slave who saw the irony in the idea of female weakness expressed at a women's rights convention in 1851: "That man over there says women need to be helped into carriages and lifted over ditches, and to have the best place everywhere. Nobody ever helps me into carriages or over puddles, or gives me the best place—and ain't I a woman?"[16]

The struggle for women's rights did, in fact, do what its opponents feared: it turned women away from being deferential ladies (if they ever were) and toward being social critics. Women were not always creatures of sentiment, nor were men always citadels of reason—as Anna Howard Shaw, President of the National American Woman Suffrage Association, often told her audiences. Dr. Shaw used to relish describing a Democratic convention she had observed. Men were carrying pictures around the room—screaming, shouting, singing the "Hown Dawg" song. Men jumped on their seats, threw hats in the air, and shouted, "What's the matter with Champ Clark?"—while other men tossed hats and shouted, "He's all right!!!!!" But all this, Shaw noted slyly, had "no hysteria about it—just patriotic loyalty, splendid manly devotion to principle." Still, women at conventions, she pointed out, never knocked off each other's bonnets, nor shouted, "She's all right!" Instead, Shaw reported, "I have actually seen women stand up and wave their handkerchiefs. I have even seen them take hold of hands and sing, 'Blest be the tie that binds.'"[17]

Women humorists from Anne Bradstreet through Anna Howard Shaw were all, in some way, angry: about the limited roles they were given, about the pious platitudes droned at them to justify their submission, about the outright false statements about women's "nature." But their responses were not truly an attack on men, not a "so's your old man" response. Theirs was an attack on patriarchal norms—on hypocrisy, on irresponsibility—in the name of a higher norm. Women humorists were not seeking domination—but equality.

By the late nineteenth and early twentieth centuries, the humorous appeals of poets and orators had crept more and more into the work of fiction writers. Anne Warner, for instance, is best-known for her Susan Clegg stories, in which

Susan—an opinionated busybody—gossips, and Mrs. Lathrop interjects an occasional, "Yes?" and "What then?" Susan Clegg spices her apparent ramblings with sharp observations. When the mother of a baby runs off with another man, Susan points out that everyone said, "How could she be so cruel as to leave it!" And then when the woman returns for her child: "How could she be so cruel as to take it!" The point as Susan sees it is that "When a woman branches out, every one's ready to go for her."[18] As for marriage, Susan Clegg tells Mrs. Lathrop that many things look different "comin' down from the altar from what they did goin' up" (p. 472)—a point Anne Warner makes even more strongly in "The New Woman and the Old" (1914), one of the most devastating satires on bourgeois marriage ever to appear in American literature.

The old-style woman, Emily Reed's mother, refuses to acknowledge that marriage is anything but the perfect future for her daughter. Then Emily's suitor describes her duties: she will be his only housekeeper, teach every one of the younger classes at his school, clean the entire school while he goes to Germany to study—and be all that marriage handbooks say a wife should be: pious, domestic, submissive. Emily complains to her mother, who gives a bald, totally unself-conscious picture of the hallowed Victorian marriage: all women work until midnight; all women suffer in drudgery; and "all men are selfish . . . Your father ate all the giblets up to the day he died." Emily protests that she doesn't want to be a slave—to which her mother replies, "But you can't be married without being a slave . . . The thing is to be married."[19] Emily decides that it is not her thing at all.

Some of the happiest characters in Mary E. Wilkins Freeman's and Sarah Orne Jewett's writings are, in fact, spinsters. The heroines of such stories as Freeman's "A New England Nun" and Jewett's "The Flight of Betsey Lane" are not conventionally pretty, nor young, nor romantically inclined. Rather, they are resourceful and free. Betsey Lane gleefully hitchhikes to Philadelphia, though at sixty-nine she has never been more than a few miles from her New England home.

Freeman's "New England nun," Louisa, finds all the adventure she ever wants by staying home—creating a tidy, smiling domestic world, a miniature art form reflecting everything she wants her life to be. Literary critics, too often judging characters by traditional norms (and therefore assuming that spinsters must be unfulfilled), have often missed the satire in Freeman and Jewett, whose targets for humor are those who insist on behaving in conventional, unthinking ways: shocked parishioners, gossipy creatures of both sexes, neighborhood carping tongues. Jewett's and Freeman's characters do not return to "normal." Rather, they create new norms. (Freeman also shows that rigid sex roles limit men—for in "A Kitchen Colonel," her seventy-eight-year-old hero loves to muddle around in the kitchen, and is unfazed by the hecklings of his neighbor. The hero's self-sacrifices, in fact, enable his granddaughter to marry the man she chooses—and in the end the hero cries, with that mixture of laughter and tears that marks Freeman's particular brand of humor.)[20]

Kate Chopin's humor is also social criticism, but in a more black-humorous vein—notably in "The Storm" (written in 1898) and "The Story of an Hour" (published in 1894). Both stories concern women who are only outwardly pleased with their marriages. The wife in "The Storm" takes refuge with a former sweet-heart during a thunderstorm—and the storm outside reawakens old desires, until both are swept away with renewed passion. Afterwards she has a particular glow when she greets her husband and son—while her lover writes to his wife that she is welcome to stay on vacation for another month. "So the storm passed and everyone was happy," the story concludes.[21] The wife in Chopin's "The Story of an Hour" is also happily married, but since she has a heart condition, people are very careful when they give her the news her husband has been in a fatal train wreck. At first she is sad, but then she watches the budding trees and thinks, "Free! Body and soul free!" She loved her husband—but loves self-assertion more. Then the door opens—and it is her husband, who was far from the scene of the accident. The wife cannot be shielded from the shock—and so, "When the doctors came they said she had died of heart disease—of joy that kills."[22]

Kate Chopin specializes in withholding information from her characters, and withholding judgment from her readers.[23] But her best writings are satiric: she shocks and delights her audience by confounding traditional expectations—particularly the view that marriage must mean self-sacrifice for a woman. The fulfilled woman is the woman alone—laughing after her illicit tempest with a man not her husband, or exulting in her room when she thinks herself freed.

Edith Wharton, on the other hand, seems to have had no particular vision of liberation for women (though she did recognize that in the highest levels of American society capitalism could be deadly). Still, in *The Custom of the Country* (1913), her finest comedy of manners, Edith Wharton shows that an unscrupulous woman can beat the system—as does Undine Spragg, who escapes her dull Midwestern town to make a killing in New York. Undine greedily marries into the old New York aristocracy, and then into the old French aristocracy, and finally into the *nouveau riche* Americans-in-France aristocracy—always pursuing the American dream, always trying to upgrade herself. As one character comments, Undine Spragg is the monstrously perfect result of the system—in which marriage is supposed to be women's only source of identity. She is neither likeable, nor intellectual (she sees the classic French theater as a bunch of people moaning about bath towels), but she is the perfect vehicle for satire as practiced by American women writers. She *chooses* to be ridiculous, and her success exposes the shallowness of her society's norms.

"Edie was a lady," Dorothy Parker said of Edith Wharton—but Dorothy Parker was not. She was perhaps the first woman writer since Marietta Holley who could truly be called a humorist—that is, a writer whose main focus was on humor, rather than a writer who used humor as one of many literary techniques. Parker is, of course, best-known for her withering one-liners. "You know that woman speaks eighteen languages?" she said about one acquaintance. "And she can't say 'No' in any of them." To a man nervous about his first extramarital affair, Dorothy Parker said soothingly, "Oh, don't worry. I'm sure it won't be the last."[24] And of *The House at Pooh Corner,* a book she reviewed for the *New Yorker's* "Constant Reader" column, Parker summarized her disgust: "Tonstant Weader Fwowed Up."[25]

Parker's funny-but-deadly poems include meditations on suicide: "Razors pain you . . . Nooses give . . . Gas smells awful . . . You might as well live."[26] Her voice is breezy, worldly, and very cynical: "I shudder at the thought of men . . . I'm due to fall in love again."[27] Her poems expect deception out of love, and her clever turns of phrase offer satire, not hope:

> By the time you swear you're his,
> Shivering and sighing,
> And he vows his passion is
> Infinite, undying—
> Lady, make a note of this:
> One of you is lying.[28]

Similarly, Parker's short stories suggest that woman's lot is not a particularly happy one. Unlike nineteenth-century heroines, her characters are not made contented through creating well-ordered solitary lives. In fact they are quite incompetent in the household: one husband, surveying the bed his wife has just made, demands: "What is this? Some undergraduate prank?"[29]

Some Parker short stories have a unique blending of humor and resentment that no other writer has ever managed—particularly in such soliloquies as "The Waltz," a young woman's cynical musings while dancing with a young man. Though she has said she would adore waltzing with him, she thinks the truth: "Being struck dead would look like a day in the country, compared to struggling out a dance with this boy."[30] Grimly, she wishes he would at least leave her shins as he found them—but at the same time she tells him his "little step" is "perfectly lovely," but just a "tiny bit tricky to follow." At the end she wonders if the dance has lasted thirty-five years, or maybe a hundred thousand—then tells him she would "adore to" dance another waltz with him. Parker shows that the young woman has no alternative—for how can she dare say what she considers saying: "It's so nice to meet a man who isn't a scaredy-cat about catching my beri-beri"? Women are expected to please men. Parker's target is neither the clumsy young man nor the bruised young woman, but the social roles they are locked into.

Human vulnerability makes much of Parker's humor poignant as well as amusing. In the short stories, she is merciless toward unthinking, self-styled do-gooders ("Arrangement in Black and White," "Clothe the Naked"). She hates the rich ("From the Diary of a New York Lady," "The Custard Heart"). But her finest subject is the gap between women and men: *she* hangs on his every word, *he* forgets what he has said; *she* waits for him to phone, *he* cannot understand why she is upset; *he* would like to tell her about his day, *she* would like to tell him about hers—but each figures the other would not be interested anyway.

Dorothy Parker emancipated women writers from the need to be nice, to hide their anger. Though her wit was often at her own expense, she nevertheless said what she thought. In fact, she paved the way for a new openness in humor—for housewives, for feminists, and for women who are both. Indeed, by the 1940s two distinct streams of American women's humor had emerged. The first, derived largely from the nineteenth-century domestic tradition, focussed on the humorous aspects of women's sphere: children, family chores, home-making. But only a decade after Marietta Holley's last Samantha book, Dorothy Parker had already pioneered in the new stream of women's humor: finding irony, humane humor, and radical criticism of patriarchal norms almost entirely in the world beyond the home. Parker's humor leads most directly to the feminist humor of such writers as Erica Jong, Toni Cade Bambara, Alix Kates Shulman, and Rita Mae

Brown—while the domestic stream has produced Betty MacDonald, Phyllis McGinley, Peg Bracken, and Erma Bombeck.

Though Betty MacDonald in *The Egg and I* (1945) and Phyllis McGinley in *Sixpence in Her Shoe* (1964) promote a grin-and-bear-it attitude toward the tribulations of housework, much of their humor seems either hateful (MacDonald) or patronizing (McGinley) in the 1980s. MacDonald makes housekeeping, even on a chicken ranch, seem trivial and dull; McGinley glorifies the many roles a housewife can play (chauffeur, gardener, cook, nurse) and says that any woman who does not find all these jobs creative and fulfilling has only herself to blame. But like Jean Kerr, author of *Please Don't Eat the Daisies* (1957), and Shirley Jackson, author of *Life Among the Savages* (1953) and *Raising Demons* (1957), McGinley was not a full-time housewife.

The domestic humorists before Peg Bracken were, in fact, telling *other* women to stay in their place—but Bracken in *The I Hate to Cook Book* (1960) said, with humor, what Betty Friedan showed seriously in *The Feminine Mystique* (1963): the home is too small a world. Not every woman is totally fulfilled with chauffering, gardening, cooking, nursing—and Bracken was among the first to say openly that cooking, in particular, is often a detestable activity. The *I Hate to Cook Book* taps what most women humorists have found: the mingling of satisfaction and resentment, of anger and amusement, that creates an ironic perspective on the "normal" world. *The I Hate to Cook Book* revels in tricks: garnishes to disguise failures, and ways to con the family into thinking something canned is original. Bracken even provides sample remarks for convincing a husband that frozen-and-heated rolls are really home-baked. "Admittedly," she writes, "this is underhanded, but then, marriage is sometimes a rough game."[31] Her goal is not to train the ideal, spotless homemaker. Rather, Bracken criticizes the norm, by showing how a woman can ignore much of it, fake the rest, and go on to the important things in her life.

Likewise, Erma Bombeck tells strong truths cloaked in humor. She analyzes traditional images of women—and demolishes them. As early as 1967, Bombeck was writing that the housewife could not win. If she complained, she was neurotic; if she did not, she was stupid. If she stayed home with children, she was an overprotective "boring clod." If she worked outside, she was selfish, and "her children will write dirty words in nice places."[32] Nor can Supermom ("Super Mom!") be an appropriate replacement for the housewife. In *The Grass Is Always Greener Over the Septic Tank* (1976), Bombeck portrays a super mother who does everything right: bakes her own bread, delivers puppies, even waxes her garden hose. But the neighbors hardly praise her. Instead, they whisper snidely—until the super mother begins to change. She buys deodorants not on sale, she secretly cooks TV dinners, and when she hears that her child is using toothpaste with fluoride on the side, the reformed super mother says, "Who cares?" Bombeck concludes: "She was one of us."[33] To be "one of us" in Erma Bombeck's world means not fitting the old mold, the nineteenth-century norm of the all-nurturing, all-perfect angel in the house. Bombeck recognizes that Super Mom can be a super sucker, no more appreciated than women whose children send Mother's Day cards to Colonel Sanders. Erma Bombeck is not the housewife's tranquillizer. Rather, she speaks the unspeakable, and says with humor what other feminists, such as Marilyn French (in *The Women's Room*), say with rage.

Erma Bombeck is the bridge between the housewife stream of humor and the new feminist stream—which is perhaps best represented by Erica Jong, whose adolescent ideal was Dorothy Parker. In her poems and novels, especially *Fear of Flying* (1973), Jong debunks myths and shatters taboos—particularly about menstruation, female masturbation, and lust. Jong uses words traditionally forbidden to women: the ultimate romantic fantasy, in which there is no mumbling, no fumbling, no outside world intruding, is called "the zipless fuck." *Flying's* heroine Isadora Wing dreams of the zipless fuck while adventuring around Europe in a parody of *The Odyssey*. She mocks the portentous and wrong-headed psychoanalytical descriptions of WOMAN, and she yearns for sexual excitement and literary success, love and laughter—but on female terms. At the end of her quest, Isadora does something no male hero ever did: she has her period. In the bathtub, Isadora gazes at the mighty artifact: "the Tampax string fishing the water like a Hemingway hero."[34]

Erica Jong traces the roots of new feminist humor to Dorothy Parker—but also to Sylvia Plath, whose novel *The Bell Jar* (1963) is one of the first pieces of women's writing to look directly at the male anatomy. When the medical student Buddy insists on undressing in front of the heroine, what she sees reminds her most of "turkey neck and turkey gizzards."[35] Again, what is being mocked is *not* Buddy's anatomy—as men have mocked the female body. Rather, Plath is mocking the norm: the belief that viewing the genitals of the opposite sex is an instant turn-on. That may be true for men—but not for women.

Most new feminist humorists of the 1970s and 1980s lack the morbid edge of Plath's writing, however. Instead, they have chosen exuberance, adventure, sex and love and laughter—and breaking many taboos simply by ignoring them.

In the literature of the 1970s, tampax insertion becomes a comical rite of passage for young women, especially in such novels as Lois Gould's *Such Good Friends* (1970) and Alix Kates Shulman's *Memoirs of an Ex-Prom Queen* (1972).[36] It is easily the equivalent of winning the big game, and in Judy Blume's *Are You There God? It's Me, Margaret* (1970), three teenagers vie to see who will have the first period. One even tries to make a deal with God, offering to be good around the house if He will give her some breasts. The heroine does finally get "it," then stops her mother from showing her how to use napkins ("Teenage Softies"): "Mom, I've been practicing in my room for two months!"[37] Thus we have a happy, if unconventional, ending: girl gets napkin.

The nineteenth-century domestic writers praised the same virtues—generosity, practicality, neatness—but could not write about menstruation or lust, nor use four-letter words. Nor could they describe the special treat Alix Kates Shulman's protagonist in *Memoirs of an Ex-Prom Queen* has, when she discovers her "joy button" (clitoris) and the pleasures of masturbation. Nor could they print what Shulman describes in "A Story of a Girl and Her Dog" (1975): the day a dog licks a young girl, Lucky, in a most sensitive place—and Lucky revels in the feeling. That is the day of Lucky's "brightening."[38]

New feminist humorists are insistently honest, especially about the first sexual experience—in which, for women, the earth rarely moves, nor is ecstatic and simultaneous communion achieved. Lisa Alther's heroine in *Kinflicks* (1976), for instance, has her first experience in a fallout shelter, with a greasy motorcyclist fresh from a den of iniquity called The Bloody Bucket. His condomed penis is "the size and shape of a small salami, lime green and glowing fluorescently." The heroine waits for the cosmic joy romances have promised, but instead hears herself saying, "You mean that's *it?*[39]

These feminist humorists are keen observers, preferring independence to snivelling and appreciating irony and role reversal. Gail Parent's *David Meyer Is a Mother* (1976), for instance, satirizes norms for men—in that David Meyer begins life as a conscienceless exploiter of women, but ends up begging his roommate to have a baby, so *he* will be fulfilled. In between, David learns that the sexual revolution has begun, and he is fighting on the losing side. Women take him out, and then neglect to call; his boss expects him to sleep with her to keep his job. In the end, he is delighted to withdraw to the sanctity of Home—the nineteenth-century haven in a heartless world becomes the most attractive place for this late twentieth-century man to be.

Sexual harassment is also a target for satire in E. M. (Esther) Broner's *Her Mothers* (1975), in which a mother attends a conference of scholars, and asks five of the men why they are attending. All have high-minded, altruistic or political motivations. The Indian wants to "buy guns" for his people ("and to fuck women"), the Black man wants to "make contacts for my people" ("and to fuck me some women"), the Jewish man wants to represent "the Jew as Eternal Immigrant" ("and to fuck some women"). Finally, the heroine meets her mentor, a charming, aging, respected friend who tells her his purpose. He wants to reacquaint himself with old friends and "fuck some women."[40] Esther Broner uses satire because it is indirect, a way to attack hypocrisy. Much of new feminist humor has been devoted to attacking hypocrisy—but more recent writers have gone beyond criticizing the foibles of society, and the other sex. Writers of feminist humor are now proposing alternatives.

Alternative worlds for women, like that in Bertha Harris' *Lover* (1976), are not an invention of the 1970s. As early as 1915, Charlotte Perkins Gilman described a women's utopia in *Herland*—a model country stumbled upon by three contemporary American men who immediately say to themselves: "This is a *civilized* country . . . There must be men."[41] Instead, the explorers find a civilization consisting entirely of women, and run along reasonable lines that make our world seem humorous, bizarre, and certainly irrational. Herlanders laugh at one explorer's constant attempts to show himself to be "a man, a real man"; they cannot understand why the frantic explorers find it so upsetting to be treated exactly the way the women treat each other. *Herland,* of course, questions the ways of the real world in which Gilman lived. Romantic love, one explorer learns, is really just "caveman tradition" (p. 93). Herlanders find sex distinctions amusing, especially the ambiguous use of "man" (pp. 60, 137), and they clearly prove one of the explorers wrong when he claims: "Women cannot co-operate—it's against nature" (p. 67).

Newer writers like Toni Cade Bambara have put into practice the values expressed in *Herland*. In Bambara's story "Raymond's Run" (1971), for instance, young Squeaky is the fastest runner on the block. She wins her big race—but she also revels in having her retarded brother share her victory, and in making friends with her strongest competitor. Squeaky's triumph celebrates physical fitness, health, and joyful activity for women—but also supports traditionally feminine values: concern for others, co-operation, and sincerity—being "honest and worthy of respect . . . you know . . . like being people."[42] "Being people" in a woman's world is what many recent feminist humorists are really writing about—as Bambara says in "Medley" (1977): "I arranged my priorities long ago when I jumped into my woman stride."[43]

Alice Walker's mother-character in "Everyday Use" (1973) has also hit her woman stride. She is big-boned and strong and proud of it: "My fat keeps me hot in zero weather."[44] Mama also has an amused love for both her daughters: the nervous, crippled, stay-at-home (Maggie), and the brisk, militant adventurer, sporting an Afro and a new African name (Wangero). Walker pokes some fun at Wangero—not for her ideas, but for her pretensions. But it is Maggie who stays with Mama, with "a real smile, not scared," and they sit "just enjoying, until it was time to go in the house and go to bed" (p. 88). The ending has women's warmth.

A true heroine, feminist humorists are saying today, has warmth and spunk and vitality—the characteristics of Molly Bolt in Rita Mae Brown's *Rubyfruit Jungle* (1973). Molly grows up poor, unloved, but full of ideas; her first childhood business is selling (for 5¢) the chance to see "the strangest dick in the world"—property of her chum "Broccoli" Detwiler, who seems to enjoy the notoriety.[45] Because she is bright and ambitious and curious, Molly soon learns that love is not confined to the opposite gender. She creates herself as she grows up lesbian, laughing at pretensions that do not hurt others—and fighting those that do. She threatens to expose the hypocrisy of her smarmy teachers caught in an adulterous rendezvous; she objects to the idea that getting married is "something you have to do, like dying" (p. 36). The only norms she accepts are those she has chosen. When she goes to the big city to seek her fortune, she meets many desperately alienated people: a woman whose fantasy is to be admired at a Times Square urinal, a man who imagines himself with stupendous breasts. A rich grapefruit freak pays Molly $100 to throw fruit at him, his path to sexual ecstasy. But *Rubyfruit Jungle* is also about reconciliation: combining love and work, bringing together mother and daughter, mixing laughter and tenderness. Being people.

There is no canon of women's humor in America, though there are two excellent anthologies: Martha Hensley Bruère and Mary Ritter Beard's *Laughing Their Way: Women's Humor in America* (1934) and Gloria Kaufman and Mary Kay Blakely's *Pulling Our Own Strings: Feminist Humor and Satire* (1980).

A comprehensive survey of American women's humor would include many writers not mentioned here—among them Harriet Beecher Stowe, Zora Neale Hurston, Flannery O'Connor, Ellen Goodman, Nora Ephron, Nikki Giovanni. Creators of one-liners would be included, such as Florynce Kennedy for "A woman without a man is like a fish without a bicycle." Very little has been written about female stand-up comedians or cartoonists.[46] And since women's humor characteristically criticizes and subverts patriarchal norms, it is not always amusing to the other sex—which may account for its absence from many humor anthologies.[47] What does seem clear is that women's humor—as a weapon, and as communion—is not apt to wither away. Pretensions and hypocrisies are still with us—and so is the anger that they create.

But women's humor has gone beyond the stage of imitating men's humor (pure mockery), and beyond attacking traditional humor (parody, role reversal), to the third stage: creating new norms, a culture.[48] In the future, American female wits may create more poems like Hisaye Yamamoto's 1949 combination of a Japanese form *(haiku)* with French *elan* and down-to-earth American needs:

It is morning, and lo!
I lie awake, comme il faut,
sighing for some dough.[49]

The gap between what *is* and what *should be* still exists, as it did when Alice Duer Miller wrote "Feminism," just before women got the vote:

"Mother, what is a Feminist?"
"A Feminist, my daughter,
Is any woman now who cares
To think about her own affairs
As men don't think she oughter."[50]

What women's humor is, ultimately, is women's seeing what they oughter: being equal, being people, being smart. Women humorists, like Marietta Holley's Samantha, will continue to have one irrepressible trait in common: "I could stop my tongue—but I couldn't stop my Thinker."[51]

Notes

1. Marietta Holley, "A Male Magdalene," in *Samantha versus Josiah* (New York: Funk and Wagnalls, 1906), p. 304. Other references to this edition will be made by page number in the text.

2. Joanna Russ, "What Can a Heroine Do? or Why Women Can't Write," in *Images of Women in Fiction: Feminist Perspectives,* ed. Susan Koppelman-Cornillion (Bowling Green: Popular Press, 1972), p. 3.

3. Patricia Williams, "The Crackerbox Philosopher as Feminist: The Novels of Marietta Holley," *American Humor: An Interdisciplinary Newsletter,* 7 (Spring 1980), p. 16.

4. Susan Koppelman, Introduction to *The Other Woman: Stories of Two Women and a Man* (New York: Feminist Press, 1984).

5. See, for instance, Enid Veron's 1976 anthology, *Humor in America* (New York: Harcourt Brace Jovanovich), which purports to survey the history of American humor—yet the only female humorists included are Flannery O'Connor (a short story); Dorothy Parker (two pages of short poems); and Judith Viorst (a minor contemporary poet, given three pages). Parker's significance is further

diminished by the inclusion of Alexander Woollcott's snide sketch, "Our Mrs. Parker."

6. Anne Bradstreet, "The Prologue to the Tenth Muse," in *Salt and Bitter and Good: Three Centuries of English and American Women Poets,* ed. Cora Kaplan (New York and London: Paddington, 1975), p. 29.

7. For the long history of misogynist humor, see Katharine Rogers, *The Troublesome Helpmate: A History of Misogyny in Literature* (Seattle: University of Washington Press, 1966).

8. Women's humor as an attack on patriarchal norms is discussed further in Judy Little's *Comedy and the Woman Writer: Woolf, Spark, and Feminism* (Lincoln: University of Nebraska, 1983).

9. Sarah Kemble Knight, "The Journal of Madam Knight," in *The American Tradition in Literature,* ed. Sculley Bradley et al., 4th ed. (New York: Grosset & Dunlap, 1974), I, 148.

10. Caroline Kirkland, "Borrowing in a New Settlement," from *A New Home—Who'll Follow?* in *Laughing Their Way: Women's Humor in America,* ed. Martha Bensley Bruère and Mary Ritter Beard (New York: Macmillan, 1934), pp. 5–6.

11. Frances Berry Whitcher, "The Widow Bedott," in *Laughing Their Way: Women's Humor in America,* pp. 6–8.

12. Fanny Fern, "Tabitha Tompkins' Soliloquy," in *Laughing Their Way: Women's Humor in America,* pp. 10–12.

13. Quoted in *Laughing Their Way: Women's Humor in America,* p. 53.

14. My discussion of Holley derives from Jane Curry, "Samantha 'Rastles' the Woman Question," *Journal of Popular Culture,* 8 (Spring 1975), 805–24. *Samantha Rastles the Woman Question* is also the title of Jane Curry's forthcoming book on Holley, to be published by the University of Illinois Press.

15. Alice Duer Miller, "A Consistent Anti to Her Son," in *Pulling Our Own Strings: Feminist Humor and Satire,* ed. Gloria Kaufman and Mary Kay Blakely (Bloomington: Indiana University Press, 1980), p. 85.

16. Eleanor Flexner, *Century of Struggle: The Woman's Rights Movement in the United States* (New York: Atheneum, 1968), p. 90.

17. Aileen S. Kraditor, *The Ideas of the Woman's Suffrage Movement, 1890–1920* (New York: Doubleday Anchor, 1965), p. 90.

18. Anne Warner, "Miss Clegg's Adopted," *Century,* 46 (1904), 471. Further reference to this story will be by page number in the text.

19. Anne Warner (French), "The New Woman and the Old," in *The Experience of the American Woman,* ed. Barbara H. Solomon (New York: New American Library, 1978), pp. 126–27.

20. Mary E. Wilkins, "A New England Nun" (pp. 1–17) and "A Kitchen Colonel" (pp. 427–47), both in *A New England Nun and Other Stories* (New York: Harper & Brothers, 1891). Mary E. Wilkins took Charles Freeman's name when she married him in 1902, at the age of fifty. Thereafter, her writing never achieved the quality of her earlier work, and in particular, she lost most of her humor. It was an unhappy marriage, finally ending in divorce.

21. Kate Chopin, "The Storm," in *The Complete Works of Kate Chopin,* ed. Per Seyersted (Baton Rouge: Louisiana State University Press, 1969), p. 596.

22. "The Story of an Hour," in *The Complete Works of Kate Chopin,* pp. 352–54.

23. "The Storm" was not published during Chopin's lifetime; "The Story of an Hour" was rejected by a magazine editor as unethical. See Per Seyersted, *Kate Chopin: A Critical Biography* (Oslo: Universitetsforlaget and Baton Rouge: Louisiana State University Press, 1969), p. 68.

24. To date, the most comprehensive source of Parker anecdotes is John Keats, *You Might as Well Live: The Life and Times of Dorothy Parker* (New York: Simon & Schuster, 1970) . Marion Meade is at work on a new and more sympathetic biography of Parker.

25. *The Portable Dorothy Parker* (New York: Viking, 1973), p. 518.

26. "Résumé," in *The Portable Dorothy Parker,* p. 99.

27. "Symptom Recital," in *The Portable Dorothy Parker,* p. 112.

28. "Unfortunate Coincidence," in *The Portable Dorothy Parker,* p. 96.

29. "Mrs. Hofstadter on Josephine Street," in *The Portable Dorothy Parker,* p. 157.

30. "The Waltz," in *The Portable Dorothy Parker,* pp. 47–51.

31. Peg Bracken, *The I Hate to Cook Book* (Greenwich, Conn.: Fawcett Crest, 1960), pp. 24–25.

32. Erma Bombeck, *At Wit's End* (Greenwich, Conn.: Fawcett Crest, 1967), p. 219.

33. Erma Bombeck, *The Grass Is Always Greener Over the Septic Tank* (Greenwich, Conn.: Fawcett Crest, 1976), p. 207.

34. Erica Jong, *Fear of Flying* (New York: New American Library, 1973), p. 310.

35. Sylvia Plath, *The Bell Jar* (New York: Harper & Row, 1971), p. 75.

36. The humor involved in tampax-insertion scenes is analyzed in Janice Delaney, Mary Jane Lupton and Emily Toth, *The Curse: A Cultural History of Menstruation* (New York: Dutton, 1976), esp. pp. 151–54.

37. Judy Blume, *Are You There God? It's Me, Margaret* (New York: Dell, 1970), p. 148.

38. Alix Kates Shulman, "A Story of a Girl and Her Dog," in *Rediscovery: 300 Years of Stories By and About Women,* ed. Betzy Dinesen (New York: Avon, 1982), p. 24.

39. Lisa Alther, *Kinflicks* (New York: Knopf, 1976), pp. 126–27.

40. E. M. Broner, *Her Mothers* (New York: Berkeley, 1975), pp. 185–86.

41. Charlotte Perkins Gilman, *Herland* (New York: Pantheon, 1979), p. 11. Other references to this edition will be made by page number in the text.

42. Toni Cade Bambara, "Raymond's Run," in *Gorilla My Love* (New York: Random House, 1972), p. 32.

43. Toni Cade Bambara, "Medley," in *Midnight Birds,* ed. Mary Helen Washington (New York: Doubleday Anchor, 1980), p. 268.

44. Alice Walker, "Everyday Use," in *Black-Eyed Susans,* ed. Mary Helen Washington (New York: Doubleday Anchor, 1975), p. 79. Further reference to this story will be made by page number in the text. "Everyday Use" will be reprinted in the forthcoming anthology *Between Mothers and Daughters: Stories Across a Generation,* ed. Susan Koppelman (New York: Feminist Press, in press).

45. Rita Mae Brown, *Rubyfruit Jungle* (New York: Bantam, 1973), p. 5. Further reference to this edition will be made by page number in the text.

46. For some discussion of stand-up comics, see my "Female Wits," *Massachusetts Review,* 22 (Winter 1981), 783–93.

47. In a recent article, Nancy Walker quotes some reasons given for omitting Marietta Holley from humor histories, despite her great importance in the nineteenth century. In *Native American Humor* (1947), James Aswell writes that Holley "most particularly . . . didn't amuse me." In *America's Humor: From Poor Richard to Doonesbury* (1978), Walter Blair and Hamlin Hill say that Holley "could never have become as popular today as she did during her lifetime." Most peculiar is C. Carroll Hollis' comment in Louis D. Rubin's *Comic Imagination in American Literature* (1973). According to Hollis, Marietta Holley's work is "of interest to historians, not citizens." Nancy Walker's study is "Wit, Sentimentality, and the Image of Women in the Nineteenth Century," *American Studies, 20* (Fall 1981), 5–22. Jane Curry's recent successes in performing Marietta Holley's stories show that there is still a large, appreciative audience for Holley's wit and wisdom.

48. The three stages in women's literature are discussed in Elaine Showalter, *A Literature of Their Own: British Women Novelists from Bronte to Lessing* (Princeton: Princeton University Press, 1977).

49. Hisaye Yamamoto, "Seventeen Syllables," in *The Third Woman: Minority Women Writers of the United States,* ed. Dexter Fisher (Boston: Houghton Mifflin, 1980), p. 486. Originally published in 1949.

50. Alice Duer Miller, "Feminism," in *Laughing Their Way: Women's Humor in America,* p. 222.

51. "The Miraculous Light," in *Samantha versus Josiah,* p. 223.

From Kate Sanborn to Feminist Psychology: The Social Context of Women's Humor, 1885–1985

Alice Sheppard

While current feminists are calling for a theoretical psychology of women, the present paper suggests that its foundation can be found in the writings of certain nineteenth-century women. Their conclusions, drawn from a different era and assuming contrasting social science paradigms, parallel and anticipate modern discoveries. This paper examines the work of Kate Sanborn (1839–1917), who edited an anthology of women's humor and crusaded for 20 years to alter the stereotype of women's humorlessness. It is suggested that her work adds to our knowledge of feminist history, as well as presaging current theoretical developments in the psychology of women.

This paper examines one aspect of American women's cognitive and social processes as shaped by historic social roles—women's sense of humor. Studying humor provides insights into historical consciousness and social attitudes, as it is an element of popular culture. It is also a trait whose significance has been recognized by contemporary psychologists as integral to a sense of well-being and as related to personality (McGhee & Goldstein, 1983; Ziv, 1984). Finally, the tradition and evolution of women's humor in America is surprisingly well-documented—although it is necessary to search for these resources.

Disregard of Women's Humor

The topic of women's humor has been virtually ignored by literary anthologists, social scientists, and the general public. By 1976, feminists themselves tried to rectify the imbalanced emphasis on men's humor by producing *Titters: The First Collection of Humor by Women* (Stillman & Beatts, 1976). The book, a collection of parody, satire, and illustration, included contributions by such notables as Erma Bombeck, Phyllis Diller, Phyllis McGinley, Gail Parent, and Gilda Radner— though it was not the "first," as will be shown. *Titters* was followed a few years later by *Pulling Our Own Strings* (Kaufman & Blakely, 1980), a volume containing selections by Nora Ephron, Gloria Steinem, Flo Kennedy, Claire Bretécher and others, and organized around themes such as menstruation, motherhood, marriage, clowning, politics, and female roles. While Stillman & Beatts (1976) regarded their selections as "humor by women" rather than "women's humor" (p. 4), Kaufman and Blakely (1980) sought a more direct rationale for their selections: "Feminist humor is based on the perception that societies have generally been organized as systems of oppression and exploitation, and that the largest (but not the only) oppressed group has been the female" (p. 13). Historic women humorists and wits were acknowledged in Kaufman's introduction, although only a few examples of early women's humor were reprinted. These were written by "Fanny Fern" (Sara Willis Parton, 1811–1872), Elizabeth Cady Stanton (1815–1902), and Alice Duer Miller (1874–1942).

Given the relative neglect of women's humor in recent years, it may be surprising to learn of repeated efforts by women over the past century to praise women humorists and call attention to their significance. In 1884, Kate Sanborn published the *The Wit of Women* to prove that American women were not devoid of humor. The book, approximately 200 pages long, was written in a casual, almost conversational style, and offered contents ranging from informal anecdotes to literary quotations, accompanied by a kind of intuitive psychological analysis. Kate Sanborn's decision to publish her collection of women's humor was prompted by an appeal for evidence of women's humor published in the *Critic* in 1884 and by two well-reasoned responses to this appeal from writer Alice Rollins. Rollins' first article, "Woman's Sense of Humor" (1884a), used literary works to prove that women could indeed have a sense of humor. The second, "The Humor of Women" (1884b), elaborated the initial theme with the further claim that women not only possessed humor, but used a distinct and more intellectual form of humor than did men!

Kate Sanborn, herself already a published author, solicited contributions from women humorists, many of them personal acquaintances, to complete her anthology. In a letter to a writer in Concord, Massachusetts (probably Harriette W. Lothrop [*sic*], "Margaret Sidney"), she explained:

> I'm trying to compile a book on the Wit and Humor of American Women—a thing never attempted before. I think I might to have [*sic*] something from you. Will you kindly mail me some selections to choose from?[1]

By the years of the Great Depression, women again collected their humor—this time in the form of a celebration. Artist-writer Martha Bruère teamed up with historian Mary Beard to edit *Laughing Their Way: Women's Humor in America* (1934). The book, nearly 300 pages, was organized by genre (verse, columns, skits, character studies, etc.) and, in addition to literary selections, was illustrated with women's humorous crafts, cartoons, and drawings. Bruère and Beard believed that women's humor was inherently different from men's, observing in their introduction:

> In spite of differences of time and condition, women's humor always bears their proprietary brand. The sexes have their own directions for toleration. . . . And among women, the flowers of their humor are as varied as their lives. . . . Yet the angle of vision from which women see a lack of balance, wrong proportions, disharmonies, and incongruities in life is

a thing of their world as it must be—a world always a little apart. (p. viii)

In light of these historical efforts, why do contemporary feminists believe themselves to lack a tradition of women's humor (e.g. Stillman & Beatts, 1976; Weisstein, 1973) or to be discovering women's humor for the very first time? Part of the answer lies in the nature of gender roles.

Gender Roles and Humor

Twentieth-century women constitute a minority in professional humor and comedy, where even Phyllis Diller and Joan Rivers are perceived as anomalies in the field (Collier & Beckett, 1980). With the women's movement of the 1960s, new interest in women humorists arose, and their rarity began to be explained through the concept of gender roles. As Naomi Weisstein (1973) explained:

> But being a funny, nasty clown doesn't go along with the definition of WOMAN that gets us our provider (beautiful, mysterious, she keeps her own counsel; a quiet stream beneath the blah, blah, blah); an independent, mocking humor is too active for the objectified role we were supposed to fill. Yes, we had an obligation to laugh endlessly at men's jokes, whether or not they were funny, insulting, crude, unpleasant, stupid. . . . (p. 6)

Paul McGhee (1979) emphasized socially derived roles in his survey on the development of female humor and showed the mechanisms that affected aspects of men's and women's humor differentially.

> It is proposed here that a clearly definable set of sex-role standards regarding humor exists for males and females in our culture. Most important along these lines is the expectation that males should be initiators of humor, while females should be responders. . . . Because of the power associated with the successful use of humor, humor

initiation has become associated with other traditionally masculine characteristics, such as aggressiveness, dominance, and assertiveness. For a female to develop into a clown or joker, then, *she must violate the pattern normally reserved for women* [italics added]. (pp. 183–184)

We tend to accept the above analysis at face value as reflecting the insights of twentieth-century psychology. A century of research and theory have culminated in such views. But now consider an excerpt written in 1885 by Kate Sanborn, writer and lecturer, who never studied the social sciences.

[T]here is a reason for our [women's] apparent lack of humor, which it may seem ungracious to mention. Women do not find it polite to cultivate or express their wit. No man likes to have his story capped by a better and fresher from a lady's lips. What woman does not risk being called sarcastic and hateful if she throws back the merry dart or engages in a little sharp-shooting? No, no, it's dangerous—if not fatal. (pp. 205–206)

Sanborn speculated on the meaning of humor as a psychological trait and denied the inherent lack of humor in women. She insisted that such traits were molded by social practices and argued as follows:

It is affirmed that "women seldom repeat an anecdote." That is well, and no proof of their lack of wit. The discipline of life would be largely increased if they did [sic] insist on being "reminded" constantly of anecdotes as familiar as the hand-organ repertoire of "Captain Jinks" and "Beautiful Spring." Their sense of humor is too keen to allow them to aid these aged wanderers in their endless migrations. (pp. 15–16)

In short, women's sense of humor was superior to men's and transcended reliance on stale jokes or borrowed material. Sanborn judged spontaneity an important characteristic of women's joking, observing that it predominated in informal settings where shared amusement was the objective.

The wit of women is like the airy froth of champagne, or the witching iridescence of the soap-bubble, blown for a moment's sport. The sparkle, the life, the fascinating foam, the gay tints vanish with the occasion, because there is no listening Boswell with unfailing memory and capacious note-book to preserve them. Then, unlike men, women do not write out their impromptus before-hand and carefully hoard them for the publisher—and posterity! (p. 207)

Intrapsychic Aspects of Gender

In a literary study of autobiography in the nineteenth and twentieth centuries, Estelle Jelinek (1980) found contrasting realities reflected in male and female consciousness. Reflecting women's experience of their own lives and roles in society, women's narratives appeared disconnected, fragmentary, and irregular. In contrast, males' experiences of life events were unified and linear, yielding chronologically organized stories. There is a parallel between nineteenth-century male humorists' structured stories of adventure and their masculine life perspectives. Women, in contrast, eschewed the dramatic episode, developing a style whose main attributes were the portrayal of ludicrous women and parodies of female roles.

Aspects of men's and women's social realities have been discussed by contemporary psychologists. For example, David Gutmann (1970) theorized that what males perceive as detached or boundaried beyond themselves (Schachtel's [1959] allocentric mode), females treat as a source of connectedness, feeling, and conveying personal significance (the autocentric mode). Moreover, this approach reveals continuity between nineteenth-century social organization and associated literary styles, and the intrapsychic structures of males and females today. In the light of personalized perception, the whimsy and absurdity commonly found in women's humor may relate to differential use of symbolism or an enhanced entry into the fantasy realm (Groch, 1974).

Nineteenth-Century Women's Humor

Although American history books and literary anthologies are generally silent on the topic of women's humor in the nineteenth century, popular women humorists existed, contributing to newspapers and magazines; writing short stories, children's books, and novels; and earning reputations as brilliant and witty conversationalists. In addition, the humor of nineteenth-century women contributes to our historical understanding, as documented by Linda Morris (1979).

> If there were no other evidence to support the conclusion, this particular vernacular humor could take us a long way toward understanding that men and women in nineteenth-century America, especially in the literate classes, lived in adult worlds that consisted almost exclusively of other members of their own sex. (p. 275)

As for these major nineteenth-century women humorists, they ranged from mid-century columnist Ann Stephens, creator of Jonathan Slick, a country youth encountering the big, industrial city, to Marietta Holley, author of approximately 20 books written between 1872 and 1914 under the name of "Josiah Allen's Wife." Holley's immense popularity was attested to in contemporary periodicals (The Lounger, 1905; Wagnalls, 1903), and her work has been reintroduced to the modern reader (Curry, 1983). Preceding Holley's work by two decades was another pinnacle of women's humor, *The Widow Bedott Papers* (1856), written by Frances Miriam Berry Whitcher and published posthumously. Whitcher's persona, Priscilla ("Silly") Bedott, is a conniving, middle-aged woman, whose one goal in life is to remarry as quickly as possible. Women's protagonists typically define themselves in relation to others; while the Widow Bedott spends her time looking for a husband, Josiah Allen's Wife is constantly tied to hers. Samantha Allen has been married for fourteen years to Josiah, a balding widower of slight build.

Samantha, a hefty 200-pounder, is a woman outspoken in her dedication to practical reason, moral values, and human rights. Yet she senses no conflict between her intense devotion to Josiah and her efforts on behalf of "wimmen's rites." Nor does she avoid a realistic assessment of her "pardner's" weaknesses.

> I knew the size and strength of his mind, jest as well as if I had took it out of his head, and weighed it on the steelyards. It was *not* over and above large. . . . But he knows that my love for him towers up like a dromedary, and moves off through life as stately as she duz—the dromedary. Josiah was my choice out of a world full of men. I love Josiah Allen. (Holley, 1885, p. 107)

Returning to the early effort to laud women humorists, we shall now outline the career of Kate Sanborn (1839–1917). Sanborn, a seventh-generation New Englander, was reared in an atmosphere of Yankee wit and humor. She was a witty woman whose professional activities included public speaking, adult education, college teaching, and writing. Her midlife introduction to farming, published in *Adopting an Abandoned Farm* (K. Sanborn, 1891), has been considered a good representative of American humor and was influential in the late-century "back-to-the-land" movement (Hanscom, 1935). She also wrote a sequel, *Abandoning an Adopted Farm* (K. Sanborn, 1894).

In Kate Sanborn's humor anthology, we find one woman's effort to assemble a representative sample of women's humor for the 1880s. She selected brief anecdotes to illustrate a particular woman's propensity for wit and included several literary excerpts, one extending to 11 pages. To some extent, Sanborn's criteria for inclusion was a disadvantage to the modern reader; for example, she cited Frances Miriam Whitcher of the *Widow Bedott Papers* (1856) as only "a familiar name," "popular," and conveying "good examples . . . of an amusing series of comicalities" and explained that Marietta Holley, by then the author of three books in her popular Samantha Allen series, "must be allowed only a brief quotation" (K. Sanborn, 1885, p. 69). Still other humorists were omitted because Sanborn felt that their work could not be excerpted without destroying the humor.

Becoming a Nineteenth-Century Woman Humorist

What about the women who managed to become humorists in the nineteenth century? Are there any common threads to their lives that would help us to understand the intricate relationships between personality, gender roles, and historical time? Most of the prominent women humorists were middle-class and well-educated, came from established families in the Northeast, and additionally showed streaks of rebellion and mischief in their characters. Young Frances Miriam Whitcher enjoyed drawing caricatures of her friends, recalling

> I can scarcely remember the time when the neighbors were not afraid that I would "make fun of them." For indulging in this propensity, I was scolded at home, and wept over and prayed with, by certain well-meaning old maids in the neighborhood; but all to no purpose. (Neal, 1856, pp. xiii–xiv)

Whitcher published anonymously and, sharing George Eliot's cohort, initially selected a masculine pseudonym, "Frank" (Stearns, 1936).

Marietta Holley, raised on a fifth-generation family farm in upstate New York, attended a nearby school but was also tutored at home in French and music. Her childhood verses and sketches were hidden "jealously from every eye," until she began publishing as "Jemyma" in the hometown paper (Willard & Livermore, 1893). She eventually turned to the name "Samantha" as symbolizing "absolute practicality" and as a contrast to the whimsical names (e.g. "Fanny Fern") then much in vogue with women writers (Wagnalls, 1903, p. 61).

Kate Sanborn, a staunch New Englander, was raised on the campus of Dartmouth College, where her much-adored father was a professor of classics. Both he and his wife (a niece of Daniel Webster) were determined to obtain a good education for their first-born, Kate. She was tutored in Greek, English literature, and elocution and was herself ready to teach by her late teens. As a child, she was "pert and audacious" (K. Sanborn, 1915, pp. 2–3). When once silenced for screaming from a burned finger, she told her father, "Put your fingers on that teapot—and don't kitikize" (p. 3). Told to go to bed at her regular seven o'clock bedtime, she retorted, "I'm going to sit up till eight tonight, and don't you 'spute" (p. 3). Her parents upheld strict standards of conduct, as is evident from her father's letter when Kate was visiting relatives.

> I hope you will be so obedient that they can send home a good report for every day. Then you will remember, I hope, to be very respectful and never reply to anything they may say. Some little girls reply to their parents and dispute what is said to them. Such children become very disagreeable and nobody ever loves them. (Letter, 15 September, 1847)[2]

We have briefly surveyed some nineteenth-century women humorists and their family backgrounds. The most persistent question remaining, then, concerns why they were repeatedly overlooked by critics and historians. It becomes more remarkable in the face of Kate Sanborn's monomaniacal efforts to counteract attitudes of her day.

Efforts to Recognize Women's Humor

Did Kate Sanborn's arguments for and numerous examples of humor diminish the stereotype of women's humorlessness? Reviews of *The Wit of Women* were scarce, and Sanborn (1915) later reflected, "If a masculine book reviewer ever alluded to the book, it was with a sneer. He generally left it without a word . . ." (p. 164). The British *Saturday Review* ("Review of *The Wit of Women*," 1886) may be typical of the general negative reaction: "If anything could induce disbelief in the reality of feminine wit, it would be the facetious poetry by various American ladies which Miss Sanborn, with more patriotism than discretion, has seen fit to publish" (p. 126).

Despite such responses, Kate Sanborn did not abandon her humor crusade but continued writing and lecturing on humor into the next decade. Her public lecture "Are Women Witty?" (1898) expanded the major themes of the book and was highly entertaining.

At the turn of the century, none other than the *New York Times* instigated discussions on women's humor, with a focus on literary aspects. "The Saturday Review" section of the *Times* ("Women Among," 1900) printed the following, allegedly based on a true conversation:

> Now, on the contrary, search the list of women writers from Mary E. Wilkins to Mrs. Aphra Behn, and *you will not find a single professedly woman humorous writer* [italics added]. Some of them may have sporadic flashes of fun, but they soon lapse into gravity or sentimentality. . . . It may be that women are deprived of the humorous sense in the same manner that a person may be born without sight or hearing or speech. (p. 40)

The commentary concluded with an invitation for readers to aid in the quest for a "real woman humorous writer" and promised that replies would be published. The next week the readers' page contained the heading "Kate Sanborn, One of Them, Makes a Defense" (K. Sanborn, 1900). She selected Marietta Holley as the strongest "professedly" humorous woman writer and presented an additional list of 82 "Real Women Humorous Writers." Other readers sent in their choices of women humorists, and several of them mentioned Sanborn. If the issue remained unresolved, it was not for lack of interest!

Throughout the early years of the century, the issue of women's humor re-emerged sporadically. In 1902, Burges Johnson introduced a two-part series on "The New Humor" with photographs of four humorists, three of whom were women (Carolyn Wells, Josephine Daskam, and Mrs. Atwood Martin). *Good Housekeeping* contained an article by Arthur Maurice (1910) in which he described the "new school" of American humor as "at least three-fifths feminine." *Woman's Home Companion* published an article by Jeannette Gilder (1912), "Women Writers as Humorists," which praised a number of women humorists: Mary Wilkins Freeman, George Eliot, Alice Hegan Rice, Anne Warner, Mary Roberts Rinehart, Josephine Daskam, Carolyn Wells, Mary Heaton Vorse, and others. The creator of a successful stage comedy and co-editor of the *Critic*, Gilder had now taken a stand in the debate. Indeed, a careful reading of her Lounger column in first the *Critic* and later *Putnam's,* into which the *Critic* was subsequently absorbed, showed her to have praised women humorists over the years.[3]

Historical Developments in Women's Humor

Kate Sanborn's campaign for the recognition of women's humor coincided with a major transition in American thought. In her memoirs some 15 years later, *Memories and Anecdotes* (1915), Sanborn exclaimed: "Now you can hardly find any one who denies that women possess both qualities [wit and humor], and it is generally acknowledged that now a few have· the added gift of comedy" (p. 164).

The issue of women's humor was debated within the relatively short span of twenty years (roughly 1884–1904). Within this period two distinct phases can be discerned. The first phase consisted of greater attention to the question of women's humor, found referred to in newspapers and periodicals of the times. Theoretical reviews, however, could still overlook women humorists, as shown by an article, "American Literary Comedians" by Henry Lukens (1890), that discussed only men.

The second phase began as women humorists were acknowledged and given a place with men. For example, the ten-volume series, *The Wit and Humor of America* (Wilder, 1907), contained 31 women out of 206 humorists, about 15%. By the turn of the century, women's magazines published a great deal of comic poetry and humorous drawings by women. In the century's second decade, humor had changed to the point that the stock vaudeville character of a very large man in petticoats and a wig wearing a "Votes for Women" banner had actually disappeared. Beatrice Hale (1914) explained the significance of the change in public attitude: "The tone of public humour is infinitely higher than it used to be, for the reason that as women learn to value themselves more, they are more valued by men" (p. 117).

Agents of Social Change

The existence of women's humor was most strongly acknowledged shortly after the turn of the century. Probably a number of factors were responsible for this rapid and effective change, and some of the important ones include: (1) education, (2) domestic science, (3) political activism, and (4) the increasing convergence between male and female social spheres. Each of these will be examined.

Education

The latter half of the nineteenth century witnessed a rapid increase in educational opportunities for women and in the founding of women's colleges. Once the belief in the potentially harmful physical effects of education on women had been dispelled, the educational "woman question" could now focus on just *how* women should be educated. By 1881, the Association of Collegiate Women, later the American

Association of University Women, was founded to promote lifetime learning for women (Frankfort, 1977). Artistic and literary studies, the more "feminine" aspects of a classical education, provided the skills for women to become comic artists and writers.

Domestic Science

The new science of home economics created professional interest in activities such as food preparation and home management, which were considered to be in the female domain. The magazine *Good Housekeeping* attested to new scientific and social benefits for women, elevating child and home to subjects for scientific inquiry. These offered a new focus for humor. For example, Josephine Daskam's *Memoirs of a Baby* (1904) was a satire on then-new child-rearing methods. The domestic humor formula has continued to this day in the work of columnist Erma Bombeck and cartoonist Lynn Johnston.

Political Activism

Dedication to the cause of woman suffrage was accelerated at the turn of the century and found representatives in the humor profession. It has been claimed that the humor of Marietta Holley did more for the women's cause than many more serious advocates (Blair, 1942). While collective political goals unified sympathies, cartoons were recognized as an effective instrument for change in the hands of early-century political cartoonists Nina Allender, Blanche Ames, and Lou Rogers (Sheppard, 1984).

Converging Social Spheres

In the late nineteenth century, women's sphere was the home and men's the marketplace. Because of these occupational and social divisions, areas of interest were different. As Linda Morris (1979) revealed, "Thus, for both sexes, the final and decisive factor that distinguishes their humor from each other's is their preoccupation with the affairs, activities, and concerns of their own sex" (p. 275).

Works of women's humor in the nineteenth century were characterized by domestic settings and an orientation toward interpersonal relationships. The contemporary blurring of these distinctions has altered the experience of both sexes and perhaps diminished the most characteristic features of "women's humor."

Women's History and Feminist Theory

There is little in theories of women's humor that recognizes its own historical evolution. A comprehensive framework, moreover, would clarify the relationship between social change and humor. To what extent has women's humor actively brought about social change, or does it passively reflect society's inconsistencies and injustices? Given the contemporary humor of women and men, what gender differences still exist? Are the dimensions that underlie gender distinctions today similar to those in the nineteenth century? Has the magnitude of these differences been reduced? Many questions remain to be answered.

Study of late-nineteenth-century writings reveals a discrepancy between the existence of women's humor and its recognition by the literary world. For example, Marietta Holley, whose works were widely read, elicited reactions from critics such as the following.

> It's up-hill work for a man to be funny through a book of ordinary size, but it is much more difficult when a woman undertakes the task in an extended way. "Samantha at Saratoga" is a peculiarly sad and depressing volume. . . . ("Review of *Samantha*," 1887, p. 14)

The number of copies sold, however, was a figure approaching the 500,000 for *Huckleberry Finn*, ranking it a "better seller" (Mott, 1947).

The main obstacle to recognizing women's humor lay in the construct "woman humorist," with its implicit gender bias. Kate Sanborn understood that society's attitudes did not reflect its behavior and pointed out the inconsistency. Concluding her discussion on Marietta Holley, Sanborn (1848) wrote as follows.

> Men, I mean publishers, find that women's wit puts much money in their pockets. As they rattle the gold and caressingly count the bills from twentieth editions, do they think of women as sad, crushed, sentimental, hero-adoring geese, who can't see the humorous side? (p. 324)

More surprising is the realization that vestiges of these stereotypes are still with us in the continued failure to acknowledge the tradition of women's humor. Because of the male-based standard, many professionals and scholars, both women and men, show an inability to perceive the tradition of women as humorists. Lois Rather (1971) explored the implications of editors and anthologists who were male. Nevertheless, she found Whitcher's work "less than uproarious" (p. 8) and settled for the conclusion, "If we come right down to it, maybe women just aren't as funny" (p. 10). *The Feminization of American Culture* by Ann Douglas (1977) deals with the influence of women on the nineteenth century intellect. Yet Douglas fails to include any reference to humor, comedy, wit, or women's humor in the 22-page index, even though she actually discusses it in her presentation of Lyman Beecher and Harriet Beecher Stowe.

> Of Beecher's children, only she [Harriet] relished the vernacular as he did; she outdid her father in her shrewd instinct for comedy, and became *the only major feminine humorist* [emphasis added] nineteenth-century America produced. (p. 294)

To some extent it is possible for feminists to reconstruct the tradition of women's humor (Curry, 1976; Dresner, 1982; Morris, 1979; Sheppard, 1984; Walker, 1984) and to document contemporary trends (Neitz, 1980; Sheppard, 1985). Yet historical research is impeded by the fact that failing to recognize the significance of women humorists causes the exclusion of their papers and correspondence from libraries and archives. Kate Sanborn may be studied today not because historians recognized the value of the women's humor question but because she happened to be the daughter of an important academic family and *their* papers were retained. She also had an admiring younger brother who submitted a full-length, illustrated biography shortly after her death (E. Sanborn, 1918). Other humorists have not fared so well, with few remnants surviving from which to reconstruct their lives. In short, only certain types of social histories are researchable because the subject matter of history itself is remolded by social forces. For those excluded from the dominant culture, as women have been, continuity with the past is frequently disrupted or lost. Jean Baker Miller (1976) knew what this meant for a psychology of women: "Most records of these actions are not preserved by the dominant culture, making it difficult for the subordinate group to find a supporting tradition and history" (p. 11).

Much of our insight into this period comes from analyses of gender roles and their history. Kate Sanborn's analysis of humor in 1885 and those by psychologists of the 1970s emphasize differences in men's and women's humor. Each demonstrates how these can be viewed as derived from sex role expectations and differential behaviors prescribed for each gender. What progress, then, has been achieved in our theories of women's humor over the past hundred years? It appears that popular beliefs about women and the stereotype of their humorlessness are changing faster than the conceptual tools offered by social scientists. Moreover, if the relevant history is not reviewed, there is constant danger of re-inventing old theories.

Identifying a social group as oppressed or for whom certain actions are disallowed does not constitute a sufficient psychological interpretation of the group's experience and perceptions. A feminist theory of psychology must move beyond mere role contrasts to an understanding of the social world as perceived by women at a given historical time. Historic humor enables one to rediscover perceived incongruities and thus reconstruct a lost perspective. It constitutes a step in understanding the processes by which those perceptions are created and altered. Consider the framework proposed by Berger and Luckmann (1966) in *The Social Construction of Reality.*

> The reality of everyday life maintains itself by being embodied in routines, which is the essence of institutionalization. Beyond this, however, the reality of everyday life is ongoingly reaffirmed in the individual's interaction with others. Just as reality is originally internalized by a social process, so it is maintained in consciousness by social processes. (p. 149)

While sociologists and psychologists have acknowledged the social origins of our cognitive experience, they cling to the universalized, i.e., male, model. Carol Gilligan (1982) has argued that women's experiences are ignored "in part from the assumption that there is a single mode of social experience and interpretation" (p. 173). Berger and Luckmann's (1966) analysis shows the progression from daily routines and social interaction to social reality. Just as the social activities and patterns of interaction differ for males and females, so do the resulting realities.

In sum, the question of women's humor becomes not "why didn't women develop a humor tradition?" but "why has the humor which was created and appreciated by women been ignored?" We have seen that part of the answer lies in the social worlds of past generations, culminating in the exaggeration of separate spheres in the late nineteenth century. Men's and women's activities were distinct, were thought to reflect contrasting spiritual and instinctive characters, and resulted in contrasting cognitive constructions of their experience. Humor, an instrument of social correction and subversion, reinforced women's shared perceptions, strengthened social bonds, and itself facilitated social change. Masculine aspects of humor—violence, power, and adventure—were deemed inappropriate for the world of women, which was properly oriented toward social etiquette, true womanhood, and sentimentality (Walker, 1981). Women created their own humor, complying with social restrictions and revealing a unique perspective.

In the course of history, new activities for women brought changes in role definition. Yet, despite these transitions, substantial continuity in women's consciousness remains, such that feminists of today may read historical women's humor and feel that they have discovered their hidden roots. By studying the development of women's humor in America, we can trace everyday realities, social consciousness, and awareness of the forces that oppress women. Feminist theory must deal with women's psychological experience across differing times in history to discover the genesis of social cognitions. As George Eliot (1876–1967) knew too well, "A difference of taste in jokes is a great strain on the affections" (p. 201).

Notes

1. Material reprinted courtesy the Trustees of the Boston Public Library. Department of Rare Books and Manuscripts, Boston Public Library.

2. By courtesy of Dartmouth College Library Archives.

3. Frank Mott (1938) identified Jeannette Gilder as the "Lounger" columnist, implying that she was the author of the *Critic's* commentary on women's humor. A contrary opinion is offered by Alfred Habegger (1982; personal communication, January 11, 1984), who believes that her brother, Joseph Gilder, was the Lounger.

References

Berger, P.L. , & Luckmann, T. (1966). *The social construction of reality.* New York: Doubleday/Anchor.

Blair, W. (1942). *Horse sense in American humor.* Chicago: University of Chicago Press.

Bruère, M., & Beard, M. (Eds.). (1934). *Laughing their way: Women's humor in America.* New York: Macmillan.

Collier, D., & Beckett, K. (1980). *Spare ribs: Women in the humor biz.* New York: St. Martin's.

Curry, J.A. (1976). Women as subjects and writers of nineteenth-century American humor. *Dissertation Abstracts International, 36,* 6681A. (University Microfilms No. 76—9379)

Curry, J.A. (Ed.). (1983). *Samantha rastles the woman question.* Urbana, IL. University of Illinois Press.

Daskam, J. (1904). *The memoirs of a baby.* New York: Harper's.

Douglas, A. (1977). *The feminization of American culture.* New York: Knopf.

Dresner, Z.Z. (1982). Twentieth century American women humorists. *Dissertation Abstracts International, 43,* 1970A. (University Microfilms No. 82–26451)

Eliot, G. (1967). *Daniel Deronda.* New York: Penguin. (Original work published 1876)

Frankfort, R. (1977). *Collegiate women: Domesticity and career in turn-of-the-century women.* New York: New York University Press.

Gilder, J. (1923, May). Women writers as humorists. *Woman's Home Companion,* p. 22.

Gilligan, C. (1982). *In a different voice.* Cambridge, MA: Harvard University Press.

Groch, A. (1974). Generality of response to humor and wit in cartoons, jokes, stories, and photographs. *Psychological Reports,* 35, 835–838.

Gutmann, D. (1970). Female ego styles and generational conflict. In J.M. Bardwick, E. Douvan, M.S. Horner & D. Gutmann, *Feminine personality and conflict* (pp. 77–96). Belmont, CA: Brooks/Cole.

Habegger, A. (1982). *Gender, fantasy and realism in American literature.* New York: Columbia University Press.

Hale, B.F. (1914). *What women want: An interpretation of the feminist movement.* New York: Stokes.

Hanscom, E.D. (1935). Sanborn, Katherine Abbott. In D. Malone (Ed.). *Dictionary of American biography* (Vol. 16, pp. 327–328). New York: Scribner's.

Holley, M. (1885). *Sweet Cicely, or Josiah Allen as a politician*. New York: Funk & Wagnalls.

Jelinek, E.C. (1980). Introduction: Women's autobiography and the male tradition. In E.C. Jelinek (Ed.). *Women's autobiography* (pp. 1–20). Bloomington, IN: Indiana University Press.

Johnson, B. (1902). The new humor, *Critic, 40*, 331–338.

Kaufman, G., & Blakely, M.K. (Eds.). (1980). *Pulling our own strings*. Bloomington, IN: Indiana University Press.

The Lounger. (1884). *Critic, 4*, 138.

The Lounger. (1905). *Critic, 46*, 6.

Lukens, H.C. (1890, April). American literary comedians. *Harper's*, pp. 783–797.

Maurice, A. (1910, January). Feminine humorists. *Good Housekeeping*, pp. 34–39.

McGhee, P.E. (1979). The role of laughter and humor in growing up female. In C.B. Kopp (Ed.). *Becoming female* (pp. 183–206). New York: Plenum.

McGhee, P.E., & Goldstein, J.H. (Eds.). (1983). *Handbook of humor research* (Vols. 1–2). New York: Springer-Verlag.

Miller, J.B. (1976). *Toward a new psychology of women*. Boston: Beacon Press.

Morris, L.A.F. (1979). Women vernacular humorists in nineteenth-century America: Ann Stephens, Frances Whitcher, and Marietta Holley. *Dissertation Abstracts International, 40*, 258A. (University Microfilms No. 79–14705).

Mott, F. (1938). *A history of American magazines* (Vol. 3). Cambridge, MA: Harvard University Press.

Mott, F. (1947). *Golden multitudes: The story of best sellers in the United States*. New York: Macmillan.

Neal, A.B. (1856). Introductory. In F.M. Whitcher, *The Widow Bedott papers* (pp. ix-xix). New York: Derby.

Neitz, M.J. (1980). Humor, hierarchy, and the changing status of women. *Psychiatry, 43*, 211–223.

Rather, L. (1971). Were women funny? Some 19th century humorists. *American Book Collector, 21*, 5–10.

Review of *The wit of women*. (1886, January 23). *Saturday Review of Literature, Science, and Art, 61*, p. 126.

Review of *Samantha at Saratoga*. (1887, September 25). *New York Times*, p. 14.

Rollins, A.W. (1884a). Woman's sense of humor. *Critic, 4*, 145–146.

Rollins A.W. (1884b). The humor of women. *Critic, 4*, 301–302.

Sanborn, E.W. (1918). *Kate Sanborn*. Boston: McGrath Sherrill.

Sanborn, K. (1885). *The wit of women*. New York: Funk & Wagnalls.

Sanborn, K. (1891). *Adopting an abandoned farm.* New York: Appleton.

Sanborn, K. (1894). *Abandoning an adopted farm.* New York: Appleton.

Sanborn, K. (1898). Are women witty? In K. Sanborn, *My favorite lectures of long ago for friends who remember* (pp. 309–338). Boston: Case, Lockwood, & Brainard.

Sanborn, K. (1900, January 27). Kate Sanborn, one of them, makes a defense. [Letter to the editor]. *New York Times Saturday Review,* p. 52.

Sanborn, K. (1915). *Memories and anecdotes.* New York: Putnam.

Schachtel, E.G. (1959). *Metamorphosis: On the development of affect, perception, attention and memory.* New York: Basic Books.

Sheppard, A. (1984). There *were* ladies present! American women cartoonists and comic artists in the early twentieth century. *Journal of American Culture, 7,* 38–48.

Sheppard, A. (1985). Funny women: Social change and audience response to female comedians, *Empirical Studies in the Arts, 3,* 179–195.

Stearns, B.M. (1936). Whitcher, Frances Miriam Berry. In D. Malone (Ed.). *Dictionary of American biography* (Vol. 20, p. 82). New York: Scribner's.

Stillman, D., & Beatts, A. (Eds.). (1976). *Titters: The first collection of humor by women.* New York: Collier.

Wagnalls, M. (1903, November). A glimpse of Marietta Holley. *Ladies Home Journal,* p. 61.

Walker, N. (1981). Wit, sentimentality, and the image of women in the nineteenth century. *American Studies, 22,* 5–22.

Walker, N. (1984). *The tradition of women's humor in America.* Huntington Beach, CA: American Studies Publishing Co.

Weisstein, N. (1973). Introduction. In E. Levine, *All she needs* (pp. 1–10). New York: Quadrangle.

Whitcher, F.M.B. (1856). *The Widow Bedott papers.* New York: Derby.

Wilder, M.P. (Ed.). (1907). *The wit and humor of America* (vols. 1–10). New York: Funk & Wagnalls.

Willard, F.E., & Livermore, M.A. (1893). Holley, Miss Marietta. In F.E. Willard & M.A. Livermore (Eds.). *A woman of the century* (p. 386). New York: Moulton.

Women among humorists. (1900, January 20). *New York Times Saturday Review,* p. 40.

Ziv, A. (1984). *Personality and sense of humor.* New York: Springer.

Why We Aren't Laughing . . . Any More

Naomi Weisstein

Why have they been telling us women lately that we have no sense of humor—when we are always laughing? Turn on the tube: there we are, laughing away, running in slow motion through warm sand with the Pacific roaring in back of us, goldenrod and grass undulating in sync with our mane of long straight hair, the camera slightly out of focus and the lights diffused and blinking. All we do is laugh. We're sudsing our hair on the color TV and laughing, we're drinking soda out of bottles and laughing, we're catching taxis in our new panty hose and laughing, we're playing with pink telephones and laughing. Laugh! We're a laffriot. And when we're not laughing, we're smiling. We're smiling at the boss, smiling at the kid (no headache is going to stop me from smiling at my kid), smiling at the old man, smiling at the dog, the baby, the gas man, the cop who just gave us a ticket, the automobile mechanic who just insulted us, the men on the street who just whistled at us, the guy with his fly open who's following us down the street (maybe if we're nice he'll go away), smiling through parties, smiling through conversations, smiling when we talk, smiling when we listen.

When I collided with puberty in the fifties (and I wish nothing worse on those who are nostalgic for those detergent, lying, tight-ass, repressive apolitical years than to *live through them again*), the first thing I figured out was that, if I were to acquire *personality*—the key to *popularity, dates,* a *steady boyfriend,* a chance for me, too, to run in slow motion with defocused lenses while whole choruses sang madrigals on my

131

behalf—I'd better start smiling. Laugh as much [as] possible, and when you can't manage a laugh, do smile. So I laughed maniacally through high school, college, graduate school, and smiled warmly through all those years when all those chairmen of all those psychology departments explained that women were not suited for academic careers.

And now they tell me I have no sense of humor.

I'm setting up a straw man. Everybody knows that laughter is a highly unreliable measure of whether or not something is funny, or of whether or not there is any comedy at all in a situation. The sight and sound of women laughing nervously after each sentence we utter is acutely painful: it is clear that we are only italicizing our timidity, our feelings of inadequacy. ("You don't think it's cancer, do you, Doctor?" the patient says, laughing a little.) I knew a Vietnam veteran who told me that after a couple of months over there his "nerves" got so bad that he couldn't keep himself from laughing when he was in combat. Laughter is one of those behaviors whose personal and social uses are almost infinitely varied. It would be an enormous task to enumerate all the situations in which we laugh, or what that laughter means.

So laughing is no index of whether or not women have a sense of humor, and, in any case, that's not what people mean when they level that charge against us. What they mean is that women have no sense of humor these days—and by *these days* they mean the days of "women's lib." (Better yet, "femlib." The term is kinda cute, isn't it? Why do you think "femlibbers" don't think it's so clever to describe a movement to stop the waste, suffering, and destruction of women's lives by such a cute little term? Many "femlibbers" just don't know "cute" when they see it.) "You women can no longer take a joke" is what they mean. Whatsamatter baby, don't you smile? Whatsamatter baby, don't you smile *any more?* There's this joke about this fat ugly old lady who tries to get on a bus, see, and—hey, whatsamatter, can't you take a joke? I'm not talking about you. You're not old, har-har. Or, in somewhat more pompous terms, as a New York *Times* reporter wrote recently,

". . . I am always distressed whenever . . . feminist leaders display such a total lack of humor."

Why is it that the Women's Movement has been charged at this time with lacking a sense of humor? Humor, like laughter, is an extraordinarily complex social and cultural form, having a variety of meanings and functions. Do they mean we don't laugh any more? (No, we've already been through that.) Do they mean that none of us in the Women's Movement is witty, or clever, or funny, or comic? (That's obviously false.) It is not simply tendentious to state that, if a charge is directed against a *political* and social movement (and is otherwise meaningless or demonstrably false), then one might do well to examine the politics behind the charge. And that, in turn, means examining the political or power-related uses of humor.

Not all humor is "political" in the sense that not all humor serves to establish, maintain, or reinforce differences in power. Humor can serve as an expression of pleasure, affection, love, play, recreation, or an aesthetic, and be used as a vehicle for wit, argument, thought. But it can also be used as an expression of social solidarity within groups, to the exclusion of others; it can define normative behavior; it can be used to establish or restate relations of power, or to question these relations; it can be used as a signal that a situation is not at all serious, or that it is so serious that we had better laugh if we are to be able to do battle with it; it can be used as a display of personal charm and attractiveness. In all these cases, humor has, in addition to its other functions, a political function.

Humor as a weapon in the social arsenal constructed to maintain caste, class, race, and sex inequalities is a very common thing. Much of this humor is pure slander. It serves to put whoever it is in their place by showing that they can't be taken seriously, that they're too stupid or dumb or ugly or childlike or smelly or mean to count as human. But some ridicule of the powerless touches on the real behavior of the people who are out of power, and the laughter is at the manifestations of their victimization. This is not because people are "naturally" insensitive to other people's pain, or "naturally" bad or cruel. It is just extraordinarily difficult to *understand* what it means to be out of power when you aren't there, to understand the behavior which accompanies such a state, to recognize in an individual's behavior the social symptoms of powerlessness. It is very difficult for someone not under personal or social or physical threat to understand why somebody else is so nervous, so jumpy, so dumb, so slow moving, so "dizzy," so careful with their speech, so careless about their speech. It is a commonplace in the Women's Movement to tell men that if they really want to understand what we mean by our total oppression, they should "pass" for women for a day and see what happens. Ignored in conversation, patronized at work, hello-babied by strangers, ogled on the street, followed into buildings, fondled in crowded buses, attacked in elevators; objects of ridicule and contempt, even the most neutral transaction is usually accompanied by abuse: "Hey, Dutch, she says do we have any pork chops. Did you hear her? Do we have any pork chops? Lady, what's your *problem?* Can't you see we don't have any pork chops?"

As women, we live in a coercive, threatening, unpleasant world; a world which tolerates us only when we are very young or very beautiful. If we become stupid or slow, jumpy or fast, dizzy or high-pitched, we are simply expressing the pathology of our social condition. So when we hear jokes against women, and we are asked why we don't laugh at them, the answer is easy, simple, and short. Of course, we're not laughing, you asshole. Nobody laughs at the sight of their own blood.

But this is a glib answer, because people *do* laugh at their own pain. The important difference is that if they are really to find it funny, *they* have to have made the joke. Humor here, too, has a political use, but its function is reversed: it is a weapon or a technique of survival used by the oppressed. It is the powerless fighting back.

There are a number of great comic traditions among oppressed groups. Lenny Bruce had a bit about why Jews and blacks were such natural comedians. It focused on the survival function of entertaining: you charm your oppressor and then you don't have to work so hard.

But it's deeper than that. My grandparents' humor drew from an Eastern European Jewish tradition. All sorts of characters appeared in this humor, many of them winning small victories over their oppressors. (The clever, gentle Jew, for instance, who, upon hearing a Prussian officer yell "Swine!" turns around, bows, and returns the introduction: "Cohen. Pleased to meet you.") In none of these stories were there kike jokes, archetypal Izzys and Ikeys: the "little Hebe" wasn't there. The humor was based on the understanding of a shared and unjust oppression. If the humor wasn't heavy on political ways to fight the oppression, it was nonetheless about people fighting back, retaining their dignity. It ridiculed those who oppressed them. This type of humor can create strength. It can assert that the roles and social categories we find ourselves in are not going to intimidate us; they are human creations, and we can play with them, challenge them, attack them, ridicule them. Historian Margaret Young Jackson quotes a beautiful example of this: an exchange between a slave and his master, who is just about to fight a duel and has dressed appropriately:

"Pompey, how do I look?"
"0 massa, mighty."
"What do you mean, 'mighty,' Pompey?"
"Why, massa, you look noble."
"What do you mean by 'noble'?"
"Why, sar, you just look like one <u>lion</u>."
"Why, Pompey, where have you ever seen a lion?"
"I seen one down in yonder field the other day, massa."
"Pompey, you foolish fellow, that was a <u>jack-ass.</u>"
"Was it, massa? Well, you look just like him."

Some humor of oppressed groups is directed against types within the group itself. There are categories of self-deprecation in the humor of the oppressed, categories, even, of the same kind of stereotype of the group held by the rest of the society.

This seems directly a survival humor, an implied under-standing that if this is what some of us have become, it is because we couldn't help it, and we're helping it by naming it and laughing at it ourselves.

I know of no comparable traditions of women's humor. By women's humor, I don't mean women being funny. I mean a humor which recognizes a common oppression, notices its source and the roles it requires, identifies the agents of that oppression. This may simply be my own ignorance; there may be traditions of women's humor in different social classes, ethnic groups, cultures, historical periods. But if such traditions existed or exist now, I have been denied them. I remember no redemptive or fighting humor about my condition.

If this is true, it is a very painful conclusion. Why didn't we develop or maintain a tradition of humor with which to fight back? Why didn't I have a culture available which would have allowed me to mock my own roles, and therefore question their sanctity, their quality of inevitability?

There may be a couple of reasons. Consider rebellious humor as a technique for survival. It would seem to require that the group with whom one identifies provide some permanent although perhaps fragile shelter, some home base from which one goes out and deals with an oppressive world. While there are many occasions when women are together—in offices, in factories, in homes—our base has not generally been a social grouping of women, but some particular man with whom we live. In fact, it is assumed that when women are together socially, they are not together out of volition; they are together either because their men prefer to be alone, or they are waiting for some man, or they are forced together by their inability to attract some man. For most of us, our livelihood depends on charming some man, having a provider. Our physical safety depends on having some man protect us; and our primary social interaction is limited to a single individual from the opposite sex. Under these circumstances, the development of an open, rebellious humor may not have been an option available to us. In addition, the charm that we had to develop was of a very special nature. For us, the definition of charm depended primarily on our being beautiful, passive, accepting, and mute. Had we just been required to be charming, without also being required to be sex objects at the same time, we might still have been able to develop some fairly subtle survival humor. But being a funny, nasty clown doesn't go along with the definition of WOMAN that gets us our provider (beautiful, mysterious, she keeps her own counsel; a quiet stream . . .).

An independent, mocking humor is too active for the objectified role we were meant to fill. Yes, we had an obligation to laugh endlessly at men's jokes, whether or not they were funny, insulting, crude, unpleasant, stupid; yes, we were supposed to laugh at what others thought we were; yes, we were supposed to be witty and pleasing—all that is part of personal charm. But to be able to mock the requirement that we be all these things is quite a different thing.

It may be, in fact, that the reason the charge "humorless" is not simply dismissed—as we would dismiss a charge that we were, for instance, stockpiling all the desk calculators in the world in order to halt commerce and industry and thereby bring on the final catastrophe—is that "having a sense of humor" in the way defined for women (that is, laughing only at those things which we are expected to laugh at) is part of maintaining our charm. Since our charm is so bound up with our survival, it may become a frightening accusation when people tell us we've lost our sense of humor—it's as good as telling us we're ugly. And it is, of course, as revealing. It means that we may actually be changing our social roles, that we have stopped trying to please. If we are no longer laughing at what is not funny to us, we may be, in a way, taking the first step in our being able to develop our own women's humor.

There's another baroque aspect of the cultural definition of woman which may have made it difficult for us to develop a fighting, saving humor. At present, in our culture, unless we are being WOMAN (beautiful, mysterious, in touch with the verities of birth, blood, and death, quiet by the seashore . . .), being a woman (actually, being a "lady" in the sense of "ladies' room," or "Listen, lady, how the hell should I know how you're going to get on that plane?") *is itself ridiculous.*

That is, part of the present social definition of woman is "ridiculous person." Women have always been in part defined as "ridiculous persons"; but there was a time when "wife" and "mother" was, in principle, honored. If having babies, being that wife-and-mother, was an oppressive role, at least it was something that had its rewards: there was a dignity attached to that social position. But wife and mother are held in less and less esteem, and are considered less and less useful socially. And until the current Women's Movement we had *no* alternate roles into which we were accepted and from which we could obtain dignity. So women fast became that residual category, socially useless and ridiculous persons.

How can you trust humor when it's a weapon used against you? I notice movie audiences laughing when a woman does anything but be WOMAN (beautiful, mysterious, a golden mist surrounds her . . .). It is quite a feat to turn what is defined as a ridiculous state of being into your own definition of the ridiculous, to take control of the *quality* of the absurdity, to turn it away from yourself. We must at the same time show that our existence has social meaning, that we agree that what we are *supposed* to be is not only ridiculous but also barbaric, that nobody is either WOMAN or "lady," and that all this is very funny indeed. That's a hard act to get together.

Finally, women have not had a tradition of fighting and rebellious humor perhaps because the humor of the oppressed is based on a knowledge of shared oppression, and this has been hidden from us in curious ways. One of the paths of coming into consciousness, into politics, of an oppressed group is the realization that their misery is not due to some innate inferiority, to their own flawed characters, but that there is something going on outside that is keeping them down, and that it is *not fair.*

The curious thing about our oppression is that we were taught that it *is fair:* that it was in the divine order of things. So even when we realized that there was something out there keeping us down, whether defined in terms of "born a woman," suffering because of men, the meanness of men, whatever, the conclusion was that this was timeless, unalterable, the way things are and always will be. It was woman's nature to suffer. We *dug* pain. How else could we really be WOMAN?

It is, of course, belaboring the obvious to explain that once a group is in a position of victim, it certainly is more pleasant for most people to believe that they like being there. Happy slaves, dumb niggers, women digging pain. God's in His heaven, all right. But, to retrace: to deny this definition, clothed as it is in WOMAN (beautiful, mysterious: See! Primal Mysteries! Ancient Wounds! Guided Tour of the House of Secrets!), to deny this idiot metaphysics means a coming into consciousness, a politicizing, a statement. No. We don't like pain. We hate it. We hate this prehistory in which we live, where all of us are born in pain, and most of us live our lives out in pain. We hate the waste and destruction of human lives, of women's lives, of our lives. And we hate it so much that we're not going to allow it to happen any more.

There have been extraordinary obstacles to the development of a women's fighting humor. We must therefore experiment with the public presentation of such a humor. We must try out forms which throw off the shackles of self-ridicule, self-abnegation; we must tap that capacity for outrage, that knowledge of our shared oppression.

We must construct a women's culture with its own character, its fighting humor, its defiant celebration of our worth. We must reclaim our history, our rights to self-expression and collective enjoyment. We must create our own humor. The propitiating laughter, the fixed and charming smiles are over. This time, when we laugh, things are going to be funny.

Mother Wit: Humor in Afro-American Women's Autobiography

Lucinda H. MacKethan

T he expression "Mother Wit" has three associations: according to Alan Dundes, it is, first, "a popular term in black speech referring to common sense"; secondly, it is "the kind of good sense not necessarily learned from books or in school"; and thirdly, "with its connotation of collective wisdom acquired by the experience of living and from generations past," it is "often expressed in folklore" (Dundes xiv). In his collection of essays related to Afro-American folklore, Dundes consistently pairs mother wit with laughter and humor, for, as he says, "it is what makes a people laugh that reveals the soul of that people" (611). When we look, however, at the word *mother,* in relation to mother wit, we might wonder how the term applies to the traditional experience of the Afro-American mother from slavery times forward; the question we could ask is, Why are these women laughing? A survey of three important autobiographical accounts of black women's existence in America, the works of Harriet Jacobs, Zora Neale Hurston, and Maya Angelou, reveals little cause for laughter. Jacobs' *Incidents in the Life of a Slave Girl,* the only woman's fugitive slave narrative verified as having been written by the slave herself, tells how Jacobs hid from her master for seven years in the narrow attic crawl space of her free grandmother's house in North Carolina; Hurston's *Dust Tracks on a Road* is in large part the story of a woman who succeeded in many ways but ultimately could not triumph over the poverty and sense of isolation that shadowed her from early childhood until her death in a county home and her burial in a segregated cemetery. Angelou's *I Know Why the Caged Bird Sings* contains the gruesome account of how Angelou, at age eight, was raped by her mother's lover; it ends with her attempts as a sixteen-year-old unwed mother to nurture and protect her newborn son.

These three autobiographies are case studies of what Elizabeth Schultz has named "the black American woman's struggle for survival and liberation . . . against the dual traditions of racism and sexism in America" (317). In Hurston's novel, *Their Eyes Were Watching God,* Janie Crawford's grandmother identifies the situation that all three works dramatize:

> "Honey, de white man is de ruler of everything as fur as Ah been able tuh find out. Maybe it's some place way off in de ocean where de black man is in power, but we don't know nothin' but what we see. White man throw down de load and tell de nigger man tuh pick it up. He pick it up because he have to, but he don't tote it. He hand it to his womenfolks. De nigger woman is de mule uh de world so fur as Ah can see." (29)

In this remark we hear echoed the words of Harriet Jacobs, remarking that "[W]hen they told me my new-born babe was a girl, my heart was heavier than it had ever been before. Slavery is terrible for men; but it is far more terrible for women" (Jacobs 110); perhaps too Hurston's thoughts on her own life went into the making of her grandmother character's words: in *Dust Tracks* she said, "I have been in Sorrow's kitchen and licked out all the pots" (Hurston 280). Maya Angelou's summation is most explicit: "The Black female," she said, "is assaulted in her tender years by all those common forces of nature at the same time that she is caught in the tripartite crossfire of masculine prejudice, white illogical hate and Black lack of power" (Angelou 231). Yet while Jacobs, Hurston, and Angelou all testify here to the truth of Janie Crawford's grandmother's words, what their autobiographies are about is the more important truth that if the black woman is the world's mule, she is, like Francis, at least a talking mule, and in her talk is the "mother wit" that is not so named for nothing: mother wit is the verbal weapon of survival that informs the experience in these works and makes them, finally, celebrations of "getting ovah," assertions of identity, proclamations of the beauty and mastery of circumstance that simply being Black and a woman can affirm.

The humor of mother wit in these three compelling versions of black female experience is the humor of the word as it has been deviously employed since slavery times by people denied access to all forms of power, but most particularly to the power of language: it was the skillful wielding of the word, in spiritual, folktale, and even harmless-seeming everyday conversation that gave the slaves their means of control over their masters. "Both in slavery times and now," Geneva Smitherman tells us, "the black community places a high value on the spoken word" (77). Slave narrators like Harriet Jacobs announced their triumphant mastery of the forbidden word through the daring act of writing out, and thereby enacting, their lives as free people. Hurston, out of her love for Afro-American folk expression, harnessed the word to the essential act of transcribing the vital sources of her culture; Angelou's story of her girlhood is in many places a lyrical testament to language as providing her one saving image of self; from a childhood in which she tried to live wordlessly as a means of protecting herself against knowledge that was certain pain, Angelou emerged armed, she says, with a "secret word which called forth the djinn who was to serve me all my life: books" (170).

The woman's brand of mother wit that we see in the works of Jacobs, Hurston, and Angelou is tied to their special sense of the capacities of language as an enabling power. That power first reveals itself in the humor of caricature, in broad slaps of ridicule applied to the backsides of oppressors who include white men, white women, and black men too. Secondly, the power of language appears in the humor of exaggeration, a device which comes into play particularly when these women writers portray the gulf that existed between what they had the right to expect and what the world was willing to allow. And finally, the power of mother wit resides perhaps most plentifully in their representations of their own mothers' words of wisdom; in all three works mother figures offer the practical, loving, yet also tough and disciplining advice for life that they know their black daughters must acquire if they are to have any hope of being more than the mules of the world. Jacobs' portrayal of her grandmother, Hurston's memories of the mother whose death altered her childhood course forever, Angelou's characterizations of both her mother and grandmother seem to enact in several ways Alice Walker's idea that "our mothers and grandmothers have, more often than not anonymously, handed on the creative spark, the seed of the flower they themselves never hoped to see" (Walker 240). Thus for all their shadows, the mother and mother-wit stories of Jacobs, Hurston, and Angelou are not tragedies; they are comic in their use of word play, caricature, and exaggeration and in their affirmation of what their mothers have handed down: "respect for the possibilities," as Alice Walker puts it, "and the will to grasp them" (Walker 242).

Harriet Jacobs' autobiography, *Incidents in the Life of a Slave Girl*, uses caricature and exaggeration as tools of invective to bring in the judgment of her very specifically targeted audience, "the women of the North," against the master class of the South. Her own master and mistress in Edenton, North Carolina, are frequently lampooned and in that way are effectively dehumanized. The master, Dr. Flint, is a villain figure of sentimental novel vintage, and while there is nothing laughable about his lust or his cruelty, he himself is a uniformly ineffectual Lothario; in his jealous rages he hisses like a snake, springs "like a wolf," and storms about like "a restless spirit from the pit." "Satan had no difficulty determining the color of his soul," we are told (Jacobs 541).

Yet Dr. Flint never had his way with Linda Brent, as Jacobs calls herself in her narrative. In order to foil his attempts to force her into bed, Jacobs allowed the attentions of another white townsman and bore two children by him. When

Dr. Flint threatened these children, who "followed the condition of the mother," Jacobs ran away, but only as far as her grandmother's house. There, for seven years, her relatives managed to keep her hidden, even from her own children who lived below. In a crawlspace only three feet high, she suffered from the cold and heat, from insect bites and cramps; still this section of her narrative contains some finely ironic scenes that Jacobs herself saw as a comedy. It pleased her to exhibit a thwarted Dr. Flint, who often visited her grandmother to vent his rage that his Linda had made her escape to the North; little did he know that she was listening just above his head. How he was tricked into believing in her disappearance is a lesson in the power that literacy conferred on the slave as well as a prime example of mother wit. Because she could read and write, Jacobs was able to concoct letters to the Doctor that would make him think she was living in New York. She included references to authentic street names and numbers that she gleaned from an old New York newspaper, and a friend carried the letters north for her, where they were mailed at intervals back to the master in North Carolina. Taking the bait, Dr. Flint would appear at the grandmother's door, often twisting what was in the letters to try to make the old woman think that Linda longed to return home. "This was as good as a comedy to me, who heard it all," writes Jacobs. For years she could enjoy watching her old tormentor's futile searches through New York and Massachusetts for his prized possession; her family tricked him, again, into selling her children to their father. Thus for all his constant ranting and raving, Dr. Flint never won in any contest with his female slave; as Jacobs remarks, "My master had power and law on his side; I had a determined will. There is might in each" (130).

One remarkable quality of *Incidents* is its presentation of a southern sisterhood which crossed racial and class lines to unite white and black women in a struggle against the tyranny of a patriarchal society. Only one woman is pictured as a cruel supporter of slavery, and that is Dr. Flint's wife, whose jealousy and indolence make her a classic shrew. Sarcasm is almost always present in Jacobs' descriptions of her:

> She had not the strength to superintend her household affairs; but her nerves were so strong, that she could sit in her easy chair and see a woman whipped till the blood trickled from every stroke of the lash. . . . If dinner was not served at the exact time on that particular Sunday, she would station herself in the kitchen, and wait till it was dished, and then spit in all the kettles and pans that had been used for cooking. She did this to prevent the cook and her children from eking out their meagre fare with the remains of the gravy and other scrapings. (22)

When she learned of her husband's interest in Linda, Mrs. Flint took the girl to sleep in her own compartments, where, we are told, she spent "many a sleepless night to watch over me" (54). Sometimes, Jacobs says, "she whispered in my ear, as though it was her husband speaking to me, and listened to hear what I would answer." Thus Mrs. Flint is reduced to a laughable cartoon of the jealous wife, driven to crawling along the floor in the dark, hoping to catch her husband and slave in "the act." While her husband was busy wooing Linda with the promise that he would make a lady of her, the lady of the house stood guard, like a surly dog, over her slave's virtue.

Jacobs' tale is a somber one, relieved only infrequently by these cartoons of the master and mistress and sometimes by the use of dialogue in which the slave's and the master's intelligence and sensitivity are contrasted through their speech. Jacobs' battle of wits against her master is a battle of words—his rage against her cool sarcasm, as when he grills her about her white lover: "'Do you love him?' said he, in a hissing tone. 'I am thankful that I do not despise him,'" Linda replies. In another scene she relates a confrontation between her grandmother and a group of rowdy poor whites who had been empowered, during the weeks following the Nat Turner uprising, with the right to search homes of blacks for evidence of insurrection. At her grandmother's house, one ruffian, speaking barely decipherable English, asks, "Where'd the damned niggers get all dis sheet an' table clarf?" The grandmother, in a rare display of sass, retorts, "You may be sure we didn't pilfer 'em from your houses" (100). The men leave, stymied by the black woman's word wielding, a power that humiliates them without ever challenging their authority.[1]

Jacobs' grandmother, very much like Maya Angelou's later, was a strong, nurturing presence who yet constantly counselled forbearance rather than rebellion, endurance instead of escape. While these two almost archetypal figures never openly challenged the double burden of racial and sexual prejudice that they were forced as black women to bear, both exude an unshakable dignity, an inner faith in their ability to prevail where it mattered most—in the preservation of their self-respect. Jacobs tells us that it was at her grandmother's house that she learned the words that carried her to freedom: "He that is *willing* to be a slave, let him be a slave." The grandmother lived long enough to see Linda Brent make her way to New York, where she was finally able to secure her and her children's freedom. Jacobs closes the book that she published in 1861 with thoughts of the woman who made the painful recollections of her past possible to bear.

Jacobs' autobiography ends with the image of home and family, with the writer's journey successfully ended in the freedom to be the mother and homemaker that the grandmother's life idealized for her. Simply in its title, Hurston's *Dust Tracks on a Road* indicates the great distance that separated not so much the wills or needs of women of the two different periods but their starting points, their directions, and their audiences. For Jacobs the road was something to leave behind, for Hurston something to embrace in a new challenge against different kinds of chains binding black women in the America of the early decades of the twentieth century. The most vibrant and least ambivalent section of Hurston's autobiography pictures her childhood years in Eatonton, Florida, a small southern town yet one light years removed from the Edenton, N.C., of Jacobs' time. Eatonton, Hurston tells us, was "a pure Negro town—charter, mayor, council, town marshal, and all" (Hurston 3), and her father was a three-term mayor who wrote the town laws. In her early years, then, she was surrounded by people who had a sense of their own importance—Eatonton was like an oasis in the desert of the South, and Hurston was bound to have imbibed some of its confidence. From her mother she received the encouragement to be the kind of woman that Harriet Jacobs became only in the face of tremendous opposition: Hurston remembers that "Mama exhorted her children at every opportunity to 'jump at de sun.' . . . She conceded that I was impudent and given to talking back, but she didn't want to 'squinch my spirit' too much for fear that I would be a mealy-mouthed rag doll by the time I got grown" (21). In her self-presentation, Hurston begins then with the assurance that she *should* be somebody: "Zora is my young 'un," her mother insisted, predicting that she would "come out more than conquer" specifically through the "sassy tongue" that everyone else deplored.

Hurston sets up the events of *Dust Tracks'* early chapters to target the three moving spirits in her life: a love of language pinned to a sense of the magic of the things of the world; wanderlust, an urge for the road that her mother could only explain as the result of a conjure; and differentness, a belief that her stars decreed that she would never be like those around her, both because she was always looking for the extraordinary in experience and because she trusted mysterious visions that told her of her destiny. It would be language and wit that provided the continuity for the lonely picaro existence that Hurston defined as her fate. The form of wit that seemed to come most naturally was a comic sense of the disparity between desires and realities—her own and others'. Speaking of her childhood dissatisfaction with life, she writes, "Stew beef, fried fat-back and morning grits were no ambrosia from Valhalla. Raking back yards and carrying chamber pots were not the tasks of Thor" (56). She used a folktale to poke fun at racial pretensions, relating a theory of how the black folks got black that was one of the many "lying stories" of the men who gathered at Joe Clarke's store: when God was giving out color to folks, the last ones to show up, being late for their appointment with the Almighty and afraid of missing their gift, crowded so close that the Old Maker hollered, "Git back! Git back!" But the folks misunderstood and thought He said, "Get black!" Thus, Hurston concludes, "they just got black, and kept the thing a going" (69).

This story appears both in an early chapter and again in one called "My People! My People!," which was originally written in 1937 and heavily edited when *Dust Tracks* was published in 1942. In the original version, the folktale ends Hurston's discussion of what it means to have every judgment and motive shaped by race consciousness, or to deny being "kinfolks" with "skinfolks" on the basis of race. Her last comment on the original version is that the folktale tells us that "we are no race. We are just a collection of people who overslept our time and got caught in the draft" (306). In both versions of "My People! My People!" (but much more in the original one), Hurston tells several racial jokes in order to confront both white and black racial attitudes: "I am the only Negro," she says at one point, "whose grandfather on the mother's side was *not* an Indian chief" (235). In the early version she announces several comic tests which might help one to recognize "My People!": most of the signs are derogatory, but one of them emphasizes her special sense of language: "If he hunts for six big words where one little one would do, that's My People. . . . Somebody didn't know the word total nor entire so they made bodacious. Then there's asterperious, and so on. When you find a man chewing up the dictionary and spitting out language, that's My People" (298). Such jokes are in-jokes, and most in this chapter indicate a level of irritation beneath the pose of tolerant acceptance. The jokes Negroes tell on themselves, Langston Hughes wrote in an essay of that title, constitute "the humor of frustration, and the laughter with which these sallies are greeted, for all its loudness, is a desperation laughter" (Hughes 639). In Hurston's case this point is underscored by what she wrote at the end of the edited version of "My People": "I maintain that I have been a Negro three times—a Negro baby, a Negro girl and a Negro woman" (237). The exasperated cry of "My People! My People!" might be an in-joke, but it is also, for Hurston, an announcement of either exclusiveness or exclusion that in any case denied her the individuality that she, particularly as Negro *girl* and Negro *woman,* found threatened all too often.

In one other area Hurston applied mother wit to puncture a particular pretension, the ideal of Love with a capital L. Again, her sense of her differentness, her problems with winning respect for her womanhood, and her eye for debunking delusions of grandeur make capital L Love a perfect target. The scene that she sets reflects the fact that in her own life, her work—her oath to "take the hard road of labor"— made her vulnerable to the sexist charge that she was unwomanly. Talking of types of lovers, Hurston first regales us with the one who "whisper[s] gustily into my ear" while "I may be thinking of turnip greens with dumplings, or more royalty checks, and here is a man who visualizes me on a divan sending the world up in smoke" (262). "There must be something about me that looks sort of couchy," she concludes. Another lover-type is the one who makes her feel "the divine urge for an hour, a day or maybe a week. Then it is gone and my interest returns to corn pone and mustard greens, or rubbing a paragraph with a soft cloth" (264). Her conclusion: "much that passes for constant love is a golded-up moment walking in its sleep. Some people know that it is the walk of the dead, but in desperation and desolation they have staked everything on life after death and the resurrection, so they haunt the graveyard" (264–65).

One of Hurston's most colorful characters is also one of the most gifted, in her experience, of those who could do what she called "specifying," a kind of "signifying" or word-wit that embeds insult and reversal of status in adroit power-plays with language. Hurston's champion in this skill is Big Sweet, a tough saw-mill town Mama who was engaged, when Hurston

met her, in bringing a man in the street "up to date on his
ancestry": she "broke the news to him, in one of her mildest
bulletins, that his pa was double-humped camel and his ma
was a grass-gut cow. . . . He was a bitch's baby out of a buzzard
egg" (187). Here is a woman using mother wit in an age-old
manner, to bring the power of the word into the arsenal of the
once weaker and more abused group—Big Sweet is good at
pistols and knives, but best in what Hurston and other Afro-
American woman autobiographers recognize as their most
effective defense in a world where, as Hurston put it, "that
white man could run faster," and "My grandma . . . being the
pursued, had to look back over her shoulder every now and
then to see how she was doing" (236).

The development of verbal humor as a survival strategy,
which Jacobs tried tentatively and Hurston celebrated
boisterously, is a unifying device for the events of her life that
Maya Angelou selected for *I Know Why the Caged Bird Sings.*
Angelou the autobiographer takes her childhood self, who
goes by many names, on a kind of quest for a name and for
words. The book's first scene is comic as well as pathetic: in
the Colored Methodist Episcopal Church, young Marguerite
Johnson cannot call up the words she is supposed to say in the
Easter pageant; at the scene's end, she runs from the church,
looking (to herself) a ridiculous figure in lavender taffeta,
wetting her pants, laughing to be free from the agonizing
turmoil of having to depend on the words of others. The
progress of this girl's life is made possible by a series of word-
bringers—her brother, her teachers, her mother's con men
friends, her mother herself—who gradually open to her the
potential of language; words alone can free her from her fear of
and dependency on others' conceptions. Thus, with no ability
to raise the words she needs, Marguerite in the first scene is
betrayed by the white world's view of beauty: "Because I was
really white," she tries to think, "and because a cruel fairy
stepmother, who was understandably jealous of my beauty,
had turned me into a too-big Negro girl, with nappy black hair,
broad feet, and a space between her teeth that would hold a

number-two pencil" (2). By the end of the book, Maya is not only talking but she has an edge on her white school mates; she and her friends "were alert to the gap separating the written word from the colloquial. We learned to slide out of one language and into another without being conscious of the effort" (191).

The most important of the word-bringers in Maya's life is her mother—a savvy, sassy, street-wise Mama who makes Black beautiful and language a gift of the body as well as an art of the mind. Vivian Baxter Johnson can dance, can shoot a crooked business partner, can make her living in the tough blues joints of St. Louis and San Francisco. Yet most of all she can talk, and unlike Maya's conservative southern grandmother's, her talk is full of hope, irreverence for tradition, and scorn for anyone who thinks they can keep her down. When she repeats the old report, "They tell me the whitefolks still in the lead," she says it, Angelou tells us, "as if that was not quite the whole truth" (175). Vivian's words are a compendium of mother wit: "She had a store of aphorisms," Angelou remarks, "which she dished out as the occasion demanded" (228): "The Man upstairs, He don't make mistakes" (237); "It ain't no trouble when you pack double" (229); "Nothing beats a trial but a failure" (225); and perhaps most to our point, "Sympathy is next to shit in the dictionary, and I can't even read" (175).

While we are given no explicit statement at the end of her story that Marguerite Johnson has fully absorbed what she needs of her mother's verbal capacities, Maya's own nascent motherhood, and her attitude toward becoming a mother, indicate that a survivor is coming into being. She tells us her feelings as a young, unwed mother who managed to hide her pregnancy from her family for almost eight months, and her words have a kind of triumph in them: "I had a baby. He was beautiful and mine. Totally mine. No one had bought him for me. No one had helped me endure the sickly gray months. I had had help in the child's conception, but no one could deny that I had had an immaculate pregnancy" (245). Gone is the girl who could see her Blackness only as some cruel fairy godmother's revenge. With a real mother, and mother wit, Maya has the preparation she needs to become the writer, the word-bringer, who created *I Know Why the Caged Bird Sings.*

One joke that the Black American community has shared for a long time shows a young black girl gazing into the fabled mirror to ask, "Who's the fairest of all?," whereupon the mirror, of course, answers back: "It's Snow White, you Black bitch, and don't you forget it." The joke, we can bet, is a trick on that tired white trope, locked as it is in the blind and self-reflexive looking glass of impotent white hate. The autobiographies of Harriet Jacobs, Zora Neale Hurston, and Maya Angelou reveal that, beginning in slavery times, women found the means, in the company of other nurturing women, to change the joke and slip the yoke. So indeed, they don't call it Mother Wit for nothing.

Notes

1. A valuable discussion of Jacobs' dialogues appears in William Andrews' forthcoming book, *Afro-American Autobiography, The First 100* Years (University of Illinois Press).

Works Cited

Angelou, Maya. *I Know Why the Caged Bird Sings.* New York: Bantam Books, 1971.

Dundes, Alan. *Mother Wit From the Laughing Barrel.* Englewood Cliffs, N.J.: Prentice-Hall, 1973.

Hughes, Langston. "Jokes Negroes Tell on Themselves." In *Mother Wit From the Laughing Barrel.* Englewood Cliffs, N.J.: Prentice-Hall, 1973, 637–641.

Hurston, Zora Neale. *Dust Tracks on a Road.* 2nd ed., with intro by Robert E. Hemenway. Chicago: University of Illinois Press, 1984.

———. *Their Eyes Were Watching God.* Chicago: University of Illinois Press, 1978.

Jacobs, Harriet. *Incidents in the Life of a Slave Girl. Written by Herself.* Miami, Fla.: Mnemosyne Publishing Co., 1969.

Schultz, Elizabeth. "Free in Fact and at Last: The Image of the Black Woman in Black American Fiction." In *What Manner of Woman: Essays on English and American Life and Literature.* New York: New York University Press, 1977.

Smitherman, Geneva. *Talkin and Testifyin: The Language of Black America.* Boston: Houghton Mifflin, 1977.

Walker, Alice. *In Search of our Mothers' Gardens.* New York: Harcourt Brace, 1983.

Humoring the Sentence: Women's Dialogic Comedy

Judy Little

For several thousand years, any woman who became literate and who ventured to write learned to "humor" the sentence which she borrowed from a culture and language very largely designed and dominated by her father, her husband, or her sons and brothers. She humored the sentence; that is, she had to get along with it, be nice to it, and give in to it enough so that she could make it give in to her at least some of the time. In doing this, women have also humored the sentence in another way—they have carnivalized it. Those women writers who have a sense of a woman's peripheral yet invested position within a male-dominated culture have given their sentences the license of carnival, a license to overturn, to mimic, and to "deconstruct." Especially in the sentences of women who write comedy, there is a double-voiced tension or "dialogic imagination," to use Mikhail Bakhtin's term, which immerses the piece in a subtle rebellious mockery.

A woman's discourse usually carries with it some hint of the language and worldview of the patriarchal structures in which she lives. There is, as Gilbert and Gubar emphasize, quoting Emily Dickinson, an "infection in the sentence."[1] But one might also say that the infection from the male language and culture produces antibodies; there is a "dialogic" tension, often comic, between the two "voices" that contend in the same sentence. In his examination of Dostoyevski's fiction, Bakhtin describes and illustrates extensively just how a character's own voice (as it muses in first-person or in third-person indirect discourse) will include phrases and sentences that show someone else's worldview and style. In texts and in life, an individual shares a language with others, with an entire culture. "The word in language is half someone else's," Bakhtin notes in *The Dialogic Imagination*. In the literary text, the voice of a character and the voice perhaps of someone with whom that character has recently been talking will collide and evaluate each other within the ongoing thoughts of the musing character. The juxtaposition of the two voices may result in ridicule of one of the voices and of the ideology it brings along, speech diversity being "an indispensable prerequisite for comic style." Indeed, parody can be used as "an exposé to destroy" the language of another.[2]

The comic style of many women writers shows some of these dialogic qualities, or deconstructive qualities, to use Derrida's more drastic term. Luce Irigaray, for instance, in *Speculum of the Other Woman,* inserts entire phrases (sometimes without quotation marks or italics) from Plato and later male philosophers into her own ongoing, teasing exposé of the oppressive effect these ideas have had on women. This dialogic, often harshly comic style is a major feature of the writing of certain French feminists like Irigaray and Hélène Cixous, those writers of an *écriture féminine.* Sandra Gilbert, in her introduction to the English translation of *The Newly Born Woman* by Hélène Cixous and Catherine Clément, asserts that some American writers, such as Susan Griffin, also employ a style similar to that of the French feminists, a style that tries to reverse the usual ideologies and strategies of discourse; Gilbert calls this style a "creative hysteria."[3] The style is essentially dialogic; it deconstructs or exposes the ideologies of authority and power, often by juxtaposing the male voice of solemn formality and the female voice of buoyant hysteria. Such double-voiced discourse relativizes the social and political hierarchies implicit in the teased (male-enunciated) ideology, and the result is a "carnivalization" of dialogue, as Bakhtin calls it in *Problems of Dostoevsky's Poetics.* [4]

In order to carnivalize the voice of authority and power, the rebel comic voice must use that authoritative voice, must parody or mimic it. As Derrida describes the process, a deconstructive discourse "borrows from a heritage the resources necessary for the deconstruction of that heritage itself."[5] What is the heritage that is most likely to be comically violated when women writers carnivalize their discourse? It is the heritage of a discourse of power and control, of law and taboo. Although some have disagreed with the details of Michel Foucault's analysis of Western culture's understanding of sex, women, and power, his overall argument is respected and convincing. He argues in *The History of Sexuality* that a culture's perception of sexual behavior, sexual "perversion," the bodies of women, and the laws that regulate sex and the family are all a matter of ideology rather than scientific fact. Our understanding of these aspects of our culture constitutes a "deployment," a "technology of sex." Modern psychoanalysis is not so much a science as an ideology, one way (among others that could have been used) of deploying the political options for controlling sexual activities.[6] The modern West has deployed a notion of power and law that has also defined a counterpart in the "hysterization of women's bodies." That is, women's bodies have been defined in terms of the uterus, fertility, and the supposed intrinsic pathology that is part of this delicate, female function. In the "creative hysteria" of women's discourse, then, it is not surprising that a comic tension frequently emerges between the (male) heritage of power and a rebellious "hysteria" that carnivalizes or mocks both itself and the phrases borrowed from a language of power.

This comic verbal tension requires a distinct self-reflective voice, a speaking or internally musing voice which can be the medium for the dialogic mimicry and parody within it. Bakhtin emphasizes this voice as a necessary medium, and he even argues that poetry and actual dialogue (as in the drama or in the dialogue passages of a narrative) are seldom fully internally "dialogic."[7] There needs to be a sense of *one* voice, but a conflicted voice in which more than one style and ideology contend. Such a voice may not be typical of realistic drama, but in some experimental plays by women juxtaposed styles occur occasionally within a voice, and the result is a carnivalized discourse. A strong dialogic comedy is also present in some of the poetry by women authors. Nevertheless, prose fiction does seem to be the richest source of women's comic discourse. Most of the following discussion deals with prose, although I want to begin with a few examples from drama and poetry.

In most dramatic literature, in texts written for performance, the major arena of tension (and of comedy) exists *between* the characters, between the bodies moving about as well as between the voices of the characters. A single character's self-reflective, internally dialogic discourse is not a necessary part of the dramatic medium, though such discourse is sometimes present. In the plays of writers such as Megan Terry and Maureen Duffy, a single voice or speech may include within it the parodied voice of (male) authority; that is, the speech is a dialogic, carnivalized discourse. Near the beginning of Terry's play *Calm Down Mother,* for instance, "Woman One" declares that she is Margaret Fuller and that she accepts the universe. The only other persons in the play are asked to respond as follows:

> TWO WOMEN *(assuming superior postures):* You had better. You had better. Carlyle said that you had better. You had better. You had better. You bet your butter. Carlyle said that you had better.[8]

This unison speech is dialogic in that Carlyle's authoritative advice (and controlling put-down) is repeated and distorted ("You bet your butter") so much that this "heritage" of power withers under the rebellious mockery that questions it. The same dialogic, conflicted speech also serves to question the assertion of "Woman One"—does she, can she, really accept the universe?

In performance, the "superior postures" (which in the performance that I saw also included "superior" facial expressions) reinforce the dialogic discourse with what we can call a *dialogic body language.* The bodies of women—of women who have not generally in our civilization spoken the words of law and power such as "You had better accept"— here assume the shoulders-back, chin-in power posture along with the power language of male authority. In so doing, the actors carnivalize both the language and the posture, and indeed the ideology of power itself. A dialogic body language will obviously be a major contributor to the impact of a performance, and to the impact of women's comic drama where verbal discourse is only one element of the medium.

There is, for instance, a vividly dialogic "body" in Maureen Duffy's *Rites.* A group of women in a public restroom beat and kill someone whom they take to be a male intruder— someone "spying" on them. After they have killed the person, who was dressed as a man, they realize it was a woman. This shocking, physical "deconstruction" of the intruder is an appropriate and powerfully symbolic climax to the play. The play's increasingly strident and comic discourse has been full of tension between the cultural presence of male authority and the desperate hysteria of the oppressed and suspicious women. The women in the play represent several classes (there are the lavatory attendants, office girls, two widows in their sixties, two younger women with a boy toddler), but all of them are in a sense "dressed" in the male-designed culture that has trivialized their lives. All of these women are disguised as men; that is, they speak the roles men have imposed on them. The dialogue and the individual discourse show the effects of the "hysterization" of women's lives. No matter what their class, these women have been preoccupied with playing the part of the womb, the fertile, comforting, unseen nourishers of men.

From time to time, various characters in Duffy's play mimic certain cultural scripts that have confined them: horoscopes, advice columns, recipes.[9] The character's voice mocks the cliché of the cultural script even while it repeats it, thus generating a kind of hysteria of resistance. And the resistance culminates in the ritual killing, a parody of a Dionysian fertility rite. In Duffy's *Rites,* however, there is little implication of rebirth and renewal. Although the women have attacked, in comic discourse and brutal action, the male-clothed culture that oppresses them, their own comic, dialogic speech still submits to that culture's clichés about women even while mocking the clichés.

A similar dialogic discourse in which submission and protest scrape against each other in violent comedy is present in poetry being written by women. In Margaret Atwood's poem "The Landlady," the writer's voice describes a sort of archetypal interior landlady whose "raw voice" is part of a "squabble going on below," and who "presides" over the writer's attempts to read, write, or dream of escaping. The landlady's power (she "presides," slams doors, stands and blocks the way) seems to exceed that of the writer. The landlady and her language imply a cultural or psychological inhibition or imprisonment, especially an imprisonment *within* womanhood, within the hysterization of women's concerns. In the writer's humorous, dialogic struggle with her, the landlady still rules the house and is "solid as bacon."[10]

Although a dialogic mingling of two languages in one voice is not a constant feature of Sylvia Plath's poetry, some of her most powerful work does have such a voice. Clearly, when the voice in "Daddy" says she "adores a Fascist," the languages of hysteria and power are colliding: "Every woman adores a Fascist, / The boot in the face, the brute / Brute heart of a brute like you."[11] Here the culture that "deployed" this sexuality of sentimental hysteria on the one hand and brute boots on the other is mocked by one voice that mimics an acceptance of such a destructive relationship.

Even more prominent is the dialogic voice in "Lady Lazarus." The speaker, like an accomplished performer of guerrilla theater, praises her own ability to capture her audience (that is, her oppressors, who have, of course,

"captured" and abused her as a Jew, woman, sideshow freak).
She mocks the language of power as she says, "O my
enemy"—a king's phrase, the words of the guilty King Ahab
when Elijah confronted him.[12] She mimics the language of the
impresario or master of ceremonies ("The big strip tease. /
Gentlemen, ladies") and the language of the learned "Doktor"
whose "opus" she is, whose "great concern" she carnivalizes.
Like a pedagogue of popular psychology, she analyzes and
trivializes her own capacity for death and resurrection ("Dying
/ is an art, like everything else"). Yet the same voice
throughout absorbs into its own zany hysteria these abusive
power images and power languages. In the last line, Lady
Lazarus declares, "And I eat men like air." She does. Literally,
she does; she eats their "letters"; with her airy words she eats
their airy words, their language. With its comic dialogic
discourse, her language of creative hysteria has been eating the
power languages of the men all along.

A much less aggressive and more domestic Lady Lazarus
tries to resurrect her inspiration in Susan Griffin's prose poem
"This Is the Story of the Day in the Life of a Woman Trying."
Here the dialogic oppositions within the narrator's voice are
not directly between male control and a resistant female
hysteria. Instead, some rather literary storytelling phrases drift
in and out of the worried mother's language of domestic oral
colloquialism. All in one day, she is trying to write, trying to
take care of a sick child, trying to line up a teaching job,
hoping to line up a lover, trying to get a baby-sitter, and finally
(climaxing this very brief piece) wondering about her
daughter's refusal to eat. The initial sentences show both
languages emerging and subsiding as the narrator's more
literary consciousness maintains a pestering dialogue with her
domestic and personal worries:

> This is the story of the day in the life of a woman trying to be
> a writer and her child got sick. And in the midst of writing
> this story someone called her on the telephone. And, of
> course, despite her original hostile reaction to the ring of the
> telephone, she got interested in the conversation which was

about teaching writing in a women's prison, for no pay of course. . . .[13]

The first four words are rather formal; they announce a story. But the sentence comes to a comic and painful halt at the colloquial "got sick." Inspiration sticks at the domestic crisis. Soon a very literary and latinate diction ("despite her original hostile reaction") jerks the story back to a remote, objective narrator, yet the "got interested" and the rambling syntax (of a very long sentence which I did not quote in full) draw us again into the nervous language of the irritated mother. The repeated, frustrated "of course" emphasizes the obvious distractions and drawbacks (becoming interested but expecting no pay), as the language veers far away from the writerly, controlled diction and back to the run-on worries. The dialogic comedy in Griffin's portrait of an artist as mother protests the painful and limiting domestication of the woman's ambition and calling.

An earlier writer whose sentences tease and humor the language of her literary inheritance is Virginia Woolf. She was one of the first writers to recognize that a woman with literary aspirations could well find herself in conflict, as a woman, with the largely male-designed literary culture. Defining a certain distance from that culture, she announced in "Modern Fiction" that a free writer must look for a style and novelistic form that would have none of the authoritative formalities, "no plot, no comedy, no tragedy, no love interest or catastrophe in the accepted style."[14] Her own style, along with that of other writers who used various forms of "stream of consciousness," is heavily dialogic; that is, a given consciousness almost always mingles his or her own language with the language and ideology of others as these languages merge or conflict with the musing consciousness. In the consciousness of Woolf's characters and narrators, these dialogic mergings are often comic, and they very frequently highlight the conventions of authority (literary, social, sexual) and a resisting freedom.

All of Woolf's novels make use of dialogic comedy. Centuries of English discourse flow through the mind of the narrator and supposed "biographer" of Orlando. The vital, long-lived Orlando, whose flexible gender alters from male to female near the beginning of the eighteenth century, maintains an evaluative dialogue with the languages and ideologies of her past and present. As she continually adjusts her clothes, behavior, and language to the gender decorum of the era, almost every sentence is dialogic. Near the end of the novel, the female Orlando at age thirty-six (but the "biography" began with Orlando as an Elizabethan boy of sixteen) drives her car toward her ancestral estate. While she tries to understand and sum up her varied experiences, she and the narrator play havoc with the usual authority structures that hold a literary work together. Many of Orlando's earlier "selves" (male, female, young, older) pop into the meditation with a single phrase or question. Every three or four sentences, the narrator, with comic irrelevance, also pops in with a parenthesis that tells us the obvious: "here another self came in."[15] While Orlando, in dialogic comedy, struggles with a "self" that is not confined to the conventional gender structures of power or hysterization, the narrator struggles with the conventions of "biography" and seems ready to concede that the biographer's authority is illusory.

Even in her first experimental novel, *Jacob's Room,* Woolf had developed a dialogic narrator who seems humorously puzzled and playful about the entire business of writing. It is as though the narrator tries, but fails, to take seriously a very serious, even tragic, story about a quite British young man who quits himself well in all the classic passages of male initiation, including the university, love, a tour of Italy and Greece, and death in the Great War. The narrator feigns ignorance of her fictional character and implies sometimes that she, as a female narrator, finds a young man's culture rather foreign and amusing. The third-person discourse, edging into Jacob's own consciousness, moves comically back and forth, for instance, between the serious young man's attempt to appreciate the Italian landscape and the narrator's tourist discourse about how "scenic" it all is:

> These Italian carriages get damnably hot with the afternoon sun on them, and the chances are that before the engine has pulled to the top of the gorge the clanking chain will have broken. Up, up, up, it goes, like a train on a scenic railway. Every peak is covered with sharp trees, and amazing white villages are crowded on ledges. There is always a white tower on the very summit, flat red-frilled roofs, and a sheer drop beneath. It is not a country in which one walks after tea.[16]

Several languages are in subtle comic conflict here, and they thoroughly disintegrate any pretensions the action may have to the status of a manful, Byronic pilgrimage. Jacob's youthful male language condemns the temperature and weighs the odds on the vehicle's achieving the summit. The (female) narrator enters with the voice of someone reading a children's story ("Up, up, up") and thus trivializes Jacob's quest. Her metaphor of the scenic railway and her urgent superlatives ("every peak," "amazing," "always") comically overstate the exclamatory response of the impressed tourist. Yet (the narrator shifts out of the tourist's language and into a fastidious reserve) no civilized British person, especially a British gentlewoman, would deign to walk in such rugged country after tea.

The comedy in the passage is dialogic in that several styles and ideologies collide in it. The contending ideologies tease and question several gender issues. Among these are the relationship of the doting mother (as Jacob's mother certainly is) to the son now going "Up, up, up" in Italy and in life; the relationship of the conventional tourist to the even more conventional and restricted Englishwoman presiding at tea; the relationship of a woman author and narrator to the powerful traditions of a male-designed culture (the tour, classic education, war) in which she lives and aspires to write. Although Woolf's dialogic comedy is more lyric and subtle, it probes the same basic conflicts that Foucault identified, conflicts that the comic sentences of Terry, Plath, and Griffin probe: the domestication of women and the established power of the male culture that has defined this "technology" of the sexes.

Many women novelists since Woolf have made effective comedy from a double-voiced discourse that teases the conventions of gender and power. Among these are Jean Rhys, Barbara Pym, and Christine Brooke-Rose, three writers who are not at all alike in the way they use dialogic comedy and for this reason will illustrate the flexibility of the double-voiced style.

The first-person narrators of Jean Rhys's novels persistently mock themselves (and all self-pitying outsiders and all self-congratulating insiders) with phrases they have picked up through the same desperate promiscuity with which they have picked up men. The comedy is bitter, and the Rhys heroine is bitter. The dialogic discourse feeds into the down-and-out woman's consciousness the malicious phrases of those (usually white British males) whose familiarity with power makes them insensitive to those who lack it. In *Good Morning, Midnight,* Sasha Jansen, after losing her job as a clerk in a Paris dress shop while "Mr. Blank" was inspecting it, repeats to herself the ancient sentimentality that somehow the suffering of *some* people contributes to a sense of fortunate well-being in others. She mimics the language of all the powerful Mr. Blanks: "We can't all be happy, we can't all be rich, we can't all be lucky—and it would be so much less fun if we were. Isn't that so, Mr. Blank? There must be the dark background to show up the bright colors."[17] The repetitions ("we can't all") mimic the rhetorical urgency and authority of a sermon or lesson, and after the repetitions collide with Sasha's smirking question, her discourse takes on the lofty tone of pedantic, philosophic illustration as she offers the poised analogy of dark background and bright colors. Sasha's dialogic, self-mocking hysteria sometimes resembles that of Plath's Lady Lazarus, except that the language of the Rhys heroine never "eats" that of her oppressor; instead, her style (and her life) is consumed by the languages and machinations of power.

At the end of Barbara Pym's *Excellent Women,* Mildred Lathrop, like Sasha, unenthusiastically argues herself into submitting to the way things are (as she perceives them), and her language is hilariously dialogic. Her words argue against themselves, like Sasha's, but the never-married Mildred, an "excellent woman" and pillar of church jumble sales, has long ago made some civilized concessions to her male-dominated society. As a result, her submission is more coy, ironic, and quiet—unlike Sasha's desperate, protesting surrender.

Gradually developing a tentative interest in Everard Bone, who is a rather stiff and self-centered anthropologist, Mildred responds to his dinner invitation and lets herself be coaxed into proofreading his manuscript. She seems to think that this will lead to something else (in a later novel of Pym's, we find that Mildred does marry Everard), and her thoughts ponder the future in understated comic horror. Bone suggests that when the proofreading becomes boring she can work on the book's index for "a nice change." Then it is as though his words (and his ideology about men and women) begin to infect her thoughts. She muses, "And before long I should be certain to find myself at his sink peeling potatoes and washing up; that would be a nice change when both proofreading and indexing began to pall. Was any man worth this burden? Probably not."[18] From proofing to indexing to peeling potatoes, Mildred seems to place her language and life at the disposal of Everard's language and life. Taking him at *his* word, her own sentence still protests with dialogic irony his definition of a "nice change." Both he and she apparently perceive a legitimacy in his authority (and his freedom to be creative) and an inevitability in the hysterization of her life. Yet Pym's distancing dialogic language preserves a sense of larger, open possibilities, even though her delicately and comically self-limiting characters (both the men and the women in her novels) usually are unadventurous and fail to take advantage of these larger possibilities.

By contrast, the characters in Brooke-Rose's comic experimental novel, *Amalgamemnon,* aggressively venture into larger possibilities. They seem confident of redefining the world with their language. They are eager to perpetrate revolutions, terrorist plots, dragon-slaying crusades, and a new "technology" of the sexes, simply by exploiting the carnivalizing power of language. The "frame" of this novel is the ongoing meditation of Mira, a professor who expects to lose her job very soon. The humanities, and hence scholars like herself, are becoming "redundant," she realizes. She invents several alter egos, some male and some female, and launches into sketchy narratives which run into each other as she imagines the future. Indeed, the entire text is written in future tense, with an occasional conditional voice thrown in.

The language of *Amalgamemnon* is dialogic in the extreme and comic in every phrase. Most of the language, and most of the overlapping narratives, are Mira's comic attempts to "deconstruct," as she says, the stifling language and ideology of men, especially of her several lovers.[19] Whether he is Willy (at the beginning of the novel) or Wally (near the end), the man in her life seems to her an "Amalgamemnon," an amalgamation of all the macho heroes, or Agamemnons, of history. In this pun, male heroism and Mira's judgment of male heroism collide dialogically in the same word. The Agamemnon in her life tends to ignore her intellectual interests. She enjoys reading and teaching Western classics, yet her own discourse is in constant comic dialogue with the phrases of male writers and the put-down phrases of her lover. Resenting that her relationship with Willy involves so much pretense, she notes, "Mimecstasy and mimagreement will always go together, like sexcommunication." Fake ecstasy and mimed agreement yield only a deceitful sex life and a relationship that resembles excommunication—outsiderhood and alienation.

The slipping and sliding comic discourse, as Mira considers possible futures, is a continual and liberating reminder of certain assumptions that Foucault and Derrida emphasize: cultural (and gender) institutions are in large part language, deployment, strategy. The language of authority preserves the social and psychological deployment of the male's power. As Mira begins to write her own story, and as her creative syllables begin to invade even the hero's name, her own sentimental hero, Willy, begins to lose his territory. He had anticipated that when she lost her job she would be dependent on him—"wholly mine," as he says, and at last "only a woman." But Mira's comically double-voiced language trespasses on the verbal preserve of the authoritative male. She experiments with a punning phrase that dialogically adopts the authority of mathematics and the godlike diction of fiat. "Let sex equal why," she says, examining the "why" of the X and Y chromosomes and questioning the usual gender myths; perhaps she envisions a new world, "ex almost nihilo," divinely creating it from nothing, merely by her authoritative word. Mira's carnivalizing of both the language of power and the language of submissive or strident hysteria constantly deconstructs these verbal and ideological gestures.

The dialogic comedy of Brooke-Rose's novel is a radical use of the double-voiced discourse which Bakhtin identified as integral to comic style, but the other writers I have considered here also play with the ideologies of style and exploit the opportunities for comic collision when these ideologies are juxtaposed. When these writers humor the sentence, they make it unsay, or partly unsay, what it seems to say. In so doing, these women expose the ambivalent structures of language and its implied worldview. Power is revealed as a linguistic posture (and a bodily posture in the case of drama), while gender categories unravel in the linguistic stripping. Whether we hear the reserved subtleties of Barbara Pym or the extravagant conflicts in the language of Sylvia Plath, whether the dialogic voice belongs to drama, poetry, or fiction, the result is a powerful comedy of a highly political nature. It is comedy that speaks a woman's voice even in a male culture and playfully overturns that culture in a deconstructive dialogue.

Notes

1. Sandra M. Gilbert and Susan Gubar, *The Madwoman in the Attic: The Woman Writer and the Nineteenth-Century Imagination* (New Haven: Yale University Press, 1979), 45–53.

2. Mikhail Bakhtin, *The Dialogic Imagination,* trans. Caryl Emerson and Michael Holquist, ed. Michael Holquist (Austin: University of Texas Press, 1981), 41–47, 293, 311, 364.

3. Sandra M. Gilbert, Introduction, *The Newly Born Woman,* by Hélène Cixous and Catherine Clement, trans. Betsy Wing (Minneapolis: University of Minnesota Press, 1986), xv.

4. Mikhail Bakhtin, *Problems of Dostoevsky's Poetics,* ed. and trans. Caryl Emerson (Minneapolis: University of Minnesota Press, 1984), 167.

5. Jacques Derrida, "Structure, Sign, and Play in the Discourse of the Human Sciences," in *The Languages of Criticism and the Sciences of Man,* ed. Richard Macksey and Eugenio Donato (Baltimore: Johns Hopkins University Press, 1970), 252.

6. Michel Foucault, *The History of Sexuality,* trans. Robert Hurley (New York: Vintage Books, 1980), 77–155.

7. Bakhtin, *Dialogic Imagination,* 285–97. Bakhtin does find occasional dialogic discourse in Pushkin's *Eugene Onegin;* see *Dialogic Imagination,* 46–47.

8. Megan Terry, "Calm Down Mother: A Transformation for Three Women," in *Plays By and About Women,* ed. Victoria Sullivan and James Hatch (New York: Random House, Vintage, 1974), 279.

9. Maureen Duffy, "Rites," in *Plays By and About Women,* 345–77.

10. Margaret Atwood, "The Landlady," in *The Animals in That Country* (Boston: Little, Brown, 1968), 14–15.

11. Sylvia Plath, "Daddy," in *Ariel* (New York: Harper and Row, 1965), 49–51.

12. Sylvia Plath, "Lady Lazarus," in *Ariel,* 6–9. (And see 1 Kings 21:20 for the encounter between Ahab and Elijah.)

13. Susan Griffin, "This Is the Story of the Day in the Life of a Woman Trying," from *Like the Iris of an Eye* (Harper and Row, 1976); rpt. in *In Her Own Image: Women Working in the Arts,* ed. Elaine Hedges and Ingrid Wendt (Old Westbury, N.Y.: Feminist Press, 1980), 127.

14. Virginia Woolf, "Modern Fiction" (1919), in *Collected Essays* (London: Hogarth Press, 1966–67), 2:106.

15. Virginia Woolf, *Orlando* (New York: Harcourt Brace Jovanovich, 1956), 310–12. For a detailed discussion of comic

discourse in *Orlando,* see my "(En)gendering Laughter: Woolf's *Orlando* as Contraband in the Age of Joyce," *Women's Studies* 16 (1988).

16. Virginia Woolf, *Jacob's Room* (London: Hogarth Press, 1945), 134.

17. Jean Rhys, *Good Morning, Midnight* (New York: Norton, 1986), 29.

18. Barbara Pym, *Excellent Women* (New York: Harper and Row, 1980), 255.

19. Christine Brooke-Rose, *Amalgamemnon* (Manchester: Carcanet, 1984), 14–15, 136, 82, 55.

III. Essays on Individual Humorists

Sarah Kemble Knight and the Picaresque Tradition

Peter Thorpe

From the appearance of *Lazarillo de Tormes* (c. 1554) to the close of the eighteenth century, those writings usually known as "picaresque" seem to have formed a persistent and fairly well defined tradition in Western literature. During this period the history of our culture is regularly punctuated by such picaresque or near-picaresque works as (to name a few of the more famous ones) *The Unfortunate Traveller, Don Quixote, Hudibras, Gil Blas, Moll Flanders, Roderick Random, Candide,* and volumes VII and VIII of *Tristram Shandy*.[1] It is safe to generalize that, with a few such notable exceptions as *Huckleberry Finn*, the picaresque tradition after 1800 is less sharply defined, although some scholars—R.W.B. Lewis and Robert Alter,[2] for example—maintain that its impulses continue noticeably even in twentieth century literature. In any case, it is clear that the great age of picaresque places itself in those two-and-a-half centuries from *Lazarillo* to the decline of Augustanism in the later 1700s. Very near the middle of this period, American literature, though still in its infancy, made what seems to me to be a significant contribution to the picaresque tradition: the *Journal* of Sarah Kemble Knight, a brief, highly amusing and frequently incisive piece of writing which follows rather closely the customary patterns of picaresque.

Although any genre is perhaps finally elusive of definition, the patterns of picaresque are clear enough to allow certain generalizations. Always present is the element of travelling, which lends to the work a certain restless excitement and vitality. There are usually numerous episodes, but these seldom have any necessary connection with each other, except they involve the same main character. Customarily the traveller serves as first-person narrator. He is frequently, though not always, a member of the lower classes. In any event, his travels bring him into contact with many different social groups, upon whose morals and manners he may comment, often in a witty or satirical vein. Bizarre comic situations are also a typical ingredient in picaresque, and no less common is a rakishly comic style. On the other hand, the piece may end on a serious note, for not infrequently the hero or *picaro* ("rogue") undergoes some sort of reform at the end of his travels.

According to Madam Knight's *Journal,* she was "five months from home"[3] in her trip from Boston to New York City and back. During part of this time she sojourned with friends or relatives, but of these pauses in her travels she makes little mention. The chief emphasis is rather on the fact and act of travelling, of moving almost hurriedly from one place to the next. The first sentence of her diary tells us, without introduction or milling about, that "I begun my Journey" (425): we are travelling at once, scarcely to pause—except for meals, lodging and short comic scenes—until we return to Boston at the end. The *Journal* derives much of its power and excitement from this headlong haste. It may be noted, although we are not yet formally considering style, that the language is fortified with vigorous expressions of motion: "pogging" (426); "rid" [i.e., *rode*] (428); "gave Reins to my Magg" (429); "made all possible speed" (431); "made Good speed along" (434); "went pretty briskly forward" (435). It is the language of typically exuberant picaresque.

Also picaresque is the episodic quality of the *Journal.* Although Madam Knight has numerous adventures, some of which repeat the same basic pattern, she makes no conscious effort to connect these episodes. Each one, though it may remind us of an adventure earlier in the *Journal,* seems entirely new to this vivacious Colonial writer—and, as a consequence, seems fresh to the reader. Less successful picaresque has a tendency to fall into a dull repetition of scene and action. Such a charge could be levelled at portions of *Lazarillo,* even though it is historically important. But Madam Knight's little-known diary reveals to us a narrator ever full of youthful expectancy. In the October 4 entry, for example, we learn that she is to be accommodated for the night at "mr. Devills, a few miles further" (431). What might have been just another routine approach to an inn (there are many inns in the *Journal*) turns into a witty linguistic exercise as Madam Knight puns on the innkeeper's name:

> But I questioned whether we ought to go to the Devil to be helpt out of affliction. However, like the rest of Deluded souls that post to ye Infernal denn, Wee made all possible speed to this Devil's Habitation (431).

Similarly, there are several points in the journey at which the narrator must cross dangerous rivers. The pattern of action is basically the same, but Madam Knight's vitality makes each fording a unique and exciting experience. One crossing, in a "Cannoo," was so terrifying that it

> caused me to be very circumspect, sitting with my hands fast on each side, my eyes steady, not daring so much as to lodg my tongue a hair's breadth more on one side of my mouth then tother, nor so much as think on Lott's wife, for a wry thought would have oversett our wherey (428).

It is the "wry thought," however, which gives the *Journal* its entertaining variety.

Another characteristic of picaresque is the use of the main character as first-person narrator, who always serves to lend coherence and order to a genre which, by its episodic nature, tends automatically to be structurally weak. In Madam Knight's *Journal,* however, we find much more consistency than we might ordinarily look for in picaresque, for we have a narrator of such brilliant force of character that she transcends the disjointed structure and pulls the variety of materials into focus. However unconnected the adventures or episodes may be, there is always in the foreground the dominant personality of Sarah Kemble Knight. Her writing does not suffer from the unconcatenated effect which one senses in, say, *The Unfortunate Traveller* and which is almost certainly caused by the subdued detachment of Jack Wilton.

Anyone who has read Madam Knight or read about her cannot but admire her powerful character. When she undertook her journey she was already thirty-eight, and that was not young in 1704. Moreover, except for hired guides and persons she met enroute, she travelled alone, frequently by night. The trip was arduous, of course, as already suggested by the river crossings; and a map produced two years before her journey indicates how frequently Madam Knight did not even have roads to travel on.[4] Nor was it a propitious time of year, for the five-month adventure began "Octb'r. ye second" (425), and at one point the heroine finds herself lost at night and "overtaken by a great storm of wind and snow" (443). But she persevered and completed her journey. Her strength of character is also attested to by her highly developed managerial and business sense; indeed, the purpose of the expedition was to settle a business affair in New York which apparently could be handled only by the presence and expertise of Widow Knight. It does not surprise us to learn that when she died in 1727 she left the not inconsiderable sum of 1800 pounds.

Her courage and business sense, however, were balanced by a fairly strong background in literature. Although her grammar is slipshod—actually a virtue of her lively style—her *Journal* is laced with classical allusions and also reveals its author as the creator of some nicely chisled couplets, very much in vogue in England (but not in America) at the time. Her "tho'ts on the sight of the moon" will serve as a sample of Madam Knight's poetic art:

> Fair Cynthia, all the Homage that I may
> Unto a Creature, unto thee I pay:
> In Lonesome woods to meet so kind a guide,

To Mee's more worth than all the world beside.
Some Joy I felt just now, when safe got or'e
Yon Surly River to this Rugged shore,
Deeming Rough welcomes from these clownish Trees,
    Better than Lodgings with Nereidees (429).

She was an accomplished lady, and the force of her character as first-person narrator lends strength and consistency to her picaresque *Journal.*

Another typical element in picaresque is that the narrator is frequently a member of the lower social classes. In America, however, even at the early date of 1704, much of the old European class structure had already broken down. Madam Knight is not strictly a member of any social group, and her travels have the effect of placing her on many social levels. At one point she may be thrown in with the most abject of bumpkins, as is the case in "a merchants house," where she encounters a tobacco-spitting "tall country fellow" and his wife, who is "Jone Tawdry" to Madam Knight (438). At another point she is invited to "stay and take a supper" with Governor John Winthrop of Connecticut (446). Because she is of no class and of all classes, she is eminently qualified as an observer of society on all levels. The customary picaresque hero is restricted to the "worm's-eye view" of things, but Sarah Kemble Knight is much more versatile; and her writing, as a result, has an advantage not enjoyed by many other works in the picaresque tradition.

It is one of the functions of the picaresque hero to comment upon the morals and manners of those he meets. Madam Knight fulfills this function admirably, for she seems to have a good balance of moral indignation and amused tolerance. She has no use for an innkeeper who is so surly that he, "had he bin one degree Impudenter, would have outdone his Grandfather" (444). She is justifiably enraged when "a surly old shee Creature" refuses to give her shelter on a stormy night (443). And in one passage which has the flavor of an older world-view, she is indignant upon learning that in Connecticut the Negro slaves sometimes dine with their masters: "into the dish goes the black hoof as freely as the white hand" (437). But Madam Knight is not essentially a narrow-minded person. For example, she can look with amused tolerance upon the strange wedding customs of Connecticut or upon the Indian religions of that area (though she disapproves of easy divorce among Indians, as well as among whites). She usually seems to have a tolerance for that which differs from her own way, provided that it does not run too strongly counter to her sense of morality, which, after all, was quite broad for that of a Bostonian born in 1666, only three years after the birth of Cotton Mather. Above all, she does not preach, either to the people she meets or to the reader. She merely relates her experiences and lets her wisdom, decency and good sense shine out as they will. And when she is morally indignant, she does not come groveling to the reader for support; rather, he is invited to draw his own conclusions. Sarah Kemble Knight knew that the world conforms to nobody's image of it, and that one must adjust himself to the shifting winds of the various settlements between Boston and New York.

Moral tolerance is usually associated with comedy, and this is very much the case in Madam Knight's *Journal*. It is pregnant with bizarre comic scenes, another common element in picaresque. At one inn, she is assigned "a little Room parted from the Kitchen by a single board partition" through which she overhears a long and tedious argument among some town drunkards about the derivation of the word "Narraganset" (430–431). At another inn, a "french Doctor," with whom she has been travelling, is "entertain'd" unceasingly by a hypochondriac hostess (432). At still another stop, a bumpkin enters the inn, fills his pipe and sits smoking "without speaking, for near a quarter of an hower. At length the old man [i.e., the host] said how do's Sarah do?" The bumpkin's response is "as well as can be expected" (433). This last is a species of humor which is far from extinct in America today. That these three examples occur within a few pages of each other suggests the frequency of comic scenes in Madam Knight's *Journal.*

Comic situations, of course, are only a part of the humor of picaresque; a rakishly comic style plays a major role in defining the genre. Although quotations already given may serve to suggest something about the style of Sarah Kemble Knight, we have not yet seen her language at its best. Her writing is decorated with images which, if not brilliant, are certainly unforgettable. When some tavern loungers refuse to leave their drinking to act as guides for her, she writes that they are "tyed by the Lipps to a pewter engine" (426). She finds that one of her guides, apparently a heavy fellow, makes such an appearance that "His shade on his hors resembled a Globe on a Gate post" (426). At the prospect of crossing a swift river, she writes that she feels as though she imagines herself to be "like a holy Sister Just come out of a Spiritual Bath in dripping Garments" (428).

But the comic style of Sarah Kemble Knight is at its highest point when it is combined with a fully worked-out comic situation. There are a number of examples in the *Journal,* two of which will be quoted in full, partly because editions are scarce and partly because their sheer virtuosity makes them pleasingly quotable. The first is an image of frontier justice (the italics are Madam Knight's):

> A negro Slave belonging to a man in ye Town, stole a hogs head from his master, and gave or sold it to an Indian, native of the place. The Indian sold it in the neighborhood, and so the theft was found out. Thereupon the Heathen was Seized, and carried to the Justices House to be Examined. But his worship (it seems) was gone into the field, with a Brother in office, to gather in his Pompions [pumpkins]. Whither the malefactor is hurried, And Complaint made, and satisfaction in the name of Justice demanded. Their Workships cann't proceed in form without a Bench: whereupon they Order one to be Immediately erected, which, for want of fitter materials, they made with pompions—which being finished, down setts their Worships, and the Melefactor call'd, and by the Senior Justice Interrogated after the following manner.

You Indian why did You steal from this man? You sho'dn't do so—it's a Grandy wicked thing to steal. Hol't Hol't, cryes Justice Junr Brother, You speak negro to him. I'le ask him. You sirrah, why did you steal this man's Hoggshead? Hoggshead? (replys the Indian,) me no stomany. No? says his Worship; and pulling off his hatt, Patted his own head with his hand, sais, Tatapa—You, Tatapa—you; all one this. Hoggshead all one this. Hah! says Netop, now me stomany that. Whereupon the Company fell into a great fitt of Laughter, even to Roreing. Silence is commanded, but to no effect: for they continued perfectly Shouting. Nay sais his worship, in an angry tone, if it be so, *take mee off the Bench* (436).

The second comic situation involves the familiar image of a backwoods couple at a general store (Knight's italics):

Being at a merchants house, in comes a tall country fellow, with his alfogeos [Spanish saddle bags, i.e., cheeks] full of Tobacco; for they seldom Loose their Cudd, but keep Shewing and Spitting as long as they'r eyes are open,—he advanc't to the middle of the Room, makes an Awkward Nodd, and spitting a Large deal of Aromatick Tincture, he gave a scrape with his shovel like shoo, leaving a small shovel full of dirt on the floor, made a full stop, Huggin his own pretty Body with his hands under his arms, Stood staring rown'd him, like a Catt let out of a Baskett. At last, like the creature Balaam Rode on, he opened his mouth and said: have You any Ribinen for Hatbands to sell I pray? The Questions and Answers about the pay being past, the Ribin is bro't and opened. Bumpkin Simpers, cryes its confound Gay I vow; and beckning to the door, in come Jone Tawdry, dropping about 50 curtsees, and stands by him: hee shows her the Ribin. *Law, You,* sais shee, *its right Gent* [genteel], do You, take it, *tis dreadful pretty* (438).

The above two passages show us a writer who is skillful indeed at combining comic style and comic situation.

Although comic situation and style comprise a large portion of Madam Knight's *Journal,* approximately the final thousand words are devoid of humor of any kind. This is not surprising in that, as mentioned earlier, the picaresque hero customarily undergoes a kind of reform or moral regeneration at the end of his travels. Sarah Kemble Knight is not, of course, a rogue or *picaro* in the strict definition of the term, but her behavior parallels that of the picaresque hero in the sense that after many a rakishly frivolous narration she takes on for her closing paragraphs a serious tone. At the end of her travels she makes it clear that in spite of the carefree attitude heretofore adopted, she knows that only God's providence has brought her safely back to Boston. The last few sentences of the *Journal* suggest that the irreverent *picaro* is gone, replaced by a humble and solemn servant of the Lord:

> . . . the next day being March 3rd wee got safe home to Boston, where I found my aged and tender mother and my Dear and only Child in good health with open arms redy to receive me, and my Kind relatins and friends flocking in to welcome mee and hear the story of my transactions and travails I having this day bin five months from home and now I cannot fully express my Joy and Satisfaction. But desire sincerely to adore my Great Benefactor for thus graciously carying forth and returning in safety his unworthy handmaid (447).

Such language is in marked contrast to the earlier portions of the *Journal*.

The *Journal* of Sarah Kemble Knight, then, although a short and little-read piece of literature, takes its place as a successful and significant contribution to the picaresque tradition just when that tradition was in its full flower. Madam Knight was not, of course, a conscious picaresque writer, nor did she write on the much broader scale of H. H. Brackenridge's *Modern Chivalry,* which was to appear nearly a century later. Nevertheless, the *Journal* of Madam Knight is a genuine work of art and an important milestone in earlier American literature.

Notes

1. For a useful general survey of picaresque writings see Frank W. Chandler, *The Literature of Roguery* (New York, 1907); for a less historical and more critical treatment of picaresque see Robert Alter, *Rogue's Progress* (Cambridge, Mass., 1964). Both books contain useful bibliographical information.

2. Lewis' *The Picaresque Saint* (Philadelphia, 1959) traces picaresque influences in Moravia, Camus, Silone, Faulkner, Graham Greene and others. Alter's *Rogue's Progress* touches on picaresque themes in Mann, Cary, Bellow, and others.

3. Thomas H. Johnson and Perry Miller, eds., *The Puritans* (New York, 1938), p. 447. Further quotations of Madam Knight will be cited by page number.

4, George P. Winship, ed., *The Journal of Madam Knight* (Boston, 1926), frontispiece.

The Return of the Widow Bedott: Mrs. F.M. Whitcher of Whitesboro and Elmira

Thomas F. O'Donnell

After slumbering quietly on the dusty Dark Shelf of American literature for eighty years, the once garrulous Widow Bedott is beginning to stir and come back to life. Mrs. F. M. Whitcher's best-seller, *The Widow Bedott Papers,* an American favorite for forty years after its original publication in 1855, is back in two reprint editions.[1] This is news to gladden the hearts of all students of New York history and literature as well as connoisseurs of American satire. Not that the new editions will mean much to the small band of faithful who long ago found their now-treasured copies of Mrs. Whitcher's book in grandma's Saratoga trunk or in the three-for-a-dollar stall of some used book emporium; these happy few will probably scorn the new editions. But they will rejoice at their appearance, knowing that modern editions will attract new readers and new appreciation for *The Widow Bedott Papers*—even in Whitesboro, Utica, and Elmira, where strong men and women once squirmed at the very sound of Mrs. Whitcher's name. And a modern audience, they also know, is bound to include perceptive readers who will recognize and comment on the book for what it is and always has been: not a mere literary curiosity, not just another collection of "Yankee papers" perversely written in upstate New York and worthy only of a chuckling dismissal by literary historians, but a muscular forerunner of literary realism and certainly one of the most incisive pieces of social criticism to surface in antebellum America.

In 1846, just as James Fenimore Cooper was finishing *The Redskins*—the final volume of a trilogy[2] in which he traces the feudal and agrarian roots of upstate New York society and finds much to complain about in both the manners and morals of his contemporary New Yorkers—in a village some fifty miles northwest of Cooperstown, an unknown country-woman of Cooper's was also casting critical glances at Yorker society, especially at the segment into which she had been born. Frances Miriam Berry (she was to become Mrs. Whitcher later) was well past thirty when her satirical sketches started to appear anonymously in *Neal's Saturday Gazette* in 1846. But the sketches were less concerned with roots and principles than were Cooper's novels. Their author was not disturbed by the quarrel about land titles that was still racking the eastern part of the state. It was, rather, the surfaces, the superficial crudities of society as she saw it in her native Whitesboro that at once fascinated and repelled Miriam Berry, as she was known to her unsuspecting neighbors.

Her village in the heart of the state—the first permanent white settlement west of the Palatine hamlets on the Mohawk—was, by the time she reached maturity, a young and vigorous community safely past the frontier stage. It was now a funnelling point on the Erie Canal not only for westward-moving settlers but for the latest ideas, fads and manners from the east. With the manners—or lack of them—of her fellow Yorkers in her representative village, and with the way the new ideas and fads shaped the surfaces of her society, Miriam Berry was very much concerned. She said so in the first group of loosely connected sketches that delighted editor Joseph C. Neal and the readers of his popular *Gazette.* In 1847, when life took her to Elmira and proved to be about the same, new pictures of life in a proud, fast-growing southern tier community moved up to *Godey's Lady's Book* and a larger audience. Finally, in 1855—three years after the author's death—the sharp pictures of central and southern New York manners were brought together and reached the public in book form as *The Widow Bedott Papers.*

The book appeared on the crest of a wave of demand for dialect humor and was snatched up by two generations of delighted readers. Its popularity "was instant and unprecedented," says one historian. "Over a hundred thousand copies were demanded, and new editions were issued in 1856, 1864, 1880, 1883, and 1893."[3] Solid citizens of Whitesboro and Elmira cringed, seeing themselves as real life models for Mrs. Whitcher's unscrupulous and hypocritical boors; but the garrulous "Widow" and her cronies captured the national fancy along with such other popular figures as Seba Smith's "Major Jack Downing," T.C. Haliburton's "Sam Slick," and B.P. Shillaber's "Mrs. Partington," as well as James Russell Lowell's "Hosea Biglow."

But *The Widow Bedott Papers* was destined to enjoy public favor only as long as the fad for dialect humor remained alive. By the turn of the century the winds of that favor had died, and the long string of new printings came to an end. Mrs. Whitcher's sharp etchings of the foibles of Yorker society in the 1840s started down the road to oblivion, helped along by the unessential characteristic that had made them popular in the first place—a dialect that dated them and dulled the keen edge of social criticism. Actually, Mrs. Whitcher's ear was as sharp as her eye, and so the dialect of her sketches is probably the most authentic representation in our literature of the speech of nineteenth century Yorker villages and farms. Nevertheless, after five decades of vigorous life, *The Widow Bedott Papers* became—for a public grown weary of the clownish phonetic spelling of Artemus Ward and his host of followers—just another book that was too hard to read.[4] The Widow grew silent, climbed morosely to the Dark Shelf, and New York came close to losing forever an incisive and respectably artistic criticism of the less pleasant aspects of antebellum upstate behavior.

Significantly enough, this second critic of upstate society—like Cooper, the first—was completely free of any inhibiting New England or Puritan strain. Yankee manners, Puritan traditions, and a transplanted New England climate were all about Frances Miriam Berry as she grew up in Whitesboro. But her forebears were neither Yankee nor Puritan, and this fact helps to account for the stinging anti-Yankee thrusts that occur so often throughout *The Widow Bedott Papers*. Miriam Berry's father had come from New Jersey, where his father had been a King's Justice turned patriot at the outbreak of the Revolution. The first Berry to reach America was an escapee from Sterling Castle, where, according to family legend, he had been imprisoned for fighting for the Stuarts against Cromwell.[5] And so, the Berry family tradition, far from being Puritan, was, in fact, the opposite.

Lewis Berry, Miriam's father, had moved north from New Jersey, first to the upper Hudson Valley, then, in 1802, to Oneida County, following the first wave of New England settlers. By 1807 he was settled in Whitesboro, already a thriving community, where he was to prosper as an innkeeper. Here Miriam was born, probably in 1811, the eleventh of fifteen children; and here, except for two years in Elmira, she was to live until her death in 1852.[6] Many of the literary historians who have glanced briefly at her *Widow Bedott Papers* have carelessly referred to her as a "New England housewife,"[7] an epithet she in no sense deserves. Although there is plenty of evidence that Mrs. Whitcher was well-traveled in New York State, there is none to indicate that she ever so much as visited New England, except through the character of her "Widow." The society in which she was born, lived, and died, was an evolving Yorker society in which the New England influence was still strong, but which was well on its way to social autonomy. Most important, it was a society she knew intimately—one which, for its crude shortcomings, deserved scolding.

Whitesboro in the second quarter of the nineteenth century was a vigorous community that had grown rapidly and awkwardly since 1784, when Hugh White and his sons, Connecticut Yankees all, had settled there, where the Sauquoit Creek empties into the Mohawk River, and had given the place their name. As young Miriam Berry grew up, the village was noisily alive and conscious of the fact that here had been founded "the first colony, outside of New England, by the Puritans, the first swarm of the Puritan hive."[8] Lewis Berry, despite his anomalous Jersey roots, had done well here and his tavern provided him with more than enough to maintain his large family. He had chosen a promising spot in the center of the village. In 1884 a local historian could record that

> At the time of Mr. Berry's . . . removal to Whitesboro, that village had become an important and prominent locality. It was one of the county seats [Rome was the other], and was the abode of some of the most influential men in this part of the state. It was a good location for a well regulated and a well kept tavern . . . and the place where judges, lawyers, and the best class would congregate when courts were held in that village, and where travelers would stop on their way through the central part of the state . . . there are yet so many among the living who remember Mr. Berry and his well kept house that it is pleasant to refer to them and to speak in unqualified praise of both.[9]

In and around this "well kept house" of her father's, young Miriam Berry could see many of the great and near-great of the 1820s and 1830s, including some of national and even international fame. She was, for example, fourteen years old on that memorable day in June, 1825, when the great LaFayette was a guest in Lewis Berry's tavern; her elder sister Elizabeth was "one of the thirteen white-robed maidens who joined in the procession that gave welcome to LaFayette."[10]

Whitesboro's climates of opinion were shaped by some formidable citizens. In a fine house next door to her father's tavern lived one of the lesser greats: Jonas Platt, Federalist leader, unsuccessful candidate for governor in 1810, and, during Miriam Berry's childhood, a justice of the New York State Supreme Court. He was also an elder in the nearby Presbyterian Church, which the Berry family attended until an Episcopal Church was established in Whitesboro.[11] Farther down and across the street lived Elon Galusha, pastor of the Whitesboro Baptist Church from 1815 to 1831, already becoming "one of the greatest Baptist preachers in the country," and destined to become one of the leaders of the Adventist movement that arose from the ruins of Millerism.[12] Still a Baptist in the 1820s, however, the Reverend Galusha was as yet untouched by the flame of Millerism and was regarded as the acme of Vermont respectability carried over into Whitestown country. As the son, nephew, and grandson of three different Vermont governors, Galusha was a member of democratic nobility.[13]

On the same street in the other direction—toward nearby Utica—lived or visited other men whose names and reputations were well known for good or ill far beyond Miriam Berry's small village. The Reverend George Washington Gale, for instance, came to town in 1827, when Miriam was sixteen, and founded his Oneida Institute, a new kind of school in which manual labor was a regular part of the curriculum. By 1833 Gale had worked out plans for a more ambitious college for both men and women and was arranging to move to the prairies of Illinois, where he was to open his college in Knox County. As he planned it in Whitesboro, Gale tentatively called his institution "Prairie College," but it opened in 1834 as Knox Manual Labor College in the Illinois village that Gale also founded.[14]

Gale's successor at the Oneida Institute was even more colorful, if less admired. Beriah Green, the fiery, craggy-faced abolitionist who had come from Western Reserve Seminary and was to live out his turbulent life here, walked the streets of Whitesboro through Miriam Berry's adult life and, indeed, until long after her death. Green, who was to gain national recognition—or notoriety—as president of the first National

Anti-Slavery Convention, held in Philadelphia in 1833, brought to Whitesboro a voice and a zeal that were both admired and feared; to the end he was to be stormily involved in the village's affairs.[15] On September 5, 1833, as he delivered his stirring inaugural address as second president of Oneida Institute,[16] most of Whitesboro crowded into the Presbyterian Church to hear him, and to applaud or condemn his radical ideas about education. Miriam Berry, who had been received into this same church a year before, could have been in the audience; she lived less than a quarter of a mile away.

But even more exciting than the regular presence of these strong men in the Whitesboro of Miriam Berry's youth were the frequent and thrilling visits to town of the great Mr. Finney. Charles Grandison Finney, the preaching sensation of American Protestantism—"that modern Paul," as one of his disciples called him—had reason to come to Whitesboro often: to visit his wife's family (he had married Lydia Andrews, a Whitesboro girl); to talk and plan with his old teacher, Mr. Gale; or to conduct one of his remarkable revivals in the Presbyterian Church down the street from Lewis Berry's tavern. In March, 1832, at the end of one of Mr. Finney's protracted meetings, Miriam and one of her sisters were "examined and received into" this church,[17] along with dozens of others, some of whose religious enthusiasm was perhaps intensified by fear of the cholera that ravaged the East that year. But cholera or no cholera, Mr. Finney, with his "great staring eyes," his "holy band" and the "anxious seat" he had instituted, and his insistence that women be allowed to pray in public meeting[18]—Mr. Finney would have had them anyway. For Charles Grandison Finney was more than just a preacher. He was a York State hero, ever since the days in 1827 when he—with the help of Mr. Gale—had talked down the arrogant Yankees, Lyman Beecher and Asahel Nettleton, at the New Lebanon Convention and sent them back to Boston, whipped but respectful.[19] Through the early 1830s—until he was called to Oberlin College in 1835—Finney carried his "streak of fire" to Whitesboro frequently, and brought with him the breath of whichever city he had most recently conquered.[20]

These are some of the men who shaped the personality of Miriam Berry's "parish-world" as they met and talked in the rectangular park—a New England common in the heart of New York—that stretched out like a great front yard to Lewis Berry's tavern as Miriam grew up. And there was plenty to talk about: first, of the new canal that was dug through Whitesboro in 1823, and was supposed to turn the village into a metropolis; then of the boatloads of westward-bound migrants drifting through the village that never grew so fast as expected; then, as Miriam Berry came of age, of the strange new ideas and fashions in reform that followed in the wake of the slow-moving boats. All kinds of new crazes settled at least briefly in Whitesboro and touched even the most respectable of the inhabitants: phrenology, mesmerism, Fourierism, per-fectionism, women's rights, Millerism, and a dozen different kinds of reform movements. These, as well as the sometimes frightening skirmishes about abolition and the always invigorating religious revivals, were all part and parcel of daily life among these Yorkers, who "were a more quarrelsome, argumentative, experimenting brood than their parents and stay-at-home cousins" in New England.[21]

Such was the atmosphere around Miriam Berry as she attended local schools, now fearing and now loving a variety of teachers. One of these, her sister recalled, was an ignorant and "sour-faced woman," another was a "stern, cruel, vindictive man who literally whipped knowledge into his pupils' noddles."[22] Later, at the academy, however, she met a friend, Peletiah Rawson, the "kindest hearted and most indulgent of pedagogues, well skilled in mathematics and learned in all classic lore." A good deal of her education she received at home from her bright older sister, Elizabeth, and a favorite brother, Morris, with some informal supervision from Rev. John Frost, pastor of the Presbyterian Church until

Miriam was sixteen. She was recognized as a precocious child with a talent for drawing and a fondness for the books she found not only in her father's bookcase but also in the "somewhat extensive [and] infinitely miscellaneous" circulating library available to villagers. Her father, who had sent two of his sons to Hamilton College, encouraged her. "The advantage of a boarding school she might have had," says her sister, "but she shrank from the thought of leaving home." Miriam Berry stayed in her father's house, and the neat village green across the street became her campus.[23]

Despite her attachment to a large and enlightened family circle, however, Miriam later recalled that her childhood was not particularly happy. "I assure you that it has never been my lot to have many friends," she wrote to editor Joseph C. Neal in response to his enthusiasm for the first Widow Bedott sketches. "And I will tell you what I believe to be the secret of it":

> I received at my birth, the undesirable gift of a remarkably strong sense of the ridiculous. I can scarcely remember the time when the neighbors were not afraid that I would "make fun of them." For indulging in this propensity, I was scolded at home, and wept over and prayed with, by certain well-meaning old maids in the neighborhood; but all to no purpose. The only reward of their labors were frequently their likenesses drawn in charcoal and pinned to the corners of their shawls, with, perhaps, a descriptive verse below . . . And yet, at the bottom of all this deviltry, there was a warm, affectionate heart—if any were really kind to me, how I loved them! . . . I became a lonely child, almost without companionship; wandering alone, for hours, in the woods and fields, creating for myself an ideal world, and in that ideal world I lived for many years.[24]

Still unmarried as she entered her thirties, Miriam Berry had nevertheless found some interesting and congenial companions in the early 1840s. Whitesboro by this time boasted of "a society of persons of literary ability, who formed a reading circle" called the Moeonian Society; the group met twice a month at one another's homes for reading, music, and conversation. At the instigation of brother Morris and sister Kate—both enthusiastic members—Miriam Berry joined the society and soon became one of its stars, regaling the circle with her humorous poems and essays. Occasionally, pieces of verse or prose produced within the group found its way anonymously into one of the newspapers in neighboring Rome or Utica.[25] "Navigation Song: I'm Afloat," a rollicking Erie Canal ballad that appeared in the Utica *Gazette* and later in the *Roman Citizen*, for instance, probably came from Miriam Berry's pen.[26]

It was for the Moeonian circle that Miriam Berry eventually decided to write a sustained satirical tale to be read at group meetings a chapter at a time. The idea stemmed from her amused reaction to Regina Maria Roche's sentimental *Children of the Abbey*, widely popular in both England and America and replete on every page "with the most exalted sentiments, favorable to religion, morality and virtue."[27] *Children of the Abbey* and its "exalted sentiments" challenged Miriam Berry's "strong sense of the ridiculous"; the result was eleven chapters of a spoof entitled "The Widow Spriggins," with a title character who foreshadows the later Widow Bedott.[28]

In the summer of 1846, one of her fellow Moeonians—himself a contributor to *Neal's Gazette*, says Kate Berry, although she does not identify him—sent some of Miriam's poems to Neal, who promptly published them, with flattering praise. Miriam was surprised to see her verses in print, and Neal's comments prompted her to think of a series of prose pieces for publication. The Widow Bedott was about to make her first appearance.

The sketch form that Miriam Berry decided to use as a medium was ideally suited to her purpose. First of all, it was marketable; Irving had popularized it and Hawthorne had demonstrated in his "twice-told" tales that it was adaptable to various uses. By 1846, the American reading public was looking for more and more "sketches" in its popular magazines. Furthermore, the form allowed the author to focus attention on situation and characters without fear of violating the unity and coherence necessary to sustained narration. For ideas for her main character and a narrative thread for the sketches she looked not only at Whitesboro life bustling outside her window, but to her own bookshelf—or the village library's—which contained plenty of literary precedent for what she intended to do. One of the authors she certainly remembered as she planned the Widow Bedott's character and adventures was the Englishwoman, Frances Trollope. Although the indefatigable Mrs. Trollope is remembered today only for her critical *Domestic Manners of the Americans* (1832), she was also the author of a number of novels. The most popular of these, entitled *The Widow Barnaby* (1839), is a picaresque account in three volumes of the social adventures of a loud and vulgar English widow in search of another husband. The Widow Barnaby is guilty of most of the vices that were about to characterize her later American counterpart, the Widow Bedott: She is loud, arrogant, cruel, hypocritical, and unscrupulous. In the words of her own sister, she is "the very vilest, great, big, coarse, hateful oyster that was ever fished up."[29] She encourages the spread of a false rumor that she is wealthy, just as the Widow Bedott later does. The Widow Barnaby even has a nephew, an Oxford student home for a few months, who sees throughout her sham just as Jefferson Maguire, a college student, sees through his Aunt Bedott's. And the Widow Barnaby, like the Widow Bedott, finally captures an "extemporary preacher" whose moral level is no higher than hers. Other parallels of detail, as well as of plot and character, are numerous enough to indicate that as she wrote her early Bedott sketches Miriam Berry was indebted to Fanny Trollope [sic], although she never acknowledged the debt.

The indebtedness extended, moreover, to the searing *Domestic Manners* itself, a book in which upstate New Yorkers had more than a passing interest. Mrs. Trollope—like many other traveling British writers, including Captain Basil Hall before her and Harriet Martineau after her—had passed through the Mohawk Valley, pausing in Utica or Whitesboro long enough to allow a visit to Trenton Falls, the internationally famous scenic spot on West Canada Creek, only a few miles to the north. Her impression of the rugged beauty of the area is recorded in some detail in *Domestic Manners of the Americans.*[30] For the young Whitesboro woman, however, the book must have had more appeal than mere local allusion could give it. The people and institutions that Mrs. Trollope observed across America were the same people and institutions that Miriam Berry observed daily in her microcosmic village: the itinerant preacher, the lady lecturer, the sturdy political leader (like the Berrys' next-door neighbor, Judge Jonas Platt), the familiar peddler, the local laureate, the gossiping and borrowing neighbor. All these elements of American life cried out for treatment by one who was part of it.

Twenty-one of the new sketches came quickly from Miriam Berry's pen in the autumn of 1846 and throughout 1847. Introduced as a garrulous but innocuous gossip with a flair for execrable verse, the Widow is soon exposed as hypocritical and malicious in her determination to find a new husband. Her true character starts to emerge in the second sketch, when she indulges her "grief" in a doggerel tribute to the late Deacon Bedott:

> And since it was my lot to be
>   The wife of such a man,
> I tell the men that's after me
>   To ketch me if they can. (p. 28)

But the real reason for her sorrow is revealed in another stanza:

> But now he's dead! the thought is killin'
>   My grief I can't control—

He never left a single shillin'
   His widder to console. (p. 30)

The next six sketches deal with her efforts to snare widower Tim Crane and with her chagrin when she learns (in sketch #8) that it is her daughter Melissa, rather than herself, that Crane has been after. Shortly thereafter, the Widow decides to leave "Wiggletown"—now "a perfect set o' Goffs and Randals" (p. 100)—and continue her search in a larger town, Scrabble Hill, the home of her sister "Aunt Maguire." Here she sets her traps for another widower, the Rev. O. Shadrack Sniffles, pursues him relentlessly through five sketches (#13–17) and finally snares him. The last four sketches of this series are about the wedding, a trip to neighboring villages, and the widow's new home in Scrabble Hill. In sketch number 21 it is the Rev. Mr. Sniffles' turn to be chagrined as he learns that his new wife is penniless instead of wealthy, as she had intimated during their courtship.

The thin story-line—a tried and true laugh-getter in American literature before and after Miriam Berry's time—is the least important element of these sketches. More important is the manner in which she pillories upstate New York society for its hypocrisies and addiction to fads. In an early sketch, for instance, the Widow explains to a visiting fellow-gossip:

> That sass aint fust-rate—you see, while 'twas a dewin' Loviney Skinner, she come in with that are subscription paper, to git up a society for "the univarsal diffusion of elevation among the colored poperlation," and while I was lookin' at it to see who'd signed and how much they gi'n, the sass got overdid. (p. 33)

In a later sketch (#6), her husband-hunt takes her to a "phreenyogical lectur," a common enough social-educational event throughout the Mohawk Valley in the years following 1837, when George Combe had attracted thousands to his lectures on the new "science" of phrenology.[31] The Widow summarizes the "lectur" for her intended prey, a late arriver:

I wish you'd a ben here sooner, Mr. Crane, to hear Mr. Vanderbump's exparigate about them heads—he gin a description of the people they belonged tew—and told how ther characters was accordin' to ther heads. That are big head—the one that runs up to such a peak on top—he says that's Scott the celebrated author—I s'pose its the one that writ "Scott's Commontaries" on the Scripters. He says it's a wonderful intellectible head. . . . (p. 63)

Like most itinerant lecturers of the time, "Mr. Vanderbump" has a working partner; his wife is a lecturer, too, and the Widow intends to hear her the next night:

. . . though I don't think much o' these here wimmen lecturers, no way . . . You remember that one that come round a spell ago, a whalin' away about human rights. I thought she'd ought to be hosswhipt and shet up in jail, dident you? (p. 67)

Phrenology is only one of the fads that attract Wiggletonians. There are reform movements galore, and some villagers, like Deacon Fustick's wife, are mixed up in several of them:

. . . Seems to me Miss Deacon Fustick's a singular woman— she seems to be entirely took up with the "anti-tea and coffee society"—she talked to me all the time she was here about it—said I might depend on't that all that made me so thin, ane have such a cough, was drinkin tea and coffee. . . . She takes up everything that comes along, and gits all engaged about it. A spell ago she was wide awake against Sabbath-breakin' and dident talk about nothin' else—then 'twas moral reform—next come Millerism—(pp. 122–123)

Later, the same Mrs. Fustick is revealed to be "Superintendent o' the Maternal Society, President o' the Daughters o' Temperance, and Correspondin' Secretary o' the Friends o' Humanity." (p. 286) And in her attraction to Millerism,[32] Mrs. Fustick has plenty of company:

> Tew or three years ago, when Millerism was makin' such a
> noise, ther was a feller along lecturin' about it—and a
> number o' the Wiggletown folks raly thought ther was
> something in it. But old Miss Green was clear filled up with
> it. She give up all bizness, and dident do nothin' but traipse
> round from house to house takin' on about the eend o' the
> world—'twas comin' afore long. (p. 123)

But hypocrisy and fad-hopping are not restricted to the
women of Wiggletown; the men are guilty, too. A rich
merchant, Captain Smalley, creates the impression that "he's a
wonderful charitable man," that he favors all good causes; and
so—

> Whenever any body goes tew him with a subscription-paper,
> he always seems highly delighted with it—says it's an
> excellent objick—an objick he feels wonderfully interested
> in—he *does* hope they'll succeed in raisin' enough for 't. . . .
> But he'd ruther not put his name down—he has an aversion
> to makin' a display—he wishes they'd go all around and
> raise what they can, and if they don't git enough, come to
> him, and *he'll make up what's lackin'*. Somehow or another
> it don't often happen he's called on to make up what's
> lackin': when he *is,* he's generally missin. (pp. 127–128)

A more likeable entrepreneur is Jabe Clark, who appears and
disappears a number of times in the sketches and becomes a
kind of roving con man. In his first appearance he is a peddler,
and an entire sketch (#11) is devoted to the manner in which
he perpetrates a petty swindle on the sharp Widow. Jabe,
taken to task for having cheated her on a previous trip, assures
the Widow that he is now a "come-outer," a new and
regenerate man. He confesses that

> I did use to get the better o' my customers sometimes in a
> bargain—I've felt quite exercised about it lately. Ye see,
> Widder, I warn't activated by religious principles then. . . . I
> experienced religion over in Varmont, at one o' brother
> Armstrong's protracted meetin's. I tell ye, Widder, them
> special efforts is great things—ever sence I *come out* I've felt
> like a new critter. (p. 108)

Then, having won her attention with some gaudy "light French silk," Jabe proceeds to "skin" the Widow again and to disappear. He appears again later, as "Mr. Augustus Montgomery, Daggertyper," "makin' money like dirt." But this time the Widow outwits him, and he disappears again for fresh woods and pastures new. (#20, "The Rev. Mrs. Sniffles at Home")

The Rev. Sniffles, whom the Widow finally snares into matrimony, is a ludicrous figure, as hypocritical as the woman he almost deserves. He is also a preacher of the pulpit-pounding, double-talking variety. The Widow, learning that he is a widower, goes to hear him preach. He is described in action by the Widow's nephew:

> We had a seat very near the pulpit. As usual, the elder whaled away through his nose—thumped the desk, and went over and over again with the same thing—using a little different words each time, without ever making the most remote approach to anything like the shadow of an idea. (pp. 104–105)

The Elder soon falls for the Widow's trap, and invites her to his parsonage in a letter that is a parody of clerical pomposity:

> It will afford me most unmitigated pleasure to converse with you privately, in regard to your mind, and to give you such instructions upon doctrinal points as may be necessary and conducive to your spiritual edification. With that view, I invite you to call at my residence on Friday evening next, when, if no unforeseen contingencies intervene to prevent, and my corporeal condition continues to improve, I shall be unoccupied and most happy to attend to your case, and enlighten you in relation to such inquiries as you may be pleased to propound. (p. 140)

The Elder has, of course, heard the carefully planted rumor that the Widow is as rich as she is lonesome.

Still another target for Miriam Berry's scorn was the pretentious and ludicrously sentimental poetry and prose that was beginning to fill the pages of both local newspapers and local periodicals. Ten years before Hawthorne complained about the "damned mob of scribbling women" and forty years before Mark Twain regaled his readers with Emmeline Grangerford's lugubrious rhymes in *Huckleberry Finn*, Miriam Berry was waging war on the mawkish in American literature, on its creators, and on publishers and editors who foisted it on an ignorant public. The terrible doggerel by the Widow herself, liberally sprinkled through the sketches, represents one obvious kind of attack. Another is represented in the effusions of "Hugelina," a rhymester whose mournful lines are widely admired by readers of *The Scrabble Hill Luminary*. Hugelina, the Widow's rival for Rev. Sniffles' attention, expresses her concern at his illness—he has a cold—in a sonnet into which Miriam Berry gleefully introduces as many as possible of the clichés that characterized the genre:

> O, lyre of mine, divulge thy saddest strain
> In melancholy thunder-tones of woe!
> In gloomiest accents deep of quivering pain,
> Thy mournful numbers on the midnight throw;
> A direful theme demands thy anguished flow;
> For sighing on his lonely couch of grief,
> Truth's champion languisheth without relief! . . .
> (pp. 152–153)

Later, after the *Luminary* has published one of the Widow's poems, she attends a literary "swearee" and meets her fellow bards, all of whom publish over alliterative pseudonyms: the Widow Reade, who signs her productions "Nell Nox," and whose sharp criticism of Longfellow is about to appear in *The Reflector*; Susan Ann Briggs, who signs her work "Fenella Fitzallen"; and "a wonderful tall, slab-sided, coarse-lookin' critter" named Samantha Hocum, who writes articles on women's rights for the *Pigeon Point Record of Genius* over the name of "Kate Kenipe." Also present are the editor of *The Reflector,* who offers Fenella Fitzallen's work as proof that "America is the only country where poetry had reached the height of its zenith"; a "fat, pudden-faced" poet who signs himself "Phil Philpotts"; and "a good-lookin' young woman that writes the amusin' articles" for the *Newville Star and Trumpet* over the name "Betsy Buttertub." (pp. 197–201) Thus did Miriam Berry burlesque the "Fanny Ferns," the "Fanny Forresters," and the "Grace Greenwoods" of her time, as well as provincial "literary" groups like the Moeonian Society she herself belonged to.

On January 6, 1847, Miriam Berry married the Rev. Benjamin W. Whitcher, an Episcopal minister who had recently organized St. John's parish in Whitesboro. Both newlyweds were thirty-five years old. They were not, however, to settle immediately in Whitesboro; only three months after their marriage, the Rev. Mr. Whitcher was assigned to Trinity Episcopal Church in Elmira, and the new Mrs. Whitcher was off on a great adventure of her own—her first extended separation from her family and native village.

By now, a number of her sketches had been published. "All the world is full of Bedott," Joseph Neal had written in September, 1846: "Our readers talk of nothing else, and almost despise 'Neal' [i.e., *The Saturday Gazette*] if the Widow be not there." Even more important, Neal reported that Louis Godey, editor of the famous *Lady's Book*, wanted material from the author of the Bedott sketches.[33] But negotiations with Godey had to wait until Mrs. Whitcher was at least partially adjusted to her new role as a minister's wife in Elmira. She nevertheless continued to write Bedott sketches satirizing life in "Wiggletown"—i.e., Whitesboro—for Neal's *Gazette.* Skillfully, however, she prepared her readers for a change of background and new characters. In sketch #21, the Widow—having snared her prey, the Rev. O. Shadrack Sniffles—makes her final appearance as a central character and prepares the way for a new series that began with the July, 1847 issue of *Godey's.*

Elmira, Mrs. Whitcher's new home, was considerably larger, and growing faster, than Whitesboro. Between 1845 and 1848 it had increased by 1,000 to a population of 3,600. By the time the Whitchers arrived there, the village was experiencing the same kind of social growing pains that Whitesboro had undergone in the 1820s. If the New England influence was a bit less evident here than in Whitesboro, the social fabric was similar. "Our society is very much like the society in all growing villages," Mrs. Whitcher observed after she had been in Elmira a year. Besides "tall, white houses" and "red brick mansions," she wrote, "we have our complement of forlorn, shabby, rickety old shells, stuffed full of beings as forlorn and shabby as themselves. Poverty, vice and intemperance abound here." In Elmira, as in Whitesboro, the love for "societies" was manifest: "We have all sorts. . . ," she noted:

> Missionary societies, Bible societies, tract societies, sewing societies, maternal societies, mutual societies, sons of temperance and daughters of temperance societies, odd fellow's societies, and an odd ladies' society, composed chiefly of ancient maidens. We have freemasons' societies, literary societies, woman's rights societies, anti-everything societies, benevolent societies for all sorts of objects, "too numerous to mention" (as the menagerie bills say when they get down to the monkeys).[34]

As central figure in her new sketches for *Godey's*, Mrs. Whitcher developed more fully the character of "Aunt Maguire," already familiar to her readers as the Widow Bedott's sister, of "Scrabble Hill." Although she speaks the same dialect, "Aunt Maguire" is less given to malicious gossip and is more likeable than her sister, who appears only occasionally in the Maguire sketches. In these, Mrs. Whitcher also resorts less frequently to burlesque and parody, relying on straight satire frequently laced with caustic irony.

Before she had been married a year, Miriam Berry Whitcher had to face problems she had never known in her father's prosperous house in Whitesboro. One of these was managing a respectable home on a clergyman's meager income. In sketch #26 a minor character reports that "there ain't mor'n half a dozen in the congregation that pay their dues regularly; and if't wan't for what the minister's wife gits for writin' for the newspapers, they wouldent be able to pay their house-rent and keep out o'debt, no way." (p. 321) An institution designed in theory to augment a minister's income was the "donation party." As a young woman in Whitesboro, Miriam Berry had seen many such affairs, but never, until she was directly involved as a minister's wife, had she realized how degrading they could be.

On November 18 and 25, 1847, the Elmira *Gazette* carried announcements that for purposes of "donating," the friends of "the Rev. B. W. Whitcher will make their annual visit to his home on the afternoon and evening of Thursday, Nov. 25th."[35] Of what happened at this "party" there is no factual account. Much can be deduced, however, from "Aunt Maguire's Description of the Donation Party," the longest, most indignant and most excoriating sketch of nineteenth century American manners in *The Widow Bedott Papers* or perhaps elsewhere—a savage indictment of a parochial institution that American ministers and their wives had come to dread. In this sketch, first published in *Godey's* for March, 1848, Parson Scrantum is alloted by his congregation an annual salary of four hundred dollars a year "and a donation party"—a kind of ecclesiastical "shower"—every winter. To the first such party, for which Mrs. Scrantum is required to provide refreshments, troop the loud and vulgar parishioners with their cheap "donations": a half pound of tea, a skein of yarn, a tiny cheese ("half o' it was a donation and t' other half was to go for pew rent.") Also present are non-church members who have brought nothing except their appetites for the free refreshments. After eating all the food in the house (the Widder Grimes even steals some, tucking it into "an awful great workbag" she has brought for the purpose) the bad-mannered townspeople in their careless merrymaking smash Mrs. Scrantum's lamps and family heirloom dishes and spill oil on her new "six-dollar bunnit," the only worthwhile donation to be made. Shortly after this humiliating debacle,

Parson Scrantum resigns his pastorate, commenting, "One more donation party would completely break me down." Aunt Maguire ends her account with the hope that the new parson's new village, Bangtown, "is a place where donation parties is a thing unknown."

In Scrabble Hill (Elmira) Mrs. Whitcher came frequently in contact with another type she had not met in Whitesboro—*nouveau-riche* parishioners, arrogant and domineering, who expected deference from less affluent neighbors. Of these, Mr. and Mrs. Samson Savage are most sharply depicted. They had come originally from "Varmount," Aunt Maguire recalls, where

> . . . he was one o' these ere specilators. Wonderful fellers to make money, the Varmounters. Husband says they come over the Green Mountains with a spellin'-book in one hand and a halter in t'other and if they can't git a school to teach, they can steal a hoss. When they first come to our place, he was a follerin' the tin-peddlin' bizness; he used to go rumblin' around in his cart from house to house, and the rich folks ruther turned up their noses at him, or he consated they did and it made him awful wrathy; so he determined he'd be richer 'n any on 'em, and pay 'em off in their own coin . . . Everything he took hold of prospered, and without actilly bein' what you could call dishonest, afore many years everybody allowed he was the richest man in the place. (p. 302)

Relishing her new wealth, Mrs. Savage soon "sot up for a lady. She was always a coarse, boisterous, high-tempered critter, and when her husband grow'd rich, she grow'd pompous and overbearin'. She made up her mind she'd rule the roost, no matter what it cost—she'd be the *first* in Scrabble Hill." (p. 303) When Parson Scrantum's successor, the Rev. Tuttle—undoubtedly modeled after the real-life Rev. Benjamin Whitcher—refuses to be ruled, Mrs. Savage retaliates. "I despise Tuttle," she tells the members of the Scrabble Hill Sewing Society, "and I'll tell him so tew his face when I git a chance. Ye don't ketch me a slanderin' folks behind ther backs." Then she goes on, Aunt Maguire reports, and "such a haulin' over as Miss [i.e., Mrs.] Tuttle and the parson got, I never heered afore in all the days o' my life." (p. 308–309)

Still another type that Mrs. Whitcher unmasks is the freeloader, exemplified by the fat Scrabble Hill physician, Dr. Lippincott, who "gits the heft of his livin' away from home— contrives to git to one patient's house just as dinner's ready, and to another's jest at tea time, and so eats with 'em." A third is the reformer who preaches better than he practices, like some that Mrs. Whitcher had known back in Whitesboro. Outside the village of Scrabble Hill, for instance, lives Professor Stubbles, a Fourierist who is "always a whalin' away about the dignity o' labor" in "such a blind, twistical way o' talkin' that a body can't tell what he means half the time." When a group of ladies visit Mrs. Stubbles to invite her to join their sewing society, they find her chopping wood. Professor Stubbles, asked for his opinion of such societies, answers in the jargon of his cause:

> Did I believe that an organization of this description would be a labor promotin' association, I would give it my heart-willin' approval. . . . it's high time that the purse-proud and vice-bloated aristocracy o' the land was compelled to toil like the hardhanded sons and daughters of honest poverty; it's high time that the artificial arrangements of society was done away, and this sin-distracted, folly-bewildered, hog-ridden world was governed by such laws as the Great Heart of the universe originally intended. Ladies, the earth-mission of mundane souls is two-fold; first, to discharge with self-interest-sacrificing zeal our duty toward downtrodden humanity; second, to perform with soul-earnest, wife-assisting, daughter-keeping, labor-loving fidelity, such domestic services as shall be to be performed at home; and I prounounce that soul who refuses to acknowledge the dignity of household labor a pride-besotted, contempt-deserving, a heaven-provoking churl. (pp. 290–291)

After hearing this speech out and scornfully commenting on the hyphen-happy Professor's failure to practice what he preaches, the ladies leave and Mrs. Stubbles presumably goes back to her woodpile.

The sketches in *Godey's,* like those in the *Saturday Gazette*, were published anonymously; nevertheless, as they continued to appear in 1848, Elmirans began to see themselves in the unflattering portraits and to suspect that the author was one of their own number. On May 25, 1848, the Elmira *Gazette* reprinted on its front page "Aunt Maguire's Description of the Donation Party"; on December 28 it reprinted "Aunt Maguire's Account of the Sewing Circle," which had just appeared in the January, 1849, issue of *Godey's*. In its local news column, the *Gazette* noted that "the question now is, about town, who is *Captain Smalley?*" On January 5, 1849, another newspaper, the Elmira *Republican,* apologized for having referred, a week before, to "J.H. Husted, alias Capt. Smalley, of this place. . . ." In its apology, the *Republican* explained that "it is well known to our village readers that the 'Sewing Society' as published in the *Lady's Book* has been accused of drawing its characters from real life in Elmira." Delighted with the tempest now abrewing, the *Gazette* even reprinted in January and February three of the ealier Widow Bedott sketches from Neal's magazine, noting on February 22, 1849, that "the author of these articles resides among us." And even as pressure in the village mounted ominously, the Rev. Benjamin Whitcher confided to some friends that his wife was the author everyone was trying to identify.[36]

Miriam Whitcher was dismayed by the storm that now broke over her head. When one angry Elmiran threatened her husband with a lawsuit, she wrote to her sister: "I am heartily sick of Bedotting and Maguiring, and only wish I could be as well paid for more sensible matter."[37] By now she had, indeed, begun a new series of sketches, "Letters from Timberville," also critical of her Elmira neighbors but containing few characters drawn from real life. Three of these would appear in *Godey's* over her initials, F.M.W.[38] But the damage done by the Aunt Maguire sketches was irreparable. In June, 1849, the

Rev. Benjamin Whitcher resigned his post at Trinity Church and he and his chagrined wife returned to Whitesboro. Here she was able to write two final sketches for *Godey's* (#26 and #27) in which Aunt Maguire describes the tumult in Slabtown when word gets out that the "sewing society" sketches were written by the minister's wife.[39] In this last effort ("Aunt Maguire's Visit to Slabtown" is actually a single lengthy sketch presented in two parts in *The Widow Bedott Papers*), Mrs. Whitcher once more dramatized the pettiness, envy, and jealousy, hypocrisy and vindictiveness that she had seen in American village life of her time. Aunt Maguire reveals, in sketch #27, that she herself is the culprit, that the offensive sketches were not written by the minister's wife after all, that they were not even about the Slabtown sewing group. But the truth comes too late: the minister's wife has already been tried and convicted of a "crime" that was never committed. The irony of the situation is compounded by the knowledge that, although the Slabtown minister's wife was innocent, Mrs. Whitcher herself was not; she was "guilty" and she knew it. She could absolve her fictitious character, but not herself. Once she had established the minister's wife's innocence, Mrs. Whitcher was through with "Bedotting and Maguiring."

She was not quite finished as a writer, however. A last "Letter from Timberville," contrasting life in Elmira (Timberville) with life in Whitesboro (here called Greenvalley) appeared in *Godey's* in April 1850. Two more sketches—"Mrs. Mudlaw's Recipe for Potato Pudding" and "Morning Calls"— were published in the *Saturday Gazette* later in 1850. Still later they would appear as sketches #29 and #30 in *The Widow Bedott Papers*, even though they are comparatively innocuous and completely unrelated to the first twenty-eight sketches in the book. These were the last sketches to be published during Mrs. Whitcher's lifetime.

In 1850, now the mother of an infant daughter, Mrs. Whitcher turned to an entirely different kind of writing, noting that "I wish to leave something that shall be useful for my child to read, when she reaches an age capable of understanding it."[40] The result of this pious intention was "Mary Elmer, or Trials and Changes," an unfinished—and all but unreadable—tale full of the sentimental clichés Mrs. Whitcher had so mercilessly parodied only four years before in the Bedott sketches.[41] Before she could finish "Mary Elmer," Frances Miriam Whitcher died of tuberculosis on January 4, 1852, in her native village. She had never seen any of her writing in book form.

In 1855, James C. Derby, New York publisher of some of nineteenth century America's most popular books, had a visitor in the person of Alice B. Neal, now the widow of Joseph C. Neal. Mrs. Neal, with the aid of Martha L. W. Whitcher—the Rev. Benjamin Whitcher's new wife—had gathered the Bedott and Maguire sketches together with the plan of having them published as a book. Derby, who had not read the sketches in their original periodical printings, took them home, read them to his family, and was convinced of their merit. He immediately offered, through Mrs. Neal, to publish them at his expense and to pay all the usual royalties to the dead writer's estate. All was well. Shortly thereafter, however, the Rev. Benjamin Whitcher himself appeared in Derby's office, asking a flat sum in advance for all rights to his dead wife's sketches. Derby paid him $500, and the sketches were his. Later that year the first edition of *The Widow Bedott Papers,* suitably illustrated by "Dallas" appeared, and the soundness of Derby's judgment was proved: the book went out to tickle hundreds of thousands, and to add to Derby's already promising fortune.[42]

But upstate New York's first female social critic was now safe from reprisals and libel suits. On the day the book appeared she had been in her grave for three years—on a hill that looks down toward Whitesboro, less than a half mile from the spot where she had been born in her father's "well-kept house."

Notes

1. In 1969, Literature House (Upper Saddle River, N.J.) announced a facsimile reprint of the 1874 edition published by Mason, Baker, and Pratt; the Gregg Press Catalog for 1973–74 announced a reprint of the 1883 edition, which was published in New York by A.C. Armstrong. The latter edition is part of Gregg's American Humorists Series, edited by Clarence Gohdes. In addition, a biographical sketch of Mrs. Whitcher by Margaret Wyman Langworthy—more accurate and solidly packed than previous ones—appeared recently in the prestigious *Notable American Women, 1607–1950* (Harvard University Press, 1971), III, 580–581.

2. The earlier volumes are *Satanstoe* and *The Chainbearer*, both published in 1845. Cooper's first fictional attack on what he considered moral shoddiness in America had already appeared in *Home As Found* (1838).

3. Fred Lewis Pattee, *The Feminine Fifties* (New York: D. Appleton-Century Co., 1940), p. 234. Pattee missed the 1874 edition mentioned in note 1 above. F. L. Mott lists *The Widow Bedott Papers* among the "better sellers" for 1855 in his *Golden Multitudes: The Story of Best Sellers in the United States* (New York: The Macmillan Co., 1947), p. 320. James D. Hart says "The public . . . was large enough to . . . bring *The Widow Bedott Papers* a sale of 100,000 copies in the 23 printings in the decade after 1855," *The Popular Book: A History of America's Literary Taste* (New York: Oxford University Press, 1950), p. 142.

4. Among the host of followers must be included not only Henry Wheeler Shaw ("Josh Billings") but also another upstate New York woman, Marietta Holley (1836–1926) of Jefferson County. Miss Holley's "Samantha," the reforming heroine of a score of popular novels between 1873 and 1914, bears a pallid resemblance to Mrs. Whitcher's "Widow." Samantha speaks a dialect, however, never heard on sea or land, to say nothing of upstate New York.

5. D.E. Wager, "The Whitestown Centennial," *Transactions of the Oneida Historical Society at Utica,* 1881–1884 (Utica: Ellis H. Roberts, 1885), pp. 127–128. This reliable essay is concerned with the history of many Whitesboro families. The Berry Family is traced in some detail, not because it produced a popular writer, but because it was so widely known and respected.

6. No biography of Frances Miriam Berry Whitcher has been published, although there are three memoirs: one written and published anonymously by her sister, Kate Berry, "Passages in the Life of the Author of Aunt Maguire's Letters, Bedott Papers, etc. In

Two Parts," *Godey's Lady's Book*, XLVII (July, 1853), 49–55 and (August, 1853), 109–115; another by Alice B. Neal in later editions of *The Widow Bedott Papers*; and a third by Martha F.W. Whitcher in F.M. Whitcher, *The Widow Spriggins* (New York: Carleton and Co., 1867). It is in the last of these that Mrs. L.M. Whitcher is said to have been born in 1811; the inscription on her tombstone says she died at the age of thirty-nine, which would make the year of her birth 1813 or 1814. Since early village records of Whitesboro were long ago destroyed by fire, the birth date cannot be firmly established.

7. See, for instance, Hart's *The Popular Book,* p. 142. In his *Native American Humor* (p.50), Walter Blair refers to the Widow Bedott as one of a group of "New England ladies."

8. William M. White, in an address delivered at the centennial celebration (1884) of the founding of Whitestown. In Wager, p. 27. The town's principal village was incorporated as Whitesboro in 1813.

9. Wager, "The Whitestown Centennial," pp. 127–128.

10. Ibid., p. 131. Elizabeth Berry later married O.L. Barbour, widely known for his *Chancery Practice, Magistrate's Criminal Law*, and other authoritative works on jurisprudence.

11. Pomroy Jones, *Annals and Recollections of Oneida County* (Rome: published by the author, 1851), p. 793. In his sketch of Platt's political career, Jones quotes from Hammond's *Political History of New York*. In *Tip of the Hill: an Informal History of Fairfield Academy and Medical College* (Boonville: Black River Books, 1953), Thomas C. O'Donnell [not related to the author of this article] calls Platt "Oneida County's master politician" and maintains that he obtained a charter in 1812 for Hamilton College in preference to Fairfield Academy (p. 59).

12. Whitney R. Cross, *The Burned-Over District* (Ithaca: Cornell University Press, 1950), p. 299. See also p. 301: "He was a giant among the Baptists."

13. See William B. Sprague, *Annals of the American Pulpit* (New York: R. Carter and Bros., 1857–1869), VI, 669–670. Galusha was the son of Jonas Galusha, the nephew of Martin Chittenden, and the grandson of Thomas Chittenden, all of them governors of Vermont.

14. See "George Washington Gale," *Dictionary of American Biography*; see also Samuel Durant, *History of Oneida County* (Philadelphia: Everts and Fariss, 1878), p. 223; and Gilbert Hobbs Barnes, *The Anti-Slavery Impulse*, 1830–1844 (New York: D. Appleton-Century, Inc., 1933), p. 9.

15. For a full account of Green's life see Muriel Block, "Beriah Green, the Reformer" (unpublished Master's thesis, American History, Syracuse University, 1935). See also D. Gordon Rohman,

Here's Whitesboro: An Informal History (New York: Stratford House, 1949), pp. 34–53.

16. In this address Green announced that the goal of education was to develop "Fitness for public service, usefulness of any sort," and developed his own doctrine of humanitarianism. "Perish the sword of caste! . . . Oh! I hate the empty parade, the idle ceremony, the senseless jargon, which holds up the scholar to his own mother's children as a man of mysterious power, as a sort of wizard, who in foreign tongues and unearthly sounds, holds communion with spirits which the unpractised eye cannot perceive! . . . In Christian education, man as *man,* is to be the object of regard." See Beriah Green, *Sermons and Other Discourses, with Brief Biographical Hints* (New York: S. W. Green, 1860), pp. 61–64. Before he was through, this anti-intellectual maverick was to abolish all textbooks except Scripture from the Institute and to substitute Hebrew for Latin in the Institute curriculum. His stubborn attachment to his own ideals of education and abolition finally forced the closing of the Oneida Institute in 1844. Among the many contemporary descriptions of the Institute in its palmy days are Thomas F. Gordon, *Gazetteer of New York* (Philadelphia: Gordon, 1836), p. 575 and one by a British traveler, John Fowler, *Journal of a Tour of the State of New York* (London: Whittaker, Treacher and Arnot, 1831), pp. 81–82. This latter account is especially interesting, because it laments the apparent death of nearby Hamilton College, which was going through a period of distress. For a modern account of Green and the place of the Oneida Institute in the history of education see Benjamin P. Thomas, *Theodore Weld: Crusader for Freedom* (New Brunswick: Rutgers University Press, 1950), pp. 18–20, and *passim.* Weld, who according to the DAB became "one of the greatest figures of his time," was a student at Oneida from 1829 to 1831.

17. *Records of the First Presbyterian Church, Whitesboro,* Vol. III, p. 87 of "Register of Church Members." In Utica, N.Y., Public Library.

18. Barnes, *Anti-Slavery Impulse,* pp. 8–10; see also Cross, *The Burned-Over District,* pp. 177–178. Cross also offers a detailed account of Finney's activities in upstate New York, pp. 151–169.

19. See Charles C. Cole, Jr., "The New Lebanon Convention," *New York History,* XXXI (October, 1950), 385–397, for an excellent account of this meeting and the far-reaching effects of Finney's victorious defense of his "new measures." After this convention, Cole points out, the religious activities of Oneida County became the concern of Boston ministers, New York congregations, Phildelphia periodicals.

20. The phrase is Lyman Beecher's, quoted in *ibid.,* p. 395. For Finney and Whitesboro, see Rev. Charles G. Finney, *Memoirs* (New York: A.S. Barnes, 1876), *passim.* The lives of Miriam Berry and C.G. Finney were curiously linked in a chain of circumstances of which neither was ever aware. Among Finney's converts in Rochester in 1841 was "one of Chancellor W—'s sons," Clarence Walworth. (*Ibid.,* pp. 367–368.) Walworth studied theology at General Theological Seminary with Benjamin W. Whitcher, but later turned Roman Catholic, became one of the original Paulist Fathers, and in 1857 welcomed Benjamin W. Whitcher (his old friend and Miriam Berry's widower) into the Church of Rome. See Ellen H. Walworth, *Life Sketches of Father Walworth with Notes and Letters* (Albany: J. B. Lyon Company, 1907), pp. 83–84; 170–71 and Benjamin W. Whitcher, *The Story of a Convert* (New York: P. O'Shea, 1875), p. 191.

21. Cross, *Burned-Over District,* p. 82.

22. "Introductory," *The Widow Bedott Papers,* with an Introduction by Alice B. Neal (New York: Derby and Jackson, 1858), p. xiii. All subsequent quotations from the work will be taken from this printing of the first edition. Note that Mrs. Whitcher's name does not appear on the title pages of early editions.

23. Information about Miriam Berry's education comes from Kate Berry, "Passages . . . etc."; Wendell Berry, Miriam's oldest brother, graduated from Hamilton in 1815; Morris M. Berry followed his brother and graduated in 1817. Morris prepared for Hamilton under Mr. Halsey of Whitesboro, but, according to Martha L. W. Whitcher, his preparation "received finishing touches from Rev. John Frost," who customarily interested himself in the education of his young parishioners. The "Necrology" in *Hamilton College Catalog,* 1881–1882, reports that Morris M. Berry (1799–1881) was admitted to the practice of law in 1820. After practicing a short time in Massena, according to Martha L. W. Whitcher, he returned to Whitesboro. Later he became a book dealer in Saratoga; still later, a librarian at Divinity Hall, in Philadelphia.

24. Kate Berry quotes from, but fails to date, this letter in "Passages . . . etc., " *Godey's* XLVII (July, 1853), 50; it is reprinted in Alice B. Neal, "Introductory," pp. xiii–xiv.

25. Information about the Moeonian Society can be found in Kate Berry, "Passages . . . etc.," *Godey's* XLVII (July, 1853), 109–115; and in Martha L. W. Whitcher, *A Few Stray Leaves in the History of Whitesboro* (typescript in Dunham Library, Whitesboro, dated "May 31st, 1884" and signed "MLW.") On p. 20 of this script Mrs. Martha Whitcher identifies other members of the Moeonian Society,

including Calvert Comstock, later editor of the Albany *Argus*. In the early 1840s Comstock was editing a weekly newspaper in Rome. Note that *A Few Stray Leaves . . .* was later published and its authorship erroneously ascribed to Miriam Berry (Mrs. F.M. Whitcher).

26. See Thomas F. O'Donnell, "I'm Afloat on the Raging Erie," *New York Folklore Quarterly*, XIII (Autumn, 1957), 177–180.

27. Caritat's *Explanatory Catalogue* (1799) as quoted in Herbert Ross Brown, *The Sentimental Novel in America, 1789–1860.* (New York: Pageant Books, 1959), p. 26.

28. Published thirteen years after *The Widow Bedott Papers* in *The Widow Spriggins, Mary Elmer, and other Sketches by Mrs. F. M. Whitcher* (New York: G.W. Carleton, 1868), this book never achieved the popularity of its predecessor.

29. Frances Trollope, *The Widow Barnaby* (3 vols.; London, Richard Bentley, 1839), I, 331.

30. Frances Trollope, *Domestic Manners of the Americans* (New York: Dodd, Mead & Co., 1927), pp. 329–333 and 350–352. Michael Sadleir's Introduction to this edition traces the publishing history of this perennially fascinating book.

31. Miriam Berry could have attended phrenological lectures in Whitesboro, Rome, or nearby Utica, where a "Utica Phrenological and Magnetic Society" was established in 1845. (See "Phrenological Magnetic Society Minute Book," in possession of Oneida Historical Society, Utica, New York.) Orson Fowler had flooded the countryside with his books on phrenology and plaster heads bearing the phrenologist's *imprimatur,* "Approved by Fowler." For a complete discussion of the evolution of phrenology into a cult of personal improvement and social reform see John Dunn Davies, *Phrenology: Fad and Science* (New Haven: Yale University Press, 1956).

32. In what was perhaps the most dramatic manifestation of the religious fervor of the first half of the century, William Miller, an uneducated farmer from Low Hampton (Washington County), New York, traveled through the Northeast in the 1830s and early '40s predicting the return of the Messiah in 1844. He based his prediction on an interpretation of the chronological books of the Old Testament, especially the book of Daniel. Invited to preach in many orthodox churches during the early stages of his career, Miller attracted at least 50,000 advocates. When the second coming failed to materialize as predicted, many of Miller's followers refused to abandon the doctrine, believing that Miller had merely miscalculated. These faithful organized into Adventist congregations. For an account of the Millerite fever in central New York, see Cross, *Burned-Over District*, pp. 287–314. For a discussion of how Miller arrived at the date of the

second coming, see Elmer T. Clark, *The Small Sects of America* (revised edition; New York: Abingdon-Cokesbury Press, 1937), pp. 34–35. For a vivid account of childhood in a Millerite family in central New York, see Jane Marsh Parker, "A Little Millerite," *Century*, n.s. XI (December, 1886), 310–317. This contains reproductions of some of the propagandistic charts and diagrams that were part of the machinery of Millerism.

33. "Introductory," pp. x–xi.

34. "Letters from Timberville: I," in *The Widow Spriggins*, pp. 297–299. This and two other "Timberville" sketches, originally published in *Godey's* in 1849 and 1850, are not included in *The Widow Bedott Papers,* where two villages, Slabtown and Scrabble Hill, are made to sound very much like Elmira.

35. Herbet A. Wisbey, Jr., "The Widow Bedott," *York State Tradition*, XXVI (Fall, 1972), 19. For information about the Whitchers' two years in Elmira I am indebted to Professor Wisbey, not only for this article but for other factual information. Fortunately, Professor Wisbey was able to examine records in the Elmira public library, Trinity Episcopal Church, and Chemung County Historical Society shortly before these records were destroyed or severely damaged in the devastating flood of 1972.

36. A short account of the episode, written by an Elmira contemporary, records that "Mr. Whitcher made known, quite unfortunately, the *nom de plume* of his wife. Then the feeling became more urgent to remove him to another parish." This account is in the Steele Memorial Library, Elmira. (Letter to the present author from Mrs. Eva C. Taylor, January 12, 1966.)

37. Introduction, *The Widow Spriggins*, pp. 27, 32.

38. See XXXVII (May, 1849), 309–312; XXXIX (July, 1849), 9–13; and XL (April, 1850), 237–242. These are reprinted in *The Widow Spriggins.*

39. Sketch #28 in *The Widow Bedott Papers* is "Mrs. Maguire's Account of Deacon Whipple"; this was actually one of the first Maguire sketches to be written; it appeared in *Godey's* XXXV (July, 1847).

40. Quoted in Kate Berry, "Passages . . . etc." *Godey's* XLVII (July, 1853), 111. Her first child, also a daughter, had died at birth in Elmira on April 1, 1848.

41. "Mary Elmer" was published for the first (and only) time in 1868 in *The Widow Spriggins*, pp. 143–293.

42. See James C. Derby, *Fifty Years Among Authors, Books and Publishers* (New York: G.W. Carleton, 1884), pp. 415–416.

Frances Miriam Whitcher:
Social Satire in the Age
of Gentility

Linda A. Morris

The Seneca Falls convention of 1848 is now widely regarded as the birthplace of the woman's rights movement in America. With only two weeks notice, 300 women and men traveled to this small village in upstate New York where they debated for two days the merits of a document—the Declaration of Sentiments and Resolutions—drawn up and introduced to the convention by Elizabeth Cady Stanton and Lucretia Mott. Echoing the Declaration of Independence, the Seneca Falls document responded to what its authors called the degradation of women in American society. The solutions they posited in their resolutions were overtly and specifically political—they called for changes in the political system, including the enfranchisement of women, and they declared of "no authority" all unjust laws that stood in the way of women's full equality with men. By the time the convention adjourned, 100 of the 300 present had signed the Declaration and agreed to convene again two weeks later in Rochester, New York. Much to the signers' surprise, the press greeted their actions with hostility and ridicule so disparaging that a number of women subsequently withdrew their endorsement for the Declaration; the majority, however, remained steadfast (Buhle and Buhle 97).

Five months later, in December of 1848, a different group of women also came in for harsh criticism in the press; this time, however, the women were not early feminists but rather the participants of a sewing society in Elmira, New York. The form this particular criticism took was a satiric story published anonymously in *Godey's Lady's Book* and written by Miriam Whitcher, the wife of an Elmira Episcopal minister. On the face of it, the events in Elmira had no connection to the earlier events in Seneca Falls, in spite of the geographical and temporal proximity of the two, but upon closer examination the two had much in common. Whitcher, in her satire, was responding to the same social ills that prompted the convening of the Seneca Falls convention: she was motivated by a similar desire to change society's ways, and her writing was charged with a deeply felt indignation.

Unlike the Seneca Falls participants, however, Miriam Whitcher did not perceive the social malaise to be a political problem with a potential political solution. Instead, she seemed to hold women responsible for their own degradation and to see social satire as a means through which she might make women aware of the foolishness of their behavior; i.e., humor became a potential corrective for society's ills. Indeed, Whitcher was by no means a feminist—one of the targets of her humor in an early sketch is a woman's rights advocate— yet the personal indignation and frustration that inform her humor originated in the same quarter as did the feminist movement: women's increasingly restricted role in mid-nineteenth-century American society. These restrictions, which have received considerable scholarly attention in recent years, warrant only a brief summary here.[1]

As the predominant farming and mercantile modes of production in the Northeastern states began to give way in the 1820s and '30s to an industrial-capitalist economy, women were increasingly relegated to the private or domestic "sphere" and cut off from the public world of their fathers, husbands, sons and brothers.[2] Whereas women had once been central to the family economy, as farmers, as producers of essential commodities for the family, as workers in home industry, by mid-century many native-born women, especially those in towns and cities, no longer viewed themselves as significant contributors to their local or family economies. It was in this era that the "Cult of True Womanhood" emerged, and in this era that women's power began to reside chiefly in their ability to "influence" men. Newly deemed the moral superiors of men, they were increasingly charged with the responsibilities of rearing and educating children and creating homes that served as havens for their men when they returned each day from the admittedly tainted world of commerce. As men gained greater wealth, women became more active consumers, and their homes and their bodies became the showpieces for their family's financial success. The values of gentility began to conflict with the values of domesticity, and women became increasingly idle and peripheral. Ironically, then, but not coincidentally, women faced a world of shrinking opportunities at the very time when political and economic doors opened wider for white males from all classes of society.

One possible response to these restrictions was to attempt, through political activity, to change the conditions that gave rise to them in the first place; this was the alternative pursued by the woman's rights movement as symbolized by the Seneca Falls convention of 1848. Another response was the one introduced by Miriam Whitcher, who sought to change the *effects* of these restrictions by persuading women to alter their behavior. Her humor decried women's preoccupation with the latest fashions, their meanspiritedness, their lack of charity toward others, their propensity to fill their days with useless and malicious gossip, to name only a few of the targets of her satire.

Whitcher was not the first woman writer to focus on a manifestation of the society's ills rather than its origins in the political arena. Jane Austen, for example, was keenly critical of the frivolity of idle women's behavior, while George Eliot, in "Silly Novels by Lady Novelists," took to task a whole host of women novelists for their "busy idleness":

The standing apology for women who become writers without any special qualification is, that society shuts them out from other spheres of occupation. Society is a very culpable entity, and has to answer for the manufacture of many unwholesome commodities, from bad pickles to bad poetry. But society, like "matter," and Her Majesty's Government, and other lofty abstractions, has its share of excessive blame as well as excessive praise. Where there is one woman who writes from necessity, we believe there are three women who write from vanity; and besides, there is something so antiseptic in the mere healthy fact of working for one's bread, that the most trashy and rotten kind of feminine literature is not likely to have been produced under such circumstances. "In all labour there is profit"; but ladies' silly novels, we imagine, are less the result of labour than of busy idleness. (218–19)

As surely as the women of Seneca Falls hoped through their political actions to correct the social and political inequalities they perceived, Miriam Whitcher used her social satire as a forum through which women might "see" themselves and mend their ways. As the feminists quickly learned, calling attention to a social wrong was no assurance that it would be cured; if one lone voice could have made such a difference, however, it might well have been Whitcher's.

Frances Miriam Berry (known to her family and friends as Miriam) was born November 1, 1813, in Whitesboro, New York, a small village in Oneida county in the midst of what has come to be called "the burned-over district," the setting for America's "Second Great Awakening" (Cross). One of eleven children (four others died in infancy), Whitcher remained a resident of her father's household for thirty-five years, until 1847, when she married the pastor of the newly founded St. John's Episcopal Church, the Rev. Benjamin William Whitcher. The Whitesboro of Whitcher's childhood and young adulthood was extraordinarily lively, and the Berry family home, a popular inn that faced the village green, offered a perfect perspective from which to observe all the local activities. As the historian Mary Ryan has demonstrated, in the decade following the completion of the Erie Canal (1825–1835), Oneida County experienced great social turbulence. "It was in Oneida County, New York, that Charles Grandison Finney first practiced those 'new measures' that have come to identify the modern evangelical tradition. It was in Oneida County, and pre-eminently Whitestown and Utica, that the fires of revivalism kindled a fervent campaign to rid the world of intemperance, slavery, prostitution, profanity, Sabbath breaking, and nearly every sin a seventh-generation Puritan-turned-Victorian was capable of imagining" (*Middle Class* 11). In 1832, Whitcher herself became a convert at one of Finney's Whitesboro revivals and joined the local Presbyterian church (O'Donnell 13).

The women of the county and of the town of Whitesboro were unusually active during this period, with female moral reform societies of every persuasion abounding in the county. By 1835, even Whitesboro with its population of only 5,000 had at least one such society with 40 members (Ryan, *Middle Class* 117). Women steadily outnumbered men at revival meetings during this period (Johnson), while in their own single-sex societies or associations, they could "band together to defend their homes" against the perceived threats posed by rapid economic change and what Ryan calls a "morally suspicious commercial culture." Through these societies women could use their "influence" in a socially accepted manner—to the community's advantage—and they could recapture, at least temporarily, some of their lost sense of importance to the society at large. "It was in the association, in other words, that the Oneidans of the 1830s and 1840s worked out their (collective) family problems" (Ryan, *Middle Class* 237).

During these same tumultuous years, Whitesboro hosted meetings by representatives of every current fad or cause, from phrenology at the one extreme to abolition at the other. Whitcher herself became an active member in a literary group called "The Moeonian Society," and while she professed to being a shy and lonely person, she was bold enough to read her early burlesque sketches aloud to this society, then published them in the newspaper of nearby Rome, New York, under the title "The Widow Spriggins."[3] Toward the end of this period, she also began to publish her most famous stories in *Neal's Saturday Gazette,* a Philadelphia publication. These sketches, all presented through the Widow Bedott's perspective and in her own language, poke fun at nearly every facet of village life and at the widow herself in her relentless search for a husband. In an 1846 sketch, for example, the widow pursues the recently widowed Timothy Crane to a lecture by a traveling phrenologist named Mr. Vanderbump. Fascinated by Mr. Vanderbump's display of plaster heads, the widow offers this version of his phrenology lecture to a friend who arrives late:

> But that are head that sets aside o' the commentater—the one that's got such a danglin' under lip and flat forrid and runs out to such a pint behind—that's old mother O'Killem, the Irish woman that murdered so many folks—she was an awful critter. He said't wa'n't to be disputed though, that she'd done a master sight o' good to menkind—he reckoned they ought to raise a moniment tew her—'cause any body that lookt at her head couldent presume no longer to doubt the truth o' phreenyology. He told us to observe the shape on't perticlerly. Tou see the forrid's dretful flat—well, that shows how't the intellectible faculties is intirely wantin'. But he dident call it *forrid.* He called it the *hoss frontis.* I s'pose that's'cause its shaped more like a hoss than a human critter—animal propensitudes intirely predominates, you know. That's what makes it stick out so on the back side— that's the *hoss* hindis I s'pose—*hoss frontis* and *hoss hindis,* you know. I felt oncomonly interested when he was a tellin' about her,'cause I've read all about her in "Horrid Murders" —a book I've got—it's the interestinest book I've read in all my life. (*Papers* 64–65)

In contrast to the Aunt Maguire sketches that followed, the Widow Bedott stories are more parodic than satiric, reflecting

Whitcher's confidence that the widow's foolishness would speak for itself.

In her use of vernacular humor as a vehicle for social criticism, Miriam Whitcher was in the vanguard of the American humor tradition that ultimately included writers as diverse as Thomas B. Thorpe, George Washington Harris, Marietta Holley, and Samuel Clemens. Her immediate and only female predecessor was Ann Stephens, who had created a fictive onion farmer named Jonathan Slick who commented on the foibles of the *nouveau riche* of New York society in a series of letters he ostensibly wrote to the folks back home in Connecticut. Like Whitcher, Stephens concerned herself with the behavior of would-be women of fashion, but from the point of view of a naive male narrator whose innocence about high society made him as much a source of derision as were the women he observed. Stephens' immediate predecessor, in turn, was Seba Smith, whose male narrator, Jack Downing, also spoke (and wrote) in his native vernacular tongue. In contrast to Stephens' preoccupation with "society," Smith's primary concern was the politics of the Jacksonian era, at both state and national levels, and his humorous sketches generated a host of imitators in the nineteenth century, most of them male and most of them politically conservative.

All the other Northeast humorists familiar to modern scholars, such as James Russell Lowell and B.P. Shillaber, wrote after Miriam Whitcher began publishing her Widow Bedott sketches.[4] In the half century that followed, women humorists such as Sara Willis Parton (Fanny Fern) and Marietta Holley (Josiah Allen's Wife) would rediscover the remarkable versatility and authenticity a female persona afforded them in their humorous social criticism, but Miriam Whitcher's particular form of social satire represented groundbreaking work: she was the first vernacular humorist to create a female narrator, and the first to focus almost exclusively upon women's domestic sphere.[5]

In May, 1847, Whitcher moved with her husband, William, to Elmira, New York, where she encountered social expectations and community values surprisingly different from those of Whitesboro. A larger town than Whitesboro, Elmira was also experiencing more dramatic social and economic changes, accompanied by rapid social mobility, as the example of one man will illustrate. In 1819, a thirty-year-old itinerant salesman named John Arnot arrived in Elmira on what his admiring biographer called "a mercantile venture" (Towner 114–15; Mellor 1261–67). In the 1820s he married the daughter of his chief business rival, Stephen Tuttle, and by the end of the decade had established himself as the foremost merchant in the town. John Arnot had a hand in nearly every business enterprise of the time: he was a stockholder, director, then president of the Chemung Canal Bank; he brought the Erie Railroad into Elmira; he took over the local gas company; and he extended the Northern Central Railroad into the lucrative coal fields of northern Pennsylvania. By the 1860s, he had become arguably the most powerful and wealthy man in Elmira, and he passed that legacy on to his sons. Such a classic rags-to-riches story would certainly have taken place in Utica during the decades following the construction of the Erie Canal, but not in the village of Whitesboro, only a few miles away; its economic structure remained remarkably stable.

Unlike the women of Whitesboro, the women of Elmira in mid-century apparently had no tradition of community involvement in reform societies, no strong sense of allegiance with their churches, and little or no interest in literary matters, making them, as far as Whitcher was concerned, not especially "agreeable companions." Instead, according to Whitcher,

> the women generally are pretty much occupied with cooking, fixing, scandal & quilting. The last named accomplishment is carried to an extent almost beyond belief (by the way my quilt was sent home the other day—I would not let them put nearly as much work on it, as they wanted to—it is thus—very pretty—) There seems to be a perfect passion for quilting among the ladies—& a great strife to

have the most elaborate patterns. Mrs Luce has one that has
more work on than any other that I ever saw—but she says it
will bear no comparison with many in the village—& their
stitches are the least—nay—less than the least you ever saw.
I wouldn't dare have them see those I brought from home,
yes I would too—for I wish them to know that I don't care
for such things.[6]

Viewed from a political perspective, the women of Elmira
as Whitcher depicted them in her humor illustrate precisely
why their relegation to the private sphere denigrated women
instead of elevating them to a superior status, as the apologists
for the status quo argued. With no significant role to play in a
community that was experiencing rapid social and economic
change, many women found little better than gossip and
scandal to occupy their time; however, without the political
point of view of the suffragettes, Whitcher assumed that the
women themselves were responsible for their own
degradation. Focusing thus on the symptoms of the ills,
Whitcher held women up to public scrutiny in her humor and
in effect asked them to see their own reflections there and to
reform accordingly.

Her humor recorded, too, her personal frustrations with
Elmira society. Separated from her family and missing
especially her sister Kate to whom she felt a life-long
closeness, she also had to adjust to her new role as a minister's
wife. Frustrated by her husband's inability to have more effect
on his congregation, by the wretched condition of their small
house, by their difficulty in managing on his small salary,
Whitcher gave a prominent role to a minister and his wife in a
new series of sketches she created at the request of Louis
Godey for his *Lady's Book*.[7] She also created a new persona,
Aunt Maguire.

Like her fictive sister, the Widow Bedott, Aunt Maguire
spoke in a rustic tongue, unaided by any narrative
intervention, but unlike her sister, Aunt Maguire was not
herself the target of Whitcher's humor. The Widow Bedott, a
recognizable if exaggerated humorous type, monopolized all

conversations, relentlessly pursued every available widower in two separate villages, gossiped unmercifully, especially about other widows, and laced her speech, unconsciously, with malapropisms that confirmed her foolishness. As a fool, as an object of humor, the Widow Bedott could personify Whitcher's sense of good-natured absurdity; however, when Whitcher became more acutely aware of the extent to which social pretentiousness had taken hold of many women's lives (and when those values that she labeled "genteel" increasingly impinged upon her own life) she needed a persona who could mediate between her own frustrations and her pointed and satiric observations about female society. What Whitcher needed, in short, was a more moderate voice and a woman endowed with greater common sense and compassion; she needed what Walter Blair has termed a "horse-sense philosopher." Thus Whitcher created Aunt Maguire: she was at once a social commentator and an established, respected figure in her fictive community, Scrabble Hill. Aunt Maguire was not Miriam Whitcher, nor did she speak with her voice, but she was Whitcher's spokesperson and, as we shall see, her apologist.

From the beginning, the Aunt Maguire sketches enjoyed popular success with both Louis Godey and the readers of his *Lady's Book,* while they chronicled Whitcher's growing dissatisfaction with life in Elmira. The third sketch, for example, which Godey claimed "called forth a general burst of praise from one end of the Union to the other," was written in anxious anticipation of an event planned for the Whitchers during their first year in Elmira (311). Because ministers were paid so little (and had such difficulty collecting their salaries, at that), local church members frequently sponsored annual "donation parties" for the minister and his family, donating to the family commodities that would help see them through the year. In reality, Whitcher was pleasantly surprised at how well their donation party went, in spite of her expectations that it would be a "trying time" (Letters, Nov. 8, 1847, 4). The parishioners were generous and inventive in their contributions: 11 loaves of cake, 24 lbs. of coffee, 1 bottle of prunes, 1 lounge from the upholsterer, dozens of yards of fabric (mostly calico) but also 1 1/2 yards "*yaller* flannel," and 2 pairs of baby shoes, to name only a few items. Never at ease in public gatherings, Miriam Whitcher nonetheless presented herself to advantage; as several people told her husband, they "were agreeably disappointed in his wife—had thought until that evening that she was distant and haughty" (Letters, Nov. 29, 1847, 2).

The donation party Aunt Maguire narrates, however, is quite a different matter, revealing Whitcher's deep distrust of her new neighbors. In "Parson Scrantum's Donation Party," the parishioners bring only the most paltry gifts (ribbons, pins, a half round of cheese), consume most of the food they donate, and generally behave badly. Especially singled out for ridicule are "seminary gals" who throw sausages around the rooms and break dishes and lamps. In the end the donation party costs the minister and his wife so much money and anguish that he resigns and announces his intention to move his family to a different parish where he hopes they will never be given another donation party.

> [Parson Scrantum]: "Brethren, since I come among you, I've done my best to be a faithful pastor—if I've failed I hope to be forgiven. At first I had an idee that I should be able to rub along, on my small salary; and I don't know, but I might a done it, if it hadn't a ben for *one thing*." Here he paused. "What was *that?*" says Deacon Peabody. Mr. Scrantum continued—"I've ben here tew years, and you've had the kindness to give me tew donation parties. I've stood it so fur, but I can't stand it no longer; brethren, I feel convinced that *one more donation party* would completely *break me down*." (*Papers* 271)

The next three sketches set off a raging controversy in Elmira, reflecting as they did not imaginary problems, as in the "Donation Party," but actual events and people of Elmira.

With what must have been the best of intentions, the Rev.
Whitcher urged his female parishioners to begin a sewing
society as a means of raising money for charity; he also
persuaded his reluctant wife to participate (Letters, Dec. 19,
1847, 5). The November 1848 issue of the *Lady's Book* carried
Aunt Maguire's account of the founding of just such a society
while a story in the January 1849 issue told about the first two
meetings of the group. One woman, Miss Samson Savage,
dominated the society (even in her absence), and she bore the
brunt of Whitcher's satiric thrust:

> She was always a coarse, boisterous, high-tempered critter,
> and when her husband grow'd rich, she grow'd pompous
> and overbearin'. She made up her mind she'd rule the roast,
> no matter what it cost—she'd be the *first* in Scrabble Hill.
> She know'd she wa'n't a lady by natur nor by eddication, but
> she thought mabby other folks would be fools enough to
> think she was if she made a great parade. So she begun by
> dressin' more, and givin' bigger parties than any body else.
> Of course, them that thinks money's the main thing (and
> ther's plenty such here and every where), is ready to flatter
> her and make a fuss over her, and approve of all her dewin's.
> If ther's any body that *won't* knuckle tew her, I tell ye they
> have to take it *about east*. She abuses'em to their faces and
> slanders'em to their backs. (*Papers* 303)

Angered because the sewing society began when she was
out of town, Miss Samson Savage "drops in" on a meeting to
"see what they're up tew." She refuses the women's invitation
to join the society until she knows its purpose, and when she
learns that the women want "to arn enough to repair the
meetin'-house and build a new pulpit," she expresses nothing
but contempt:

> "I'd look purty wouldent I, a workin' to fix up that meetin'-
> house for Tuttle to preach in! . . . He don't know nothin'—
> can't preach no mor'n *that stove-pipe*"—(she hates Parson
> Tuttle 'cause he hain't never paid no more attention to her
> than he has to the rest o' the congregation)—"he's as green as
> grass and as flat as a pancake. . . . I despise Tuttle, and I'll

tell him so tew his face when I git a chance. Ye don't ketch me a slanderin' folks behind ther backs and then soft-soapin' 'em to their faces, as some folks dew . . . . And where's his wife, I'd like to know? Why ain't *she* here to work today? A purty piece o' bisness, I must say, for you all to be here a diggin' away to fix up Tuttle's meetin-house when *she's* to hum a playin' *lady*." . . . And from that she went on and blazed away about Miss Tuttle at a terrible rate. Miss Stillman and Polly Mariar, and a number more o' the wimmin, sot tew and helped her whenever they could git a word in edgeways; and such a haulin' over as Miss Tuttle and the parson got, I never heerd afore in all the days o' my life. (*Papers* 307–09)

Heretofore, Whitcher scholars have assumed that Miss Samson Savage was a wholly fictitious character, or at most a composite figure. Whitcher's letters, however, reveal that within days of the *Lady's Book* arriving in Elmira, she was identified as the author of the sketch, and

Mrs Arnot was recognised at once, to her infinite rage and that of her friends & *toad-eaters*. As she is almost universally disliked of course there is a deal of crowing & triumphing at seeing her taken off. William's enemies are making a handle of it to injure him, & some of his friends are so much afraid of the miserable woman, & such worshippers of money, that they are dreadfully alarmed. There are some who are bold enough to stand by their minister & tell him to fear nothing, but let the "galled jade wince." It is not very pleasant for me, who have hitherto been so retired & unnoticed here, to be thus hauled into notoriety, & subjected to all sorts of mean insults from Mrs Arnot & her clique, as I shall be. (Letters, Dec 28, 1848, 2)

The complexities of the issue unfold in layers as one digs further into the details of history and biography that underlie the sketch and the characterization of Miss Samson Savage. Mrs. Arnot, Whitcher's life model, was the wife of the Horatio Alger figure mentioned previously; he, too, is described in the sketch:

When they first come to our place, he was a follerin' the tin-peddlin' bisness; he used to go rumblin' round in his cart from house to house, and the rich folks ruther turned up their noses at him, or he consated they did, and it made him awful wrathy; so he detarmined he'd be richer'n any on'em, and pay'em off in their own coin. Old Smith says he's heerd him time and agin make his boast that he'd ride over all their heads some day—dident seem to have no higher eend in view than to be the richest man in Scrabble Hill. He sot his heart and soul and body on't, and knowin' how to turn every cent to the best advantage, and bein' wonderful sharp at a bargain, he succeeded; every thing he took hold of prospered, and without actilly bein' what you could call dishonest, afore many years every body allowed he was the richest man in the place. (*Papers* 302)

Whitcher transforms Mrs. Arnot into a Vermont-born seamstress, while the minister whom Miss Savage maligns in the sketch is given Mrs. Arnot's maiden name, Tuttle. With a clever but thinly disguised twist, Whitcher has Mrs. Arnot (Miss Samson Savage) malign her own family (Tuttle).

Whitcher could not have seriously expected to get away with her portrayal of Mrs. Arnot, nor could she have been seriously surprised to have her authorship revealed. She knew in advance that one of her neighbors had visited Whitesboro and learned there that she was the author of the Widow Bedott sketches, which was the only identification given to the author of the Aunt Maguire sketches, and her "Donation Party" story had been reprinted on the front page of the Elmira *Gazette* in May of 1848. She also had been forewarned that the characters in the "Sewing Society" sketch were too thinly veiled: "The first article I wrote, William wouldn't let me send—he thought the characters would certainly be recognized and make trouble. The last one too, he thought too personal, and would not consent to my sending it for some time. I tried a third time, but I was discouraged & gave it up in despair. So after suggesting some slight alterations he permitted me to send the second" (Letters, Oct. 12, 1848, 3).

As this letter suggests, Whitcher sent off her second version of the article knowing that it might ultimately expose her authorship, but she was willing to take that risk in order to satirize the behavior that so offended her; she also believed that its comic potential was too great to pass up. The Elmira *Gazette* fueled the rumors that "the author of these articles resides among us" by publishing the "Sewing Society" sketch in their December 28 issue, then reprinting two Widow Bedott stories in January and February of 1849. Neither Miriam nor William Whitcher could have anticipated, however, how fully the humor would hit home, and not only in Elmira:

> I wrote him [Godey] yesterday & gave him an account of the fuss here, & begged him to notice in the Dollar that several villages were contending for the honor of being the birth place of "Mrs Samson Savage," which is an amusing fact. A man from a village in Seneca county, came into one of our bookstores the other day to get some Lady's Books, saying that they were all alive about it in his place, because they had a Mrs Samson Savage there. And we have heard from Havana—a village twenty miles from here—they have fitted the coat to a woman there. . . . (Letters, Dec. 28, 1848, 3)

"The commotion caused by the article," Whitcher wrote her Whitesboro family, did not subside, partly because of the fury of the Arnots and their friends, and partly because the townspeople took great delight in identifying their Elmira neighbors by the names given them in the sketches: "Every body insists upon applying Mrs Samson Savage to Mrs Arnot. She goes by the name every where, & her admirers or echoes, are called the 'Stillman family.' The young man Capt. Hasted of whom I spoke in a letter some time ago as being the beau of Mrs T. . . . is called universally 'Cappen Smalley,' & they say it cuts him to death" (Letters, Jan. 1, 1849, 1). Nor was the fire extinguished for many years to come. A resident of Elmira who was interviewed nearly half a century after the sketch was published still held a grudge against Miriam Whitcher, but for a curious mixture of reasons.

"Know her? Yes I did! She was an awful woman. She slandered everybody. It was awful. She put me and my sister in the book. We were the Peabodys." "But," [the interviewer] says, "she didn't say so much about the Peabodys did she?" "Of course she didn't! You'd a thought our family didn't amount to anything. But we were just as prominent as anybody and I guess we were thought as much of." (Palmer)

In large measure, however, the controversy remained alive because the humor was decidedly on target. Godey could not keep up with the demands for back orders for the January 1848 *Lady's Book,* and subscriptions to his magazine jumped to 40,000 copies monthly by June of the same year, an unprecedented high. Whitcher did acknowledge that it was "imprudent" for her to have written the piece, but, she said, "I could not help it. I thought it a good subject for ridicule. . ." (Letters, Jan. 1, 1849, 1).

By February the Whitchers were still at the center of controversy. Determined to leave Elmira at the first possible opportunity, and actively looking for a new church, they were equally determined not to appear to be driven out by their "enemies," a hope that was not entirely realized. William Whitcher called a vestry meeting at the request of parishioners who wanted him to resign, and summarized the proceedings in these terms:

I called upon the senior warden to state the object of the meeting . . . but he could not tell any object, but that it [seemed] best to meet & talk over the state of the Parish. I then read to them my statement of its affairs which made two of them bite their lips, i.e. Mr Luce and Mr Hatch. Mr Hatch had appropriated $140, of the churches money to his own use, my allusion to this sealed his mouth effectually when he began his complaints. Mr Luce next began to complain of my unpopularity, and I convinced the rest of the vestry if not himself, that he had been the main cause of it, which shut him up for the rest of the evening. . . . The conversation then became more general, and the merits of "Aunt Maguires" Article were fully discussed, both as to its local and literary merits, Mr Hatch thot it was silly, (an

opinion in which I suppose all the Stillman family will
agree) others thought it to the life, whether considered as
local or general, and the grand result in regard to it was that
it was a very small affair for ten grave men to talk seriously
of allowing it to disturb the harmony of a Parish. (Letters,
Feb. 12, 1849, 4)

At the end of the meeting, William Whitcher asked for a vote
of confidence from the vestry, which he received, then
announced his intention to resign as soon as possible. "All
went home apparently well satisfied" (Letters, Feb. 12, 1849,
5). Miriam Whitcher's opportunity to leave came almost
immediately, for she was called home to Whitesboro in March
to attend to her dying father. When she left Elmira, she vowed
privately never to return again, and she did not. Her husband
stayed on for a few more months, then still unable to find a
position in another church, nevertheless resigned his Elmira
parish and joined his wife in Whitesboro.

From the greater security of Whitesboro, Whitcher wrote
her final words on the Elmira events in a sketch that reflected
a new understanding on Whitcher's part that the way women
behaved in Elmira was symptomatic of a larger social malaise.
Capitalizing on the fact that villages other than Elmira thought
their own sewing societies had been satirized in the *Lady's
Book,* Whitcher has Aunt Maguire travel to a neighboring
village to visit her husband's relatives. While she is there, the
latest issue of the *Lady's Book* arrives, and the village gossips
have a field day because it contains a story that they think is
based on *their* sewing society.

> "Oh," says Miss Hawkins, "as true as I'm a live woman, it's
> got every one of our members in, and shows us all up
> shamefully, only jest me and Sary Ann. I can't see as ther's
> any body in it that resembles us a mite. But you're drawed
> out, Miss Teeters; and Cappen Sapley, he's down large as
> life; and the Bomans are in for't, and so's Bill Sweezen's
> wife, and Samanthy Cooper, and Tom Baily's wife, and Miss
> Ben Curtis; and there's a Miss Stillman and her daughter,
> that's meant for the Longs. They're all fictitious names, to be

sure, but it's easy enough to tell who's who. But the squire's wife ketches it the worst of all. I tell ye, it takes her off to fits. Nobody can mistake it."

"But how do you know it actilly means your Society?"

"Oh, that's plain enough," says Miss Hawkins, "for it tells things that was positively said and done at some o' the meetin's. Jest how the squire's wife went on; calls her 'Miss Samson Savage.' . . . But the mystery to me is, how the minister's wife got hold on't. She wa'n't there. Somebody that *was* there must a told her. I wonder who't was?" (*Papers* 317–18)

As in Elmira, the local minister's wife is "blamed" for writing the story, only this time it is a different town where the minister's wife is in fact innocent. She is, however, maligned by the townspeople in much the same terms Whitcher was in Elmira:

"I say," says Miss Teeters, says she, "it's high time we got rid o' the minister; he ain't the man for us. A ginteel and intellectible congregation like our'n had ought to have a man o' great eloquential powers. And as for his wife, I never could bear her, with her old stripid dress that she wears every Sunday, rain or shine. I don't believe she was ever accustomed to ginteel society."

"Nor I neither," says Miss Hawkins. "I took a dislike tew her when they first come here. I don't like yer mum characters that never say nothin' about nobody. It seems she's ben savin' on't up to let off in the newspapers. Bethiar Nobles says she told her she thought our congregation drest tew much; and I shouldent wonder if she did, for she' stuck to that old straw bunnit and everlastin' stripid dress all winter, and I s'pose it's to set an example o' plainness afore us, jest as if we'd foller *her* lead. For my part, I think she might better spend more time a dressin', and less a writin' for the newspapers. And they say he incourages her in it, and likes to have her write. I wish they was both furder off."

"I wish so tew," says Miss Teeters; "and I guess ther's a good many that wish so. She ain't popilar at all in our set. She never runs in sociably, as Miss Van Duzen used to. They say she goes a great deal more among the poor folks, than she does among the ginteel part o' the congregation. And that's a sure sign, *I think,* that she's ben more accustomed to minglin' with them sort o' folks, than with such as we be." (*Papers* 319–20)

Aunt Maguire's cousin comes to the minister's defense (after all the other neighbors have left, of course), giving Whitcher one more chance to blaze away at the hypocrisy of the villagers and to make a curious but familiar apology for her own writing—it brought in much-needed income:

> As soon as they'd gone, Eunice burst out laughin', and says she: "Well, if that ain't the best piece o' news I've heerd this many a day. I've always heerd that that Sewin' Society was a reg'lar slander-mill, where the principal busines is to brew mischief against the minister; and I'm glad they've got showed up at last. The minister's a good man, and a smart man tew; but the biggest part o' the congregation is such a set of ignoramuses, that they don't know a smart man from a fool. They always make a great fuss over their minister when he first comes; but if he don't preach smooth things tew'em all the time, they soon contrive to starve him out or quarrel him off. When they gin this one a call, they agreed to give him five hundred dollars a year, and pay it quarterly. And it is a solemn fact, that half on't hain't ben paid yet. Betsey Hall, a girl that used to wash for'em sometimes, told me so. She said she'd often listened to the door, and heerd the minister and his wife a talkin' over their troubles; and she says that ther ain't more'n half a dozen in the congregation that pay their dues reglarly; and if't wa'n't for what the minister's wife gits for writin' for the newspapers, they wouldent be able to pay their house-rent and keep out o' debt, no way." (*Papers* 320–21)

The story then takes a curious and improbable turn: Aunt Maguire suddenly realizes that she herself may be to blame for all the trouble because she once "told" Mr. Godey about her own sewing circle back in Scrabble Hill; she surmises that he wrote up her conversation in the form of a story and published it in his magazine. Ashamed of the harm she unintentionally caused the innocent minister's wife, she decides to seek her out and apologize for the trouble she has caused. The minister's wife immediately absolves her of all responsibility:

> "Well I'm glad you feel so," says I; "but ain't it curus that the Slabtown folks should take it all to themselves as they dew?"
>
> "Not at all," says she; "human natur's the same every where."
>
> "I guess so," says I. "Any how, your Sewin' Society must be wonderfully like our'n, or they wouldent be so detarmined it means them; but what hurts my feelin's is, that you should have to suffer for't. I was so distrest when I heerd they was a layin' on't to you, and usin' on't to injure yer husband, that I felt as if I must come right over and see you, though you was a stranger. If any body's to blame, I'm willin' to bear it."
>
> "O fie" says she, "don't you fret yourself a bit about it. If people choose to fit your coats to their own backs,'t ain't your fault; and if they fit nice and snug, perhaps they'll do as good service as if they were made expressly for'em."
>
> "Jest so," says I. "But it does seem tew bad that you should suffer for't. Ain't ther no way o' puttin' a stop tew it?"
>
> "Never you mind," says she; "we minister's folks must have our trials, of one sort or another, wherever we go. If we hadent this perhaps we should have somethin' still worse."
>
> "But," says I, "what if they should drive you away from here?"
>
> She smiled, and dident say nothin'.
>
> "Well," says I, "to judge from what I've seen o' Slabtown since I come here, I'm bold to say that, if they do drive you away, they can't possibly drive you to a worse place."
>
> "Hush, Aunt Magwire," says she, "human natur's the same every where; we must expect trouble wherever we go. I feel prepared for almost any thing." . . .
>
> I come away a few days after that, and I ruther guess it'll be a good while afore I go a visitin' to Slabtown agin. The place is tew awful *ginteel* to suit my taste. (*Papers* 342–44)

In spite of the Slabtown minister's wife's brave statements, Miriam Whitcher was not ultimately prepared for the fate that awaited them; during the next several years, the Whitchers suffered irreparable harm as a result of the events in Elmira.

William Whitcher was unable to find another permanent position, as word of his wife's satiric writing preceded them at every available parish. Impoverished, Miriam Whitcher remained at home in Whitesboro with her mother, unmarried sisters, and infant daughter, while William accepted temporary assignments that kept them apart for long stretches of time. The letters that passed between them reveal the strains of the separation and the bitterness of their poverty, and Miriam Whitcher soon lost heart for satire; she wrote only a few more Widow Bedott stories for the *Saturday Gazette,* then turned all her energies to writing a pious novel that she never finished. In January of 1852, at the age of 39, Miriam Whitcher died of tuberculosis.

When modern feminists first encounter the humor of Miriam Whitcher, they often express impatience with her propensity to cast her satiric barbs almost exclusively at women. Aside from a pompous minister who marries the Widow Bedott, the only men who come in for sustained humorous criticism are reformers or faddists, such as the phrenologist, Mr. Vanderbump. Women were always at the heart of her work as both the subjects and objects of her humor, but they were held up to ridicule so they might "see" themselves and mend their ways. The growing harshness with which she judged other women was at once a reflection of her own experience of genteel society and her growing disappointment at the way women behaved in that society. Her humor, then, was not only an outlet for personal frustrations and disappointments but was also intended to serve as a social corrective.

In the last analysis, that Whitcher did not have the political perspective enjoyed by her contemporaries at Seneca Falls makes her no less a critic of the restricted role women occupied in mid-nineteenth-century American society. It would be a quarter century later before another American woman humorist, Marietta Holley, would add that political, feminist perspective to the rich legacy she inherited from

Miriam Whitcher: a robust sense of humor; a primary focus on women and women's concerns; a strong-minded, common-sensical, outspoken female protagonist; and a clear sense that women's lives were demeaned by the tenets of gentility.

Notes

1. See, for example, Cott, Fetterley, Harris, Ryan, Sklar, Smith-Rosenberg, and Welter.

2. Mary P. Ryan, for example, notes that between 1820 and 1835 in Oneida County, "home manufacturing of textiles declined to one-fourth of its former volume" (*Middle Class* 64).

3. Rome *Democratic Sentinel* (April 30–August 20, 1839). This novella was posthumously reprinted in *Widow Spriggins, Mary Elmer, and Other Sketches*.

4. Lowell's first *Biglow Papers* was published in 1848, while Shillaber's popular Mrs. Partington appeared in book form first in 1854.

5. Although not strictly speaking a Northeast humorist, Caroline Kirkland did publish *A New Home—Who Will Follow?* in 1839, the year Whitcher published her Widow Spriggins series in the Rome newspaper; Kirkland is widely considered to be America's first woman prose humorist.

6. Letter of June 27, 1847, 1–2, to her sister. Whitcher Letters, Manuscript Collection, New York Historical Society. I am especially indebted to Jenny Lawrence for giving me a copy of the official typed transcription she prepared for the New York Historical Society. All further references are to the typed transcription.

7. For a discussion of the declining influence of the American clergy during this period, see Ann Douglas, especially Chapter 1.

Works Cited

Blair, Walter. *Horse Sense in American Humor, from Benjamin Franklin to Ogden Nash*. New York: Russell & Russell, 1962.

Buhle, Mari Jo and Paul Buhle, eds. *The Concise History of Woman Suffrage: Selections from The Classic Work of Stanton, Anthony, Gage and Harper*. Urbana: U of Illinois P, 1978.

Cott, Nancy F. *The Bonds of Womanhood: "Woman's Sphere"* in *New England, 1790–1835*. New Haven: Yale UP, 1977.

Cross, Whitney R. *The Burned-Over District: The Social and Intellectual History of Enthusiastic Religion in Western New York, 1800–1850*. Ithaca: Cornell UP, 1950.

Douglas, Ann. *The Feminization of American Culture*. New York: Knopf, 1977.

Eliot, George. *Essays and Uncollected Papers*. Boston: Houghton Mifflin, 1908. Vol. 22 of The Writings of George Eliot.

Fetterley, Judith, ed. *"Introduction." Provisions: A Reader from 19th-Century American Women*. Bloomington: Indiana UP, 1985. 1–40.

Godey, Louis. *Godey's Lady's Book 36* (1848): 311.

Harris, Barbara J. *"The Cult Of Domesticity"* in *Beyond Her Sphere: Women and the Professions in American History*. Westport: Greenwood P, 1978.

Johnson, Paul E. *A Shopkeeper's Millenium: Society and Revivals in Rochester, New York, 1815–1837*. New York: Hill & Wang, 1978.

Mellor, George A. "The Arnots of Elmira." *Chemung County Historical Journal* (1964): 1261–67.

O'Donnell, Thomas F. "The Return of the Widow Bedott: Mrs. F.M. Whitcher of Whitesboro and Elmira." *New York History* 55 (1974): 5–34.

Palmer, Mrs. George Archibald. *Elmira Telegram 4* Nov. 1923.

Ryan, Mary P. *Cradle of the Middle Class: The Family in Oneida County, New York, 1790–1865*. Cambridge: Cambridge UP, 1981.

———. *"Creating Woman's Sphere,"* in *Womanhood in America: From Colonial Times to the Present*. 2nd ed. New York: Watts, 1979.

Sklar, Kathryn Kish. *Catharine Beecher: A Study in American Domesticity*. New Haven: Yale UP, 1973.

Smith-Rosenberg, Carroll. *Disorderly Conduct: Visions of Gender in Victorian America*. New York: Oxford UP, 1985.

Towner, Asburn. *Our Country and Its People: A History of the Valley and County of Chemung from the Closing Years of the Eighteenth Century*. Syracuse: Mason, 1892.

Welter, Barbara. "The Cult of True Womanhood: 1820–1860." *American Quarterly 18* (1966): 151–74.

Whitcher, F.M. *Whitcher Letters. MS Collection*. New York Historical Society, New York City.

———. *The Widow Bedott Papers*. New York: Mason, 1880.

———. *Widow Spriggins, Mary Elmer, and Other Sketches*. New York: Carleton, 1867.

The Play's the Thing:
Anna Cora Mowatt Catches the
Fashion Conscience

Jacqueline O'Connor

Anna Cora Mowatt's play *Fashion*, an American social comedy written and performed in 1845, holds an important place in the history of American theater; the entry on Mowatt in *American Women Writers* calls it the "first American social comedy" (482). Not all critics give it this status. In John Hartman's study of this dramatic genre, he includes *Fashion*, but sees it as part of a tradition that began with *The Contrast*, produced eighty years earlier (47). Critics do agree, however, that Mowatt's play furthered the development of American drama; prior to it, Margaret Opasta tells us, "native plays were blatantly imitative of European models. There was little to mark them as American and little to recommend them at all. *Fashion* was refreshingly different" (44).

American audiences at the time seemed especially skeptical that a play by one of their women could interest or please them. Nothing more adequately shows the prejudice Mowatt faced than the prologue written for *Fashion* by the playwright's friend, Epes Sargent, quoted in *The Lady of Fashion:*

> *Fashion a Comedy*— I'll go, but stay—
> Now I read farther, 'tis a native play!
> Bah! Homemade calicoes are well enough,
> But homemade dramas must be stupid stuff.
> Had it the London stamp, 'twould do—but then,

"For plays we lack the manners and the men!"
Thus speaks one critic. Hear another's creed:—
What! From a woman's pen? It takes a man
To write a comedy—no woman can. (Barnes, 138)

The prologue points out Mowatt's double disadvantage, as American and woman, nonetheless imploring the audience to give the play a chance, and grant "that some wit may grow on native soil, / And Art's fair fabric rise from woman's toil" (Barnes, 139). The play proceeded to dispel the doubts that a piece burdened by such liabilities could succeed, and *Fashion* enjoyed profitable runs in New York and Philadelphia.

When the play was staged in London a few years after its opening in New York, one critic approvingly noted that "America is worthily repaying the dramatic debt she owes us" with a play "worthy to take its place by the side of the best of English comedies" (Barnes, 288). While not every London critic was as kind, Mowatt tells us in her autobiography that "of twenty-seven criticisms by the London press, twenty were favorable," modestly adding that perhaps "the quality of mercy was strained" (Mowatt, 324). Mr. Jenkins of the *Morning Post* began by informing his readers that since "genius is of no sex," he would judge Mowatt's work impersonally; he goes on to attack her for appearing at the final curtain "ready dressed for the occasion." Jenkins was then attacked by another critic for not being "manly" in criticizing a woman so (324–25). The author's gender clouded critical opinion, and it was easier to overcome the prejudice against her nationality than against her sex.

"Scribbling women" often prompted the kind of prologue statement I quoted earlier; the void of scholarly material available on these women, including Mowatt, gives evidence that the bias continues in this century. Eric Barnes' book is the only one, besides her own autobiography, written about Mowatt, and Barnes concerns himself less with assessing her work than with reconstructing her life as a romantic melodrama. While the book proves useful for the facts he provides about her careers (she was both playwright and actor), serious criticism is sacrificed to dramatic frivolity.

Most critical surveys of American drama do include some mention of *Fashion,* noting its historical importance and the quality of its construction. Even though theater historians, in their surveys of this period, often focus more on Mowatt's acting skills, they document the success of the play. While Barnard Hewitt claims her most important contribution was that "she proved that a lady could be an actress and by inference that an actress could be a lady," he also acknowledged that *Fashion* was outstanding, for in a "day when three or four performances were good for a new play, it ran three weeks and was withdrawn, still popular, to make way for previously engaged stars" (140–41).

Daniel F. Havens, in his 1931 study of the development of American social comedy, writes that "Mrs. Mowatt has herself shaped the old tradition toward the newer, more sophisticated and polished tradition of social comedy on the American stage today" (148). Arthur Quinn's assessment of the play's content is representative, stating that the play "is that rare thing, a social satire based on real knowledge of the life it depicts, but painting it without bitterness, without nastiness, and without affectation" (312). Finally, Perley Issac Reed maintains that "it was not until the popularity of 'Fashion' and similar succeeding pieces that the society play as a genre could be recognized" (121).

The play's popularity is one reason that Karen Halttunen includes mention of it in *Confidence Men and Painted Women*, a study of 19th century middle-class culture. Her book charts the anxiety resulting from the class fluidity of the early part of the century, an anxiety embodied in the figure of the confidence man. He was a trickster figure who said one thing and meant another, coercing those around him to do likewise. To battle his evil, ante-bellum advice manuals promoted the cult of sincerity: a guard against hypocrisy, a "new code of conduct, within which men could meet without suspicion, without fear of betrayal by confidence men" (51).

Halttunen goes on to argue that as society approached the half century mark, however, this sentimental code eventually became itself a source of anxiety, for it grew artificial and hypocritical. As Halttunen points out in her conclusion: "Despite its hostility to fashion, sentimentalism was, in sociological terms, a form of fashion" (194). Her interest in fashion seems ample reason for her to discuss Mowatt's play with that title, but she makes it clear that there is another reason for its inclusion, as the play provides a "useful focal point for a discussion of the cultural transformation of the American middle classes at mid-nineteenth century" (153). She maintains that the popularity of the play testified to society's newfound ability to have a "broad sense of humor about social issues that had been the source of profound anxiety a few years earlier" (153).

Essentially, then, Halttunen agrees with Quinn that the play, despite its satirical view of society, should not be taken too seriously. She claims that *Fashion*, by its very existence and by its popularity, demonstrates that "the sentimental culture of the early Victorian period was yielding by mid-century to the new theatricality of high Victorian middle-class culture" (195). But my discussion will suggest that Mowatt's play covertly attacks the cultural norms that it upholds on the surface, and that *Fashion* dramatizes gentility and vulgarity and finds fault with both. Paradoxically, it is through a study of the humor of the play, the humor that earns *Fashion* its reputation as a "good-natured satire," that I will uncover the work's ambiguity: while the playwright attacks the fashionable pretentiousness of the nouveau riche overtly, with considerable subtlety she also undermines the home-spun values that counter the mores of fashion.

Nancy Walker's observations in her aptly named study on women's humor, *A Very Serious Thing*, provide a context for classifying Mowatt's comic style. In Chapter Two of her book,

Walker cites a number of critics who identify the clash between the vulgar and the genteel traditions as perhaps the most distinctive characteristic of American humor (42). She argues that "the dominant tradition of American humor, then, turns upon the freedom of the male to enjoy, to joke, to criticize, to question" (44). Her discussion of female humorists focuses on the fact that women's humor is distinct from men's, and uses different forms that do not appear in the male tradition; these forms express "women's sense of isolation from the dominant culture and frustration with their assigned role" (48). *Fashion* appears to be an interesting exception, a work in the male tradition written by a woman.

Certainly, *Fashion* dramatizes the conflict between the vulgar and the genteel traditions, for its plot centers around a would-be fashionable social climber, Mrs. Tiffany, whose goal is to bury her vulgar past (she was a milliner) and show the world how genteel she has become. Her pretentiousness is foiled by her own stupidity, her sister's insistence on remembering their humble past, but most of all by the appearance of a country farmer friend of her husband, a man who reveres simplicity and abhors fashion. The play contains a generous helping of the conventional complications and resolutions of social comedy (a foolish impostor, a secret rendezvous, and the discovery of long-lost relations), and all seems to end as it should with honesty and plainness rewarded, and deceit and affectation reprimanded.

Since the vulgar triumphs over the genteel, Mowatt's play seems to imitate the male tradition; also, the subject matter does not fit the pattern of domestic humor usually identified with women authors. The play features the Stage Yankee Adam Trueman, a "Jonathan" figure whose type was well known to the audience of 1845, but who most often appeared in literature by men. My discussion will show that although Mowatt appropriates male tradition humorous types, she adapts them to her own end: she uses them to point out gender inequalities and to expose the contradictions of both vulgar and genteel values.

In the opening scene, Mowatt draws a complex comparison of Zeke, the black servant, and Mrs. Tiffany, the lady of the house. The latter epitomizes the artificial sense of fashion that the playwright explicitly attacks in the work: Mrs. Tiffany's first words and actions demonstrate her foolish embrace of everything French. She butchers French expressions by Americanizing them in her pronunciation, and Millinette, the French maid on whom she depends for advice, praises her to her face and mocks her in asides. Mrs. Tiffany's speech and extravagant dress demonstrate her belief that external shows of style convince others of one's sense of fashion, and from the outset Mowatt represents this attitude with irreverence and irony.

Mrs. Tiffany is mirrored by the black servant Zeke. Zeke is overwhelmed by the dashing livery he has been given for his new job as the Tiffanys' servant, and indeed the first lines of the play point to his belief that his costume will serve to improve his status, "a coat to take de eyes ob Broadway . . . it am de fixin's dat make de natural born genman" (*Fashion,* 34). He also resembles his mistress in his language, for he aspires to a vocabulary that he has not mastered, much as Mrs. Tiffany aspires to speak French. He fails miserably, as she does, and thereby exposes his foolishness: he asks Millinette her "publicated opinion," inquires about her "special defunctions," and asks her to "lustrify my officials" (35).

We laugh at Zeke and Mrs. Tiffany's foolish aspirations, but the similarities between them suggest that they share more than a need to impress those around them. On the surface Mrs. Tiffany clearly occupies a higher social place than Zeke: she is the employer and he is the employee. But their strikingly similar striving for upward mobility underscores the fact that as woman or as black man, there are limitations to advancement. Zeke cannot be more than a servant, he can only hope to be a dignified one. Mrs. Tiffany can only improve her condition by becoming a more genteel woman—she can rise on the ladder of fashion. Their efforts make them look ridiculous, and we laugh at them, but behind the humor lurks the futility of their situations.

Another point of comparison demonstrates the similarity between these characters and their attempted transformations. Mrs. Tiffany changes Zeke's name to Adolph, claiming Ezekiel "too plebeian an appellation to be uttered in my presence" (36). This name change becomes a source of humor in the play, for the other characters (and Mrs. Tiffany herself when she gets flustered) continue to call him Zeke. Beneath the comic confusion, however, lies a subtle suggestion that social identity is fixed and therefore not as fluid as American myths of upward mobility have suggested.

Mrs. Tiffany also has a more "plebeian appellation" that her sister Prudence reminds her of, much to the former's displeasure. Prudence insists on referring to her sister as "Betsy" rather than Elizabeth, a nickname that Mrs. Tiffany calls "the height of vulgarity" (36). She does not wish to be reminded of her past as a milliner, but Prudence dwells on the subject. Her sister undercuts Mrs. Tiffany's social standing while ostensibly expressing admiration, saying that "I always told you so, Betsy, I always said that you were destined to rise above your station" (36). Mrs. Tiffany's shame about her past explicitly points out her pretentiousness; the details also reveal the illuminating fact that Mrs. Tiffany could improve her status only by marrying a prosperous merchant. Once more this suggests the problems Mrs. Tiffany faces as a woman seeking to advance herself. While her behavior is too foolish for us to condone it, we recognize the limitations the society imposes on her.

Prudence's situation further highlights the prejudices of this social system, for she epitomizes the common spinster stereotype; her character is listed as a maiden lady of a certain age, and her residence in her married sister's home emphasizes her place of no place (34). Her character and actions compare and contrast with the figure of Mr. Snobson, Tiffany's confidential clerk. Both actively but unsuccessfully seek marriage: Prudence blatantly offers herself to Adam Trueman, and Snobson attempts to trade his continued secrecy about his boss's illegal business affairs for Tiffany's daughter, Seraphina. Prudence desires marriage for position rather than money, for she disregards Trueman's wealth; in fact she offers to help run his farm, unconcerned that she will have to work. Snobson surely wants the access to the Tiffany money that would come with the marriage (although he knows of Tiffany's impending financial ruin) but he also wants to upgrade his social status, and vows to become "as fashionable as Mrs. Tiffany herself" (42).

Both Prudence and Snobson are targets of ridicule for Adam Trueman, and both fail in their attempts to improve their condition, but Mowatt does not draw them simply foolish, which we see by comparing them to Mrs. Tiffany. Next to her, Prudence's honest acceptance of their humble past, and her desire to be a farm wife, evokes a certain admiration. If indeed the play attacks pretentiousness, we cannot accuse Prudence of this. She upholds native values but is not rewarded for them; Mowatt's suggestion could be that men profit from embracing simplicity, but women do not profit likewise.

Snobson represents an even more ambiguous social figure. His name implies that he does have social aspirations, and he expresses a desire to be fashionable (he drinks mint juleps daily), but in his encounter with Mrs. Tiffany, he undercuts her adherence to French customs. He speaks plainly, and insists that "we're none French" and that no one be obliged to follow foreign fashions "when they are foreign to their interests" (48). The characters of both Prudence and Snobson resist simple categorization, and the contradictions provide evidence that the play is not simply a victory of vulgarity over gentility.

We should note that Prudence and Snobson come to different ends, and their fates seem to depend upon their respective genders. Both are foiled in their marriage efforts by the actions of Adam Trueman—he spurns Prudence, and sends Snobson packing with a threat to expose the clerk as an accomplice to Tiffany's forgery. But a clear distinction emerges, for Snobson heads for California, banished from this society but hopeful, for "they want men of genius at the West" (61). Though not explicitly stated, Prudence cannot exercise the same kind of option. She must accept her fate as a spinster, powerless to shape her future, and dependent on others for sustenance and social position. With humor, camouflaging the issue with the play's light, comic tone, Mowatt addresses serious gender distinctions that plague the society.

The two young women characters in the play make a sharply contrasting pair for considering further the marital prospects of females. Seraphina, the Tiffanys' daughter, and Gertrude, the governess, the latter ultimately revealed to be Adam Trueman's granddaughter, are objects of matrimonial desire; we can assess these young women by considering which men prefer them, and the women's responses to the males' advances. Seraphina professes affection for every man who tries to claim her, and lacks the intelligence to discriminate among her own feelings, or to judge the men's sincerity. She agrees to marry the count impostor and elopes with this two-timing confidence man, the marriage prevented only by the fact that they must return for her jewels (the count's falseness has by then come to light). The play closes with no promise of a marriage for Seraphina, for her other suitors have since disappeared. Trueman recommends that Tiffany take his wife and daughter to the country to learn "home virtues," a development that puts Seraphina out of the marriage game, back with her family for more preparation. The only hope for Seraphina is that the additional time will provide the necessary reform and education, and thus give her a chance for marital success.

Gertrude's behavior towards her pursuers differs considerably from Seraphina's. She vehemently rejects the count's advances (he wants to marry Seraphina and have Gertrude as his mistress) and she even coyly deters the upright Colonel Howard's professions of affection. In the latter case, however, she betrays her reciprocal feelings for him when alone, wondering "why should I prevent his saying, what I would most delight to hear?" (43). Despite Gertrude's virtue and caution, however, she gets caught in a compromising position with the count while enacting a plan to expose him as a fraud. Even Trueman temporarily loses faith in her and refuses to hear her explanation.

In the end, however, Gertrude gets her chance to explain and receives her reward, assuming her rightful position as Trueman's granddaughter and heir, and Colonel Howard's wife. This resolution suggests that honesty and plainness, not the pretentiousness of fashion, provide the key to upward social mobility. But before we make a final judgment, we must consider Adam Trueman's questionable behavior: while on the surface he seems to be the exemplification of native virtues, his past makes him suspect.

Fashion's critical history has been kind to Trueman; Barnes' account of the play calls this Stage Yankee "the soul of virtue," and he summarizes the prevalent nineteenth-century opinion of Trueman:

> Judging by the reactions of audiences and critics, Trueman was the most appealing character in the play. By the mid-nineteenth century the ideal of American manhood had become fixed; and Trueman personified that ideal, since in addition to being virtuous and shrewd he was also rich. (127)

Although the critics correctly identify Trueman as a popular stereotype, and his name reinforces this perception, it has been noted by James J. Quinn that "Adam Trueman is more than a mere caricature of the rustic. He reveals more than once a three-dimensional personality and takes on the guise of an actual human being" (59). Others substantiate Quinn's assessment: the rounding out of type characters elicits praise for Mowatt from Margaret Opasta, who notes that "the playwright relied upon her gift for social commentary and her familiarity with the lifestyle she was satirizing to create a realistic spoof of three-dimensional characters" (44).

Fleshing out Trueman's character involved some serious complications these critics have overlooked, however. Trueman has a personality, because Trueman has a past. From one perspective, he *is* a rich farmer who has retained his simple values, and all comes to good when he claims his virtuous granddaughter Gertrude as his rightful heir. Subverting this simple conclusion, though, are the details of his past relationship with Gertrude, whom he claims to love.

He assures the group that "I never coveted wealth—yet twenty years ago I found myself the richest farmer in Catteraugus" (*Fashion*, 58). He further explains that his wealth caused his daughter's unhappiness and death, for she married a man who wanted her money and died broken-hearted after he abandoned her. She left the child Gertrude to Adam, who "swore that my unlucky wealth should never curse it, as it had cursed its mother! It was all I had to love—but I sent it away—and the neighbors thought it was dead" (58).

Are we as readers not expected to question old Adam's judgment in this situation—he chooses to keep his corrupting wealth and sends his granddaughter packing! His resolve "not to claim her until she had made her choice and found the man who was willing to take her for herself alone" is an admirable sentiment on the surface, but we have witnessed Gertrude's precarious position (58). She is a governess, forced to earn her own living unprotected by family connections, and her unfortunate episode with the count deprives her of the meager security this job offers.

Trueman defends her with his cane from the advances of the count early in the play, but this appears a rather "lame" substitution for the security she would have if she knew her true identity. Ironically, Trueman acknowledges this security when he temporarily loses faith in her, admonishing her by exclaiming, "You had more rights than you thought for, but you have forfeited them all! All right to love, respect, protection, and to not a little else that you don't dream of" (55). He disregards the fact that he forfeited his granddaughter, and thus his accusations of her are positively heartless, considering his hand in delivering Gertrude to the winds of chance.

Yet Trueman is the character who contrasts with Mr. Tiffany, and he instructs the latter throughout the play, acting as corrective for Tiffany's behavior. In their first scene together, Adam admonishes Tiffany for his extravagant lifestyle, accusing him of surrendering to the power of wealth, and losing himself, saying that

> You look as if you've melted down your flesh into dollars, and mortgaged your soul in the bargain . . . You have traded away your youth—your hopes—your tastes, for wealth! And now you have the wealth you coveted, what does it profit you? (42)

These statements are charged with irony, considering Trueman's own choices, for he forfeits a life with his granddaughter, sending her off to be raised by others, rather than forfeiting his wealth. He most certainly trades his youth and his hopes (in the form of Gertrude) to maintain his status as a wealthy farmer.

At the play's conclusion, when we know of the tie between Adam and Gertrude, Tiffany begs for Trueman's financial aid to get out of debt, appealing to Adam's emotions:

> You, Mr. Trueman, you will be my friend in this hour of extreme need—you will advance the sum which I require—I pledge myself to return it. My wife—my child—who will support them were I—the thought makes me frantic! You will aid me? You had a child yourself. (60)

Trueman responds with an emotional outburst, claiming that "I did not sell her . . . Shame on you Antony! Put a price on your own flesh and blood!" (60). What undercuts this noble sentiment is the knowledge that Trueman gave away his granddaughter, cutting her off from knowledge of her family and rightful heritage. The comparisons and contrasts between Trueman and Tiffany are not as simple or straightforward as they may first appear, and a detailed analysis of the play involves reckoning with the ambiguities so produced.

James Quinn deals with the discrepancy in the play by misreading the situation, for he maintains that Adam's granddaughter was lost to him without his knowledge, and that it is as he "listens to her account of her own life and background, Adam realizes that Gertrude is in truth his granddaughter" (57). This interpretation ignores Adam's clear explanation that he sent the girl away, and his assertion that he has now decided to claim her, since she has found herself an honest man to marry in the form of Colonel Howard. It is significant that Quinn gives Trueman the benefit of the doubt, for the critics want to insist that Mowatt wrote a straightforward light comedy, and nothing more.

By expanding the character of the Stage Yankee, however (for Quinn is correct in claiming that Trueman "reveals more than once a three-dimensional personality" and "the guise of an actual human being"), Mowatt cleverly undercuts the heroic portrait of this American literary figure. While she has been consistently praised for her ability to construct well-rounded figures, the critics have ignored the real implications of the playwright's choices. By placing on the stage a figure common in the masculine humorous tradition, and by complicating his personality in the particular way she does, Mowatt succeeded in pleasing a large popular audience of both sexes, while attacking social pretense without wholeheartedly endorsing its opposite. Trueman points out a glaring contradiction in the epilogue of the play, for when Prudence claims that, "I told you *Fashion* would the fashion be," Trueman counters with "Then both its point and moral I distrust" (62). While this verifies what Halttunen argues, that "this attack on social theatricality was itself presented within a theatrical performance," it also suggests that the play is built upon a series of contradictions, and does not render a coherent moral message (153).

According to reviews of the time, audiences chose to ignore the serious implications and accusations underlying the overt action of the play. With the objective distancing of time, we can reassess *Fashion* and uncover the ways a humorous social comedy directs attention to cultural oppression and anxieties about conflicting values, reinforcing Nancy Walker's opinion that humor is "a very serious thing."

Works Cited

Barnes, Eric Wollencott. *The Lady of Fashion*. New York: Charles Scribner's Sons, 1954.

Halttunen, Karen. *Confidence Men and Painted Women: A Study of Middle-class Culture in America, 1830–1870*. New Haven and London: Yale UP, 1982.

Hartman, John Geoffrey. *The Development of American Social Comedy from 1787 to 1936*. New York: Octagon Books, 1971.

Havens, Daniel F. *The Columbian Muse of Comedy: the Development of a Native Tradition in Early American Social Comedy, 1787–1845*. 1931. Carbondale and Edwardsville, IL: Southern Illinois UP, 1973.

Hewitt, Barnard. *Theater U.S.A. 1665 to 1957*. New York: McGraw-Hill, 1959.

Koon, Helene. *American Women Writers: A Critical Reference Guide from Colonial Times to the Present*. Vol. 3. New York: Frederick Ungar, 1981.

Mowatt, Anna Cora. *Autobiography of an Actress*. Boston, 1853.

———. *Fashion, or Life in New York*. The Longman Anthology of American Drama. New York: Longman, 1982.

Opasta, Margaret. "Genteel Iconoclast." *American History Illustrated* 17.10 (1983).

Quinn, Arthur Hobson. *A History of The American Drama from the Beginning to the Civil War*. New York: F.S. Crofts, 1946.

Quinn, James J. Jr. *The Jonathan Character in The American Drama.* Ann Arbor, MI: Doctoral Dissertation Series, 1975.

Reed, Perley Isaac. *The Realistic Presentation of American Characters in Native Plays Prior to Eighteen Seventy.* The Ohio State University Bulletin. Vol. XXII No. 26. Columbus, Ohio: University at Columbus, 1918.

Walker, Nancy. *A Very Serious Thing.* Minneapolis: University of Minnesota, 1988.

The "Scribbling Women" and Fanny Fern: Why Women Wrote

Ann Douglas Wood

I n January 1855, Nathaniel Hawthorne penned a protest which was to be often quoted in later years, against the "d—d mob of scribbling women" who were, in his opinion, both capturing and corrupting the literary market. In a subsequent letter to the same correspondent, his publisher William Ticknor, he made an exception to the indictment he had leveled against his feminine rivals in favor of "Fanny Fern" who had just published a novel entitled *Ruth Hall.* His comments, which explain not only why he admired her, but why he disliked many of her scribbling sisters, are worth quoting in full:

> I have been reading *Ruth Hall,* and I must say I enjoyed it a good deal. . . . The woman [Fanny Fern] writes as if the Devil was in her; and that is the only condition under which a woman ever writes anything worth reading. Generally women write like emasculated men, and are only to be distinguished from male authors by greater feebleness and folly; but when they throw off the restraints of decency and come before the public stark naked . . . then their books are sure to possess character and value. . . . If you meet her [Fanny Fern], I wish you would let her know how much I admire her.[1]

Other more conventional critics agreed heartily with Hawthorne's assessment of the shock value of the novel, but their reaction was hardly, like his, one of praise. The *Putnam's* reviewer found the book full of "unfemininely bitter wrath and spite."² Fanny Fern was clearly "not sufficiently endowed with female delicacy," another reviewer felt; she had "demeaned herself as no right-minded woman should have done, and [as] no sensitive woman could have done."³ The *Protestant Episcopal Quarterly Review* was shocked to learn that such a woman, a "Bedouin authoress" existed "elsewhere than among the heathen." She had defiled the "sacredness" of the home by the baseness of the work she undertook, worst of all, "for the sake of profit."⁴ The influential Mrs. Sarah Josepha Hale, for over thirty years the co-editor of *Godey's Lady's Book,* and the champion of a decorous although determined campaign for women's advancement, politely but publicly refused to review the novel in the columns of her magazine.⁵

The novel, one of several sensational best sellers of the decade now all but forgotten, may at first hardly seem to justify to a modern reader the critical uproar it occasioned in 1854 when, in the words of one reviewer, it was hotly discussed "from the Penobscot to the Mississippi."⁶ It is an account, at times sentimentalized, at times bitterly ironic, of the development, difficulties and final success of a woman writer, written by a woman who is clearly drawing heavily on her own experience. Why, in its own time, was this subject and this approach so controversial? It is important to realize here that the significant discrepancy between Hawthorne's response and that of the reviewers is not that his was favorable and theirs unfavorable. It is rather that Hawthorne was insisting that Fanny Fern, unlike her feminine competitors, was daringly true to her fundamental experience as a woman, while her critics accused her of betraying and lowering her feminine nature, and hence of being *un*feminine, *un*womanly. There was clearly a conventional set of preconceptions as to why women should write and what kind of literature they could write which Hawthorne disliked, and which Fanny Fern challenged and even attacked in her novel about a woman writer. *Ruth Hall* consequently gains what interest it still possesses today precisely because it is a kind of test case, questioning the validity and value of a genteel tradition in itself deserving of consideration.[7]

Fanny Fern in a mock review of one of her later books neatly summed up the preconceptions her work failed to meet:

> When we take up a woman's book, we expect to find gentleness, timidity, and that lovely reliance on the patronage of . . . [the male] sex which constitutes a woman's greatest charm—we do not desire to see a woman wielding the scimiter blade of sarcasm.[8]

This "timidity and . . . Lovely reliance" was clearly what Hawthorne had in mind when he asserted that women's writing was distinguished from men's only by its "greater feebleness and folly." It should be stressed at the outset that neither Hawthorne nor Fanny Fern in their comments was *interpreting* the nature of this feminine literature; they were, in effect, simply echoing what the women themselves and their male reviewers said about it. Its "feebleness," if not its folly, was advertised as a virtue by its practitioners. Sarah Hale cautioned aspiring poetesses in her *Lady's Magazine*, a precursor of *Godey's:*

> The path of poetry, like every other path in life, is to the tread of woman, exceedingly circumscribed. She may not revel in the luxuriance of fancies, images and thoughts, or indulge in the license of choosing themes at will, like the Lords of creation.[9]

"Grace Greenwood," born Sara Clarke, a popular authoress of the day, wrote spirited, occasionally unconventional sketches and stories, but when she came to describe what "true feminine genius" should be, she slipped into line behind Mrs. Hale. In her first collection of sketches, *Greenwood Leaves,* she explains that "true feminine genius is ever timid, doubtful, and clingingly dependent; a perpetual childhood. A true woman shrinks instinctively from greatness." Carried away for a moment in praising "the joys of creation" and "the heaven-born soul of song," she soon retreats, and cautions, "but this is for the *masters* of the lyre; it can never be felt by woman with great intensity; at least, can never satisfy her."[10]

Both Sarah Hale, one of the most successful editors in mid-19th century America, and Grace Greenwood, a noted abolitionist and lecturer, were urging other women to do as they said, not as they did. Why? The half-conscious purpose behind their rationale is given away by the graceful references both of them make to the "Lords of creation" and the "*masters* of the lyre" who are to have privileges of creativity denied to women. These two women are assuaging a half-felt sense that they as writers are threatening to men,[11] that they will be seen as women who have left the world of home to challenge the exclusive right of men to the joys of intellectual and emotional self-expression, and even to compete directly with them, as Hawthorne knew they did, for a limited literary market. If the emergence of a group of feminine writers who threatened to corner the market alarmed men, it alarmed the women as well. The women writers themselves wanted to have their cake and eat it too: stay "feminine" and write successful best sellers. On one level, this desire was rooted in shrewd analysis: "feminine" books got better reviews from male reviewers. On another, it genuinely expressed their own ambivalent guilt that they were not leaving the field to the "lords of creation," but taking it over, and enjoying the conquest. As a result of this complex pattern of motives and reactions, most of the women writers of the day, like Sarah Hale and Grace Greenwood, subscribed to a rationale, heartily supported by their male reviewers, that attempted to prove how justifiable, innocuous and even elevating their work was.

Literary duties, these women assured their readers, need not and did not draw them from their proper "sphere" of home. Their hearts remained there, not in their books. Catharine Maria Sedgwick, one of the most popular and interesting American writers of the 1820s and 1830s, undeservedly neglected today, can assure her friends that her books "constitute no portion of my happiness"—this she found rather in the "dearest relations of life." In fact, cooking was the only accomplishment of which she admitted to being vain.[12] Mrs. Hale loved to satirize the *"would-be-literary lady"* who affected to "despise the dull routine of domestic duties her sex enjoined upon her."[13] Indeed, domestic cares apparently could provide the sort of artistic "inspiration" suitable to woman. Mrs. A. D. T. Whitney, who rivaled Louisa May Alcott in her popularity with female readers, showed in a novel called *The Other Girls* (1873) how a young maid becomes a successful poetess, but still refuses to quit her cooking and cleaning, because, as she tells her mistress, "The best and brightest things I've ever thought have come into my head over the ironing-board or the bread-making."[14]

Women in becoming writers were not leaving the home for the marketplace, according to this reasoning, but bringing the home *into* the market. Men's concerns, such as politics, were not suitable subjects for lady writers, as Mrs. Hale rather pointedly reminded the noted abolitionist writer Lydia Maria Child: "The precepts and examples of the Saviour should be the guide of woman's benevolent efforts. In no case did He lend aid or encouragement to the agitation of political questions."[15] Women were to eschew direct criticism of the *status quo,* Mrs. Hale argued, in favor of a quiet transmutation and sanctification of life by the "painting of domestic scenes and *deep* emotions."[16] As a result, ladies were urged toward children's literature, books on child care and household management, and works of sensibility steeped in depoliticized and lofty patriotism and misty, death-oriented and non-sectarian religious fervor. The feminine writers responded gallantly to the call, and turned out such works in staggering numbers to the polite applause of their reviewers, who complacently praised their piety, lack of energy and resolute disregard of conflict.

One reviewer paid tribute to Catharine Maria Sedgwick for her "unambitious style" and "bland, religious spirit."[17] Another gave her the highest compliment one could give a woman writer when he remarked that "there are few books which make better Sunday reading than hers."[18] W. B. O. Peabody, praising Lydia H. Sigourney, the "sweet singer of Hartford," notes that she makes no claim to "the very highest attributes of poetry," but shows rather an "unassuming" tone of "calm reflection" and, best of all, "a pure and unostentatious faith." Hers, the reviewer points out, is true feminine genius, which, in contrast to man's "militant" spirit with its "fierce energy," "will always be found on religion's side."[19]

In masking and hallowing their activity, these women writers reached the paradoxical point where, by a mysterious transmutation, they were somehow hardly writing at all. As they told it, they stumbled accidentally on the stanzaic or novel form in the course of musing about "domestic scenes and deep emotions," and picked it up, not really knowing what they had. Caroline Lee Hentz, a popular southern novelist of the day, can hardly explain what she is doing in her book *Ernest Linwood,* and has to ask herself:

> Book! Am I writing a book? No, indeed! This is only a record of my heart's life, written at random and carelessly thrown aside, sheet after sheet, sibylline leaves from the great book of fate. The wind may blow them away, a spark consume them. I may myself commit them to the flames. I am tempted to do so at this moment. [20]

Needless to say, she overcame the temptation. Mrs. Sigourney was said to write in the same unwitting way, naturally heedless of any sense of literary form. A contemporary lauded her because, "ever hurrying along on some urgent errand of affection or duty," she never worried about the "mere style of her expression" or her "literary reputation."[21]

What is happening is clear: women's motives in writing are being stripped of all their aggressive content, until the woman writer seems practically anesthetized, or rather hypnotized, responding only to the calls of home and God, calls so close to her instinctive womanly nature that she hardly needs consciously to hear them. She writes because she cannot help it, and is apt, like the consumptive young poetess Lucretia Davidson, to appear "the inhabitant of another sphere" as she "writes."[22] Whittier explains why he could not discourage the budding writer Alice Cary, who was later to become New York's best known poetess, when she first appeared on his doorstep:

> Foredoomed to song, she seemed to me;
> I queried not with destiny. . . .
> What could I other than I did?
> Could I a singing-bird forbid?
> Deny the wind-stirred leaf? Rebuke
> The music of the forest brook?[23]

Such descriptions give the whole mystique in a nutshell. The woman writer is hardly a flesh-and-blood competitor in a literary market, but a songbird, a leaf, or, like Lucretia Davidson, the inhabitant of another sphere altogether. Nor is she a willful creator, bent on self-expression; rather she is "foredoomed to song," a suffering instrument for the still, sad music of humanity. All her writing is, in a sense, automatic writing, and, hence, not only inevitable, but holy. When Harriet Beecher Stowe finally announced that "God wrote" *Uncle Tom's Cabin,* she was putting herself in a long-standing tradition. Susan Warner's sentimental best seller, *The Wide, Wide World,* published in 1850, was written, as her sister explained, "in close reliance upon God: for thoughts, for power and for words. . . . In that sense, the book was written upon her knees."[24] Catharine Maria Sedgwick confessed to the solemn feeling that she was "but the instrument" of God.[25]

Women were not only forced into writing, but they were then frequently forced into print. A woman writer was particularly admirable if, like the young and sickly poetess Martha Day, daughter of President Day of Yale, she "aimed rather to repress than to cultivate her poetic genius."[26] Her journals and poetic works were published only posthumously, by an adoring and grieving family. This situation seemed so ideal that Mrs. Sigourney made use of it in a fictionalized work called *Lucy Howard's Journal,* published in 1857. The public is only allowed the chance to peruse the exemplary, chaste and retiring thoughts of this young housewife because she died and her husband felt he could not, in all good conscience, withhold such a source of inspiration from the world. In fact, if the lady were living at publication date, one could often assume that, as in the case of Lydia Maria Child or Catharine Maria Sedgwick, relatives had urged or even betrayed her into print.[27]

The most delicate aspect of this whole rationale was that which dealt with the economic motives of the woman writer. As Helen Papashvily has pointed out in her valuable study, *All the Happy Endings,* many women writers were widows, suddenly forced to support themselves and their children, or women otherwise unexpectedly robbed of male support.[28] The situation here was very complex. On the one hand, economic necessity was a better excuse for writing than a sheer burning unladylike desire for self-expression. On the other hand, it was, as we have seen, taboo for the lady writers to appear to be what Hawthorne realized they were: shrewd competitors in the literary market. Hawthorne felt his work would "have no chance of success while the public taste is occupied with their trash."[29] An earlier, extremely telling comment on his feminine rivals shows how clearly he felt their innate aggressiveness: "the ink-stained Amazons will expel their rivals by actual pressure, and petticoats wave triumphantly over all the field," he prophesied bitterly in a biographical sketch of Anne Hutchinson.[30] Various women writers took different ways of repressing awareness, in their readers and in themselves, of this facet of their literary activity. The widowed Mrs. Hale, an astute business woman and self-advertiser, was given to dropping little personal explanations in the midst of articles on varied subjects. A consideration of Anne Boleyn, for example, leads somehow to this dignified statement:

> It is only in emergencies, in cases where duty demands the
> sacrifice of female sensitiveness, that a lady of sense and
> delicacy will come before the public, in a manner to make
> herself conspicuous. There is little danger that such a one
> will be arrogant in her pretensions. These remarks may be
> considered as allusions to our own case.

She engages in her literary and editorial work, a pursuit
"foreign to the usual character and occupations of her sex,"
only in order to "obtain the means of supporting and
educating her children in some measure as their father would
have done."[31] Clearly anxious that she has somehow usurped
her husband's role, she stresses that her only real source of
happiness in her fame is the sweet thought "that *his* name
bears the celebrity."[32] Yet she is not above using her declared
maternal motivation for a shrewd bit of advertising: the public
is given the "surest pledge" that she will deserve its patronage:
"The guaranty of a mother's affection."[33] She is indeed having
her cake and eating it too.

The financial imperative offering itself as the maternal (or
sometimes filial) impulse, mysteriously disconnected from
what Mrs. Hale gingerly refers to here as "pecuniary
remuneration," makes a frequent appearance in this literature.
Above all, a woman writer was not to display her economic
need. If she did, she was clearly threatening, reminding an
absent husband or a neglectful father, or men in general, of
their failure to support her in the graceful domestic sphere for
which she was presumably formed, and implying that she
might now actively take from them what they refused to give.
"Fanny Forrester," born Emily Chubbuck, a popular New York
writer of the 1840s, who later became the third Mrs. Judson
and a missionary to Burma, provides a telling example of the
advertising techniques an impoverished woman writer might
employ. Raised in New Hampshire by a father lacking in all
"practical shrewdness and energy," she knew poverty young.
She later recalled digging "broken wood out of the snow" to
keep her family from freezing, and she started work at eleven

in a woolen factory (p. 20).[34] Not surprisingly, she combined, as her biographer recorded, "shrinking sensitiveness" with the "masculine energy of action" (p. 54) her father so notably lacked. She early took over his role as breadwinner for the family. While teaching young ladies at the Utica Female Seminary in New York, she began to write pious Sunday school tales that found a small but dependable market. Her assessment of her motives given to friends was candid in the extreme: she planned to sell "brains for money" (p. 57). Although she was proud of the "iron" toughness she had gained in her struggles with a harsh world, she felt there was "little of the poetry of life" left in her (p. 48). Indeed, she occasionally felt that writing had become "such a matter-of-fact dollars and cents business" with her, that she hated her pen: "Oh, there is nothing," she exclaimed to a sympathetic correspondent, "like coining one's brain into gold—no, bread—to make the heart grow sick" (p. 72).

Yet when she entered the New York market by submitting two trial sketches to Nathaniel Willis' *New York Mirror,* the organ of New York's would-be fashionables, this impoverished schoolteacher publicly denied all pretensions to being a "blue," and coyly explained that, although her friend "Bel" had urged her to pretend poverty to win sympathy, she has decided to tell the "truth"—she is a charming young thing who simply wants a little cash for a new hat! She prefers to disarm her readers and Willis with a false confession of feminine frivolity rather than to expose a need and a determination which would be seen as unfeminine. Her subsequent sketches of the woman artist all deal with girls who are a compound of Little Eva and Ariel, wandering amongst dense mists of poetry and totally eschewing any aspect, economic or otherwise, of the real world.[35] She herself became a romantic figure whose consumption was seen, not as a badge of poverty and overwork, but of poetic genius. An admiring sister poetess spoke of the "shadow wan and deep" on her brow, her "hollow temples" with their "darker violet veins," and her "fairy feet," falling "faint and low/ As the feathery flakes of the drifting snow."[36]

No one should or could minimize the fact that dying poetesses and consumptive storytellers were hardly a figment of the feminine imagination: they existed, in staggering numbers, and were as genuine a part of the feminine experience as the hearth and altar which provided the chief themes of these women's work. Yet it is equally undeniable that these facts of life also yielded a complex symbolic value and served an important double function. The consumptive ladies, for example, presented a tacit reproach to a masculine world that murderously trampled on their delicate sensibilities, and yet, at the same time, their wan faces and decaying limbs hinted that if they had offended by their literary ambitions, at least they were dying for it. The reality of this guilt as a component of the woman writer's psyche seems undeniable. Grace Greenwood wrote a long and fascinating story for the *Atlantic Monthly* in 1859 called "Zelma's Vow," probably based in part on her own unhappy marital experiences.[37] Zelma, a noble but wild English girl of gypsy descent, runs away from her foster father's home with a young actor. He turns out to be worthless, selfish and flagrantly unfaithful, and when she herself becomes a great actress, he is bitterly and undeservedly jealous of her. In fact, interestingly enough, it is precisely his scorn of her capacities which stings "like a lash" into her first triumph (p. 333). On stage, she plays a character in Congreve's *The Mourning Bride* who defies and triumphs over the character her husband plays, but off-stage, she is at once "the loving wife, yearning for one proud smile, one tender word" (p. 334). The split between the artist and the wife, one aggressive and defiant, the other asking to be forgiven for her aggression and defiance, could not be clearer. As her acting, to which she allegedly turns for "consolation" for his coldness, improves, his grows worse and worse. In some psychic fashion, she is sapping him of his vitality, and finally, he dies. Although Grace Greenwood has given us no overt hint that Zelma is in any way to blame, she clearly *feels* that her heroine is guilty, for the rest of the story is concerned with Zelma's deterioration as an actress and as a woman. Dying of consumption, she is reduced to playing in cheap, provincial theaters. In a terrible scene, after accidentally using her husband's skull as a stage prop in a scene from Rowe's *Fair Penitent,* she dies murmuring, "he will forgive me . . . when he sees that all the laurels have dropped away" (p. 344).

This guilt and the kind of soft-pedaling and blurring it imposed on the woman writer's need to express and finance herself were of course evidences of deep-rooted alienation and of genuine psychological conflict within these women, but, in a curious way, the resulting rationale, as I have suggested, also furthered their original impulse. Authoresses like Sarah Hale and Fanny Forrester presumably unconsciously believed that they could succeed better, be more assertive economically, by hiding behind a conventional "feminine" facade. Hence, the importance of the rationale for strategic as well as psychic reasons was very great. It enabled hundreds of women to write without understanding all the frightening and unacceptable implications of their desire to do so, and it helped them make a profit from their writing as well. So it is hardly surprising to find one woman author after another, from Lydia Maria Child to Harriet Beecher Stowe, subscribing in large measure to the Hale doctrine, no matter how outspoken or even subversive her own work might be. One woman, however, refused to accept it. This woman was "Fanny Fern," whose novel *Ruth Hall* Hawthorne so much admired, and she built her work openly on the defiance her fellow authoresses labored to conceal. Although she created a nine-days' sensation, she had no effect on the formulators and followers of the rationale, nor did she particularly want to do so. Never an analytic critic like the abrasive essayist Gail Hamilton, she was as unconscious of what she was doing, as fully acting out her own needs and tensions as they were. It is perhaps for this reason that she and her novel provide a kind of litmus test, a photographic negative, so to speak, for the work of her feminine contemporaries.

It was Fanny Fern's own experience that produced *Ruth Hall* and led her to cry from the rooftops what other women writers hardly wished to whisper in the basement.[38] She was born in 1811 and christened Sara Payton Willis. Her father, Nathaniel Willis, was an editor of religious periodicals, a friend of Lyman Beecher's, and a deacon in Edward Beecher's Park Street Church in Boston. He was apparently a "rather wooden person," characterized by a "formal and narrow piety."[39] His daughter Sara never accepted his harsh theology. Like many other women of her day who revolted against Calvinism, she mentally pitted her mother Hannah Willis as a "Christian" against her father as a "Calvinist."[40] With her mother, "Hell was forgotten, harshness was softened, fear was cast out," and her children "found the radiance of heaven in her eyes."[41]

Her father was apparently cut off from this source of light. Indeed, Fanny Fern seemed to take a certain histrionic and morbid pleasure in recalling in later years a terrible moment in her childhood when Mr. Willis addressed his saintly wife in terms "so rude, so brutal, so stinging" that all the blood in Sara's body "seemed to congeal as the murderous syllables fell." The killer male had revealed himself to Sara's fascinated young gaze, a figure she was to know better after her own "baptism [into] . . . a woman's lot." At such moments her mother retreated to her Bible for solace, but she had other resources as well. She could have been a writer, her daughter believed, because "she *talked poetry unconsciously!*"[42] But here too she was repressed, and a load of domestic cares prevented her from developing this talent. Sara was to be different.

As a girl, Sara Willis was extremely attractive, mischievous and unconventional. Sent to several "female seminaries" and remaining long at none, in 1838 she married "Handsome Charlie" Eldredge, a charming and successful young banker. From all accounts, the marriage was an enthusiastic love match. The couple had three little girls— Sara claimed she had determined to have no boys—and all went well until 1844 when Sara's favorite sister died, followed quickly by her adored mother. In 1845, her daughter Mary died, and two years later Charles Eldredge died of typhoid fever, leaving his wife with almost no means of support. Although accounts vary,[43] it seems clear that neither her father nor her father-in-law gave her the kind of financial aid she needed. Totally without any real vocational training, she tried teaching and sewing, the traditional resources of genteel ladies in difficulty, and failed at both. In desperation and urged on by her own family, in 1849 she married Samuel Farrington, a widower with two children, although no love was felt on either side. Farrington was jealous and possessive, Sara Willis was difficult and neurotic, and the marriage ended in a separation, publicized by Farrington in a humiliating advertisement in the *Boston Daily Bee* on February 25, 1851, forbidding anyone to harbor or trust his wife. He obtained a divorce in Chicago in 1853.

The years after Eldredge's death and preceding her final separation from Farrington were terrible ones for Sara Willis. Her third and last husband, the biographer James Parton, explained in his *Memoir* of her that those years "left deep traces upon her nature, never wholly obliterated."[44] Grace Greenwood in a biographical sketch referred to the "ugly ditches" and "hurdles she had to leap" in her "desperate race."[45] Never stable, her sudden confrontation with deprivation and the harsher side of reality made her "unquestionably neurotic."[46] For the rest of her life until her death from cancer in 1872, she was haunted by insomnia, tormented by an acute oversensitivity to noise, and incessantly, although humorously, referring to the possibility of insanity.[47] Her central crisis in these desperate years seemed to focus on what she clearly felt as the repeated defection of the men in her life. Her father had failed to help her, her first husband had failed her, if only by dying, her second by slandering her, and last but not least, her famous brother Nathaniel Willis, the well known poet and editor, had coldly tried to squelch her rising literary ambition. In July of 1851, shortly after the dissolution of her second marriage, she had started to write short, racy sketches for two Boston papers, the *Boston True Flag* and the *Olive Branch,* beginning at a rate of fifty cents an article. Having a decided success, she wrote to her brother in New York City, enclosing some of her work and asking him if he would help her find a market there. He wrote back a frank if somewhat brutal reply. After telling her that New York was "the most overstocked market in the country for writers," he went on to warn her that her sketches

> would do only in Boston. You overstrain the pathetic, and your humor runs into dreadful vulgarity sometimes. I am sorry that any editor knows that a sister of mine wrote some of these which you sent me. In one or two cases they touch very close on indecency. For God's sake, keep clear of that.

In closing, he remarked that the only "chance" for her was perhaps with "the religious papers." Sara Willis seized on this rejection as the archetypal moment for which all of her experience had been preparing her: the male had fully revealed himself in all his treacherous cruelty. It was clearly with a sense of acting in a crucial moment of her history that she elaborately and somewhat inaccurately endorsed the letter: "from Nathaniel Parker Willis when I applied for literary employment . . . being at the time quite destitute."[48] At this point, "Fanny Fern" was baptized if not born, and she soon went on to New York, to be a regular and highly paid contributor to Robert Bonner's wildly successful *New York Ledger* and to be known coast to coast for her stories and sketches—and her ability to make money.[49]

Nathaniel Willis was clearly mistaken about his sister's box-office appeal, but he was right in thinking that hers was not the tone he encouraged in his literary weeklies designed for feminine consumption. Although Willis, like his sister, came from a relatively undistinguished background, unlike her, he gravitated both in America and in Europe toward the socially elite. Dressing in the height of fashion, presenting himself as a dandy with flashes of irony often quite lost on his audience, he was, in Oliver Wendell Holmes' wonderful phrase, "something between a remembrance of Count D'Orsay and an anticipation of Oscar Wilde." Contemporary reactions to him varied tremendously: Charles Fenno Hoffman found nothing but "cold speculation" in his eyes which seemed to be "two holes, looking out through a stone-wall," while James Russell Lowell praised him as "the topmost bright bubble on the wave of the town."[50] What no one could question, however, was that Willis was the high priest of the feminine subculture and its mystique which I described earlier. He recognized that "the republic of letters" was "fast coming under female dominion" and paid tribute to *Godey's* as a "powerful gynocracy."[51] After working in the late 1820s with the famous publisher S. G. Goodrich on such "gemmy" albums as *The Token,* where he split a first prize with Mrs. Sigourney, he contributed to other annuals like the *Opal,* the *Thought Blossom* and the *Gift,* and to magazines like *Godey's* and the *Ladies' Companion.* He also ran a series of literary newspapers in New York City that sought contributions from ladies such as Frances Osgood, Anne Lynch, Fanny Forrester and Grace Greenwood, while writing much literature in a similar, if occasionally ironic vein himself.[52] By the time of his first European trip in the early 1830s he had announced the "ornamental" as his "vocation" and he never renounced his choice. Maginn, the notorious reviewer for *Fraser's Magazine,* could satirize Willis unkindly, yet with some point, as the "namby-pamby writer in twaddling albums."[53]

In earlier years, Willis tried to tame his younger sister's writing into his own style in a graceful poem entitled "To My Wild Sis" which Sara Willis saved for years. Urging her to "Be like the wild rose—[which] . . . doth not burst/ In to full pride of life at first," he promised her that if she would be in her "budding years" as "purely faultless as [her] . . . tears," she would have in a "future hour/ A perfect woman's hallowed power."[54] There probably was, as Willis' early biographer points out, "an original opposition in character and taste between the two,"[55] and certainly the violent, "coarse" (as her critics loved to call them) and fractured sketches she sent him could hardly have seemed to him evidences of "woman's hallowed power."

Her brother's rejection of her, so different from the kindly puffing the brothers of literary aspirants were supposed to provide, clearly helped shift Fanny Fern's attitude toward the polite fictions of the feminine subculture, which were Willis' own chosen weapons, from dislike to active hostility.[56] She waged a curious and confused battle in which she often utilized the techniques of this subculture to fight against it. For example, why did she pick out the nom de plume "Fanny Fern"? Such alliterative, woodsy and flowery names were already regarded as typical of a certain kind of woman writer, and the provocative essayist Gail Hamilton would refer some years later to the "fluttering, . . . ephemeral . . . stories" by "Maggie Marigold and Kittie Katnip."[57] Fanny Fern herself gave the most acceptably sentimental and probably sincere account of her choice:

> I think the reason I selected the name "Fern" was because, when a child and walking with my mother in the country, she always used to pluck a leaf of it, to place in her bosom for its sweet odor; and that gloomy morning, when I almost despaired of earning bread for my children, I had been thinking of her, and wishing that she were living, that I might lay my head upon her bosom and tell her all my sorrows; and then, memory carried me back, I scarce knew how, to those childish days, when I ran before her in the woods, to pluck the sweet fern she loved; and then I said to myself, my name shall be "Fanny Fern."

This nostalgic scene, with its veiled emphasis on an ingrown and exclusively feminine world, is staple fare in the feminine literature of the day.[58] But of course it does not account for all of her choice: why the "Fanny"? She gives the answer in a sketch when she has a young man remark, "I never saw a 'Fanny' yet that wasn't as mischievous as Satan."[59] The half-confused, half-deliberate union of the sentimental and the mischievously Satanic was to be Fanny Fern's trademark.

Furthermore, she probably had another motive in picking the name she did. The two women writers her brother patronized most extensively had also chosen alliterating and floral nom de plumes. "Fanny Forrester" dubbed Willis the "foster-father" of her intellect, and he kept her, as he told her, in the "chamber of my better nature."[60] "Grace Greenwood" was the other authoress whom Willis most lavishly praised. Indeed, he called her the "fairest blossom on the rose-tree of women," personifying the "elegant uselessness" and "brilliant trifling" he so admired.[61] Grace Greenwood recognized at once that Fanny Fern was "poaching" on her "Greenwood preserves."[62] Fanny Fern was of course trying to cash in on their market, but she was mocking it, even as she captured it. In her first book, she could satirically caution her imitators, "In choosing your signatures, bear in mind that nothing goes down, now-a-days, but *alliteration*. For instance, Delia Daisy, Fanny Foxglove, Harriet Honeysuckle. . . ."[63] She parodied the name even as she exploited it, and thus could get her audience both going and coming; work on their sentimentality, then satirize it. She summed up her game in a short piece called "A Bid for an Editorship": "I should insist on being treated with the deference due to a woman, though in all respects I should demand the untrammeled-seven-leagued-boots freedom of a man."[64]

This attack on two fronts was only subconsciously planned, if at all, and her earliest work reads like an exercise in artistic schizophrenia. Like Grace Greenwood's Zelma, she had two selves, two voices, one strident and aggressive, the other conventional and sentimental, although both are equally well publicized. She divides *Fern Leaves from Fanny's*

Portfolio, a collection of her earliest newspaper-sketches published in 1853, into two distinct sections, "Part I" and "Part II," with a rather frightening neatness. Part I is packed with tales of lonely widows and dying and saintly children, who are described with a sentimental abandon which might make even Mrs. Sigourney blush: "How sublime! How touching! Holy childhood! Let me sit at thy feet, and learn of thee"[65] is but a minor effort. Suffering womanhood is extolled in the person of a patient victim of an alcoholic husband: "O, all-enduring power of woman's love! No reproach, no upbraiding—the slight arm passed around that reeling figure," etc. (p. 146). In Part II, we leave the "Fern" behind and encounter the "Fanny": she is no longer drawing her readers into her sacred inner chamber of sorrow and sisterhood, but is lecturing them, hectoring them, from a podium. Her style changes markedly: she is humorous, satirical, crude in her language. Instead of ruminating, she is attacking an invisible opponent: "fiddlestick!" (p. 326) and "Don't you do it!" (p. 331) are characteristic openings for these essays. She has turned from the praise of suffering (pp. 180–81) to the advocacy of fighting (pp. 362–63). The subject matter is the same but viewed from a radically different angle. She satirizes the widow she had been weeping over in Part I (pp. 30–31), while the suffering wife is now merely a pathetic sniveler whom she upbraids with heavy-handed irony: "You miserable little whimperer! What have you to cry for! Ant-you-married? Isn't that the *summum bonum*—the height of feminine ambition?" (p. 324).

In her first novel, the autobiographical *Ruth Hall,* however, Fanny Fern was able, if not to heal, at least to utilize this split in a way best suited to accomplish her purposes. The heroine when we first meet her seems to come from Part I of *Fern Leaves.* She appears but one of the innumerable literary descendants of Charlotte Temple, a persecuted orphan, and, as her name indicates, tender-hearted and loving. We learn, indeed, that "Ruth could remember when she was no taller than a rosebush, how cravingly her little heart cried out for love!" (p. 16).[66] Needless to say, her little heart is disappointed, and the men in her life are responsible for it. Her mother, who had lived in fear of her father, apparently dies in despair (p. 17). Her foppish brother Hyacinth, a dandy clearly patterned on Nathaniel Willis, who does not like her to kiss him lest she rumple his dickey, has no heart to give. And her father is the dour, selfish figure who is every sentimental heroine's dream: Ruth can only think "I never had [a father]" (p. 30).

In a moment of deceptive promise, Ruth marries a young man named Harry, clearly modeled on "Handsome Charlie" Eldredge, who adores her and makes her happy, despite the persecution inflicted on her by her jealous and narrow-minded mother-in-law and a father-in-law who is as flinty-hearted as Ruth's own parent. Not surprisingly, her father-in-law, Dr. Hall, in effect murders her oldest child by his negligence (pp. 78 ff.). Then her husband dies of a fever, just as Charles Eldredge did, and, in describing his sickness and death, Fanny Fern makes it clear that on some level she regards his death as an act of hostility against her heroine. Harry has paroxysms, and the doctor in charge warns Ruth that he may "injure" her. Although his violence is only expressed by his "white teeth glittering through his unshorn beard" (p. 100), the purport is clear. In fact, in a sketch written by Fanny Fern just before *Ruth Hall* which describes the same scene, the woman in Ruth Hall's situation bears "on her delicate breast . . . the impress of an almost deadly blow from the hand that was never before raised but to bless her."[67] This is the wound that Harry is in reality inflicting on Ruth by dying and deserting her. The atmosphere of male cruelty has already been intensified by Ruth's meeting just prior to her husband's death a rich and beautiful, but unhappy, woman named Mrs. Leon whose husband maltreats and oppresses her. She and Ruth are at once drawn together, she as a confirmed, and Ruth as a potential member of the suffering sisterhood.

After her husband's death Ruth comes face to face, just as her creator did, with a cruel world that Fanny Fern describes with graphic bitterness. Neither Ruth's father nor her father-in-law, despite their religious pretensions, is willing to give her more than a pittance. She is living in a slum with her two little girls:

> The prospect was not one to call up cheerful fancies. Opposite was one of those large brick tenements, let out by rapacious landlords, a room at a time at griping rents, to poor emigrants, and others who were barely able to prolong their lease of life from day to day.... tier upon tier the windows rose, full of pale, anxious, care-worn faces—never a laugh, never a song—but instead, ribald curses and the cries of neglected, half-fed children. From window to window outside were strung on lines articles of clothing, pails, baskets, pillows, feather-beds, and torn coverlets; while up and down the door-steps . . . passed ever a ragged procession of bare-footed women and children, to the small grocery opposite, for "a pint of milk" . . . a few onions or potatoes, a cabbage, some herrings, a six-pence worth of poor tea, a pound of musty flour . . . for all of which the poor creatures paid twice as much as if they had the means to buy by the quantity. (pp. 171–72)

Ruth in her defenseless position gives various classes a chance to grind their heels on her face; they do so, and Fanny Fern delights in catching them at it. The upper-class women who refuse to employ her as a seamstress because they feel they cannot offer her the starvation wages they usually pay; her rich relatives who kindly allow her to do her laundry in their kitchen while they buy forty-dollar jackets; her in-laws, stifling themselves and others in their middle-class mediocrity adorned with pious literature and poor needlework; the smug and quarrelsome Board of Education, too lost in petty infighting to give Ruth's qualifications as a teacher a fair examination; the group of editors, headed by her fashionable brother Hyacinth, who refuse to help her despite her talents—all these receive some of the best satire at Fanny Fern's command. She has no patience for the mild, womanly rebukes and faint, but pious admonitions Mrs. Sigourney and others liked to pass off as social criticism; instead, she gives vent to the "unfemininely bitter wrath" her critics were to deplore.

There is, at this point, however, a gap between the writer's viewpoint and her heroine's. While Fanny Fern has clearly been angered and what we would call radicalized by what she describes, Ruth is still patiently staggering around under huge loads of laundry, "looking . . . pale about the mouth" and intermittently "holding on to her side, as if she would never move again" (p. 159). But the gap finally closes and in a very significant way. Ruth Hall accidentally discovers her old friend, Mrs. Leon, dead in an insane asylum "where her husband put her simply to get rid of her."[68] The asylum is a nightmare of man's cruelty to woman. When Ruth hears a terrible scream, the keeper informs her casually that it is "nothing . . . only a crazy woman in that room yonder, screaming for her child. Her husband ran away from her, and carried off her child with him, to spite her" (p. 212). Ruth and her two little girls are the only people at Mrs. Leon's funeral: three silent witnesses to the sufferings of their sex. Not surprisingly, it is right after this experience that Ruth determines to try to support herself by writing. She asks Hyacinth for his help, and he sends back a letter almost echoing Nathaniel Willis' to his sister. It is at this moment that Ruth's conversion experience takes place. In an extremely significant line, we learn that a "bitter smile disfigured her gentle lip" (p. 222); her transformation has begun, and she resolves: "I *can* do it, *I feel* it, I *will* do it . . . but there will be a desperate struggle first" (p. 222).

We now enter into the "Part II" of the novel, dominated by a shrewd, bitter, business-oriented and aggressive woman whom Grace Greenwood tellingly described as "Ruth*less* Hall."[69] This Charlotte Temple can *write*, and hence claw her way back out of the ditch and fight men on their own terms, and Fanny Fern, far from masking her heroine's effort, glories in it. Taking "Floy" as her nom de plume, perhaps an echo of Nathaniel Willis' early pen name "Roy," Ruth surprises those who think with her father-in-law that she is "nothing but a parlor ornament" with no "business talent" (p. 249). As a phrenological analysis of her reveals, she has immense "will" and "tenacity of purpose" as well as sensibility and maternal devotion (pp. 310–25). Although she acquires a devoted lackey called John Walters whose function is to remind the reader of what a sensitive and suffering little woman she has been, she is now clearly, as one tough editor remarks admiringly, "sharp" (pp. 253–54). Realizing that "business is accumulating" (p. 293), she exploits her burgeoning popularity as skillfully as Fanny Fern did her own. No longer burdened with laundry or feminine submission, she outwits experienced editors with calm aplomb (pp. 300–1), and even John Walters praises her as "sagacious and business-like." "Our heroine" has indeed, as Fanny Fern tells us, "become a regular business woman" (p. 330) as well as a shrewd satirist of the social scene. The moment in which she buys her first shares in a bank is treated as one of the two emotional climaxes of the book (p. 396). The other comes with her visit to her husband's grave which follows the bank-share episode and closes the novel. It would seem that, like Zelma, the grieving woman tries to follow up the successful artist.

One might be tempted to think at this point that Ruth Hall has slipped into the familiar pattern I described earlier. She has, after all, like Mrs. Hale, always insisted that "her *mother's heart* was goading her on" in all her labors (p. 331) and now she is making the appropriate pilgrimage to her husband's grave. But, unlike Zelma, she does not come to apologize or atone. In fact, this is the first time we have seen her at her husband's grave, and it is appropriate that it is a moment of victory for her. She is about to leave "this part of the country" forever, presumably to conquer wider fields, and there is a sense that she is taking farewell of her own past roles as sentimental orphan, loving wife and suffering widow, as well as of her husband's memory. Unlike Mrs. Hale, she has not tried to enhance the luster of her husband's name through her own fame; indeed, she does not even use it. Significantly, as she leaves the graveyard, a bird "trill[s] forth a song as sweet and clear as the lark's at heaven's own blessed gate," and her friend John Walters takes it as an "omen" that "Life has much of harmony" yet in store for Ruth (p. 400). In a sense, Ruth Hall has triumphed over her husband as well as over all the other men who left or failed her, and the bright future is hers alone.

Yet even the sentimentalized Ruth Hall of the earlier portions of the book, now dead and buried, had served a definite function. She was the needed midwife to the successful and shrewd Ruth Hall of the novel's later chapters. In her suffering, she represented a reproach to the male world. If woman's place is really in the home, why don't men enable her to stay there?, Fanny Fern is implicitly demanding. No one could have been more frail, loving and dependent than Ruth Hall originally was. If men will not even protect and aid a clinging creature such as this, the book's logic seems to suggest, they deserve what they get, for it is what they themselves have forced into being: a smart business woman capable of outwitting them in *their* sphere. Fanny Fern made her point crystal-clear in an article called "A Bit of Injustice," printed seven years later:

> As a general thing there are few people who speak approbatively of a woman who has a smart business talent or capability. No matter how isolated or destitute her condition, the majority would consider it more "feminine" would she unobtrusively gather up her thimble, and, retiring into some out-of-the-way-place, gradually scoop out her coffin with it, than to develop that smart turn for business which would lift her at once out of her troubles; and which, in a man so situated, would be applauded as exceedingly praiseworthy. The most curious part of it is, that they who are loudest in their abhorrence of this "unfeminine" trait, are they who are the most intolerant of dependent female

relatives. . . . [In this situation] might well be born "the smart business woman." And, in truth, so it often is.[70]

This is clearly in itself a kind of rationale, but it is one very different from that put forth by Grace Greenwood or Fanny Forrester—the *men* are the guilty parties, not the women writers, and any defense on the latter's part is justifiable self-defense.

Hawthorne's admiration for Fanny Fern's first novel now comes into clearer focus. She was indeed true to what she saw as her own experience. Her heroine competes with men, and refuses to feel guilty about it. Ruth Hall writes in large part because she needs money, and, unlike Fanny Forrester, Fanny Fern was devastatingly honest about this fact. She herself had found out about poverty, and the bitterness and anger and ambition it produced in her, and "unfeminine" as it all was, she wrote about that as well. She exposed what her feminine peers, and her brother, were trying to conceal. Little wonder Hawthorne was fascinated by

> this spectacle of Fanny Fern in little more than her bare bones, her heart pulsating visibly and indecently in its cage of ribs. Still there are ribs and there is a heart. Here is not merely silk and suavity and surface.[71]

Ruth Hall was undoubtedly Fanny Fern's finest and most central book. The rest of her career need not concern us here except to say that she went on talking frankly, if hysterically, about why women should write. Time after time, she expressed not only the financial, but the emotional needs and frustrations that drove her and her sisters to the pen, and she characteristically emphasized that craving for *self*-expression so carefully veiled by women like Grace Greenwood and Mrs. Hale. God's dictation has little part in the writing process she describes:

> Look around, and see innumerable women, to whose barren and loveless lives this would be improvement and solace,

and I say to them, write! . . . write! it will be a safe outlet for
thoughts and feelings that maybe the nearest friend you have
has never dreamed had place in your heart and brain. . . . it
is not *safe* for the women of 1867 to shut down so much that
cries out for sympathy and expression, because life is such a
maelstrom of business or folly or both, that those to whom
they have bound themselves, body and soul, recognize only
the needs of the former. . . . One of these days, when that
diary is found, when the hand that penned it shall be dust,
with what amazement and remorse will many a husband, or
father, exclaim, I never knew my wife, or my child, till this
moment.

Fanny Fern is frankly urging women to write both to
compensate themselves for male cruelty and to reproach the
men who exercise it. Writing is the only weapon for women
whose husbands expect them "once wound up by the
marriage-ceremony . . . to click on with undeviating monotony
till Death stops the hands." Women are to write because their
writing will someday stand as an accusing witness to the finer
sensibility their fathers and husbands ignored or brutalized.
But, finally, Fanny Fern is saying, women must write simply
to survive, and the sources of her own hysteria become clearer
as she exclaims

Write! . . . to lift yourselves out of the dead-level of your
lives . . . to lessen the number who are yearly added to our
lunatic asylums from the ranks of misappreciated, unhappy
wcmanhood, narrowed by lives made up of details. Fight it!
Oppose it, for your own sake's and your children's! [72]

She is proclaiming loudly that writing served precisely that
purpose for women which Sarah Hale and so many others
publicly most strongly abjured: it provided for women a way
out of the home, and a campaign, even a crusade, against the
men who wanted to keep them there.

Notes

1. Caroline Ticknor, *Hawthorne and His Publisher* (Boston: Houghton Mifflin Company, 1913), pp. 141–43.

2. "Editorial Notes—American Literature," *Putnam's Monthly: A Magazine of American Literature, Science, and Art, 5* (1855), 216.

3. Quoted in *The Life and Beauties of Fanny Fern* (New York: H. Long and Brother, 1855), pp. 180, 222.

4. Quoted in Patricia I. McGinnis, "Fanny Fern, American Novelist," *Biblion: The University Library Journal: State University of New York at Albany* (Spring 1969), p. 26.

5. "Literary Notices," *Godey's Lady's Book, 50* (1855), 176.

6. Quoted in Fred Lewis Pattee, *The Feminine Fifties* (New York: D. Appleton-Century Company, Incorporated, 1940), p. 119.

7. For a discussion of this tradition see Pattee, *Feminine Fifties,* Helen Waite Papashvily, *All the Happy Endings* (New York: Harper, 1956) and Herbert Ross Brown, *The Sentimental Novel in America 1789–1860* (Durham, N.C.: Duke University Press, 1940).

8. Quoted in Ethel Parton, "Fanny Fern: An Informal Biography," Chap. 8, unpublished MS in Parton Collection in Sophia Smith Collection, Smith College, Northampton, Mass.

9. *Lady's Magazine, 2* (1829), 142. See also her *Woman's Record* (New York: Harper & Brothers, 1876), which discusses many women writers from this angle.

10. *Greenwood Leaves* (Boston: Ticknor, Reed, and Fields, 1850), pp. 310–312. Grace Greenwood was capable of satirizing the kind of literature this critique produced (see *Greenwood Leaves,* pp. 303–8), but not of altering the critique.

11. Helen Papashvily treats the anti-men aspect of this literature as do William R. Taylor and Christopher Lasch, "'Two Kindred Spirits': Sorority and Family in New England, 1839–1846," *New England Quarterly, 36* (1963), pp. 231–41.

12. Mary E. Dewey, *Life and Letters of Catharine M. Sedgwick* (New York: Harper & Brothers, 1871), pp. 250, 330.

13. "Sketches of American Characters, No. 7: The Belle and the Bleu," *Lady's Magazine*, 1 (1828), 305.

14. *The Other Girls* (Boston: J.R. Osgood and Company, 1873), p. 434.

15. *Woman's Record,* p. 620.

16. *Lady's Magazine, 2* (1829), 143.

17. *Ibid.,* p. 235.

18. "Clarence," *North American Review, 32* (1831), 79.

19. "Mrs. Sigourney and Miss Gould," *North American Review, 41* (1835), 441–43.

20. *Ernest Linwood* (Boston: J.P. Jewett and Company, 1856), p. 69.

21. The Rev. E. B. Huntingdon, "Lydia H. Sigourney," in *Eminent Women of the Age* (Hartford, Conn: Betts, 1869), p. 96.

22. Catharine M. Sedgwick, "Lucretia Mott Davidson," *The Library of American Biography,* ed. Jared Sparks, 7 (Boston: Hilliard, Gray, and Co., 1837), p. 238.

23. Quoted in Mary Clemmer Ames, *A Memorial of Alice and Pheobe Cary* (New York: Hurd and Houghton, 1874), p. 27.

24. Quoted in Pattee, pp. 55–56.

25. Dewey, p. 250.

26. "Literary Remains of Martha Day," *Lady's Magazine, 7* (1834), 278.

27. See Dewey, pp. 150–51, and Margaret Farrand Thorp, *Female Persuasion* (New Haven: Yale University Press, 1949), pp. 216–18.

28. Papashvily, p. xvi. For some contemporary evidence, see Hale, *Woman's Record, passim;* Gordon S. Haight, *Mrs. Sigourney: The Sweet Singer of Hartford* (New Haven: Yale University Press, 1930), p. 36.

29. Ticknor, p. 141.

30. *Works of Nathaniel Hawthorne, Standard Library Edition,* 12 (Boston: Houghton, Mifflin and Company, c. 1883), p. 218. For evidence that his fears were not unfounded, see J.C. Derby, *Fifty Years Among Authors, Books and Publishers* (New York: G.W. Carleton & Co., 1884) and James D. Hart, *The Popular Book* (New York: Oxford University Press, 1950), as well as Pattee.

31. *Lady's Magazine, 4* (1831), 3–4.

32. *Woman's Record,* p. 687.

33. "The Beginning," *Lady's Magazine, 2* (1829), 5.

34. This and all subsequent references about Emily Chubbuck's life will be to A.C. Kendrick, *The Life and Letters of Emily C. Judson* (New York: Sheldon & Company, 1860).

35. See particularly "Ida Ravelin," "The Poetess" and "Dora," in her collection of sketches, *Alderbrook* (Boston: W.D. Ticknor & Company, c. 1846).

36. Kendrick, p. 121.

37. See Thorp, pp. 157 ff. All references to "Zelma's Vow" will be to the *Atlantic Monthly, 4* (1859), 73–84, 327–44.

38. The main sources for Fanny Fern's life are in the Parton Collection in the Sophia Smith Collection which contains valuable personal letters, including a lengthy correspondence from Harriet Beecher Stowe and an unpublished biography, already referred to, by

Fanny Fern's granddaughter, Ethel Parton. Valuable secondary sources are as follows: Florence Bannard Adams, *Fanny Fern: A Pair of Flaming Shoes* (W. Trenton, N.J.: Hermitage Press, Inc., 1966); Elaine Breslau, "Popular Pundit: Fanny Fern and the Emergence of the American Newspaper Columnist" (M. A. thesis, Smith College); Milton Flower, *James Parton: The Father of American Biography* (Durham, N.C.: Duke University Press, 1951); Grace Greenwood, "Fanny Fern—Mrs. Parton" in *Eminent Women of the Age;* James Parton, *Fanny Fern: A Memorial Volume* (New York: G.W. Carleton & Co. 1873); Elizabeth Bancroft Schlesinger, "Fanny Fern: Our Grandmother's Mentor," *New York Historical Society Quarterly* (1954), reprint in Schlesinger Library, Cambridge, Mass.

39. Henry A. Beers, *Nathaniel Parker Willis* (Boston: Houghton Mifflin and Company, 1885), p. 11.

40. For similar conflicts see Elizabeth Stuart Phelps, *Chapters from a Life* (Boston: Houghton Mifflin and Company, 1897) and *The Autobiography of Lyman Beecher,* ed. Barbara M. Cross (Cambridge, Mass.: Belknap Press of Harvard University Press, 1961), pp. 1, 40–60.

41. Ethel Parton, chapter 2.

42. Fanny Fern, *A New Story Book for Children* (New York: Mason Brothers, 1864), pp. 13–16.

43. An anonymous satiric contemporary answer to *Ruth Hall,* entitled *The Life and Beauties of Fanny Fern* (New York: H. Long and Brother, 1855) insisted she had never been really poor and cited her own well known extravagance. More recently, Robert P. Eckert, Jr., in "Friendly, Fragrant Fanny Ferns," *Colophon, 18* (1934), n.p. upheld a modified version of this view.

44. James Parton, p. 49. For an article dealing with his own relation to Fanny Fern, see Harriet Prescott Spofford, "James Parton," *Writer, 5* (1891), 231–34.

45. Greenwood, "Fanny Fern—Mrs. Parton," p. 78.

46. Ethel Parton, chapter 7.

47. Some of the more interesting of these references can be found in the *New York Ledger,* Apr. 4, 1868 ("A Maniac Authoress"), and Feb. 18, 1871 ("Female Insanity"), in Trinity College Library, Hartford, Conn.; in *Fern Leaves from Fanny's Portfolio* (Auburn, N.Y.: Miller, Orton & Mulligan, 1854), pp. 83 ff.; in *Fern Leaves . . . Second Series* (Auburn, N.Y.: Miller, Orton & Mulligan, 1854), p. 156.

48. Unpublished letter in Parton Collection, n.d.

49. Anya Seton in *The Turquoise,* for example, was still remembering Fanny Fern as the woman "who made more money from her writings than any other authoress" (Typewritten extract in

Parton Collection). Patricia I. McGinnis in "Fanny Fern, American Novelist," already cited, shows how skillfully her publishers promoted *Ruth Hall,* and a contract found in the Parton Collection proves that Fanny Fern had them promise to "use extraordinary exertions to promote the sale" of the book "to make it exceed the sale of any previous work."

50. Beers, pp. 75, 293, 302.

51. Cortland P. Auser, *Nathaniel P. Willis* (New York: Twayne Publishers, 1969), p. 63.

52. For an example of his ability to satirize the feminine literary style he himself often assumed see "The Spirit Love of 'Ione S'—" in *Fun Jottings* (New York: C. Scribner, 1853), pp. 62–71.

53. Beers, pp. 123, 195.

54. Fanny Fern's copy in Parton Collection.

55. Beers, p. 335.

56. She mocked the much praised manuals with such titles as *Guide to Wives* as "Moral Molasses" (*New York Ledger,* Feb. 21, 1863); she satirized magazine like *The Lady's Garland* (*Rose Clark* [New York, 1856], p. 210); she heaped scorn on the popular sentimentalized heroine, "embroidering the worsted dogs and cats and singing doubtful ditties, rolling her eyes at the chaste moon" (*Folly as It Flies* [New York, 1868], p. 264).

57. *A New Atmosphere* (Boston: Ticknor and Fields, 1865), p. 53.

58. *A New Story Book,* p. 8. For examples of similar scenes and sentiments see the opening chapters of Susan Warner's *The Wide, Wide World* (New York: G.P. Putnam, 1851), describing the relationship between young Ellen Montgomery and her mother.

59. *Life and Beauties of Fanny Fern,* p. 150. This notion about the name seems to have been a common one.

60. Kendrick, p. 101.

61. Pattee, p. 278.

62. "Fanny Fern—Mrs. Parton," p. 73.

63. *Fern Leaves from Fanny's Portfolio* (Auburn, N.Y.: Miller, Orton & Mulligan, 1854), p. 334.

64. *Ginger-Snaps* (New York: Carleton, 1870), p. 60.

65. This and subsequent references are to the edition of *Fern Leaves* already cited.

66. This and subsequent references are to *Ruth Hall: A Domestic Tale of the Present Time* (New York: Mason Brothers, 1855).

67. *Fern Leaves,* p. 44.

68. This was apparently not an uncommon practice at the time. See Harvey Wish, *Society and Thought in America* (New York: Longmans, Green, 1950), 1, 416–17. For contemporary evidence, see

Mrs. E.P.W. Packard, *Modern Persecution: or Insane Asylums Unveiled* (2 vols.; Hartford, Conn.: Case, Lockwood, & Brainard, Printers and Binders, 1873).

69. "Fanny Fern—Mrs. Parton," p. 74. The reviewer of the novel in the *Southern Quarterly Review 11* (1855), 449, stresses the change of character Ruth undergoes.

70. *New York Ledger,* June 8, 1861.

71. Ethel Parton, chapter 7.

72. *New York Ledger,* Aug. 10, 1867. Reprinted with some additions in *Folly As It Flies,* pp. 61–64.

Introduction to *Samantha Rastles the Woman Question**

Jane Curry

A writer for *The Critic* of January, 1905, said of Marietta Holley: "As 'Josiah Allen's Wife,' she has entertained as large an audience, I should say, as has been entertained by the humor of Mark Twain." That puts Holley and her folksy, common-sense character Samantha Allen in illustrious company. Marietta Holley made a special contribution to nineteenth-century American humor—not because of innovative comic style or technique, for even in her own time the mother-wit, dialect style was anachronistic; nor because she was our only woman humorist, for the nineteenth century claimed Frances Whitcher, "Fanny Fern," and others; but rather because she was the only humorist whose main character was a woman who spoke specifically about women's rights.

Much of Holley's humor strikes a resonant note of familiarity with modern readers—in terms of language and images as well as in terms of some conservative ideas that have stubbornly persisted into late-twentieth-century culture—and establishes her kinship with latter-day feminists,

---

*A different version of this introductory essay was published in the *Journal of Popular Culture,* VIII:4 (Spring, 1975). For most of the biographical information on Marietta Holley, I am indebted to Margaret Wyman Langworth's article in vol. II of the series on *Notable American Women 1607–1950,* edited by Edward T. James, Janet Wilson James, and Paul S. Boyer, and to an unpublished Ph.D. dissertation entitled "Marietta Holley" by Katherine G. Blyley, University of Pittsburgh, 1936, Ch. I, pp. 2–37.

some of whom sound the same arguments but withhold the same good humor. When one reads the Samantha books, she begins to view the nineteenth century not as "then" so much as it was the beginning of "now." One may be struck by the same confusion Ann Douglas notes in *The Feminization of American Culture* when she describes the process of researching and writing her book on nineteenth-century America: "I expected to find my fathers and my mothers; instead I discovered my fathers and my sisters. The best of the men had access to solutions, and occasionally inspiring ones, which I appropriate only with the anxiety and effort that attend genuine aspiration. The problems of the women correspond to mine with a frightening accuracy that seems to set us outside the process of history; the answers of even the finest of them were often mine, and sometimes largely unacceptable to me. . . ."[1]

Of course, in certain ways, Holley's humor is definitely dated. Her comic style, like that of other mainstream nineteenth-century American humorists such as Seba Smith, Josh Billings, and Artemus Ward (Browne), utilized a dialect dependent on misspellings to conjure sounds of the spoken word and hence reflect (or affect) the rustic flavor so popular among the horse-sense-loving public. Thus, "says" becomes "sez," "was" becomes "wuz," and "medium" becomes "megum." Since twentieth-century humor eschews reliance on "spelling dialect" to convey regional or class linguistic peculiarities, modern readers may at first need to read a few sentences aloud to catch on to the dialect aspect of Holley's work.

Likewise, some of her issues, such as suffrage and temperance, belong particularly to movements and events of the late nineteenth and early twentieth centuries. Indeed, her humor can be seen as a reflection of and argument against late-nineteenth-century social and political reality. But Holley's verbal wit transcends both the situational provenience and the stereotypical characters, thereby providing a freshness that reminds us that the "woman question" goes beyond social mores and politics to the most basic assumptions of our culture.

Marietta Holley, born on the family farm in Jefferson County, New York, in 1836, very early began writing verses generally of pious and sentimental poetry. Her brothers teased her endlessly about these verses, and she later blamed that unmerciful teasing for her life-long case of extreme shyness that even in the height of her popularity inhibited her from making public appearances. Her formal education at the district school ended when she was fourteen because of family financial difficulties, but she developed a passion for music and was assisted by an uncle who paid for piano lessons. Teaching seemed an appropriate way for a young lady to make a living, and she did so with her family's approval. Holley apparently admired a local young schoolteacher who did not follow the approved route and instead quit teaching in order to become a book agent. She was, of course, considered by the community to be "forward." A woman's place was by the "fireside where sheltered by a man's personality she could labor from dawn to dark safe from the vulgar gaze of the public."[2] This woman likewise claimed other-world spiritual communication which also impressed the young Marietta. A religious woman, like Samantha, Holley thoroughly believed both in direct divine guidance via the Bible and in spiritualism. "Every morning she picked up her Bible, held it in her left hand, and opened it with her right. The verse upon which her right thumb rested was the law for the day."[3]

When her first book, *My Opinions and Betsey Bobbet's,* appeared in 1873, it was sold by subscription and found its greatest appeal in rural sections of the country. It was published and circulated by the American Publishing Company, the same publisher that sold 150,000 copies of Twain's *Innocents Abroad* and 80,000 copies of *Roughing It.* The Samantha books, which eventually numbered twenty-one and came out regularly until the last in 1914, were a popular success as evidenced by her large sales, frequent public readings, the success of a Neil Burgess dramatization,[4] and the eagerness of publishers to bring out her new work. Holley was offered a $14,000 advance by Funk & Wagnalls for her 1893 book called *Samantha at the World's Fair*.[5] The propaganda value of her feminist view early caught the attention of Frances Willard and Susan B. Anthony. Willard invited her to be a delegate at the 1877 WCTU (Woman's Christian Temperance Union) convention and Anthony urged her to attend the 1878 National Woman Suffrage Association, but Holley never attended a convention and was terrified at the idea of being on a public stage. Even Anthony's suggestion that she come "incog" couldn't persuade her to attend.[6]

She became famous and financially comfortable, but she still refused to attend conventions or appear publicly and in fact refused the offers of various publishers to send her to Europe or St. Louis or Chicago in order to write her books on travel and expositions. With the exception of her trips to Saratoga and to Coney Island, she never visited any of the places before she wrote about them. Instead, she assiduously studied maps, guidebooks, descriptions, etc., and then wrote her narratives without the encumbrance of directly observed reality.

Though her success and fame were attached to her humorous work, Holley continued to write poetry throughout her life and considered poetry the far more valid literary form. She allowed Samantha to speak her ideas and thus endow her principles with personality, but she resembled Samantha in neither appearance, culture, nor status. "Miss Holley is more like a Grand Duchess than the homely character she has immortalized. Her spectacles are a pair of gold lorgnettes, her gowns are made by a French modiste, and she has no need of a cap."[7] Though she chose to remain in the country, her society was not the local society of country folk but rather people of prominence. And though Samantha praised the "cast-iron affection" that bound her to Josiah and glorified the virtues of home and family, Marietta Holley never married. Aside from the good humor and solid common sense they shared, Samantha seems to have exhibited precisely those traits not attributable to Holley. Samantha is aggressive, loquacious, well traveled, and plain.

By the time she died in 1926 at the age of ninety, Holley's books were scarcely read. The ideas and issues so relevant to late-nineteenth-century America had become by then commonplace and lacked the urgency and appeal that had preceded the war and the Nineteenth Amendment. Her later books had become endlessly repetitious and her rustic philosopher, an anachronistic comic convention even in 1900, was yet more incongruous in the increasingly urban 1920s.

My Opinions and Betsey Bobbet's (1873) introduces us to the rustic philosopher of sound country stock whose ideas on various issues are grounded in an affection for common sense and faith in its applicability to problems. Jonesville's Samantha Smith Allen is hefty in both principles and weight. By her own admission, she is a wise, religious, compassionate, loyal, faithful, and loving 204-pound wife. She is possessed of endless good judgment, is adept at moral "eppisodin'," and is a first-rate housekeeper and cook. Though she protests both categories, she is also immodest and ceaselessly talkative. She proclaims immediately that "sentiment ain't my style, and I abhor all kinds of shams and deceitfulness."[8] She is a good Christian Methodist who reserves judgment on people until all the facts are known and refuses to participate in malicious gossip feeding upon unfounded rumors. On the other hand, she recognizes the genuinely foolish or destructive qualities of her "sect" such as the use of corsets, bustles, and pantaloons in order to be stylish, and the tendency to gossip. She extols the virtues and recognizes the duties of wives and mothers, and prides herself on being a loyal wife to Josiah and a good mother to his children. At the same time, she sees no conflict between devotion to one's "pardner" and family and a belief in women's rights. She does, however, see a conflict between devotion to family and the licensing of liquor by the government. Thus, Samantha is both prosuffrage and protemperance.

One of the foolish foils whose opinions are set against Samantha's is her husband, Josiah Allen. A widower with two children when she married him, he is a lightweight both as "measured by the steelyards" and as measured by intelligence. He and Samantha have been married fourteen years or so in *Opinions* and forty years by the time the last book is published. This 100-pound, bald weakling displays a tendency toward sentimental foolishness and impractical, adventuresome schemes that Samantha is of course obliged to break off. He is naturally vain, proud, and egotistical and can be easily swayed even from moral good sense by his yearnings to be fashionable. Samantha complains that he is "clost" with his money, and he is continually inventing schemes to acquire more. He is a good pardner, but he's incapable of exercising good judgment. Since he also fails to heed Samantha's reliable advice, his plans are generally utter catastrophes.

Josiah presents the egotistical masculine argument that would keep women strictly in the home because that's what it says in the Bible, because women have weak minds, and because they are constitutionally fragile and must be protected by their stronger menfolk. He is, on the one hand, portrayed as the reversal of the standard male stereotype: he is smaller, dumber, prouder, and more irrational than his female counterpart. On the other hand, he fits the comic stereotype of the small, weak husband henpecked by his larger wife. Whenever they have a discussion in which Samantha has logically boxed him into a corner, he nearly always remembers that he has to milk the cow, or plow the field, or devour his dinner. This is a clear reversal of the usual stereotype of the female who, when losing an argument on rational grounds, will dissolve in torrents of tears guaranteed to soften the heart of her beloved.

Betsey Bobbet is weak sentimentality set against Samantha's absolute practicality. In a glaring understatement, Samantha described her: "Betsey haint handsome." Samantha goes on to depict the stereotypical skinny, ugly old maid whose complexion isn't good, whose eyes are little and deep set, whose large nose has remained steadfastly in place though both teeth and hair have long since fallen away. She mouths the views of the genteel female whose "gushings of a tendah soul" display affectation of speech and agreement with the view that "women's speah" is to cling, to coo, to smile, and to soothe. She agrees with the masculine argument that "it is wimmen's duty to marry, and not to vote." She has a sentimental and impractical picture of marriage and, like Frances Whitcher's Widow Bedott, writes "dretful" poetry and is reduced to vulgar coquetries in her desperate pursuit of the dignity that the state of marriage would bring her. Unfortunately for Betsey, though she is more than willing to be a clinging vine, there seem no men willing to become her stately tree.

To make one's ultimate goal in life the snaring of a husband, Holley suggests, is to transform women into ridiculous buzzards swooping voraciously on their prey; into lonely, bitter people who feel totally defeated because of unhappy love matches contracted for the wrong reasons; into showpieces who have been socialized to value the status of a title—Mrs.—over the quality and dignity of honest loving relationships. Girls must have self-respect and be industrious. "Marryin' ain't the only theme to lay holt of. . . . No woman can feel honorable and reverential toward themselves, when they are foldin' their useless hands over their empty souls, waitin' for some man, no matter who, to marry 'em and support 'em."[9]

No husband can make up for the loss of self-respect. But Betsey does not heed Samantha's advice. She considers it her "duty" to marry, and so she relentlessly pursues eligible men and finally snares Simon Slimpsey, dooming herself to a hard life caring for his several children and coping with his laziness, poverty, and drunkenness. But, pitifully, she still would never part with the "dignity" she has achieved simply by becoming a married woman.

Samantha's constant stance is that of "megumness" ["mediumness"]. She avoids the extremes of any idea and circles all the way around to see all sides. For example, she includes both corsets and pantaloons in her category of female foolishness. Both the genteel ladies of fashion who obstruct normal breathing patterns and the more immodest, boyish women who wear trousers in public are slapped on the hand for failing to be "megum" and sensible. She admits that men are "curious, vain and tejus" but also admits that "so be women." Both "sects" are about equally foolish and disagreeable, good and noble.

Representatives of various viewpoints take their turns confronting and arguing with Samantha, with Samantha's opinions nearly always seeming eminently sane and correct. Samantha's persona as sensible, reasonable sage provides a distance from her various foils. Additionally, the distance between Holley and Samantha as a literary as well as a personal fact allows the reader to perceive Samantha's shortcomings, malapropisms, and loyalties that may seem inimical to her self-perceived stature. For example, the reader sees that though Samantha outdid herself in eloquence while chastizing Victoria Woodhull regarding free love and divorce (Selection 12),* Victoria remains unconvinced and un-converted. Samantha may think she has won the debate, but the reader knows better. In Selection 1, Holley has her rustic character use an abstract literary device—allegory—to make her point to a decidedly dull-minded Josiah. Though she uses stereotypical characters like Josiah, Holley makes him more than a mere whipping boy for feminist ideas by repeatedly

---

*Editor's note: Curry makes reference throughout her *Introduction* to "Selections" that follow in her text. I have retained them here to be faithful to Curry's essay.

showing Samantha's genuine, warm affection for him, even
while she roundly criticizes his ideas. And in such instances
as the discussion about the gender of the courthouse "figger of
liberty" (Selection 33), Holley allows Josiah to miss the point
and claim victory, Samantha to remain smug about her verbal
wit while tending the tea kettle, and the reader to discern the
real point while being amused at both of them. Such uses of
characterization, wit, and irony give more dimension to
subjects and situations than the genre of humor often allows
and offer the persona of Samantha as a woman of genuine
good nature who would not be mistaken (even by anti-
suffragists) for a termagant wife who browbeats the long-
suffering husband.

And she also displays that good nature (and didactic bent)
when she confronts the Mrs. Flamms of the world. Mrs.
George Washington Flamm in *Samantha at Saratoga*
represents the cosmopolitan genteel scatterbrain who has to go
to the watering spa in stylish splendor. Her only criticism of
the Statue of Liberty, that defective Goddess, is that she
should really have a tapered waist, a skirt looped over a
bustle, and a flowered hat on her head. Samantha protests that
if she were thus gussied, Liberty couldn't lift her torch over
her head and enlighten the world (Selection 15).

The extremes of the feminist view are also discouraged. A
wild-eyed feminist appears with characteristically short hair,
flailing vituperative barbs at those tyrants who oppress
women. She is the man-hating radical bent upon immediate,
militant tactics that would eventually give women dominance
over men by rescinding male voting rights (Selection 13).
Samantha listens attentively, remembers that after all Josiah is
a man, and argues with innate mother-wit for a moderate
approach that insures equality and eradicates subordination of
either "sect." She also avoids any threat to the stability or
sanctity of the family by pointing out in that interview with
Victoria Woodhull that liberal divorce reforms and any
overtones of free love are misguided.

Various townsmen, particularly elders in the Meetin'
House, side with Josiah on the "woman question" and provide
rationales for women's place. But in all her books, Holley
insures that the male argument is in blatant, glaring
contradiction to perceivable reality. Occasionally, Samantha
will appeal to a politician to exert his position to "do the right
thing." Though some are educable, like Horace Greeley, still
they are politicians whose position is likely to vary according
to pressure from interest groups, and Samantha knows that the
liquor trade wields the most powerful lobby.

So, on the "woman question" Samantha sets herself
squarely in the reasonable middle and makes foolish the
masculine argument for female submission, the sentimental
female argument for adherence to that defined role, and the
radical feminists whose views and tactics might threaten the
sanctity of home and family. In her sketches on women's
social position, suffrage, temperance, powerlessness before the
law and the church, the double standard, female symbols in
public life, and traditional roles, Samantha's (and Holley's)
stand on women's sphere becomes quite clear.

Holley exposes the contradiction between a democracy
based on consent of the governed and the disenfranchisement
of half of the members constituting that democracy. The
government, because it denies the basic right of the vote to
women, perpetuates women's powerlessness before the law.
Common law provides that a woman's property, her body, her
children, even her clothing belong to her husband, and she has
no recourse under the law to take exception. She is not
allowed equal education, equal job and professional opportunities, or equal pay for work done. Samantha illustrates
women's place in the land of liberty in several ways and then
proposes solutions: the vote, economic independence, freedom to speak publicly against wrongs.

In *Sweet Cicely* (1885), Samantha shows how helpless
women are to change their condition, exercise their own
principles, or influence society in any significant direct

manner. The Cicely saga also illustrates the link Samantha nearly always draws between suffrage and temperance. Cicely is a sweet young mother whose good husband is brought to ruin and murder through the temptation of drink. After his death, she is helpless to do anything to save her young son from future temptations because she cannot vote. She cannot even control the estate to which she had brought considerable property. She is encouraged to influence society through training her son. The executor, though he knows of her strong feelings against liquor, nevertheless rents her property for saloons because it is financially advantageous. Thus she is powerless to insure that even her own property dealings will be consistent with her principles. And in a story that accumulates grievance upon grievance, Samantha tells of the Burpy women who have suffered humiliation, imprisonment, and poverty—all legal according to the workings of the law.

Basic rights, therefore, are withheld from women by the government. Holley's characters give personality to the four predominant anti-suffragist arguments delineated by Aileen Kraditor in her book *The Ideas of Woman Suffrage 1890–1920.* Kraditor argues that, like the suffragists, the anti-suffragists had no one ideology. Unlike the suffragists, the rationale representing anti-suffragism was not characterized by mass activity. There were, however, four standard arguments made by anti-suffragists that, significantly, also appear in folksy form in the Samantha books.

One argument held sacred the sentimental vision of Home and Mother. Women were destined from birth to become full-time wives and mothers. The theological argument, Kraditor maintains, was merely pronouncement that God had ordained man and woman to perform different functions. Women were intended for home, men for the world. Advocates of this argument maintained that this division did not indicate superiority or inferiority. Quite to the contrary, if she remained in her proper sphere, woman was insured supremacy therein.[10]

The biological argument was based on two assumptions: souls as well as bodies have sexual attributes; women are physically incapable of undertaking various duties concomitant with voting. Consistent with the first assumption, femininity is identified with emotionalism and illogicality. Women's intuition is a higher faculty than male logic. However, though their method of arriving at truths is superior to men's, it is nevertheless useless in the political realm. Consistent with the second assumption, anti-suffragists argued that "the weakness, nervousness, and proneness to fainting" of the fragile sex would be out of place in voting booths and conventions.[11]

The sociological argument proclaimed that indeed men and women should occupy different spheres, but that their respective spheres were equal. Social peace and welfare of the human race depended upon women staying at home, having children, and staying out of politics. Female suffrage represented a threat to the very structure of society, the basic unit of which was seen to be the family rather than the individual. The man voted as political representative of his family. Women were not deprived of the privilege to vote as were idiots, aliens, and criminals: women were exempt from the burden of being involved in the dirtiness of politics.[12]

Samantha's anti-suffragists say it in the following ways. Since those who make the laws—men—also interpret the law, women inevitably become angel designates who can confidently look to men as their legal representatives. The male response to female dissatisfaction is to describe the consequences of voting which would outrage and destroy women's modesty by placing them in the same street with a man every election day. Man's sacred privilege is to protect woman's weakness. Josiah assures Samantha that he votes as her representative (a declaration from which she takes little comfort). Women are weak, helpless angels, "seraphones," sweet, delicate, coo'n' doves who can't rastle with difficult questions. The angels of our homes are too ethereal, too dainty to mingle with rude crowds. Women should have husbands instead of rights; voting would only lower women in the opinion of men. (Samantha replies that since women are already the lowest class in society, they could hardly consider this a threat.) It is flyin' in the face of the Bible not to marry and "stay to home." It is the Law of Nater for the female of the species to stay at home. Since women are naturally frivolous and weak-minded, they probably wouldn't even know how to fold the ballots right and would instead be leanin' over to the next booth to find out what kind of trimmin' the other lady had on her dress. Women can influence the world through their sons; it is unwomanly to suggest the vote. Women must leave to men the difficult task of interpretation. Entering the public sphere ". . . would endanger her life, her spiritual, her mental and her moral growth. It would shake the permanency of the sacred home relationship to its downfall. It would hasten anarchy, and . . . sizm."[13]

In order to claim their rights heretofore withheld, women clearly must have the vote. The two major suffragist arguments were one based on justice and one based on expediency. Kraditor claims that while the earlier suffrage movement held primarily to the natural rights argument, there was a shift in the later movement to an essentially pragmatic argument of expedience. The early suffragists, therefore, had stressed the natural inalienable rights of the common humanity shared by men and women while later arguments underscored the differences between men and women, seeing the vote as primarily a means to the ultimate goal of reform. The suffrage movement was, then, linked to temperance and to the general progressive movement as a means of influencing public morality.

Though Samantha argues for equality of the sexes because it is a natural human right, the vote itself is primarily advocated on grounds of expediency. It is a means to justice and social purity. The licensing of liquor is undermining the family structure. If women could vote, the family would remain inviolate because the whiskey trade would be smashed. Contrary to those who say suffrage would mean aproned men confined in kitchens amid suds and babies, Samantha maintains that suffrage is the way to insure that traditional morality and the sanctity of the home will be guaranteed. Liquor threatens both.

Samantha (and Holley) accepts the concept of women as moral and cultural guardians, and argues that women will be better wives and mothers when they can actively participate in making society a healthier place in which to rear their children. The truly benevolent natures and duties of women in caring for the sick and nurturing the young will be given more significance when the bad men are turned out of office by right-thinking women.

In only one book, *Samantha Among the Colored Folks,* does Holley propose a limited suffrage based on educational qualifications and general intelligence. The assumption clearly is that all white women and some black women would measure up. The fact that she articulates limited suffrage only in her work specifically concerning the race question shows that there are indeed limits to her concept of human equality. The "Southern Question" in the later suffrage movement involved issues of states' rights and maintenance of white supremacy. Though Holley is humanely sympathetic to the plight of the emancipated but generally uneducated black man, she sees temporary solutions in colonization and at least implicitly nods in the direction of southern women whose interests lie in keeping whites in power.

Like the suffragists of the 1890s, Holley was optimistic about what female suffrage could accomplish, and she was essentially conservative in ideology. The argument that women who vote would be better wives certainly implies no radical change in sex roles. Though she considered herself "megum" in all things, Samantha was rejecting only the frivolous, overdone, and sentimental characteristics of the genteel tradition. The morality and conservatism were still hers. Like the suffragists, who were primarily white, middle-class Anglo-Saxon Protestants, she encouraged social reform, not social revolution. The basic structure of society was not attacked, merely women's lack of participation in it.

In *Samantha Among the Brethren* (1890), Holley exposed the rights withheld from women by the church and the incredible reasoning that accompanied the blanket denial of those rights. The 1888 General Conference of the Methodist Episcopal Church had refused to seat four duly elected women delegates on the grounds that admission of women was not in accord with the constitutional provisions of the church embodied in the Restrictive Rules. A special investigative commission was appointed, but it eventually reported adversely on the admission of women delegates. In a publisher's appendix to *Brethren* six of the arguments—three for and three against admission—are cited.[14] Holley obviously just added her keen good humor to some already laughable arguments. Samantha describes a situation in which the Meetin' House is in disrepair and the women set out to fix it up. Through this narrative, she obliterates the argument that women are too weak to sit on the conference and exposes the lengths to which women who are economically dependent on men must go in order to secure the necessary monies. Women are reduced to self-sacrifice and even deceit, Holley implies, because they are unpaid labor dependent on the generosity of husbands or fathers in a society that values both money and independence.

Holley's point is clear. If women are to reclaim from the Church the rights and privileges denied them, they must have voting power on governing conferences; they must maintain some measure of economic independence, and they must be allowed to speak publicly without fear of being labeled "unwomanly." In the religious sphere as in the secular sphere, women have not been accorded equal human rights—ironic in terms of democracy, demonic in terms of salvation.

Thus, Marietta Holley transformed moralizing tracts into humorous sketches. However, her sketches involving problems of drinking, white slave traffic, race, imperialism, conflict between capital and labor, and insensitivity to and oppression of the poor are almost never humorous. She doesn't hesitate to eliminate even small children through violent death in order to make a moral point about injustice. One insensitive rich man loses his adored daughter to disease in the very tenement house he failed to repair. A wealthy industrialist who had refused to take safety precautions to reduce deaths caused by his trolleys loses his son in a trolley accident. Both men reform. Even Samantha's own granddaughter is killed by the inaccurate bullet of bigoted southern whites who want to keep the blacks down. These stories and the many stories involving the consequences of the liquor trade are dim reminders of what Holley's work would have been without her humor. They are sentimental, melodramatic episodes of didactic moralizing that seek to manipulate emotions and point the way to justice and reform.

Fortunately, her treatment of women's sphere, suffrage, the double standard, fashions, rural life, corruptions in government, and so forth do not fall victim to the same moribund moralizing. Though Holley turns again and again to the issue of suffrage, there are numerous sketches and images of women that relate to symbolic representations of women and to role assumptions about women.

In *Samantha at the World's Fair* Josiah Allen's Wife admires the achievements of women as exhibited by the Woman's Building. Josiah articulates male expectations of the extent of female productivity. He had anticipated seeing light and triflin' things like gauzes, artificial flowers, and tattin', but instead he saw that he had vastly underrated women's creative talents. Josiah, who had assumed that it wouldn't take long "to see all that wimmen has brung here," was astonished to learn that women had designed the building, decorated the interior with carved panels, and written the books shelved in the library. In noticing the many statues on the fairgrounds, Samantha remarked that she felt "dretful well, to see how much my sect wuz thought on in stun." Then she describes various statues symbolic of Truth, Liberty, Diligence, Tradition, etc. She finds that abstract properties are assigned to male and female in complete accord with assumptions about male and female roles. Samantha would probably be disappointed to know that Columbia, the female figure that used to be cosymbol with Uncle Sam, has met a quiet and apparently unnoticed demise.

In the later suffrage movement, the conservative ideology which supported women's sphere as in the home was reconciled with the ideology of social reform because some, such as Jane Addams, perceived the workings of the government as essentially "enlarged Housekeeping" that required the experience of the nation's housekeepers.[15] Though she never makes an explicit connection to a specific suffrage argument of reform as housekeeping, Samantha does, significantly, use Columbia as symbol of the United States in *Samantha at the Centennial.* Columbia is the housekeeping metaphor: ". . . (she) has got her high heeled shoes on, as you may say, and is showin' off, tryin' to see what she can do. She has been keepin' house for a hundred years, and been a addin' to her house every year, and repairin' of it and gettin' housen stuff together, and now she is havin' a regular house warmin', to show off, what a housekeeper she is."[16]

Furthermore, Samantha is optimistic that things will go better for women now that "Justice is beginnin' to peek out and notice that 'male and female created He them.' Bein' so blind, and believin' jest what wuz told her, Justice had got it into her head that it read: 'Male created He them.'"[17]

Because Justice has been so blind and because the accounts have been "writ down by males and translated by 'em," the deeds of women have been ignored and/or forgotten. In a sketch about the wives of the Old Testament prophets, Samantha points to the function of woman as healer and nurturer, comforter and guardian, workhorse and hostess that remains constant over historical time in society's eyes (Selection 28). Furthermore, the efforts and sacrifices of these faithful "helpmeets" are not acknowledged in any historically significant way because their contribution was not in the political, religious, *public* sphere and because from a male point of view things are as they were created to be. Besides, men write the books. She understands (and understates) that women were probably overlooked because "it's sort o' naterel to stand up for your own sect."

So, Holley took the "woman question" and walked clear around it to see all sides as it was being enacted in late-nineteenth-century America. There is a strong temporal attachment to the issues of suffrage, temperance, and the holdover Victorian female virtues of piety, purity, submissiveness, and domesticity.[18] The use of Columbia as symbol of America is likewise dated because for some reason Columbia has fallen away or returned to the closet while Uncle Sam still wants you.

But though certain issues and symbols reflect a specific historical time, others that have persisted seem strikingly modern. Or at least modern feminists use language, imagery, and reversals that are amazingly akin to those of Holley. The story of the nurturing wives of the prophets obviously transcends a fixed historical time period. Samantha's use of the term "Revolutionary 4 Mothers" was no doubt shocking both because the term "forefathers" was so universally used and accepted and because any alternative that excluded the male gender was unthinkable (Selection 19). Holley points to the fact that women are assumed to be included in the term "man." Men, of course, would not automatically and unquestioningly feel included in the term "4 Mothers" and in fact have written history so that only our male ancestors really did anything worthwhile anyway. The current pressure for genderless terms (such as "chairperson") reflects the same concern that women be recognized as distinct people who should not automatically be subsumed under male titles.

Generally, an institution or a building is genderless. But Samantha jolts Josiah by referring to the Meetin' House as "she." His protest that it should be "he" because it "stands to reason" is only immediately acceptable to other "he's" (Selection 23). Holley would not have gone so far as to call God "she"; however, it is obviously but a short jump to the current "Our Mother who arte in Heaven." Holley questioned not the Deity, "Himself," but the interpretation of divine word so as to subordinate women in the social sphere and exclude them in the hierarchical structure of His institutional church. Nevertheless, the shock value of calling the Meetin' House a "she" was undoubtedly not lost upon an audience that would have considered a change in God's gender both blasphemous and sacrilegious.

In a sketch that elucidates via role reversal, Holley captures an image bearing noticeable resemblance to the caption of a recent British family-planning poster showing a man pregnant: "If it were you, how would you feel?" In "A Male Magdalene" (Selection 16), Samantha attacks the irrational double standard by simply reversing the traditional tale of the fallen woman. Nelt Chawgo, "that young he-hussy," is a lost man, a "ruined feller." He was ruined by Angerose Wilds who had deceived him by promising marriage, had used him, and then had deserted him. Samantha urges that neither Angerose nor Nelt is guiltless, nor should either bear the entire blame. There should be no double standard of conduct. She claims that men and women do and should perform different functions in society, but that qualities of soul and character and basic humanity have no sex identification. Women should not be above or below men—they should sit side by side as equals.

In *My Opinions and Betsey Bobbet's,* Samantha said in the preface that she had been persuaded by a deep inward voice that she must write about "Wimmen's Rights." She resolved to "set her shoulder blades to the wheel" and write what that voice of the heart knew must be authored. The cover page announces that *Opinions* is "designed as a beacon light, to guide women to life liberty and the pursuit of happiness, but which may be read by members of the sterner sect, without injury to themselves or the book."

For the mother-wit who exposed as preposterous many of the arguments against suffrage, current objections to the Equal Rights Amendment would be an enticing challenge. One wonders how Samantha would "rastle" with objections that passage of the ERA would mean unisex public bathrooms, women fighting beside men in the trenches of war, and the destruction of the family unit. Or, she would once again tackle the always current scriptural argument of fundamentalists who object that the ERA would be flyin' in the face of the Bible, which clearly shows woman's place to be subordinate to man's. Certainly, the current women's movement would elicit both her support and criticism, just as the earlier movement did. She had in common with modern feminists a sympathy for and commitment to ideas and projects that encouraged and demanded equal status as human beings. She would probably be distraught at current divorce rates, permissive sexual mores, the instability of the family structure, and militant feminist tactics. But my hunch is that Samantha would set her shoulder blades to the wheel and "resoom" the struggle, though of course, "eloquence is dretful tuckerin'."

Notes

1. Ann Douglas, *The Feminization of American Culture* (New York, 1977), p. 11

2. Quoted by Blyley from Holley's posthumously published autobiography, *The Story of My Life,* 1931, Chapter 1.

3. Blyley, p. 28. Blyley was able to interview Holley's longtime gardener and others who provided first-hand accounts of her daily habits.

4. Neil Burgess was a popular comedian who often dramatized humorous works. Among those he chose were Frances Whitcher's Widow Bedott and Holley's *Betsey Bobbet*. According to Blyley, Burgess agreed to pay a weekly royalty to Holley for the use of names of characters in the book and for the plot material which he was to adapt into a dramatic version. The author insisted that there be nothing "off color" in the adaptation. With Burgess playing Samantha, the Providence premiere was highly successful. In 1878 he moved the play to New York City, but he broke his contract by changing Samantha from a dignified philosopher to a grotesque termagant. The version, renamed *Vim,* ran for 200 performances at Bijou in 1883 and was revived periodically in both New York and Boston down to 1888.

5. *Notable Women,* p. 203. Although sales records are not available from Funk & Wagnalls publishers, there is further evidence of her popularity. In *Golden Multitudes,* Frank Luther Mott cites as best-sellers books believed to have had a total sale equal to 1 percent of the population of the continental United States for the decade in which it was published. Best-sellers in the decade 1880–89 required a sale of at least 500,000 to make the list. Better-sellers don't quite match that number but are believed to be 1 percent of the population. *Samantha at Saratoga* made the better-seller list for that decade.

6. *Notable Women,* p. 203; Blyley, pp. 2–37. A recent article evaluates Holley's value as a propagandist. See Shelley Armitage, "Marietta Holley: The Humorist as Propagandist," *Rocky Mountain Review,* 34:4 (Fall, 1980), 193–201.

7. Mable Wagnalls, "A Glimpse of Marietta Holley," *Ladies Home Journal* (Nov., 1903), 61.

8. Marietta Holley, *My Opinions and Betsey Bobbet's* (Hartford, 1973), p. 24.

9. Marietta Holley, *The Widder Doodle's Love Affair* (New York, 1893), p. 43.

10. Aileen Kraditor, *The Ideas of Woman Suffrage 1890–1920* (New York, 1971), pp. 12–26. Two general survey accounts of the campaign for suffrage are Eleanor Flexner, *A Century of Struggle* (Cambridge, Mass., 1959) and Andrew Sinclair, *The Emancipation of the American Woman* (New York, 1965), originally published as *The Better Half.* For documents pertaining to the suffrage movement, many reprinted from the multi-volumed *History of Woman Suffrage,* see Section III, "Woman and Government," in Kraditor, ed., *Up From the Pedestal* (New York, 1968).

11. *Ibid.*

12. *Ibid.*

13. Marietta Holley, *Samantha Among the Brethren* (New York, 1890), p. 20.

14. See headnote to Section V for specifics on these arguments.

15. Kraditor, *Ideas,* pp. 38–57. Samantha uses the housekeeping metaphor in *Samantha on the Race Problem* as follows:

> "I know the law is there. [She refers to the law passed by men that made the age of consent for children the venerable old age of seven.] But let wimmen have a chance to vote; let a few mothers and grandmothers get holt of that statute-book, and see where that law would be."
>
> Sez I eloquently, "No spring cleanin' and scourin' wuz ever done by females so thorough as they would cleanse out them old law books and let a little of God's purity and justice shine into their musty old pages" (p. 238).

16. Marietta Holley, *Samantha at the Centennial* (Hartford, 1887), p. 496.

17. Marietta Holley, *Samantha Among the Colored Folks* (New York, 1894), pp. 317–18.

18. These four virtues were described by Barbara Welter in "The Cult of True Womanhood: 1820–1860," *American Quarterly* (Summer, 1966), 151–174. They seem appropriate to mention in this context because Samantha emphasizes all but submissiveness as admirable ideals. She does not, however, equate piety with subordination in church affairs nor purity with exclusively female mandates. She is proud of her domestic skills (and boasts of them periodically) but though she argues for suffrage on the grounds that the family and domestic sphere can be saved because of the votes of moral women, she is obviously not relegated to a nonpublic existence.

Welter's article was representative of a predominant theme in writings on women's history, often based on published didactic literature regarding woman's place and the home, which cited the changing status of nineteenth-century women that in fact diminished them when compared to their eighteenth-century mothers. Women became victims of an ideology of domesticity that served man's view of the social order. Nancy Cott, in *The Bonds of Womanhood* (New Haven, 1977), sees three successive interpretations of "woman's sphere," with Welter's perspective representing the first. The second, she contends while apologizing for the injustices of over-simplification, "observed that women made use of the ideology of domesticity for their own purposes, to advance their educational opportunities to gain influence and satisfaction, even to express hostility to men." This perspective was generally based on the published writings of women authors. The third, drawing primarily from diaries, letters, and other "private documents of nonfamous women," turns tables on the first by viewing "woman's sphere as the basis for a subculture among women that formed a source of strength and identity and afforded supportive sisterly relations; this view implied that the ideology's tenacity owed as much to women's motives as to the imposition of men's or 'society's' wishes." See Cott's discussion, "On 'Woman's Sphere' and Feminism," 197–206.

Among those who show "true womanhood" to have been less monolithic than Welter's assessment are Carroll Smith-Rosenberg, whose article "The Female World of Love and Ritual: Relations Between Women in Nineteenth-Century America," *Signs,* 1:1(1975), 1–29, describes long-lived, intimate same-sex relationships among eighteenth- and nineteenth-century women that were casually accepted by American society. Though women possessed little status or power in the larger world, the continuity of female closeness and support networks signified their value, dignity, status, and power within the specifically female world.

A forthcoming book (working title, *"Liberty, A Better Husband": The Single Woman in America, 1780–1860*) should expand and revise still more our understanding of options for the nineteenth-century woman. Lee Chambers-Schiller discusses the "cult of single blessedness" and argues that the assumption that single women were denigrated is false. There was more flexibility in the social mores than has been thought and in fact many women chose to live single lives (as missionaries, teachers, artists, scientists, writers) and were socially approved.

Heterodite Humor: Alice Duer Miller and Florence Guy Seabury

Zita Dresner

Since humor has traditionally been considered, especially by men, an unorthodox mode of expression for women, it is not surprising that two of the wittiest exponents of woman's equality should be members of Heterodoxy, a club, as Mabel Dodge Luhan wrote in her autobiography, "for unorthodox women."

Founded by Marie Jenney Howe, Heterodoxy flourished in Greenwich Village from 1912 to approximately 1940. In her monograph, *The Radical Feminists of Heterodoxy* (1982), Judith Schwarz describes the club as "a meeting place for women of widely divergent political views" and professional occupations (authors, lawyers, journalists, physicians, stockbrokers, educators, social reformers, psychologists, anthropologists, visual and performing artists). In addition, Schwarz notes, the membership included "conventionally married heterosexual women . . . , scandalously divorced members and free-love advocates, . . . [and] never married women, several of whom were lesbians involved in long-term relationships with each other or non-Heterodoxy women." Yet, despite these political, professional, and personal differences, all of the members of Heterodoxy, Schwarz maintains, were "ardently pro-women supporters" whose involvement in Heterodoxy was important to their lives and whose "collective memories of Heterodoxy meetings conjure up images of often uproarious meetings just this side of bedlam, witty comments, and hotly debated political opinions tossed back and forth . . ." (1).

These two major characteristics of Heterodoxy—the expression of pro-woman sentiment and the exercise of woman's wit—are epitomized in the writing of two of the club's members who chose humor and satire as a medium of expression: Alice Duer Miller and Florence Guy Seabury. Miller's pro-suffrage verse and Seabury's humorous essays on the roles, images, and status of men and women in the 1920's are clear evidence not only of the quality of women's literary humor but also of the feminist nature of that humor—the term "feminist" being used here as defined in Alice Duer Miller's poem "Feminism":

> "Mother, what is a Feminist?"
>   "A Feminist, my daughter,
> Is any woman now who cares
> To think about her own affairs
>   As men don't think she oughter."

Poet, playwright, screenwriter, and highly successful author of traditionally romantic popular fiction, Alice Duer Miller gained initial recognition through the pro-suffrage verse she published from 1914–1917 in a *New York Tribune* column entitled "Are Women People?" Like many humorists of the period, Miller was able to take advantage of the shift in humor that began to appear by the turn of the century as urban populations grew, rural populations declined, and new humor publications were introduced to speak to the values and concerns of a more cosmopolitan middle-class culture, as well as to a "New Woman." Moreover, like many of Heterodoxy's members, Miller worked for the suffrage cause, not only as an active lecturer but as chair of the committee on resolutions for the National American Suffrage Association. The combination of her political work, talent for satire, accessibility to new outlets and audiences for political humor, and support group of Heterodites who shared her sentiments undoubtedly stimulated the quality and success of her column.

Collected in two volumes, *Are Women People?* (1915) and *Women Are People!* (1917), Miller's verse satirizes the arguments against woman's rights promoted mainly, but not exclusively, by the male population. One of Miller's frequent techniques in these verses is to present a then current quotation from a newspaper, magazine article, book, or pamphlet about woman's role, image, nature, or rights, followed by a poem that ridicules the point or "argument" of the quotation. Using one of the most common tools of women humorists before and after her—pointing up the incongruity between images and realities, particularly in women's lives—in addition to displaying a trenchant wit, Miller reveals in her pro-suffrage satiric verse a penetrating perception of the ways in which gender stereotypes were (and have continued to be) manipulated to keep women in a subordinate place and men in positions of status and power.

For example, one popular argument against woman's equality was that it would encourage females to leave their homes and work, as one anti-suffrage leaflet stated, simply "to win pin money." In "Selfish Creatures," Miller reduces this argument to absurdity with stanzas like the following, which underline the discrepancy between the assumption that women work for trivial causes and the reality of many women's position as sole support of themselves and their children:

> I stopped to ask a scrub-woman
> "Why labour like a man?
> You cannot feed your children? Well,
> There must be some one can."
> She said: "I merely work because
> I need a feather fan."

Another anti-suffrage concern that Miller frequently targeted was the fear that women's equality would kill chivalry. Of Miller's numerous responses to this concern, the following two demonstrate her effective use of both direct and indirect irony to achieve her satiric purpose. "To Chivalry" begins

> Chivalry, I don't abuse you,
>   Not at all—the only rub
> Is that those who praise you, use you
>   Very often as a club.
> As a club or stick of candy,
>   As a punishment or prize
> Finding you extremely handy
> When they want to sermonize.

The more facetious tone of "The Demise of Chivalry" can be heard in the following stanza, which presents an almost cartoon image to the mind that, in evoking laughter, destroys the false notion being promulgated:

> The courteous policeman on my beat
> Who always helps me cross the crowded street,
> Had I the ballot—as I understand—
> Would throw me underneath the horses' feet.

This technique of pretending to take seriously what is patently ridiculous is also apparent in Miller's attacks on the hypocrisy of those who hide behind slogans about the sanctity of the home and the frailty of women. In "Protect the Shrine," for example, Miller targets a congressman from North Carolina, Mr. Webb, who, following an anti-suffrage speech about a mother being an "uncrowned queen" presiding over "the fireside shrine," voted against a bill to restrict child labor. Again, Miller undermines the validity of the chauvinist position by exposing the incongruity between Mr. Webb's professed sentiments about the family and his actions against the exploitation of children:

> O woman, O mother, we love and respect you
> As queen and as goddess we long to protect you,
> And how can we give you a pleasanter day
> Than by keeping your dear little children away?

CHORUS

O, come all ye factory owners, combine;
Though the world misinterprets your noble design,
Keep children away from a spot so divine,
So potential and pure as the fireside shrine.

Similarly, in "Independence Day: A Patriotic Hymn for Girls,"
Miller underscores the discrepancy between the slogans about
American life and the reality of the position of women:

Come, little girls, and let me teach
   The truths of Independence Day
Lest patriotic song and speech
   Should lead your little minds astray,
Lest you should fancy you would be
   Extolled for wishing to be free.

You've learnt whence governments derive
   Their powers—their just powers, rather;
And how your fathers had to strive
   (But never imitate your father),
And how we've all enjoyed since then
Democracy—at least for men.

Another way in which Miller undermines the cliches
about woman's status and image is through reversing gender
roles, as illustrated in "A Mother to Her Son: On His Request
for a Latchkey" and in "A Consistent Anti to Her son." In the
first poem, the mother uses the same arguments in denying her
son a latchkey that the son has used to justify denying women
the vote:

A woman likes her offspring
   To cling, and who can tell—
If you could open the door yourself
   I might not love you as well.
Waiting upon you, Georgie,
   Is such a pleasure to me,
I shouldn't enjoy life half so much
   If you were given a key.

315

In the second poem, the "Anti" is made to unwittingly satirize both herself and the anti-suffrage position by issuing to her son the same warnings about voting that were issued to women:

> You must not go to the polls, Willie,
>   Never go to the polls,
> They're dark and dreadful places
>   Where many lose their souls,
> They smirch, degrade and coarsen,
>   Terrible things they do
> To quiet elderly women—
>   What would they do to you!

Miller's ultimate use of role reversal to attack the anti-suffrage position, however, is found not in her verse but in an unpublished one-act play entitled "His Place in the Armory." Set in the year 2100, when women are running the government, the play recounts a special session of Congress called to consider men's repeated petition for the vote. The following anti-male suffrage argument by one of the female senators is representative of Miller's sustained burlesque of the arguments advanced against women's suffrage by the male Congressmen of the period:

> Men are so terribly hysterical. If anything goes wrong, they must swear. If anything goes right, they must shout. I went to one of their football games the other day, and you cannot imagine the hysterical exhibition that took place at the end. Men of fifty—fathers of families—dancing about—the field, . . . screaming and singing. And I said to myself: And this is the sex that is asking for the ballot!

Miller also employs burlesque in verses which do not reverse roles to undermine the validity of the anti-suffrage viewpoint. A series of poems entitled "Love Sonnets of an Anti-Suffragist" not only reduce to rubble the cliches about women that constitute the bricks of the "pedestal" men build to keep women in their place, but also expose the crumbling mortar of male vanity that holds these bricks together. The first sonnet in the series, "To His Love, Complimenting Her on Her Lack of Intelligence," is typical of Miller's method of mocking male-constructed feminine "ideals" by revealing the insulting and self-serving assumptions upon which they rest:

> Mabel, my love burns with this flame intense,
> Not for your beauty, though I find you fair,
> Not for your charming lack of common sense,
> Not for your ignorance, beyond compare.
> I love you, not because I think your mind
> Is empty as a flawless cup of glass,
> Not for the fascination that I find
> Hearing you talking like a perfect ass.
> No, but because with you, as in a dream,
> I seem a giant, dominant and strong,
> As in real life I very seldom seem,
> Or only after effort hard and long,
> But you admire everything I do,
> And all I say you greet with "Oh, how true!"

It is not just masculine vanity that Miller attacks, however. Feminine vanity, self-righteousness, and indifference are also the targets of her satire. Like Marie Jenny Howe's mock antisuffrage monologue, Miller's verse suggests that the women of Heterodoxy understood that a good part of the battle for women's rights had to be fought not just against men but against women who feared equality. Thus, Miller's verse also derides different types of the female "anti." In "The Anti Speaks," for example, Miller targets women who are terrified that female activism will lose women men's protection, failing to understand that such "protection" is oppression. "Antis We Have Known" presents an unflattering portrait of women who are unsympathetic to women's rights issues because their money and social position protect them from want, suffering, and having to work to support themselves or their children. Finally, "Ode: Recollections of Anti-Suffrage Speeches Heard in Early Childhood" targets the woman who accepts and revels in the cliches about women's weakness, frivolity, and childishness because they excuse her own selfishness and irresponsibility.

Although these examples provide only a limited sense of the scope of Miller's concerns and techniques in her pro-suffrage work, what unifies all of this writing is her conscious choice of humor and satire as her strategy for promoting the cause of woman's equality. Using humor as an instrument for change, Miller also understood its aggressive and subversive potential, particularly for women who, along with being considered unfit for mental and physical exertion, for participation in public life, and for the vote, were also, as at least one antisuffrage speech noted, "not supposed to be humorous." Miller pokes fun at this assumption in "The Code," noting again how the double standard devised by men functions to support their claim to superiority:

> Ladies, true to the tradition
> 　　Of the ivy and the oak,
> Never make the dark admission
> 　　That you see a joke!
> Laugh and smile, for that's beguiling,
> 　　If the teeth are good;
> But not knowing why you're smiling—
> 　　That's true womanhood.
> Humour must remain a stranger
> 　　To the loving female mind,
> If we would avoid all danger
> 　　Of a thought unkind.
> Chivalry would go to Hades
> 　　Very, very quickly then.
> Men may laugh at us poor ladies;
> 　　We must not at men.

In suggesting the true reason why men have denied or denigrated woman's sense of humor—their fear of being laughed at, exposed—Miller also implies the speciousness of arguments that use other supposed characteristics of women to deny or denigrate their petitions for equal rights.

Like Alice Duer Miller, Florence Guy Seabury exhibited some of the new trends in humor that characterized the first quarter of the twentieth century. Active in the suffrage movement, Seabury served for a time as editor of *The Woman Voter,* as well as contributed satirical articles to *The New Republic, McCall's,* and *Harper's,* some of which were collected in *The Delicatessen Husband and Other Essays,* published in 1926. Written after the passage of suffrage, Seabury's essays are concerned not with the vote but with what commentators on the 1920's have termed the "war between the sexes" in American humor, set off in large part, as Nancy Walker argues in *The Tradition of Women's Humor in America* (1984), by "the antagonism created by women moving into man's realm" (15) and characterized by the emergence of new humorous types: a caricature of the "New Woman" and a new representative American male, identified by Norris Yates, in *The American Humorist* (1964), as a "Little Man" (38).

While *The Delicatessen Husband* reflects many of the elements and concerns of the humor of the 1920's, it also incorporates Seabury's formal study of and work in social welfare and psychology and her involvement in women's rights. The essays comprising the volume gain a unique perspective from this mix of interests and influences with Seabury's dry wit, mastery of ironic understatement, and use of mock case studies and scientific method to explore issues and questions concerning relations between the sexes in an era of changing ideas about sex roles, morals, and manners. The fact that these same elements of style and tone are evident in a humorous piece Seabury wrote in 1919 for Heterodoxy, entitled "Marriage Customs and Taboo Among the Early Heterodites," suggests that she, like Miller, may well have been influenced and encouraged by her co-members in her choice of humor as a literary mode.

The opening article, "Men Nowadays," sets up the framework and point of view of the collection in using a "case history" (three generations of the fictional Wade family) to document the shift from a time when the images, roles, and functions of men and women in American society were clearly defined and accepted to 1926, when "men and women seemed to be all mixed up"—not just in appearance, but in personality and place. Although Seabury presents the changes (and the confusion and resentment resulting therefrom) in a sympathetic and unbiased way, she also makes clear, in this and succeeding pieces, that the way to cope with the chaos is not by sending women back to the home or by encouraging men to go slack and let women take over, but by men and women cooperating to find constructive ways to accommodate the changes brought about by women's fight for equal rights, freedoms, and opportunities.

Finding these ways, for Seabury, involves the exploration of some of the causes and effects of the problems that she sees creating chaos in relations between the sexes in order to discover some possible steps toward solutions. As a "scientist," she proceeds from "data" to conclusion, using humor to strip away illusions and expose the truth. In "The Cave Manikin," for example, she begins by discussing the ways in which fairy tales indoctrinate boys and girls at an early age with dangerously unrealistic ideas about masculine and feminine roles—ideas which parents and society continue to reinforce. She goes on to suggest that, even though these roles and images have been challenged, parents still try to push and intimidate their children to fit given gender molds, with the result that people still feel humiliated and frustrated if they do not meet fairy tale expectations of what a man or woman should be. Like Miller, she juxtaposes fantasies and realities to emphasize the lack of congruence between them and, therefore, the inevitability of failed expectations. Then she concludes by suggesting that society look again at the fairy prince: "Was there ever such an invincible he, or was he only a cave manikin put over on us all?"

Seabury's recognition of and concern with the clash between the realities of people's lives and their illusions about their roles as men and women, marriage, and the opposite sex not only inform and unify the collection of articles but also establish the structure in which the humor operates. In the title piece of the collection, for example, the pseudo-objective voice of the investigator/writer underscores the foolishness of the husband of the couple being "case studied"—a man made miserable by his wife's career and his subsequent dependency on delicatessen take-out dinners. Although his wife had told him prior to marriage that she preferred a career to homemaking, the narrator reports that "he didn't believe it; sure that she didn't understand the depths of her own nature. Nor the influence of his. All women, he believed, are domestic at heart and if the desire for cooking and dish washing has been unnaturally suppressed, marriage will miraculously unfold it" (32). Without overt commentary, Seabury uses a deceptively detached tone to depict a "Little Man" diminished not by his wife's dominance or aggression but by his inability to give up false expectations based on illusions that are destructive to both himself and his marriage.

In addition to revealing the incongruity between men's traditional notions of woman's domestic roles and the non-domestic, career-oriented lives many women were leading, Seabury also points out the incongruity between the masculine images promoted by society and the realities of many men's lives. In "The Sheltered Sex," for example, Seabury, like Miller, uses role reversal to turn topsy-turvy the idea of man as protector, illustrating again with "case studies" the ways in which women must constantly protect men from the unpleasantnesses of life. There is Arnold Hutchins, whose wife has to protect him from onions—not only in his own home, but everywhere else. There is Helen Field, who has to protect her husband from his own family whenever *he* invites them to visit. In almost every American home, Seabury writes, "you will find grandmothers, mothers, wives, sisters, aunts, daughters and female servants consecrated to one great purpose—saving the male members of the family from the vicissitudes of everyday life" (48). Even the business world, Seabury asserts,

> is built upon the theory of masculine protection. In every well-regulated office a cordon of women employees vie with each other to keep the outside world from permeating the inner sanctum. A young girl answers the telephone and prevents access of any but the acceptable; a woman secretary is always on duty as a buffer and custodian of the sacred presence; feminine stenographers, bookkeepers and file clerks carry on the drab routine while "he" sits majestically in an inner chamber. (49)

Then, reversing the stereotypes, Seabury concludes,

> Naturally, this easy and secure life of men and their years of sheltered living have made them more or less helpless. They have been brought up, poor dears not to do little personal things for themselves. In many ways, an average man could put a Victorian female to shame. (49)

At the same time that she exposes masculine strength and independence as a sham, Seabury also targets women for conspiring to both hide and promote men's helplessness, thus contributing to their own victimization by bullying males. In "Uncle Edward's Principles," for example, Seabury mocks both Uncle Edward's wife and the conventions that motivate her behavior: "Aunt Isabel belongs to a generation of women whose marriage has been a sort of funeral for their minds. She buried her last individual opinion in the early twenties along with a decided musical talent; so, of course," Seabury concludes sardonically, "they have been a beautifully happy couple" (122).

There are numerous other conventions that Seabury burlesques, based as they are on false or no longer operative gender roles and images. In "A White, White Rose for Mother" she contrasts the conventional image of mother, the sweet white-haired old lady of sentimental pictures and songs, to the vital, active women, who are the real mothers of men who still cling to the illusory image. Seabury's satire of these men is further sharpened by her observation that "the symbolic figure is usually shown alone. The father is absent and the son is away. Men admire complete domestication, but they seldom like to stay with it. They'd rather see than be it." In "The Clinging Oak" she attacks the notion that the male should necessarily be the prime bread winner, arguing that men should not lose "manly prestige" if they are supported by a woman who wants a career and is capable of earning enough for two. This idea is further illustrated by the role reversal of "In Minor Key," in which a husband contentedly serves as secretary to his wife, who is the mayor of their town, a prospective candidate for governor, and a delegate to the national convention to nominate a presidential candidate.

What Seabury is by implication arguing for in these and other pieces is an integrity in men's and women's approach to self and others based on an honest assessment of each individual's abilities and desires. Because of this concern, Seabury subjects what she calls "the Professional Understander" to an especially large and hilarious share of jibing. The most fatuous of all her types, Dr. Peters, her prototypical professional understander, like Miller's Mr. Webb, is a hypocrite who uses women and women's issues to promote himself. Considering himself "an efficiency expert on women," Dr. Peters claims that "there is nothing hidden that shall not be revealed—to him. He knows what any woman will do under any set of circumstances, what she will think on any given subject and exactly how she will solve her personal problems" (190). He makes his living lecturing around the country on women's issues and selling his books: *Have Women Brains? Do Women Contribute to Civilization?* and his "great work," *How It Feels To Be a Woman*, "a graphic presentation of women's innermost thoughts and feelings." While also poking fun at the women who support Dr. Peters' scam by paying his lecture fees and purchasing his books, Seabury most strongly attacks Peters' hypocrisy and megalomania, for example, in describing his lecture on marriage, in which all of the chauvinist cliches are exposed to ridicule:

> He worked up finally to the great question of the hour: Can a man marry the college-bred, economically independent woman of today and find his needs cared for as they were in the olden days when there were three slabs for the Marthas of each patriarch in the village grave-yard? Dr. Peters asserted authoritatively that it could be done successfully. He had done it, although he added parenthetically that owing to complications of modern domestic service, Mrs. Peters was obliged to spend her time in a New England suburb attending to the furnace and the needs of the little Peters. However, the point was that Mrs. Peters preferred to have her career through him. For after all, a man is the greatest career a woman can have. (194)

In the end, Seabury offers no clear-cut solutions to the problems she discusses. Like the anthropologist she pretends to be, her method is descriptive rather than prescriptive, but her use of humor lets us see what she believes needs to be exposed as absurd, incongruous, or fatuous. What she targets indicates what needs to be changed, and how she targets her subjects indicates avenues for change.

In the final analysis, what Seabury seems to envision is the possibility of a truly egalitarian society, in which gender plays no part in how people evaluate each other, treat each other, allocate roles and responsibilities, and make choices about the work they want to do and goals they wish to pursue.

For both Miller and Seabury, the first step toward achieving such a society is to do away with the gender conventions and stereotypes that justify and promote inequities, unhappiness, disharmony, hypocrisy, and generally boorish behavior. For both writers, humor and satire were potential methods of annihilation as well as of cohesion. At the same time as their barbs strike and deflate what had seemed strong and solid, they unite in understanding and camaraderie those who see and appreciate the points of the barbs. Through their membership in Heterodoxy, Miller and Seabury must have experienced the pleasure and power of this dual aspect of humor, as well as enjoyed some sense of what an egalitarian society would be like. Toward the end of her piece entitled "The Dodder," Seabury says, "There are two kinds of bachelor women: those who can get along happily without men and those who cannot. The former have created a Utopia of feminine society, a woman's world of clubs, manless dinner parties, a whole gamut of gay and glorious activities of their own with few of the emotional difficulties of bifurcated social life." While neither Miller nor Seabury was a "manless" woman, it appears that the kind of mutual respect, support, encouragement, intellectual stimulation, and uninhibited laughter they enjoyed as members of Heterodoxy served as a model for the kind of society they hoped would develop from an acceptance and implementation of the principle of human equality.

"I Am Outraged Womanhood": Dorothy Parker as Feminist and Social Critic

Suzanne L. Bunkers

Dorothy Parker, who once called herself "a little Jewish girl trying to be cute," is perhaps best remembered for remarking that "men seldom make passes at girls who wear glasses" or for reacting to the news that Coolidge had died with, "How can they tell?" Then too, Parker's most famous poem, "Resume," is often quoted to attest to her matter-of-fact view of life and death:

> Razors pain you;
> Rivers are damp;
> Acids stain you;
> And drugs cause cramp.
> Guns aren't lawful;
> Nooses give;
> Gas smells awful;
> You might as well live.[1]

Occasionally a modern fiction anthology will include a Parker story such as "The Waltz" to typify the witty sarcasm inherent in her work. For the most part, however, Dorothy Parker and her works have been forgotten by both readers and critics. Those who have heard of Parker associate her with the Algonquin Round Table and *The New Yorker,* but few can remember even the title of her most famous short story, "Big Blonde," which won the O. Henry Prize in 1929. So little attention has been paid to Dorothy Parker in recent years that, as Brendan Gill comments, most people are surprised to learn that she died as recently as 1967—a woman of seventy-three, alone in a New York hotel room.[2]

Why unearth Dorothy Parker now, more than ten years after her death and over thirty years since her collected poems and stories were first published? Because her work deserves re-examination. Dorothy Parker was not only a wit but also a chronicler and a harsh critic of 1920s–1930s social roles. Her poems and short stories are not simply "cute" or "funny"— they also function as a vehicle for social criticism. Of particular importance is Parker's use of stereotypical female characters to satirize, more bitterly than playfully, the limited roles available to American women during the Twenties and Thirties, decades when the predominant image of the American woman was that of the sexually free, even promiscuous, flapper.

In keeping with her purpose as a satirist, Parker's poems and short stories criticize the status quo rather than define new, three-dimensional female roles. As a result, her women characters generally evoke mixed reactions from the reader: they seem pitiable, yet they grate on the reader's nerves. They appear to be victimized not only by an oppressive society but also by their inability to fight back against that society. It would be easy to conclude that Dorothy Parker is hostile toward the "simpering spinsters" or "rich bitches" she portrays in her poems and stories, but to do so would fail to take into account her satiric purpose and technique. Dorothy Parker is not satirizing women per se; rather, she uses her pitiable, ridiculous women characters to criticize the society which has created one-dimensional female roles and forced women to fit into them.

My first encounter with Dorothy Parker was in 1965. A high school student competing in the state speech contest, I was assigned "The Waltz" as my humorous declamation speech topic. I learned from others who had previously used "The Waltz" that this perennial favorite was a sure bet for "Superior" ratings from the judges. So I began practicing, first reading aloud to perfect the two opposing tones used by the persona, then memorizing the material, and, finally, learning the waltz step that would accompany the speech. The judges, true to form, laughed themselves into near-exhaustion and awarded me with Superiors. Although happy about the ratings Dorothy Parker and I had received, I began to wonder if "The Waltz" were really as funny as everyone thought. The persona, a young woman, at first seems to be the stereotypical chatterbox until one notices that the bulk of her "chattering" consists of a serious discussion with herself. Even though she speaks politely to the clumsy man with whom she is dancing ("Why, I'm simply thrilled. I'd love to waltz with you"), her thoughts reveal her distaste for the social role she is expected to fulfill:

> Ah, now why did he have to come around me, with his low requests? Why can't he let me lead my own life? I ask so little—just to be left alone in my quiet corner of the table, to do my evening brooding over all my sorrows. And he must come, with his bows and his scrapes and his may-I-have-this-ones. And I had to go and tell him that I'd adore to dance with him . . . But what could I do? Everyone else at the table had got up to dance, except him and me. There I was, trapped. Trapped like a trap in a trap. [sic][3]

As the pair dances, the speaker's comments to her partner are the usual amenities deemed appropriate to the social situation: "Yes, it's lovely, isn't it? It's simply lovely. It's the loveliest waltz. Isn't it? Oh, I think it's lovely, too." But her witty and sarcastic thoughts reveal her true inner rage:

> I wonder what I'd better do—kill him this instant, with my naked hands, or wait and let him drop in his traces. Maybe it's best not to make a scene. . . . I've led no cloistered life, I've known dancing partners who have spoiled my slippers and torn my dress; but when it comes to kicking, I am Outraged Womanhood. When you kick me in the shin, smile. (pp. 48–49)

The pattern of sharply conflicting overt and covert messages in "The Waltz" characterizes the ironic tone of Parker's fiction, a tone also evident in poems such as "Love Song." In this poem the persona seems to be the ingenue-in-love, extolling her lover's virtues; however, she ironically undercuts this glowing admiration in the eighth and final line of each stanza. The tone of this line, playfully sarcastic in the first two stanzas, becomes decidedly bitter in the last stanza:

> My love runs by like a day in June,
> And he makes no friends of sorrows.
> He'll tread his galloping rigadoon
> In the pathway of the morrows.
> He'll live his days where the sunbeams start,
> Nor could storm or wind uproot him.
> My own dear love, he is all my heart—
> And I wish somebody'd shoot him.[4]

Here, as in "The Waltz," a tension exists between the surface and subsurface of Parker's satire. The lyric quality of "Love Song" is stopped short by the surfacing of the speaker's suppressed rage. Thus, the eighth line of each stanza conveys the irony of the speaker's situation as well as her dissatisfaction with social conventions, conventions which Parker mocks by her choice of style and tone in the seven preceding lines.

This conflict between surface convention and the desire to break through it is even more evident in Parker's short interior monologue, "A Telephone Call."[5] Here the speaker is torn between her desire to break with convention by phoning the man she loves and her fear of violating this social taboo. She addresses God throughout this sketch, alternately pleading with him to let the phone ring and threatening to step out of her passive role by making the call herself. She views the man's failure to call her as her own fault, the result of some "sin" she has committed without knowing it; and she begs for God's forgiveness, promising to atone in a socially acceptable way:

You see, God, if You would just let him telephone me, I wouldn't have to ask You anything more. I would be sweet to him, I would be gay, I would be just the way I used to be, and then he would love me again. And then I would never have to ask You for anything more. (p. 121)

But even as the speaker promises to "be better," her repressed rage begins to surface. First she threatens the telephone: "Damn you, I'll pull your filthy roots out of the wall. I'll smash your smug black face in little bits. Damn you to hell." Then she turns her anger on her lover: "I wish to God I could make him cry. I wish I could make him cry and tread the floor and feel his heart heavy and big and festering in him. I wish I could hurt him like hell." Yet every time she threatens someone or something, she relents and repents. "A Telephone Call" is a tug-of-war between the speaker's social self and her inner self, seemingly a light-hearted game but actually a deadly battle. The battle's tension remains unresolved, however. "A Telephone Call" ends with the speaker still determined to make the all-important call, but still unable to do so.

The tension between social role expectations and the desires of the inner self does seem to be resolved in Parker's eight-line poem, "Observation."[6] This poem's structure parallels that of "Love Song": the first six lines depict the role which the female persona is expected to fulfill, while the last two lines reveal her reaction to this role:

If I don't drive around the park,
I'm pretty sure to make my mark.
If I'm in bed each night by ten,
I may get back my looks again.
If I abstain from fun and such,
I'll probably amount to much;
But I shall stay the way I am,
Because I do not give a damn.

331

Once again, the initially buoyant tone becomes more cynical at the poem's end, a characteristic of many of Parker's poems, notably "Men":

> They hail you as their morning star
> Because you are the way you are.
> If you return the sentiment,
> They'll try to make you different;
> And once they have you, safe and sound,
> They want to change you all around.
> Your moods and ways they put a curse on;
> They'd make of you another person.
> They cannot let you go your gait;
> They influence and educate.
> They'd alter all that they admired.
> They make me sick, they make me tired.[7]

In "Men," Parker uses cliches such as "safe and sound" and clever rhymes such as "curse on/person" to establish a jaunty tone which she then destroys in the poem's final line. Despite the poem's generally light-hearted tone, its message is quite serious. Men put women in an impossible situation, first encouraging them to exhibit certain types of "appropriately feminine" behavior and then punishing them for that behavior by insisting they change it.

Poems such as "Love Song" and "Men" belie the low estimation that critics such as Edmund Wilson have made of Parker's verse: "Her poems do seem a little dated. At their best, they are witty light verse, but when they try to be something more serious, they tend to become a kind of dilution of A.E. Housman and Edna Millay."[8] Dorothy Parker's poetry ranges from two-line witticisms to serious, technically excellent sonnets. A careful examination of her poems reveals that Parker did not take writing poetry any more lightly than she did writing fiction. In her hands, poetry, like fiction, becomes an effective tool for social criticism.

In addition to first-person monologues such as "The Waltz" and "A Telephone Call," Parker's fiction includes longer stories. Many of these are third person narratives which allow the reader to glimpse several characters from the perspective of an omniscient, somewhat cynical narrator. In these stories, as in her monologues, Parker uses female stereotypes to criticize social norms. In "The Wonderful Old Gentleman," the long-suffering Griselda figure, Allie Bain, is contrasted with the domineering bitch, Hattie Whittaker.[9] These sisters share a vigil at the deathbed of their father, the "wonderful old gentleman."

The reader soon discovers from the sisters' dialogue that Hattie is a self-assured schemer, quite conscious of appearances: "Mrs. Whittaker always stopped things before they got to the stage where they didn't look right." She has arranged for their father to live with the poorer Bains rather than with her husband and herself, and she has persuaded her father to leave her his entire estate. Hattie Whittaker, the stereotypical bitch, dominates everything and everyone around her.

Allie Bain, by contrast, is timid and submissive. Her life has not been happy, but she never complains. In fact, she seems to revel in her sorrows. Her father and sister use her because she allows herself to be used. Although Allie's situation is wretched, the reader cannot completely pity her, because she is such a Griselda figure. Nor can the reader completely hate the cold and proud Hattie, whose life consists of manipulating others. Despite her bad qualities, Hattie remains a forceful, assertive woman who knows exactly what she wants and exactly how to get it. Both characters evoke mixed reactions from the reader, which indicates that Parker does not merely intend these figures to be ridiculed but that her criticism goes beyond mocking specific satiric types. By satirizing the Griselda and the Bitch, Parker criticizes the American society which has produced these stereotypes and forced women into them. "The Wonderful Old Gentleman" is a serious indictment of American society, not an amusing portrayal of a sado-masochistic relationship between sisters.

In another intriguing story, "Horsie," the stereotypes used are those of the Old Maid and the Galatea. Miss Wilmarth, an "old maid nurse," is described in terms of confinement and limitation:

> She was tall, pronounced of bone, and erect of carriage; it was somehow impossible to speculate upon her appearance undressed. Her long face was innocent, indeed ignorant, of cosmetics, and its color stayed steady. Confusion, heat, or haste caused her neck to flush crimson. Her mild hair was pinned with loops of nicked black wire into a narrow knot, practical to support her little cap, like a charlotte russe from a bakeshop.[10]

Parker focuses on the nurse's facial features in particular to reinforce the image of the unattractive, even grotesque, woman:

> . . . her face was truly complete with that look of friendly melancholy peculiar to the gentle horse. It was not, of course, Miss Wilmarth's fault that she looked like a horse. Indeed, there was nowhere to attach any blame. But the resemblance remained. (p. 260)

Miss Wilmarth, "sure and calm and tireless," has been hired by the wealthy Crugers to care for their infant daughter. The gawky, unattractive nurse stands in sharp contrast to Mrs. Camilla Cruger, the epitome of the sweet, dainty, and mesmerizing American woman:

> . . . she had always been pale as moonlight and had always worn a delicate disdain, as light as the lace that covered her breast. . . . Motherhood had not brought perfection to Camilla's loveliness. She had had that before. (p. 265)

While Nurse Wilmarth idolizes the Crugers' seemingly perfect existence, they call her "Horsie" behind her back and joke about her ugliness. She is their workhorse, and they use and abuse her much as they would an animal. Her physical appearance might make Miss Wilmarth seem repulsive, but she is also pitiable because of her social position. Neither married nor independently wealthy, she must work to support herself, her mother, and her aunt. She must fit into society as best she can, in the role of the undesirable "old maid" who is grateful for any recognition of her humanity from the rich sophisticates she serves.

Ironically, Camilla Cruger, the beautiful little rich girl, is no happier with her state in life than is Miss Wilmarth. In fact, Camilla's attitude throughout the story is that of boredom: boredom with her husband Gerald, with her baby Diane, and with her life in general. To everyone around her, Camilla represents the Galatean ideal of beauty, grace, and elegance. Yet she is dissatisfied. Her role, although more socially acceptable than Miss Wilmarth's, is just as confining.

The story's climax reveals how trapped both women are in their roles. As the nurse prepares to leave the Cruger household, Gerald, exuberant at the thought of being alone with his Galatea at last, brings Camilla a bouquet of dainty yellow roses and, as an afterthought, gives Miss Wilmarth a small corsage of gardenias. To the nurse, this gift signifies that the Crugers at last view her as a person rather than as an object that has outlived its usefulness. However, her reaction to the gift horrifies Mr. Cruger because it breaks down the formal barrier between them:

> Her squeaks of thanks made red rise back of his ears. . . .
> Gerald was in sudden horror that she might bring her head
> down close to them [the flowers] and toss it back, crying
> "wuzza, wuzza, wuzza" at them the while. (p. 272)

Gerald, embarrassed, quickly re-establishes the necessary social distance as he packs Miss Wilmarth, her face "like that of a weary mare," into a taxi. Then he rushes inside to "get back to the fragrant room and the little yellow roses and Camilla." The story's final focus is on the nurse sitting in the taxi—a small, pitiful figure cradling her gift:

> Miss Wilmarth's strange resemblance was not apparent, as she looked at her flowers. They were her flowers. A man had given them to her. She had been given flowers. They might not fade for days. And she could keep the box. (p. 275)

On the surface, "Horsie" seems to satirize the egocentric and unfeeling Galatea while holding the long-suffering Old Maid up for sympathy and even pity. Parker's satire, however, goes deeper. By using the Galatea and Old Maid stereotypes, the author criticizes the self-centeredness and callousness of the society that has created and sustained these two female roles.

Hazel Morse, the principal character in Parker's short story, "Big Blonde," differs from the stereotyped female characters already discussed in that she incorporates several stereotypes.[11] Parker describes Hazel as "a large, fair woman of the type that incites some men when they use the word 'blond' to click their tongues and wag their heads roguishly." The only relatively small thing about Hazel is her feet, which she jams into "snub-toed, high-heeled slippers of the shortest bearable size." Since there is no hope for her as an aspiring Galatea, Hazel takes another route toward her hoped-for acceptance by the American male. She becomes a "good sport":

> Men liked her, and she took it for granted that the liking of many men was a desirable thing. Popularity seemed to her to be worth all the work that had to be put into its achievement. Men liked you because you were fun, and when they liked you they took you out, and there you were. So, and successfully, she was fun. She was a good sport. Men liked a good sport. (p. 187)

Terrified at the prospect of not being dainty and marriageable, and aware that the good sport role will ingratiate her with men, Hazel plays this role even though it is unnatural to her. She believes that others expect it of her, and she wants desperately to fulfill their expectations. She soon finds security in a circle of female friends, all of whom are "other substantially built blondes," thus assuring that she will not have to face competition from petite, fragile beauties. Yet Hazel longs for marriage, and her fear of being an "old maid" increases with the years:

> She was delighted at the idea of being a bride; coquetted with it, played upon it. . . . She wanted to be married. She was nearing thirty now, and she did not take the years well. She spread and softened, and her darkening hair turned her to inexpert dabblings with peroxide. (p. 188)

The "Big Blonde" is a grotesque version of the Galatea, blonde but bloated, simply too large for the sex goddess mold.

At last, Hazel marries Herbie Morse, "thin, attractive, with shifting lines about his shiny, brown eyes and a habit of fiercely biting at the skin around his fingernails." For the first time in years, she feels she can relax and stop worrying about being a social misfit. She drops the "good sport" role but adopts another stereotypical role, that of the tender and submissive wife:

> Wedded and relaxed, she poured her tears freely. To her who had laughed so much, crying was delicious. All sorrows became her sorrows; she was Tenderness. She would cry long and softly over newspaper accounts of kidnapped babies, deserted wives, unemployed men, strayed cats, heroic dogs. (p. 189)

Herbie, however, does not like this change in his wife; he wants a "good sport," not a "crybaby." The marriage fails and Hazel, single again, reverts to the "good sport" role, the only role she knows. She joins a poker-playing group of drinkers, takes on a series of paunchy lovers, and frequents *Jimmy's,* a meeting place for others like her: aging women, wrinkled and fat, no longer able to affect the role of the youthful, buxom woman:

> They were all big women and stout, broad of shoulder and abundantly breasted, with faces thickly clothed in soft, high-colored flesh. They laughed loud and often, showing opaque and lusterless teeth like squares of crockery. There was about them the health of the big, yet a slight, unwholesome suggestion of stubborn preservation. (p. 198)

Although Hazel's appearance brands her as somewhat ridiculous, the reader's sympathy remains with her even when she gives up and attempts suicide. Here, as in all else, Hazel is doomed to failure. Parker's description of the scene portrays the "Big Blonde" as grotesque yet quite pathetic:

> The bed covers were pushed down, exposing a deep square of soft neck and a pink nightgown, its fabric worn uneven by many launderings; her great breasts, freed from their tight confiner, sagged beneath her arm-pits. Now and then she made knotted, snoring sounds, and from the corner of her opened mouth to the blurred turn of her jaw ran a line of crusted spittle. (p. 206)

The story of Hazel Morse is Dorothy Parker's most bitter indictment of 1920s–1930s American society and the roles to which it expected women to conform. The "Big Blonde" is defeated before she has begun because there is no suitable role for her. Her attempts to fit into various stereotypical roles fail because each role is too limited and confining for a real human being. Hazel Morse is the victim of a society which has not provided her a reasonable place within it.

What, then, has Dorothy Parker accomplished by using stereotypes of women in her poems and short stories? First, by satirizing certain types, Parker can draw what seems to be playful attention to them while actually making a serious statement about her disenchantment with the roles forced on American women during the Twenties and Thirties. Parker's satire obligates the reader to look beneath the surface of her sarcastic humor to the social criticism, criticism which should not be ignored.

Second, because Parker's work is decidedly more feminist in its orientation than that of many other writers of the Twenties and Thirties, Parker uses female stereotypes differently from many writers. For instance, her use of the Bitch and the Galatea stereotypes differs in an important way from Hemingway's Bitches, such as Lady Brett Ashley and Mrs. Francis Macomber, or Fitzgerald's Galateas, such as Judy Jones and Daisy Buchanan. In Hemingway's and Fitzgerald's works, stereotypical women characters are not portrayed as women whose roles have been dictated by society but as women who have chosen their own roles. In contrast, Parker's women characters are clearly products of their society's limited visions of acceptable, "proper" female roles. Thus, Parker's stories are a valuable addition to an accurate historical perspective on women's roles and the effects of those roles during an important period in American literature.

Finally, Dorothy Parker's use of female stereotypes establishes her skills both as a writer and as a social critic. That she was awarded the 1929 O. Henry Prize for "Big Blonde" suggests that her work was receiving some serious attention during the late 1920s and early 1930s. However, her residual fame has come to rest on her sarcastic quips rather than on her social criticism. A re-examination of Parker's poems and short stories is in order. Perhaps this study will serve as a part of that re-examination.[12]

Notes

1. Dorothy Parker, "Resume," in *The Portable Dorothy Parker, Revised and Enlarged Edition* (New York: The Viking Press, 1973), p. 99.

2. Brendan Gill, "Introduction" to *The Portable Dorothy Parker, Revised and Enlarged Edition* (New York: The Viking Press, 1973), pp. vii–xxii.

3. Dorothy Parker, "The Waltz," in *The Portable Dorothy Parker, Revised and Enlarged Edition* (New York: The Viking Press, 1973), pp. 47–51. All references to "The Waltz" are to this edition.

4. Dorothy Parker, "Love Song," in *The Portable Dorothy Parker, Revised and Enlarged Edition* (New York: The Viking Press, 1973), p. 106.

5. Dorothy Parker, "A Telephone Call," in *The Portable Dorothy Parker, Revised and Enlarged Edition* (New York: The Viking Press, 1973), pp. 119–124. All references to "A Telephone Call" are to this edition.

6. Dorothy Parker, "Observation," in *The Portable Dorothy Parker, Revised and Enlarged Edition* (New York: The Viking Press, 1973), p. 112.

7. Dorothy Parker, "Men," in *The Portable Dorothy Parker, Revised and Enlarged Edition* (New York: The Viking Press, 1973), p. 109.

8. Edmund Wilson, "A Toast and a Tear for Dorothy Parker," *The New Yorker*, 20 May 1944, pp. 75–76.

9. Dorothy Parker, "The Wonderful Old Gentleman," in *The Portable Dorothy Parker, Revised and Enlarged Edition* (New York. The Viking Press, 1973), pp. 52–64. All further references will be to this edition.

10. Dorothy Parker, "Horsie," in *The Portable Dorothy Parker, Revised and Enlarged Edition* (New York: The Viking Press, 1973), pp. 260–275. All further references will be to this edition.

11. Dorothy Parker, "Big Blonde," in *The Portable Dorothy Parker, Revised and Enlarged Edition* (New York: The Viking Press, 1973), pp. 187–210. All further references will be to this edition.

12. Besides this article, the only recent academic work on Parker is Emily Toth's "Dorothy Parker, Erica Jong, and New Feminist Humor," *Regionalism and the Female Imagination 3* (Fall 1977/Winter 1977–1978), pp. 70–85.

Hurston, Humor, and the Harlem Renaissance

John Lowe

> With a few exceptions . . . black fiction has failed to produce the full, self-sustaining humorous hero, primarily because humor is out of place in what is basically a tragic literature.—Roger Rosenblatt[1]

> I am not tragically colored. There is no great sorrow dammed up in my soul, nor lurking behind my eyes. I do not mind at all. I do not belong to the sobbing school of Negrohood who hold that nature somehow has given them a lowdown dirty deal and whose feelings are all hurt about it. . . . No, I do not weep at the world—I am too busy sharpening my oyster knife.—Zora Neale Hurston[2]

I. Zora Comes to Harlem

The world has finally rediscovered Zora Neale Hurston. Her books are back in print, a new wave of black women writers have claimed her as their literary ancestor, and today's generation is eagerly exploring Eatonville and its citizens in the nation's classrooms. Zora must be somewhere, ridin' high and having the last laugh. Appropriately, when the *New York Times Book Review* recently published a front-page piece on Hurston, they included a great photo: Zora looks out at us, laughing, from the front seat of her Chevy, during one of her folklore collecting trips in the South.[3]

Why did readers turn away from this supremely gifted artist? Although Zora Neale Hurston suffered some outrageous slings and arrows for being born black and female, she also had to be silenced for her outrageous sense of humor. This no longer surprises when one realizes the extensive role that humor plays in virtually all her works. We now know too, thanks to Cheryl Wall, that Hurston pulled a really fantastic trick on the world by pretending to be ten years younger than she was; census records reveal that she was born in Eatonville, Florida, on January 7, 1891, rather than January 1, 1901. This means, among other things that she was actually thirty-four when she entered Barnard College, although people around her thought she was in her early twenties.[4]

This element of Hurston's personality and aesthetic did not cause her much real trouble until she arrived in New York in 1925, poised to plunge into the currents of the Harlem Renaissance. Significantly, Robert Hemenway begins his superb biography of Hurston at this critical juncture, picturing her arrival in the city in January with $1.50 in her purse, without a job or friends, "but filled with 'a lot of hope,'" carrying a bag of manuscripts, and with "the map of Florida on her tongue."[5]

Although one would never know it from the various accounts we have of this age of "The New Negro," Hurston was only part of the Harlem literati for a few years; she looms larger in histories of the period because she represents many of the movement's best qualities. Moreover, her rapidly reappearing works now reveal her as one of the most productive, and surely one of the finest writers the group produced. Why then, have so many scholarly studies, literary biographies by other Renaissance celebrities, and literary histories failed to do her justice? Again, one of the answers lies in how one reacts to her brand of ethnic humor.

Humor is a basic, continuing component in Hurston; to her, laughter was a way to show one's love of life, and a way to bridge the distance between author and reader. But more than this, she was determined to create a new art form based on the Afro-American cultural tradition, something she helped recover and refine, as an anthropologist. I shall here analyze Hurston's concept of humor and its importance in her works, using an anthropological and literary perspective. It now seems clear that humor played a crucial role in her initial reception by, and later relations with, the other members of the Harlem Renaissance; in her sense of folklore and its functions; in the anthropological aspect of Hurston's humor, which grew out of her training as a professional folklorist; and in the ever changing and increasing role humor played in her fiction, including her masterworks, *Their Eyes Were Watching God* and *Moses, Man of the Mountain.*

Zora Hurston would quite probably be surprised to hear herself mentioned as one of the more important figures of the Harlem Renaissance; she devotes all of one paragraph to this seminal literary event in her autobiography, *Dust Tracks on a Road* (1942).[6] Others, however, speaking of the period, have frequently noted Hurston's contagious sense of fun, her dramatic appearance, and her store of folktales, anecdotes, and jokes; all this made her a favorite at the fabled Harlem "rent" parties, salons, and gab-fests. Surprisingly, only a few writers in the group were actually from the South. Thus Zora brought a special resonance to the movement, for her "down home" qualities meshed rather well with the new interest in the so-called "primitive," a word that had much more of a cachet in the 1920s. Eventually, however, this at first refreshing quality became embarrassingly close to white stereotypes of blacks.[7]

Unfortunately for Zora Neale Hurston, people have always found stereotypes lurking in folklore as well, and this eventually happened when her colleagues and critics began to scrutinize her fiction, which was so heavily influenced, first, by the Eatonville milieu of her childhood, and then by her anthropological studies and field work. Hurston's critics have failed to understand that stereotypes may also be positive, favorable, even overvalued, as well as negative.[8]

Alain Locke, one of the elder statesmen of the Renaissance and one of Hurston's mentors, touched on these matters in a contribution to *The New Negro* of 1925:

> The elder generation of Negro writers expressed itself in . . . guarded idealization . . . "Be representative": put the better foot foremost, was the underlying mood. But writers like Rudolph Fisher, Zora Hurston . . . take their material objectively with detached artistic vision; they have no thought of their racy folk types as typical of anything but themselves or of their being taken or mistaken as racially representative.[9]

Implicit in Locke's comments is a denial that rural blacks are representative of the race. Gradually, this stance began to affect the literati's view of Hurston herself; at first charmed by her wit and appearance, they began to have reservations about her "seriousness." Sherley Anne Williams offers a sensible explanation of how this concept developed and proliferated in literary history:

> For a long time she was remembered more as a character of the Renaissance than as one of the most serious and gifted artists to emerge during this period. She was a notable tale-teller, mimic, and wit, confident to the point of brashness (some might even say beyond), who refused to conform to conventional notions of ladylike behavior and middle-class decorum. To one of her contemporaries, she was the first black nationalist; to another, a handkerchief-head Uncle Tom . . . To Alice Walker and others of our generation, Zora was a woman bent on discovering and defining herself, a woman who spoke her own mind.[10]

Williams suggests that Hurston's humor was enjoyed, but found suspect, partially because it was "unladylike." Women very rarely are permitted to take on such a role, in any society. The traditional effort to place normative restrictions on women has sought the model "good girl" who is "Chaste, gentle, gracious, ingenuous, good, clean, kind, virtuous, noncontroversial, and above suspicion and reproach."[11]

Virtually all of these communal goals for women are antithetical to the qualities associated with the humorist; it therefore comes as no surprise that women around the world almost never engage in verbal dueling or ritual insult sessions, that no female trickster or clown figure exists in the group narratives of any culture, or that the many trickster figures in world folklore are overwhelmingly male. This prejudice goes so deep that in some cultures women who laugh freely in public are considered loose, even wanton.[12] In American society, moreover, there is a widely held belief that women generally are unable to tell jokes correctly in any case. A female folklorist discovered that even in all-female gatherings, women "consistently began and ended with apologies: for speaking, for the content of their speech, for speaking too long. . . ."[13]

If a woman humorist, per se, is offensive, she can only become more so if she somehow uses this stance to obtain money. Much of the long-term damage to Hurston along these lines ultimately came from Wallace Thurman's *roman à clef* of the Harlem Renaissance, *Infants of the Spring* (1932). Thurman, a sharp-tongued, bitter, but brilliant man, almost certainly felt a kind of sibling rivalry towards Hurston. His caricature of her, the figure of Sweetie Mae Carr, a leading light of "Niggerati Manor," severely damaged Hurston's literary image until Hemenway's long-needed biography corrected the picture in 1978:

> Sweetie Mae was a short story writer, more noted for her ribald wit and personal effervescence than for any actual literary work. She was a great favorite among those whites who went in for Negro prodigies. Mainly because she lived up to their conception of what a typical Negro should be. It seldom occurred to any of her patrons that she did this with tongue in cheek. Given a paleface audience, Sweetie Mae would launch forth into a saga of the little all-colored Mississippi town where she claimed to have been born. Her repertoire of tales was earthy, vulgar and funny. Her darkies always smile through their tears. . . . Sweetie Mae was a

345

> master of southern dialect, and an able reconteur [*sic*], but
> she was too indifferent to literary creation to transfer to
> paper that which she told so well. The intricacies of writing
> bored her, and her written work was for the most part turgid
> and unpolished. But Sweetie Mae knew her white folks. . . .
> "It's like this," she had told Raymond. "I have to eat. I also
> wish to finish my education. Being a Negro writer these days
> is a racket and I'm going to make the most of it while it lasts.
> Sure I cut the fool. But I enjoy it, too. . . . Thank God for this
> Negro literary renaissance! Long may it flourish!"[14]

Thurman's portrait had an element of truth in it; Hurston *was*
interested at this point in finding patrons—but Sweetie's
coldly selfish pose is strictly a fiction.

Larry Neal's assessment of Hurston's role during the
Renaissance, written a few years before the corrective of
Hemenway's biography, shows how lingering the effect of
reports like this were. Although he begins by stating that her
reputation was perhaps hurt by the "complexity of her
personality and the controversy that attended her career," he
carries on the tradition by repeating all the old stories, and
makes the old charges. "Miss Hurston" is said to be "very bold
and outspoken, an attractive woman who had learned how to
survive with native wit. . . ." Moreover,

> Zora could often be an inveterate romantic [a traditional
> male term of derogation for women writers]. . . . the
> historical oppression that we now associate with Southern
> black life was not a central aspect of her experience . . . she
> was no political radical. She was, instead, a belligerent
> individualist who was decidedly unpredictable [another
> favorite male charge against women] and perhaps a little
> inconsistent.[15]

Neal also accuses her, as others had before, of being
"opportunistic," because she had been Fannie Hurst's
secretary and Carl Van Vechten's friend. He then quotes
Langston Hughes's oft-cited dig at her, which blithely fails to
mention that Hughes himself was the benefactor of the same
white patron:

In her youth, she was always getting scholarships and things from wealthy white people, some of whom simply paid her just to sit around and represent the Negro race for them, she did it in such a racy fashion. She was full of side-splitting anecdotes, humorous tales, and tragicomic stories, remembered out of her life in the South as the daughter of a traveling minister of God. She could make you laugh one moment and cry the next. To many of her white friends, no doubt, she was a perfect "darkie," in the nice meaning they give the term—that is a naive, childlike, sweet, humorous, and highly colored Negro.[16]

Hughes's remarks are revealing; he mentions Hurston's ability to make people laugh, her rural background, and implies a connection between them. He also infers that someone who is funny and from the South therefore comes off as naive, childlike, *humorous*—as if it were a package deal. Hughes, having arrived in Harlem from Cleveland and Washington, here seems to share his contemporaries' stereotypes of the South and Southern Blacks.

Using Hughes and Thurston as his expert "eye-witnesses" to the events of the Renaissance (something many commentators on the period have done), Neal asserts that Hurston commercially popularized Black culture. He is appalled to hear a story about Zora hosting a racially mixed party wearing a red bandana—and he adds, pejoratively, "Aunt Jemima style," obviously forgetting that many other people besides Aunt Jemima wore and wear kerchiefs, especially in the South. Worst of all, she served her guests "something like collard greens and pigs' feet."[17]

Much of the above reveals a sexist, anti-Southern bias among the intelligentsia; fairness, however, demands yet another qualification. A further factor that worked against Hurston was the residual impact of Van Vechten's *Nigger Heaven* (1926). His well-meaning but mistaken emphasis on the exotic and the sensual led him, and many readers and writers, back to old stereotypes, and caused quite a few Black writers and leaders to eschew anything that smacked of the "primitive." It was difficult for many of these people, when confronted with Zora Neale Hurston's comic folk figures, not to see parallel lines of development. Even though she dealt, for the most part, with positive elements of folk culture, they saw only stereotypes; the baby had to go out with the bathwater.

We should also remember that very few Black people of this time really understood the true greatness of Black folk culture—Hurston was one of the first writers or scientists to assess its riches and map its contours.

What led Hurston into her eventual role in Harlem and her subsequent anthropological adventure? Her autobiography, which frequently obscures rather than illuminates her past, does provide clues in this area. *Dust Tracks on a Road* won a race relations award, partly because Hurston quite consciously "accentuated the positive" and avoided bitterness, a quality she scorns in humorous, incongruous terms: "To me, bitterness is the underarm odor of wishful weakness. It is the graceless acknowledgement of defeat" (p. 280). One delights in the absurdity of the combination but also in the unexpected similarities we find in Hurston's equation of bitterness and underarm odor.

This brings us to a central aspect of Hurston's humor, which is virtually identical to her greatest gift as a novelist. She truly "made it new," combining the resources of Afro-American folklore with her own fictional agenda. One of the ways she did this was by using unconventional and unexpected verbal combinations. The juxtaposition of apparently dissimilar objects or concepts is a classic cause of humor.[18]

Similarly, as Hemenway stresses, Zora Hurston was keenly aware of the coexistent cultures of America.[19] Indeed throughout her text, she functions as a kind of guide and translator, initiating a presumably white reader into the mysteries of Black language and folklore.

Dust Tracks never bores the reader, largely because the book, in celebrating Zora Neale Hurston, also salutes the culture that made her. The text is larded with humor, both as structure and adornment. Hurston uses comic expressions, jokes, and [an] entire collection of humorous effects, to amplify, underline, and sharpen the points she makes. These deceptively delightful words often contain a serious meaning, just as the slave folktales did. Hurston skillfully trims and fits folk sayings into integral parts of her narrative; on the first page, for instance, she describes her home town by saying "Eatonville is what you might call hitting a straight lick with a crooked stick. The town . . . is a by-product of something else" (p. 3). This type of description becomes more pungent when she combines these materials with her own imaginative coinages, as in the following description of her father's family: "Regular hand-to-mouth folks. Didn't own pots to pee in, nor beds to push 'em under. . . . No more to 'em than the stuffings out of a zero" (p. 13). This utterance alone gives proof to Hurston's assertion that the Negro's greatest contributions to the language were (1) the use of metaphor and simile ("hand-to-mouth folks"); (2) the use of the double descriptive ("pot . . . nor beds"); and (3) the use of verbal nouns ("stuffings").[20] It also reveals the way such tools can be used to revitalize language by working simultaneously in the comic mode.

Additionally, this metaphoric and frequently hyperbolic language may be combined with a comically ironic presentation of the discrepancy between appearance and reality in daily bi-racial life, as in this description of what happened when white visitors came to observe at Hurston's Black elementary school:

> We were threatened with a prompt and bloody death if we cut one caper while the visitors were present. We always sang a spiritual, led by Mr. Calhoun himself. Mrs. Calhoun always stood in the back, with a palmetto switch in her hand as a squelcher. We were all little angels for the duration, because we'd better be. She would cut her eyes and give us a glare that meant trouble, then turn her face towards the

visitors and beam as much as to say it was a great privilege
and pleasure to teach lovely children like us. (pp. 46–47)

The description amuses, partly because of the language and
tropes, also partly because (along with the narrator and the
black teacher) we know the truth that is hidden from the white
visitors. Another aspect of this principle may be seen in
comedically sugar-coated scenes that are really put-downs of
insipid white culture. When wealthy whites give the young
Zora an Episcopal hymnal, she reports "Some of them seemed
dull and without life, and I pretended they were not there. If
white people like trashy singing like that, there must be
something funny about them that I had not noticed before. I
stuck to the pretty ones where the words marched to a throb I
could feel" (p. 52).

The biggest gap, however, for the young Zora to bridge is
that between her fictional/imaginary world and her real one:

> My soul was with the gods and my body in the village.
> People just would not act like gods. Stew beef, fried fat-back
> and morning grits were no ambrosia from Valhalla. Raking
> back yards and carrying out chamber-pots, were not the tasks
> of Thor. (p. 56)

This momentary distaste for the real world is dispelled,
however, when Zora becomes initiated into Black adult coded
language on the porch of Joe Clarke's store, where the males of
Eatonville congregated to swap gossip and have a "lying
session," i.e., straining against each other in telling folk tales.
"I would hear an occasional scrap of gossip in what to me was
adult double talk, but which I understood at times. There
would be, for instance, sly references to the physical condition
of women, irregular love affairs, brags on male potency. . . . It
did not take me long to know what was meant when a girl was
spoken of as 'ruint' or 'bigged'" (p. 62). She was also hearing
the double talk of animal tales, black interpretations of the
Bible,[21] and "tall tales." It wasn't long before she was making
up her own "lies" and getting roundly chastised for it by her

grandmother (surely a prototype of Nanny in *Their Eyes*), who even utters a malapropism, one of Hurston' favorite devices: "I bet if I lay my hands on her she'll stop it. I vominates a lying tongue" (p. 71). The forced coupling of abominate and vomit creates a delightfully expressive non-word.

Further clashes with authority receive similarly comic treatment: "I just had to talk back at established authority and that established authority hated backtalk worse than barbed-wire pie" (p. 95). It wasn't long, however, until Zora Neale began to see a way to be *rewarded* for her saucy imagination. Leaving home quite early, she became a governess, and soon discovered she could get out of housework by entertaining the children with humorous stories; as a lady's maid for a Northern Gilbert and Sullivan company, she found out that she had a gift:

> I was a Southerner, and had the map of Dixie on my tongue. . . . It was not that my grammar was bad, it was the idioms. They did not know of the way an average Southern child, white or black, is raised on simile and invective. They know how to call names. It is an everyday affair to hear somebody called a mullet-headed, mule-eared, wall-eyed, hog-nosed, 'gator-faced, shad-mouthed, screw-necked, goat-bellied, puzzle-gutted, camel-backed, butt-sprung, battle-hammed, knock-kneed, razor-legged, box-ankled, shovel-footed, unmated so-and-so! . . . They can tell you in simile exactly how you walk and smell. They can furnish a picture gallery of your ancestors, and a notion of what your children will be like. What ought to happen to you is full of images and flavor. Since that stratum of the Southern population is not given to book-reading, they take their comparisons right out of the barnyard and the woods. When they get through with you, you and your whole family look like an acre of totem-poles. (pp. 135–36)

This passage provides a deeper understanding of Hurston's comic dimensions and her conception of communal humor. It shows her awareness of the comic possibilities of accent, idiom, dialect, inflection, simile, invective, the tall tale, the boast, and comic anthropomorphism; more importantly, it suggests an awareness of the toast, the dozens, signifying, and marking, all key elements in both Afro-American culture and her fiction.[22]

Hurston, in her anthropological research in the South, found multiple examples of these cultural/verbal genres, which she had always known about; now, however, she was seeing them from the viewpoint of a trained anthropologist. One notes here that Hurston was able to put all this into her fiction only after studying anthropology with Franz Boas and Ruth Benedict at Barnard; there, she found the "spy glass" she needed to re-see her own culture, which had heretofore fit her "like a tight chemise. I couldn't see it for wearing it."[23] Hurston also knew that she would have to find a way to present this material to a white audience that knew little about such verbal conventions. She solved this problem in her autobiography by letting her persona in the book play dumb:

> I heard somebody, a woman's voice "specifying" up this line of houses from where I lived and asked who it was. "Dat's Big Sweet" my landlady told me. "She got her foot up on somebody. Ain't she specifying?" She was really giving the particulars. She was giving a "reading," a word borrowed from fortune tellers. She was giving her opponent lurid data and bringing him up to date on his ancestry, his looks, smell, gait, clothes, and his route through Hell in the hereafter. My landlady went outside where nearly everybody else of the four or five hundred people on the "job" were to listen to the reading. Big Sweet broke the news to him, in one of her mildest bulletins that his pa was a double-humpted camel and his ma was a grass-gut cow, but even so, he tore her wide open in the act of getting born, and so on and so forth. He was a bitch's baby out of a buzzard egg. (p. 186)

Hurston, supposedly an innocent, then asks her landlady what it means to "Put your foot" up on a person, and she and we learn that this refers to putting your foot on the victim's porch while you "play in the family," that is, play the dozens (p. 187).

II. The Short Fiction, 1921–1933

> The brother in black puts a laugh in every vacant place in his mind. His laugh has a hundred meanings. It may mean amusement, anger, grief, bewilderment, chagrin, curiosity, simple pleasure or any other of the known or undefined emotions. —*Mules and Men* (pp. 67–78)

Hurston's literary career began in 1921, when Howard University's *Stylus* published her short story, "John Redding Goes to Sea" (reprinted in 1924 by *Opportunity*).[24] The story features an ambitious, yearning central figure in a rural setting, whose wish to go to sea is opposed by tradition-bound women. The tale prefigures Hurston's later work, in that it presents male-female conflicts, a plethora of local-color touches, and references to conjuring and superstition. What's missing is Hurston's fully developed use of dialect, mature mastery of metaphor, and distinctive, humor-laden voice. In some ways the story seems derivative; the wailing, clutching mother is curiously like old Nora in Synge's *Riders to the Sea*. The tale is notable, however, for its depiction of a warm relationship between a black father and son (which Hurston would reprise in *Moses*), and for its aura of irony. The only joker in the story is Nature herself, for John gets his wish to go to sea when a storm knocks him off a bridge, and his dead body sweeps downriver atop a pine tree.

By contrast, "Drenched in Light" (1924) demonstrates all the qualities that were lacking in "John Redding," perhaps because Hurston here begins to use materials from her own experience; the central character, Isie Watts, clearly resembles the young Zora.[25] Considered a "limb of Satan" by her wizened grandmother, Isie spends long hours, as Hurston did (see *Dust Tracks*, 36, p. 45) hanging on the gate-post, looking down the beckoning and shining shell road toward the horizon.

Isie displays her impish and impulsive nature when, egged on by her brother, she attempts to shave the straggling whiskers on her sleeping Granny's chin. The old woman awakes "to behold the business face of Isie and the razor-clutching hand. Her jaw dropped and Grandma, forgetting years and rheumatism, bolted from the chair and fled the house, screaming" (p. 372).

Knowing this alone will bring on a whipping, Isie steals Granny's red tablecloth, drapes it around her shoulders, and runs off to a barbecue, where she amuses everyone with her antics and her dancing. A white woman, travelling through with her obviously bored and boring husband, is entranced; she eventually stops Granny from whipping Isie, pays for the ruined tablecloth, and carries the child off to their hotel to dance for her: "I want brightness and this Isie is joy itself, why she's drenched in light!" (p. 373).

We see a number of new elements in this story, including a more sophisticated use of dialect and metaphor, sharply individualized characters, and most importantly, a buoyant exuberance and energy that emanates from a stronger release of Hurston's comic imagination. The story is also oddly prophetic of the major criticism she would attract in the twenties—posturing for her white patrons and/or audience—for Isie escapes punishment and in fact wins rewards because of her antics/artistry, whichever you prefer. Hemenway considers the tale evidence of Hurston's considerable thought about her identity as she began to function in the Harlem literary scene.[26]

"Drenched in Light" also begins Hurston's focus upon joking relationships, crucial in pre-literate or largely oral societies, such as those Hurston would later encounter in Jamaica and Haiti, but after her Barnard training, she recognized the importance these structures played in her Eatonville, where folks valued oral ability highly, especially verbal duelling. Isie and her grandmother amuse partly because Isie seems impudently intent on establishing a joking relationship, a sentiment the elder figure adamantly refuses to recognize, so much so that her rigidity becomes a source of humor.[27]

"Spunk," Hurston's award winning 1925 story, deals with a romantic triangle between Spunk, a macho saw-mill worker, the sexy Lena, and her cowardly older husband, Joe.[28] Significantly, the community plays an important role in this story, by using cruel humor to goad Joe into seeking revenge. He attacks Spunk from behind with a razor and is killed. Spunk, convinced that Joe has returned from the dead as a black bob-cat to haunt him, loses his customary aplomb and is killed by the circular-saw. The story shows Hurston's mastery of dialect proceeding, and introduces the concept of communal humor as an instrument of torture. The ending chills with irony: "The women ate heartily of the funeral baked meats and wondered who would be Lena's next. The men whispered coarse conjecture between guzzles of whiskey" (p. 173).

"The Eatonville Anthology," a series of short sketches describing colorful events and characters in Hurston's hometown, is much more amusing and detailed, even though there is no central narrative line in the collection.[29] "The Pleading Woman" pictures a wife who begs merchants for scraps of food, pretending her husband doesn't provide for her: "Hits uh SHAME! Tony don't fee-ee-ee-ed me!" (Hurston reprised the scene for *Their Eyes,* as we shall see.)

Other sketches describe various local eccentrics, but there is also a charming animal tale about the rivalry of Mr. Dog and Mr. Rabbit over Miss Nancy Coon. During the courting ritual, Mr. Dog proposes matrimony by asking "'which would you ruther be—a lark flyin' or a dove a settin'?'"; Hurston would use this particular scene in a more serious way in *Jonah's Gourd Vine,* when John proposes to Lucy.[30]

Despite the obvious differences and relative successes of these early stories, all of them differentiated Zora Neale Hurston from her Harlem Renaissance colleagues. Not only was she from the South; she chose to *write* about the South, from the perspective of a native. Jean Toomer had set his magnificent *Cane* (1923) in Georgia, but it was written from the viewpoint of an outsider. He was never thought of as "down home."

Hurston's one attempt at the time to write about the Harlem scene (the favored subject of her contemporaries), the 1926 "Muttsy," rather sentimentally details the arrival in New York of a timid "down home" greenhorn, Pinkie; she unfortunately finds lodging at the disreputable Ma Turner's place, a combination jook/speakeasy.[31] Pinkie's virginity survives intact until the end of the story, when the title character, a gambler, unable to seduce her, rather improbably marries her. The immigrant-type humor in the story more frequently occurs in Jewish-American fiction, but there was certainly a rich fund of country-type-arrives-on-Lenox-Avenue-from-subway's-womb stories around. "Muttsy" is more notable, however, for its Southern materials (one character informs Pinkie and us how properly to eat a fish—straight out of Eatonville lore) than for its Harlem touches. Hurston would later master the latter in "Story in Harlem Slang" (1942),[32] but most of her early successes, unlike "Muttsy," were set in the South.

Appropriately, Hurston really caught fire as a writer with her contributions to *FIRE!!*, the magazine/manifesto issued by Hughes and others in 1926. "Sweat," the more gripping of her two pieces, details the grim story of hard-working Delia Jones and her no-good, philandering husband, a macho devotee of practical jokes.[33] Hurston cleverly transforms this aspect of her villain into a structural device, for the entire story turns on the idea of jokes and joking. She begins with one: Sykes throws his "long, round, limp and black" bullwhip around Delia's shoulders as she is sorting the white folks' clothes she must wash in order to support herself (p. 197). Sykes's prank, based on Delia's abnormal fear of snakes, also adds sexual imagery, and thereby makes the story more complex. Is Delia's phallic fear a sign of her frigidity, which in turn has driven Sykes to the bed of other women?

In any case, Sykes's cruel laughter fills the story; he repeatedly slaps his leg and doubles over with merriment at the expense of the "big fool" he married. Delia too, although grimly serious in her defiance of Sykes, uses comic rhetoric; referring to his mistress, she states "that ole snaggle-toothed black woman you running' with aint comin' heah to pile up on *mah* sweat and blood. You aint paid for nothin' on this place, and Ah'm gointer stay right heah till Ah'm toted out foot foremost" (p. 199). Later, alone, Delia takes comfort in folk wisdom: "Oh well, whatever goes over the Devil's back, is got to come under his belly. Sometime or ruther, Sykes, like everybody else, is gointer reap his sowing" (p. 199).

We notice another significant development in this story: the appearance of a communal comic chorus in the personages of the loiterers on the porch of Joe Clarke's store. When Delia passes by with her pony cart delivering clothes they render the community's sense of pity for her and contempt towards Sykes via a startling collage of everyday objects and actions: "How Sykes kin stommuck dat big black greasy Mogul he's layin' roun' wid, gits me. Ah swear dat eight-rock couldn't kiss a sardine can Ah done throwed out de back do'way las' yeah" (p. 200). The men's joint verdict that Sykes "aint fit tuh carry guts tuh a bear" finds confirmation when he brings his mistress Bertha to the store to buy her provisions, and then enjoys it when Delia happens to pass by and witnesses the scene.

After this drama is played out, the men again analyze the ongoing story and its characters, mixing metaphors freely: Bertha is judged to be "a hunk uh liver wid hair on it," who "sho' kin squall. . . . Whyen she gits ready tuh laff, she jes' opens huh mouf an' latches it back tuh de las' notch. No ole grandpa alligator down in Lake Bell ain't got nothin' on huh" (p. 202).

To drive Delia from her house, which he has promised to Bertha, Sykes plays his final joke by keeping a caged rattlesnake on the premises, knowing she is frightened even of earthworms. When she asks him to kill the rattler, he replies with a comically coined word and devastating irony: "Doan ast me tuh do nothin' fuh yuh. Goin' roun' tryin' tuh be so damn asterperious. Naw, Ah aint gonna kill it. Ah think uh damn sight mo' uh him dan you! Dat's a nice snake an' anybody doan lak 'im kin jes' hit de grit" (p. 203).

Normally comic expressions can be used to deadly effect as well. When Delia's fury overflows into courage, she tells Sykes, "Ah hates yuh lak uh suck-egg dog" (p. 204). The imagery is apt, for Sykes, a male (the gender usually associated with dogs) preys on women (egg bearers). When he replies with insults about her looks, she answers in kind, joining a verbal duel that silences him: "Yo' ole black hide don't look lak nothin' tuh me, but uh passle uh wrinkled up rubber [a devastating metaphor of impotence] wid yo' big ole yeahs flappin' on each side lak uh paih uh buzzard wings. Don't think Ah'm gointuh be run 'way from mah house neither" (p. 204).

The final, terrible Freudian joke also comes at Sykes's expense. He places the rattler in one of Delia's laundry baskets and makes sure there are no matches in the house to light the lamps. Delia discovers the snake, which significantly slithers onto the bed; she flees to the barn, and from there hears a drunken Sykes, confident that his trap has done Delia in, return. Once in the darkened room with the whirring snake, thinking the bed his safest refuge, he leaps onto it and meets his doom. His obsession with male, phallic power finally kills him, in a doubly figurative and dreadfully comic way.

Hurston's short story apprenticeship finally led to her first novel, *Jonah's Gourd Vine,* after the last tale in this early series, "The Gilded Six-Bits," was published in *Story* in 1933; it so intrigued Bertram Lippincott that he wrote her asking if she had a novel in progress.[34] What made this story special?

For one thing, it was written after Hurston had been collecting black folklore for several years in the South. Although this material had played a central role in her previous fiction, it now became an even more important element, for she had learned, through scientific observation, how integral and important the *process* of folklore was to black culture, and how pervasive it was in all types of communal functions.

How is this evident in "The Gilded Six-Bits"? The story concerns a young married couple, Missy May and Joe, who create a clean, sunny, happy home out of ordinary ingredients: "Yard raked so that the strokes of the rake would make a pattern. Fresh newspaper cut in fancy edge on the kitchen shelves" (p. 208). Like Janie and Tea Cake in *Their Eyes,* they keep their relationship fresh and lively through elaborate games, jokes, and rituals. Each payday Joe hides and throws money into the door; Missy May pretends to be mad and gives chase, which results in a comic tumble. They speak in hyperbolic but culturally specific terms to express ordinary facts: "Ah could eat up camp meetin', back off 'ssociation, and drink Jurdan dry" (p. 210).

When Joe praises the proprietor of the new ice-cream store, Mr. Otis D. Slemmons, who apparently has a lot of gold teeth and money, Missy May expresses her initial contempt through folksy imagery, creating a caricature: "Aw, he don't look no better in his clothes than you do in yourn. He got a puzzlegut on 'im and he so chuckle-headed, he got a pone behind his neck. . . . His mouf is cut cross-ways, ain't it? Well, he kin lie jes' lak anybody else. . . . A wouldn't give 'im a wink if de sheriff wuz after 'im" (p. 211).

Hurston creates a little physical comedy too; while Missy May dresses, Joe, who *admires* a "puzzle-gut" as a sign of prosperity, makes his "stomach punch out like Slemmons' middle. He tried the rolling swagger of the stranger, but found that his tall bone-and-muscle stride fitted ill with it" (p. 212). Later we find that Joe admires Slemmons for his comic/verbal ability as well; he quotes him as saying "who is dat broad wid de forte shake?" (p. 212).

Slemmons succeeds in seducing Missy May one night; Joe unexpectedly comes home and discovers them in the act. His stunned reaction? He laughs, before punching his rival out and grabbing his gold watch-chain. It is a last laugh, in more ways than one; although the marriage continues, its changed state is reflected by the absence of laughter and banter. After a long period of abstinence, Joe returns to Missy May's bed and leaves her the gold watch-chain, and its attached coin, which she discovers to be a gilded half dollar. The whole thing has been a joke; Slemmons was an impostor.

When Missy May delivers a son that is "de spittin' image" of Joe, everyone breathes a sigh of relief, especially Joe's formerly suspicious mother, who confesses her previous doubts in a rush of folk-warmed euphemisms: "And you know Ah'm mighty proud, son, cause Ah never thought well of you marryin' Missie May cause her ma used tuh fan her foot round right smart and Ah been mighty skeered dat Missie May wuz gointer git misput on her road" (p. 217). All of this richly metaphorical language lends a great deal of humor and interest to the story, yet is never intrusive as it sometimes is in the more sprawling pages of *Jonah's Gourd Vine;* moreover, although Hurston creates the impression of a natural spontaneity, the metaphors actually work in a system of reference. For example: the rather refined "road" euphemism used by Joe's mother had been employed by Missy May earlier, when she speculated to Joe that they might discover some gold like Slemmons's: "Us might find some gon' long de road some time," for it is indeed in her misbehavior in the "road" with Slemmons that she obtains the gold.

Joe's total forgiveness floods forth after the birth of his son. As he buys a load of candy kisses with Slemmons's gilded six-bits for Missy May, he boasts about the way he outsmarted Slemmons; his story amuses the callous clerk, who remarks to his next customer, a white, "Wisht I could be like these darkies. Laughin' all the time. Nothin' worries 'em" (p. 218), little suspecting the pain that underlies Joe's brave laughter. The story ends when Joe resumes the ritual of throwing money on the porch, accompanied by Missy May's game reply: "Joe Banks, Ah hear you chunkin' money in mah do'way. You wait til Ah got mah strength back and Ah'm gointer fix you for dat" (p. 218). Laughter thus becomes the barometer of success or failure in marriage.

III. The Novels: 1934–1937

Now that we have seen the way Hurston developed her expanding use of humor and folklore in the early short stories, we may discover how this came to fruition in her novels, beginning with *Jonah's Gourd Vine* in 1934.[35]

Here, the novel form permits Hurston to elaborate joking relationships, using kin and non-kin systems and patterns to create a vibrantly textured sense of community and communal wisdom while forming a vehicle both for the narrative and for commentary upon it. We see Hurston working with relatively simple relationships in *Jonah,* and with more complex sets in *Their Eyes;* finally, in *Moses,* she develops a complete system of humorous relationships that combines the features of both networks, for the "chosen" people are simultaneously kin and non-kin with every other member of the "family of God," i.e., the family of Israel.

In a 1934 letter to James Weldon Johnson about her new book, Hurston confided:

> I have tried to present a Negro preacher who is neither funny nor an imitation Puritan ram-rod in pants. Just the human being and poet that he must be to succeed in a Negro pulpit. I do not speak of those among us who have been tampered with and consequently have gone Presbyterian or Episcopal, I mean the common run of us who love magnificence, beauty, poetry and color so much that there can never be enough of it.[36]

Thus, while the book itself offers an abundance of laughter, the central character and his profession are never the ultimate butt of Hurston's humor, although his fall from grace within the community is partly measured by the qualitative change in their joking relationship with him.

Jonah tells the story of John Pearson, a rural lad who is called to preach by God; his mission is strengthened and sustained by his wife Lucy, a saintly but strong figure. She and John resemble Hurston's parents, although there are significant differences, partly because *Jonah* was written after the years of folklore research in the South; Hurston was intent on using this material fictionally. Moreover, she had just written, but had not published, *Mules and Men.* This text had originally been conceived as a straightforward presentation of the research findings, but the publishers wanted a livelier narrative, so Hurston inserted herself into the book, and worked out a whole series of connective conversational tissues for the various components. This makes the book much closer in form to the novel, but it improved Hurston's anthropological technique as well. Both *Mules and Men* and *Tell My Horse,* Hurston's later examination of Caribbean folklore, impress us by putting folkloric material into contextual perspective. She lets us know when a joke was told, by whom, and to whom. This practice especially succeeded when she began to incorporate the very same materials into her fiction, for it ensured that the humor found in the novels developed naturally out of the narrative, and indeed, frequently carried the narrative, either overtly or covertly.

The humorous dimensions of *Jonah,* in many ways a great rehearsal for Hurston's masterworks *Their Eyes Were Watching God* and *Moses, Man of the Mountain,* deserve extended analysis.[37] I shall summarize here, however, some of the more important humorous conventions that Hurston employs in the book: verbal duels between the sexes (first with John's parents, Ned and Amy, later between John and Lucy, then John and Hattie); coined expressions; black on black humor; country vs. city humor; courtship riddles and rituals; call and response comic sayings; references to the dozens; a tirade against "book larnin'" *à la* Papp Finn of Twain's masterwork; and many other ingenious modes of humor. Perhaps the two most important comic devices used in the novel are folk proverbs (sometimes piled on rather too thickly, and impeding the narrative) and signifying.

Hurston's purpose in *Jonah* was to show the world the glory of black folklore and language, and their central role in sustaining the community, particularly in the rhetoric of the minister and in the metaphors of everyday games and verbal exchanges. It was meant to demonstrate what Hurston had challenged Blacks in general to do in her December, 1934 article in *The Washington Tribune:* recognize the fact that Afro-American folk expression had an integrity that was every bit as fine as that of Anglo-American culture.[38]

The central battle of the sexes in *Jonah,* which is ultimately tragic, but frequently depicted using a comic technique, includes a declaration by John that becomes a central theme in Janie's story:

> "Jus' cause women folks ain't got no big muscled arm and fistes lak jugs, folks claims they's weak vessels, but dass uh lie. Dat piece uh red flannel she go hung 'tween her jaws is equal tuh all de fistes God ever made and man ever seen. Jes' take an ruin a man wid they tongue, and den dey kin hold it still and bruise 'im up jes' es bad." (p. 158)

This assessment is confirmed in *Their Eyes,* where Janie, the central figure, achieves maturity, identity and independence through the development of a voice, one that ultimately resonates with laughter. She uses this voice, however, in ways that both embrace and transcend the male/female relationships of *Jonah.*

Their Eyes, a book about a quest, ends with the heroine returning to the community for re-integration, whereby she is made whole once again, while enriching society with her newfound wisdom.[39] While the various articles and sections of books that deal with Janie's identity problem have been quite persuasive and illuminating,⁴⁰ most critics have entirely neglected the fact that she also excels as a narrator who entertains, indeed, mesmerizes, and much of this comes from her considerable gifts as a humorist. In this respect she is providentially armed, for the community has an arsenal of scorn waiting for her: "Seeing the woman as she was made them remember the envy they had stored up and swallowed with relish. They made burning statements with questions, and killing tools out of laughs" (p. 10), thereby returning us with a vengeance to Freud's concept of humor as an aggressive force. After Janie wordlessly enters her gate and slams it behind her "Pearl Stone opened her mouth and laughed real hard because she didn't know what else to do" (p. 11). Like Hester Prynne in the opening scaffold scene of *The Scarlet Letter,* Janie will be the victim of cruel, unthinking humor until she silences it, and unlike Hester, she must "cap" the discussion by having the last laugh herself, as in the finale of the dozens.

Significantly, her friend and initial audience, Pheoby, represents Janie's case to the other women with a scornful humor: "De way you talkin' you'd think de folks in dis town didn't do nothin' in de bed 'cept praise de Lawd" (p. 13).

She greets Janie's arrival more positively: "'Gal, you sho looks *good*. You looks like youse yo' own daughter.' They both laughed" (p. 14). The irony and therefore the doubling of the joke lies in the fact that Janie, in a metaphorical sense, *is* her own daughter, in that she has created a new persona out of the woman who left the town some time earlier with Tea Cake. Janie's exuberant appreciation of the dish Pheoby has brought her ("Gal, it's *too* good! you switches a mean fanny round in a kitchen" [p. 15]) inaugurates her in the reader's mind as a woman versed in folk wisdom and humor, and also demonstrates humor's power to quickly initiate intimacy and warmth. (The dish itself, Mulatto rice, is a joke too, since Janie's white blood relates her to the food and causes jealousy within the community.) Hurston extends the food/eating metaphor further; as Janie eats, she comments that:

> "... people like dem wastes up too much time puttin' they mouf on things they don't know nothin' about. Now they got to look into me loving Tea Cake and see whether it was done right or not! They don't know if life is a mess of corn-meal dumplings, and if love is a bed-quilt! ... If they wants to see and know, why they don't come kiss and be kissed? Ah could then sits down and tell 'em things. Ah been a delegate to de big 'ssociation of life. Yessuh! De Grand Lodge, de big convention of livin' is just where Ah been dis year and a half y'all ain't seen me." (pp. 17–18)

The retrospective story of Janie's life begins when she remembers a joke that was played on her as a child. Raised with the white Washburn children, she doesn't know she is Black until all the children view a group photograph. When she exclaims, "Where is me?"—Janie's distinguishing question throughout the book—the assembled group laughs at her. "Miss Nellie ... said, 'Dat's you, Alphabet [the comic, all-purpose nickname they have bestowed on her], don't you know yo' ownself?' ... Ah said: 'Aw, aw! Ah'm colored!' Den dey all laughed real hard. But before Ah seen de picture Ah thought ah wuz just like de rest" (p. 29). The frame story of the novel repeats this situation, for once again Janie's identity is at stake for a circle of questioning faces, but this time it is Janie herself who provides the answers, fighting the fire of cruel, aggressive laughter with narrative, uniting, communal laughter. Her voice, multiplied by those of the characters who have shaped and been shaped by her life, does indeed become an alphabet at last, one that spells out the human comedy and condition.

As in Balzac, or Faulkner, Hurston's human comedy is replete with tragedy as well, but virtually everyone in the book has some comic lines. Even Nanny, whose grim revelation of her own history is monumentally tragic, communicates in a dialect-driven, metaphor-drenched language. Fearing that

Janie has been beaten by Logan Killicks, Nanny erupts with comic invective, signifying, and using a wrong but curiously right word: "Ah know dat grass-gut, liver-lipted nigger ain't done took and beat mah baby already! Ah'll take a stick and salivate 'im!" (p. 40). Logan, however, is notably lacking in humor and quite a few other traits, and Janie falls for the flashy but ambitious Jody Starks, even though he "did not represent sun-up and pollen and blooming tress, but he spoke for horizon. He spoke for change and chance" (p. 5). Moreover, "it has always been his wish and desire to be a big voice" and he intends to develop it in Eatonville, an all-Black town where a man can have a chance. His abundant humor adds an ingredient; he makes Janie laugh: "you behind a plow! You ain't got no mo' business wid uh plow than uh hog is got wid un holiday! . . . A pretty doll-baby lak you is made to sit on de front porch and rock and fan yo' self . . ." (p. 49). Over the next twenty years, however, this joke pales, for it is grimly prophetic. Jody, now Mayor of Eatonville, soon banishes any sense of fun or joy from their marriage. He, even more than her first husband, wants a proverbial "nice girl" for public view, and "nice" girls don't joke in public.

There is humor aplenty, however, in the salty, gossipy tale-telling, or "lyin'" that goes on on Jody's store porch, which becomes the town center of Eatonville and the new Mayor's bully pulpit as well. But he quickly silences Janie; at the meeting where he is elected Mayor, Janie is called on to make a speech, but Jody intervenes: "Thank yuh fuh yo' compliments, but mah wife don't know nothin' 'bout no speech makin'. Ah never married her for nothin' lak dat. She's uh woman and her place is in de home" (p. 69). Janie forces herself to laugh in response; apparently this is what a decorative woman does—giggle and be still—but she is inwardly disturbed. Appropriately, these pages of the book are relatively humorless, until the introduction of Matt Bonner's skinny yellow mule, the object of a whole series of jokes played on Bonner:

"De womenfolks got yo' mule. When Ah come round de lake 'bout noon-time mah wife and some others had 'im flat on the ground usin' his sides fuh uh wash board." . . . Janie loved the conversation and sometimes she thought up good stories on the mule, but Joe had forbidden her to indulge. He didn't want her talking after such trashy people. "You'se Mrs. Mayor Starks Janie." (p. 85)

Joe does respect Janie's outrage, however, over the physical torture of the old mule; he buys him and pastures the animal just outside the store, as a gesture of largesse. As the mule fattens, new stories are concocted. In one version, he sticks his head in the Pearsons' window (the central family in *Jonah*) while the family is eating; Mrs. Pearson mistakes him for Rev. Pearson and hands him a plate!

When the mule dies, the reader finds out that Jody's combination of a big voice and a sense of humor that originally won Janie is effective with the town as well; at a funeral that mocks "everything human in death," Jody leads off with a great comic eulogy on "our departed citizen, our most distinguished citizen" (p. 95). The result: "It made him more solid than building the schoolhouse had done."

In a daring move, Hurston extends the scene into the realm of the surreal, by adding a parody of the parody: a group of vultures headed by their "Parson" descends on the carcass. "What killed this man?" is the first "call" from the "minister." The response: "'Bare, bare fat.' 'Who'll stand his funeral?' 'We!!!!' 'Well, all right.' So he picked out the eyes in the ceremonial way and the feast went on" (p. 97). When we remember, however, that Janie is telling the book to Pheoby, this becomes *her* added touch and revenge against Jody, who forbade her to attend the ceremony, much less speak of it.

A revealing passage, central to our consideration of Hurston as humorist, occurs next. Jody, who seemed to relish the mock-funeral, takes on a smug, "dicty" attitude of disapproval after the fact. "Ah had tuh laugh at de people out dere in de woods dis mornin', Janie. You can't help but laugh at de capers they cuts. But all the same, Ah wish mah people would git mo' business in 'em and not spend so much time on foolishness" (p. 98). Janie's response is no doubt Hurston's as well, and we may be sure she is thinking of those critics in the Harlem Renaissance circle who accused her of "cuttin' the monkey" for the white folks. "Everybody can't be lak you, Jody. Somebody is bound tuh want tuh laugh and play," and she is one of them (p. 99).

Jody "has to laugh," too, at the verbal duels of Sam Watson and Lige Moss, regulars on the store porch. Hurston gives them some choice lines from her Eatonville folklore collections, in tales of sheer hyperbole. "The girls and everybody else help laugh." Hurston the anthropologist thereby signals to us the ritualized nature of Eatonville humor and the value it has for the community.

One of the funniest episodes in the book reprises "Mrs. Tony," the begging woman from "The Eatonville Anthology." Once again, she begs the store owner (Jody this time) for some meat—for "Tony don't fee--eed me!" Hurston adds some delicious details too: "The salt pork box was in the back of the store and during the walk Mrs. Tony was so eager she sometimes stepped on Joe's heels, sometimes she was a little before him. Running a little, caressing a little and all the time making little urging-on cries." But when Jody cuts off a smaller piece than she wants "Mrs. Tony leaped away from the proffered cut of meat as if it were a rattlesnake. 'Ah wouldn't tetch it! Dat lil eyeful uh bacon for me an all mah chillun!' . . . Starks made as if to throw the meat back in the box . . . Mrs. Tony swooped like lightning and seized it, and started towards the door. 'Some folks ain't got no heart in dey bosom.' . . . She stepped from the store porch and marched off in high dudgeon!" (pp. 113–115).

Some of the men laugh, but another says that if she were his wife, he'd kill her "cemetery dead," and Coker adds, "Ah could break her if she wuz mine. Ah'd break her or kill her. Makin' uh fool outa me in front of everybody" (p. 116).

Although Mrs. Tony's caricature is meant to be amusing, it has much to do with several levels of the plot, and offers a fine example of the way Hurston uses humor to convey a serious meaning. Mrs. Tony, urging Jody on, telling him he's a "king," exposes Stark's enjoyment in playing the "great man," the man who can afford to be generous in public, as he was earlier when he paid for the mule's "retirement" fund. Furthermore, the scene brings out Jody's falsity (he charges Tony's account anyway) and comically underlines Jody's marital stinginess towards Janie—he doesn't "fee--eed" her spiritually or emotionally. Finally, the men's communal insistence on the propriety of using violence to "break a woman," and the shared assumption that it's Mr. Tony rather than his wife who is the ultimate butt of their humor, lends male communal sanction to Jody's prior slapping of Janie for speaking out of place, and prepares the reader for Janie's final public showdown with Jody.

When Jody's youth and good health begin to wane, he tries to draw attention away from himself by publicly ridiculing Janie. "I God almighty! A woman stay round uh store till she get old as Methusalem and still can't cut a little thing like a plug of tobacco! Don't stand dere rollin' yo' pop eyes at me wid yo' rump hangin' nearly to yo' knees" (p. 121). Such a ritual insult directed at a male would possibly initiate a game of the dozens, or physical violence, but Jody, assuming Janie will know her place and not engage in a forbidden joking relationship, expects her silence. Instead, she accepts his challenge, and powerfully concludes a spirited exchange of charges with him: "'You big-bellies round here and put out a lot of brag, but 'taint nothin' to it but yo' big voice. Humph! Talkin' 'bout *me* lookin' old! When you pull down yo' britches, you look lak de change uh life.' 'Great God from Zion!' Sam Watson gasped. [Sam, we remember, is the chief comedian of the porch] 'Y'all really playin' de dozens tuhnight'" (p. 123).[41] Not only has Janie dared to play a male game, she has "capped" Joe forever with this ultimate insult, and in fact, in the eyes of the community, has effectively emasculated him. "They'd look with envy at the things and pity the man that owned them. . . . And the cruel deceit of Janie! Making all that show of humbleness and scorning him all the time! *Laughing at him!* [my emphasis] and now putting the town up to do the same" (p. 124).

What Jody expresses here is more than a sense of betrayal; he is actually casting Janie in the diabolical role of Trickster, that omnipresent menace of folktales, who, like Brer Rabbit, one of his avatars, strikes down his physical superiors, as David slew Goliath. Significantly, however, Joe can't consciously give her this much credit, and so compares Janie to Saul's scheming daughter.

When Janie later tells this story to Pheoby in the framing device, and thereby, by extension, tells the community, she is doing so from a somewhat privileged position, which she doesn't have earlier in the book. Although multiple restrictions exist against women expressing themselves humorously in public, as we have seen, these are usually relaxed as women age. In many cultures, older women, especially after menopause, are permitted much more verbal freedom, and eventually are allowed to compete with men, if they so choose.[42] In this sense, Janie's challenge of Jody in the male territory of tall tales, verbal dueling, and finally, the doubles and capping, isn't as outrageous to the community as it might be, for she is mature, experienced, and widely recognized as a relatively wealthy, independent woman, who isn't vulnerable to sexual manipulation and appropriation.

At the time of Jody's death, however, some men in the community don't understand this. Janie learns to laugh again after the funeral, partly because of the hypocrisy of her abundant suitors: "Janie found out very soon that her widowhood and property was a great challenge in South Florida . . . 'uh woman by herself is uh pitiful thing,' she was told over and again . . ." (p. 139). Janie laughs, because the men know plenty of widows, but this one has money.

Her relationship with her eventual third husband, Tea Cake, is central to the book's meaning, and it begins on a note of humor. He walks into the store on a slow day; most of the community is off at a ball game in Winter Park. "'Good evenin', Mis' Starks,' he said with a sly grin as if they had a good joke together. She was in favor of the story that was making him laugh before she even heard it" (p. 144). Their entire first interchange is a series of little jokes, and Janie's thrilled reaction to his invitation to play checkers could just as well apply to his subsequent willingness to admit she is his comic equal: ". . . she found herself flowing inside. Somebody wanted her to play. Somebody thought it natural for her to play. That was even nice" (p. 146). Tea Cake wants her to play in every sense of the word, thereby ending the long line of nay-sayers that stretches back to Nanny.

It interests us that Janie doesn't learn his name until they've spent the afternoon together in play; when she learns it is Vergible Woods but he's called Tea Cake, she laughs, and makes a joke:

> "Tea Cake! So you sweet as all dat?" She laughed and he gave her a little cut-eye look to get her meaning. "Ah may be guilty. You better try me and see. . . . B'lieve Ah done cut uh hawg, so Ah guess Ah better ketch air." He made an elaborate act of tripping to the door stealthily. Then looked back at her with an irresistible grin on his face. Janie burst out laughing in spite of herself. "You crazy thing!" (p. 149)

But Tea Cake doesn't leave. "They joked and went on till the people began to come in. Then he took a seat and made talk and laughter with the rest until closing time" (p. 150).

It seems important to note here that Tea Cake's courting is done both in private and in public. His second visit again involves a game of checkers, but this time they play in front of an audience. "Everybody was surprised at Janie playing checkers but they liked it. Three or four stood behind her and coached her moves and generally made merry with her in a restrained way" (p. 154).

371

What Janie and the rest of the community like about Tea Cake is his spontaneity, creativity, and positive attitude toward life. In a moving scene, Hurston pinpoints this, and his teaching quality. Tea Cake combs Janie's hair for her, and says "Ah betcha you don't never go tuh de lookin' glass and enjoy yo' eyes yo' self. You'se got de world in uh jug and make out you don't know it. But Ah'm glad tuh be de one tuh tell yuh" [see I Corinthians: 13:12]. When Janie objects that he must tell this to all the girls, he replies, "Ah'm de Apostle Paul tuh de Gentiles. Ah tells 'em and then again Ah shows 'em" (pp. 157–58). Tea Cake's gospel of laughter here becomes the New Testament revision of the Black aesthetic; it is meant to replace the tragic, "Old Testament" litany of Nanny and others like her who still labor under the stubborn heritage of slavery. Nanny, we remember, believes that "folks is meant to cry 'bout somethin' or other" (p. 43), and Tea Cake's creed reverses this. His doctrine is profoundly American and hopeful, even though he too has been and will be the victim of white racism—indeed, one could argue that his ultimate death is due to it—but that doesn't blind him to the glories of the world or the possibilities of the self. Like Emerson and Whitman, he believes in living in the "NOW," but his self-love and sheer joy in living comes out of a Black heritage, and his admonishment to Janie is echoed in a traditional blues lyric: "Baby, Baby, what is the matter with you? You've got the world in a jug/Ain't a thing that you can't do."

This sense of possibility functions importantly in the world of play. Huizinga has proven play to be a basic human need, which strongly relates to laughter; play, he flatly states, is an instinctual impulse that must be satisfied.[43] Janie, who said as much to Jody, is no exception to this rule, and relishes her third husband's sense of play and laughter. She learns as much as she can from him on this subject during their brief two years together. The verb "to laugh" crops up again and again in the chapters devoted to their marriage. Play is frequently conducted within social parameters (as with the communal game of checkers, card games, the evenings with the people in the Everglades), but it often takes place on the periphery of convention or even outside it (the "widow" Janie and Tea Cake go fishing in the middle of the night). But the games Janie loves most are those that involve Tea Cake's imagination and creativity. Early on in their relationship he pretends to play on an imaginary guitar. Later, arriving in a battered car, he jumps out and makes the gesture of tying it to a post.

The widow Starks's neighbors, however, are not amused; this gets expressed in a litany of play-disapproval: they've seen her "sashayin off to a picnic in pink linen"; "Gone off to Sanford in a car . . . dressed in blue! gone hunting . . . gone fishing . . . to the movies . . . to a dance . . . playing checkers; playing coon-can; playing Florida flip . . ." (p. 166–67). Janie has flipped the town's expectations; instead of mourning atop the pedestal Jody created for her, she has lost her "class" by gambling on Tea Cake and love. They want her back as an icon of respectability, but that isn't what they say; Pheoby, their emissary, warns Janie, ". . . you'se takin' un awful chance," to which Janie, twice-married already, replies, "No mo' than Ah took befo' and no mo' than anybody else takes when dey gits married. . . . Dis ain't no business proposition, and no race after property and titles. Dis is uh love game," thereby setting the play element of their relationship out for the community.

Janie's faith is sorely tested in Jacksonville, for during their honeymoon there, Tea Cake vanishes with her hidden two hundred dollars. Janie, learning to trust herself and others, but also to take chances, bears up under the strain of the risk, and is still there, waiting, when Tea Cake comes home to tell her of the party he's given for his friends. Showing her the guitar he's bought and the twelve dollars he has left, he discloses that she's married one of "de best gamblers God ever made. Cards or dice either one" (p. 187). Watching him practice his dice throwing in preparation for an outing is exciting to Janie. He terrifies her when he comes back from his gaming wounded, but as she tends to him he shows her the three-hundred and twenty-two dollars he has made out of her twelve.

Their removal to the Everglades to work on the "muck" with the common people completes Janie's transformation. There, folks "don't do nothin' . . . but make money and fun and foolishness," and Janie grows there, like everything else: "Ground so rich that everything went wild . . . People wild too" (p. 193).

Tea Cake, with his guitar, his songs, his infectious laughter, plays Orpheus for the folk. Janie's growing ability to joke and laugh soon makes her a favorite with the people too, especially after she starts working alongside Tea Cake in the fields. When she and Tea Cake carry on behind the boss's back, "It got the whole field to playing off and on," recalling the role humor played in relieving the drudgery of work in the fields during slave times. Soon, Janie joins Tea Cake in story-telling for the appreciative audience that gathers each night at their shack: "The house was full of people every night. . . . Some were there to hear Tea Cake pick the box; some came to talk and tell stories, but most of them came to get into whatever game was going on or might go on . . . outside of the two jooks, everything on that job went on around those two" (pp. 200–201). Janie learns to "woof," to "boogerboo," to play all the games, and through it all, "No matter how rough it was, people seldom got mad, because everything was done for a laugh" (p. 200).

Even when Janie gets mad over Tea Cake's apparent flirtation, their fight ends with Tea Cake's joking dismissal of the presumed rival: "Wut would Ah do wid dat lil chunk of a woman wid you around? She ain't good for nothin' exceptin' tuh set up in uh corner by de kitchen stove and break wood over her head. You'se something tuh make uh man forgit tuh git old and forgit tuh die" (p. 206).

An extremely important passage regarding Hurston's feeling about Black laughter comes in this section, when Janie meets the near-white Mrs. Turner. This racist, who hates her own race, urges Janie to marry a whiter man than Tea Cake. When Janie asks her, point-blank, "How come you so aginst black?" she immediately replies ". . . dey makes me tired. Always laughin'! Dey laughs too much and dey laughs too loud. Always singin' ol' nigger songs! Always cuttin' de monkey for white folks. If it wuzn't for so many black folks it wouldn't be no race problem. De white folks would take us in wid dem. De black ones is holdin' us back" (p. 210). She brags about her almost white brother, who tore Booker T. Washington to pieces in a speech. "All he ever done was cut de monkey for white folks. So dey pomped him up. But you know whut de old folks say, 'de higher de monkey climbs de mo' he show his behind' so dat's de way it wuz wid Booker T." (p. 212). Mrs. Turner thus becomes Hurston's surrogate for all those critics who accused *her* of "cuttin' the monkey for white folks," and it reminds us that although Janie is Hurston's surrogate in the novel, so is Tea Cake, for here he becomes the polar and positive opposite to Mrs. Turner, as an agent of the laughter she hates, and it is he who plots her banishment.

Hurston doesn't stop with Mrs. Turner, either; she exposes the similar racist and sexist view of Black men, whose repository of "black black women" jokes she despised.[44] Sop-de-Bottom complements Tea Cake on having a light-colored woman, for when the latter slaps Janie for supposedly flirting with Mrs. Turner's brother, "Un person can see every place you hit her . . . Ah bet she never raised her hand tuh hit yuh back, neither. Take some uh des ol' rusty black women and dey would fight yuh all night long and next day nobody couldn't tell you ever hit 'em. Dat's de reason Ah done quit beatin' mah woman. You can't make no mark on 'em at all. . . . Mah woman would spread her lungs all over Palm Beach County, let alone knock out mah jaw teeth. . . . She got ninety-nine rows uh jaw teeth and git her good and mad, she'll wade through solid rock up to her hip pockets" (p. 219). Yet after this Sop-de-Bottom agrees that Mrs. Turner is "color-struck" and helps to run her off the muck! Hurston's clever juxtaposition of these sentiments could hardly be more ironic or more damning.

The wild melee the men start in Mrs. Turner's restaurant is just an excuse to wreck the place; while the destruction is going on they pay elaborate compliments to their distressed hostess. It's a scene right out of the Marx brothers. Mrs. Turner is soon on her way to Miami, "where folks is civilized" (p. 226), and presumably, less humorously inclined.

Significantly, when the folk on the muck fear the coming hurricane, they turn to the cheering resources of their culture; they sit in Janie and Tea Cake's house and tell stories about Big John de Conquer and his feats and tricks, listen to Tea Cake's guitar, and then sing a song that comes from the Dozens:

> Yo' mama don't wear no *Draws*
> Ah seen her when she took 'em *Off*
> She soaked 'em in alco*Hol*
> She sold 'em tuh de Santa *Claus*
> He told her 'twas aginst de *Law*
> To wear dem dirty *Draws*. (p. 233)

The combination of John de Conquer stories and snippets of Dozens lines helps the figures gird up their loins against cosmic forces; John is traditionally a daring figure who frequently gambles with both God and the Devil, and the defiance of the Dozens humor is directed against a malevolently approaching Nature. Culture is attempting to ward off the storm.

In the aftermath of the hurricane, whites impress Tea Cake for a burial squad, and several other examples of racial oppression are raised. When Tea Cake comments on the dangers of being "strange niggers wid white folks," Janie adds "Dat sho is de truth. De ones de white man know is nice colored folks. De ones he don't know is bad niggers," which causes Tea Cake to laugh too, helping both of them to bear an unbearable situation (p. 255).

The wrong kind of humor comes into Hurston's range before the book ends. Tea Cake, bitten earlier by a mad dog, lies abed, and a white doctor is called to make a diagnosis. He initially greets his patient with some racist jocularity: "'Tain't a thing wrong that a quart of coon-dick wouldn't cure. You haven't been gettin' yo' right likker lately, eh?' He slapped Tea Cake lustily across his back and Tea Cake tried to smile as he was expected to do but it was hard" (p. 261). The biggest joker of all, however, seems to be God. Janie ponders, "Did He *mean* to do this thing to Tea Cake and her? . . . Maybe it was some big tease and when He saw it had gone far enough He'd give her a sign" (p. 264).

After Tea Cake dies and Janie, acquitted by a white jury, buries him, she knows she has to return to Eatonville, for there she can sit in her house and live by memories.

Janie knows what to expect from the town, however; "sitters-and-takers gointuh worry they guts into fiddle strings till dey find out . . ." and Janie's tale, told to Pheoby, is meant to function like Tea Cake's bundle of seeds, which Janie has brought with her; their story is meant for planting in the community, which needs their laughing, loving example. This is implicit in Pheoby's reaction: "Lawd! . . . Ah done growed ten feet higher from jus' listenin' tuh you, Janie. Ah ain't satisfied wid mahself no mo'. Ah mean tuh make Sam take me fishin' wid him after this. Nobody better not criticize yuh in my hearin" (p. 284).

We readers know this telling is necessary for another reason; earlier, Mrs. Annie Tyler brought out the cruel side of the community's humor. An older woman who is seduced, abandoned, and robbed by a series of young men, she had gone off laughing on her final fling with a younger man named, appropriately, Who Flung. Two weeks later a pitying Eatonville man finds her abandoned and penniless in Tampa; she is the laughingstock of the community upon her return.

Similarly, at the beginning of the frame story, when Janie first returns, alone, the neighbors' "burning statements" and killing laughter once again create mass cruelty (p. 10). Janie's transformation, however, gives her words to soothe these sentiments, and to turn them to her favor, since her story, which cheers and illuminates, points the way toward personhood.

Individual achievement finds its ultimate fulfillment in conjunction with others, and as Mary Helen Washington wisely observes, "the deepest and most lasting relationships occur among those black people who are most closely allied with and influenced by their own community."[45] Throughout *Their Eyes Were Watching God,* Hurston indicates that to refuse one's heritage is cultural suicide, and the loss of laughter represents an early symptom. In a unique way, Zora Neale Hurston recognized and harnessed humor's powerful resources; using its magical ability to bring people together, she established the intimacy of democratic communion.

Notes

1. Roger Rosenblatt, *Black Fiction* (Cambridge: Harvard Univ. Press, 1974), p. 101.

2. Zora Neale Hurston, "How it Feels to Be Colored Me," 1928; rpt., in *I Love Myself When I Am Laughing,* ed. Alice Walker (Old Westbury, N.Y.: Feminist Press, 1979), p. 153; *Dust Tracks On a Road,* ed. Robert Hemenway, 2nd ed. (1942; Urbana: Univ. of Illinois Press, 1984, ed. Robert Hemenway), p. 281. All subsequent citations are to this edition.

3. Henry Louis Gates, Jr., "A Negro Way of Saying," *The New York Times Book Review,* 21 April, 1985: 1, 41.

4. Hemenway, Introduction, *Dust Tracks,* pp. x–xi.

5. Robert Hemenway, *Zora Neale Hurston: A Literary Biography* (Urbana: Univ. of Illinois Press, 1978), p. 9.

6. *Dust Tracks,* p. 168.

7. According to Walter Lippmann's classic definition, a stereotype is a set of mental pictures formulated by human beings to describe the world beyond their reach, which are at least in part

culturally determined. Lippmann stresses that stereotypes are factually incorrect products of a faulty reasoning process, and that they tend to persist despite new knowledge and education. *Public Opinion* (New York: Harcourt, Brace, 1922).

8. W.E. Vinacke, "Stereotypes as Social Concepts," *Journal of Social Psychology, 46* (1957), 229–43.

9. "Negro Youth Speaks," in *The New Negro,* ed. Alain Locke (1925; rpt. New York: Atheneum, 1970), p. 50.

10. Sherley Anne Williams, Introduction, *Their Eyes Were Watching God,* by Zora Neale Hurston (1937; rpt., Urbana: Univ. of Illinois Press, 1978), pp. ix–x.

11. G. Fox, " 'Nice Girl': Social Control of Women through Value Construct," *Signs 2,* 4 (1977), 807.

12. For a penetrating analysis of female humor, a subject that only recently has attracted scholarly attention, see chapter 2, "Sexual Inequality in Humor," in Mahadev Apte, *Humor and Laughter: An Anthropological Approach* (Ithaca, N.Y.: Cornell Univ. Press, 1985), pp. 67–81.

13. R. Lakoff, *Language and Woman's Place* (New York: Harper & Row, 1975), p.56; S. Kalcik, "'. . . Like Ann's Gynecologist; or, The Time I Was Almost Raped': Personal Narratives in Women's Rap Groups," *Journal of American Folklore, 88,* 347 (1975), 56.

14. *Infants of the Spring* (New York: MacCaulay, 1932), pp. 229–230.

15. Larry Neal, "Eatonville's Zora Neale Hurston: A Profile," *Black Review No. 2,* ed. Mel Watkins (New York: William Morrow, 1972), 11–24.

16. *The Big Sea* (New York: Hill and Wang, 1940), p. 239.

17. Neal, p. 23.

18. For Freud's classic statement on the subject, see *Jokes and Their Relation to the Unconscious,* trans. and ed. James Strachey, std. ed. (New York: Norton, 1963), pp. 9–15.

19. Robert Hemenway, Introduction, *Dust Tracks,* p. xvii.

20. Zora Neale Hurston, "Characteristics of Negro Expression," in *Negro: An Anthology,* ed. Nancy Cunard (London: Wishart, 1934), p. 40. Barbara Johnson has recently published a fascinating related study, "Metaphor, Metonymy and Voice in *Their Eyes Were Watching God,*" in *Black Literature and Literary Theory,* ed. Henry Louis Gates, Jr. (New York: Methuen, 1984), pp. 205–219.

21. An example, How God made Blacks: arriving late on the day He handed out color, they crowded in, and thought he said "Git Black" when He said "Git back!" (*Dust Tracks,* pp. 65–69).

22. For discussions of these and related terms in Black humor, see Claudia Mitchell-Kernan, "Signifying, Loud-talking and Marking," in *Rappin' and Stylin' Out: Communication In Urban Black America,* ed. Thomas Kochman (Urbana: Univ. of Illinois Press, 1972), pp. 315–335; Thomas Kochman, "Toward an Ethnography of Black American Speech Behavior," in *Afro-American Anthropology: Contemporary Perspectives,* ed. Norman E. Whitten, Jr., and John F. Szwed (New York: The Free Press, 1970), pp. 145–62, and Roger D. Abrahams, "Playing the Dozens," in *Mother Wit from the Laughing Barrel,* ed. Alan Dundes (Englewood Cliffs, N.J.: Prentice-Hall, 1973), pp. 295–309.

23. Zora Neale Hurston, *Mules and Men* (1935; rpt. Bloomington: Indiana Univ. Press, 1978), p. 3.

23. *Dust Tracks,* p. 281.

24. "John Redding Goes to Sea," 1921; rpt., *Opportunity, 4* (Jan., 1926), 16–21.

25. "Drenched in Light," *Opportunity, 2* (Dec., 1924), 371–74.

26. Hemenway, *Zora Neale Hurston,* p. 11.

27. For a cogent summary and discussion of research on this topic, see Apte, *Humor and Laughter,* pp. 29–66. The classic definition comes from A.R. Radcliffe-Brown, who describes a joking relationship as one "between two persons in which one is by custom permitted, and in some instances required, to tease or make fun of the other, who in turn is required to take no offense." "A Further Note on Joking Relationships," 1949; rpt. in *Structure and Function in Primitive Society* (London: Cohen West, 1965), pp. 105–116.

28. "Spunk," *Opportunity, 3* (June, 1925), 171–173. This story occupies a central place in Hurston's career, for it was reprinted in the ground-breaking anthology, *The New Negro* (1925).

29. "The Eatonville Anthology," 1926; rpt. in *I Love Myself,* pp. 177–88.

30. See Hemenway's penetrating analysis of this scene, "Are You a Flying Lark or a Setting Dove?" in *Afro-American Literature: The Reconstruction of Instruction,* ed. Dexter Fisher and Robert B. Stepto (New York: MLA, 1979), pp. 122–152.

31. "Muttsy," *Opportunity, 4* (Aug. 1926), 7–15.

32. "Story in Harlem Slang," *American Mercury, 55* (July, 1942), 84–96.

33. "Sweat," 1926; rpt. in *I Love Myself,* pp. 197–207.

34. "The Gilded Six-Bits," 1933; rpt. in *I Love Myself,* pp. 208–218.

35. *Jonah's Gourd Vine* (Philadelphia: Lippincott, 1934).

36. Letter from Zora Neale Hurston to Alain Locke, April 16, 1934, cited in Neale, p. 16.

37. I shall deal at length with the comic aspects of *Moses* in a future essay.

38. Zora Neale Hurston, "Race Cannot Become Great Until It Recognizes Its Talent," *Washington Tribune,* Dec. 29, 1934.

39. Joseph Campbell's formulation of this principle is enumerated in his *The Hero With a Thousand Faces* (1949; rpt. Princeton, N.J.: Princeton Univ. Press, 1972).

40. See especially Missy Dehn Kubitschek, "'Tuh De Horizon and Back': The Female Quest in *Their Eyes Were Watching God*," *Black American Literature Forum, 17,* 3 (Fall, 1983), 109–114.

41. As Michael G. Cooke notes, however, Janie and Jody are not technically playing the dozens. She *categorizes* him ("big-bellies"); as Cooke states, she "seems to crash through signifying and into denunciation." Michael G. Cooke, *Afro-American Literature in the Twentieth Century: the Achievement of Intimacy* (New Haven: Yale Univ. Press, 1984), p. 77.

42. Apte, p. 79.

43. For the full elaboration of his theory, see Johan Huizinga, *Homo Ludens: A Study of the Play Element in Culture* (Boston: Beacon, 1970. Orig. published in Dutch in 1938; trans. from the German ed., 1944).

44. Anyone who doubts this should consult *Dust Tracks,* pp. 225–26.

45. Mary Helen Washington, introduction, *Black Eyed Susans: Classic Stories by and About Black Women,* ed. Mary Helen Washington (New York: Anchor, 1975), p. xxx.

There's a Joker in the Menstrual Hut: A Performance Analysis of Comedian Kate Clinton

Linda Pershing

The world is always humor-poor. There is never enough of it. Yet, without humor we cannot survive. Our world is too relentlessly cruel, too callous, too uncivilized, and feminists who contemplate it will die of depression or lapse into cynicism and inaction without our humor. By joking, we rehumanize, recivilize ourselves. By joking, we remake ourselves so that after each disappointment we become once again capable of living and loving.[1]

February 20, 1985. It is after 8:00 P.M., the time Kate Clinton's performance is scheduled to begin, when the doors are opened to the Ritz Theater in downtown Austin, Texas. Streams of women rush in to find seats. Within minutes the theater is full downstairs, and there are people sitting in the balcony, making a total crowd of between two and three hundred. The audience is comprised almost entirely of women, with the exception of about a half-dozen men scattered throughout the crowd. A range of signifying haircuts, jewelry, and clothing suggests that the audience is largely lesbian. Although there are a few women of color, most of the audience is white. Many women have come together in groups; many know one another and greet friends with hugs and affection. The theater is buzzing with the voices of women who sound happy, excited, and expectant. There is an atmosphere of celebration. As we wait for the show to begin, I am aware of the exhilarating sensation of being in a large public gathering of women. Only upon later reflection do I come to realize that the menstrual hut Clinton jokes about during her performance is a metaphor for this theater full of women:

> Now, we have this new album out. . . . But the new album—
> we had some problems with the titles, okay?—some "artistic
> differences" about the title, also known as big fights. . . . See,
> I tried to call the album "There's a Joker in the Menstrual
> Hut." And can you see the video? Alright, the menstrual hut
> is where tribesmen sent their menstruating women because
> they were "unclean," for God's sakes, and they'd go in these
> little huts, and there'd be a lot of women in there, and they'd
> talk, you know, sing a few songs, tell a little gossip, give a
> low back massage now and again. I say: BRING BACK THE
> HUT! I think the Astrodome would be just fine! Now, can't
> you just see some guy outside going, "Honey, you've been in
> there for twenty-three days! We're practically out of
> casseroles. When are you coming out?" And she'd say: "Hey,
> I can't come out now. There's a joker in the menstrual hut!"
> (1985)[2]

Kate Clinton is a contemporary stand-up comic, originally from upstate New York, who is attracting widespread attention for her distinctive brand of humor. She describes herself as a "feminist humorist" or "fumerist"; celebration of women's experiences and using comedy to encourage feminist awareness are characteristic of her approach. This article is an exploration and analysis of Kate Clinton's February 20, 1985, and April 4, 1987, Austin appearances using concepts that have been central to performance theory as it has developed in folklore studies, most clearly articulated by Richard Bauman.[3] My analysis is also informed by the somewhat limited but growing body of research that is available concerning women's humor.

Performance theory, as it emerged in the 1970s study of American folklore, is built on an organizing principle that includes within a single conceptual framework the artistic act, expressive form, and aesthetic response, all within its own locally defined, culture-specific context.[4] This approach is predicated on the belief that it is essential to understand not only the content but also the context of the humorous event or joke and its relation to particular patterns of social reality in which it occurs.[5] The concept of performance has enabled folklorists and other scholars to shift their focus from concentration on texts or products to verbal art as action or process. I use the term *performance* in its dual sense to mean not just the event but also the act of communication: "the term 'performance' has been used to convey a dual sense of artistic *action*—the doing of folklore—and artistic *event*—the performance situation, involving performer, art form, audience, and setting—both of which are basic to the developing performance approach."[6]

I treat the verbal art form that Clinton uses—stand-up comedy—as a genre in its own right. Although this is a commercial and formalized performance form that would not conventionally be studied by folklorists, I have found that performance theory offers valuable insights into the study of verbal artists on and off stage.[7] My discussion will include analysis of the context, performer-audience relationship, subject matter, and functions of Clinton's comedy. I suggest that analysis of Clinton's humor within a performance theory orientation reveals that her work is shaped by her self-definition in the public and private spheres as a lesbian feminist, and that this distinguishes the style, content, and rendering of her humor. Constraints of time and space make it impossible for me to compare Clinton's performances with those of particular male stand-up comedians, although that would make an interesting and useful study.[8] However, I will discuss the ways in which she operates within what has traditionally been a male-dominated genre.

Finally, I make no attempt here to conceal my own bias. I think Kate Clinton is enormously funny. There were times during her performances that I was gasping for air from laughing so much. This was only compounded by friends who were sitting next to me holding their sides and hooting with laughter (one moaned, "I've got a headache from laughing so hard!"). I am hungry for the comic relief Clinton offers. As a feminist who often goes through the day feeling like a stranger on an alien planet, I was moved by Clinton's worldview and enamored of her ability to use wit as a tool for survival. In attempting to write a summary about feminist humor for the book *Pulling Our Own Strings: Feminist Humor and Satire,* Mary Kay Blakely eloquently describes the difficulty I share in removing myself from my subject:

> I couldn't write because I kept hearing the voices, the fascinating intonations, the fluctuating moods, and yes, yes, yes, I listened to the tremors of revolution that our humor inspires. I lost interest in diagramming the sentences, explicating the themes. . . . I wanted to listen. I heard the faint voice of self-consciousness in our humor, the nervous laugh of the messenger who doesn't want her head cut off for reporting damaging news: The natives are restless. We use our humor to deliver our complaints about the status quo. We tend to be a bit edgy at times because we know from experience just how many potential toes we are stepping on.[9]

The Setting

Popular notions about Austin as a politically progressive city with a visible feminist community, a sizable lesbian and gay community, and a strong intellectual faction (Austin is a university town) play an important role in providing a framework for Clinton's performance.[10] The overtly sexual and political content of much of her humor is specifically designed for an audience who will be receptive and, moreover, will share her viewpoint. Clinton suggests this in a 1985 parody of the television show "Bloops, Blunders and Practical Jokes": "[In an overly enunciated emcee-type voice.] Hello, welcome to 'Heterosexual Bloops, Blunders and Practical Jokes.' My name is Dyke Clark. Tonight we're going to play a practical joke on comedian Kate Clinton. Now, Clinton thinks tonight that she's going to go out and face an audience of radical lesbian separatists. In fact, the entire audience is filled with born-again, fundamentalist women from Little Rock, Arkansas. And they've been told that Clinton will be preaching in tongues!" (1985)

As with most touring performers, Clinton's actual contact with her audience is limited. Her shows are usually one- or two-night engagements. She mentions often that she is on tour, and during the introduction to her act the announcer tells the audience that Clinton "travels extensively throughout the country," thus conveying her mobility and lack of geographical affiliation with any one audience. One-time interaction with her audience is significant in light of Clinton's attempts to do more than simply entertain. Her closing exhortation to act upon the newly shared experience of her performance is bounded by the fact that she will be elsewhere, doing another show for a different group of people. Even though she mentioned that she would like to return to Austin—and I believe she makes this comment as a way of expressing her desire for continuity with the audience—they know that this is an indefinite commitment. Clinton performs in Austin once every two years. The audience is left to return to their everyday lives without her, and to make their own decisions about how the experience of that evening will (or will not) be integrated into their daily existence.

Clinton's Performance as "Situated Behavior"

Comedy is a business that has traditionally been the domain of males, and their influence still dominates—in numbers, in attitude, and in determining the way things are done and who does them. [11]

> And a lot of it has to do with being a woman. Why are they upset with what I'm doing when Richard Pryor is being deified and Eddie Murphy is being deified? [12]

Clinton is a verbal artist who practices her craft within clearly bounded parameters. She performs during a scheduled event that occurs in a restricted setting (a theater or club) and is open to the public (although I will argue that only a specific segment of the general public is meant to participate). Citing the work of Milton Singer, Bauman describes such performances as "cultural performances," those "involving the most highly formalized performance forms and accomplished performers in the community."[13] Clinton exhibits considerable skill as a verbal artist within this context, using the traditional performance to her advantage. Her routine includes memorized material and improvisation; both contribute to her success as a stand-up comedian. It is evident from her delivery that her routine and stage presence are the result of years of practice and the careful honing of her material. However, I contend that the particular significance of her performance lies not in the way she has mastered her craft in the traditional sense (although that in itself is formidable) but in how she manipulates it in original ways to go beyond the boundaries of "cultural performance" to a performance that calls those boundaries into question.

The idea of a feminist humorist is an intriguing one. Although historically there have been and continue to be notable exceptions (Gracie Allen, Phyllis Diller, Joan Rivers, and Whoopi Goldberg come to mind), the field of highly paid, mass media stand-up comedy has been dominated largely by men (Johnny Carson, Richard Pryor, George Carlin, Bill Cosby, Steve Martin, David Brenner, Don Rickles, Bob Newhart, Eddie Murphy—the list goes on). Much of the significance of Clinton's humor is dependent on its context and on the way she negotiates her performance against cultural and social expectations. Like all humor, it is useful to consider her performance as "situated behavior, situated within and rendered meaningful with reference to relevant contexts."[14]

In examining Clinton's work as "situated behavior," four aspects of her humor are striking: (1) she is a woman operating within a predominantly male domain; (2) she is a self-defined and outspoken feminist; (3) she is a lesbian; and (4) she uses the first three personal characteristics in a public way as the basis of her humor.

First, as a woman performing in a male domain, Clinton faces comparison by her audience, the media, and herself against societal expectations about male stand-up comedians. It is somewhat unusual for women to go into this line of work, although their numbers are increasing.[15] Some people have even suggested that humor itself is alien to "woman's nature." In a 1966 analysis of the interrelationship of gender and humor, for example, David Zippin wrote: "Comediennes [16] are numerically rare compared with male comics. This suggests that humor is somehow alien to femininity. When the woman is a comedienne, she takes on the male role."[17] Rose Laub Coser's data support this notion about women's lack of participation in joking behavior. Among women and men in the workplace, Coser attributed the lack of humor she observed among women to their passive social enculturation: "In this culture women are expected to be passive and receptive, rather than active and initiating. A woman who has a good sense of humor is one who laughs (but not too loudly!) when a man makes a witticism or tells a good joke. A man who has a good sense of humor is one who is witty in his remarks and tells good jokes. The man provides; the woman receives. Thus at the meetings, men made by far the more frequent witticisms—99 out of 103—but women often laughed harder."[18] The fact that so many authors support the contention that there is no long-standing tradition of American women's humor is testimony not to the veracity of this belief but rather to the way in which women's humor, like so many other expressive forms used by women, has been overlooked or ignored in our cultural history. Even some feminist writers seem to feel that there is no history of American women's humor, or that they are discovering women's humor for the first time. Other scholars acknowledge the existence of women's humor, while simultaneously suggesting that it has been confined primarily to the private domain: "Although women are no less capable of developing and appreciating humor than men, women have been denied similar opportunities for publicly engaging in humor. Because modesty, passivity, and virtue are associated with ideal womanhood, women have been confined to the private domain, with many constraints imposed upon them. Only marriage, old age, and the greater freedom of behavior granted to women in groups to some extent alleviate this inequality of the sexes."[19] However, contemporary feminist scholars, such as Alice Sheppard and Nancy A. Walker, have begun to identify the long-standing historical tradition of American women's humor. Sheppard, for example, argues that there *is* a tradition of women's humor, which she has partially reconstructed by digging through archival materials, and that scholars ought to be asking not "why didn't women develop a humor tradition?" but "why has the humor which was created and appreciated by women been ignored?"[20]

The popular conception that women are not funny presents particular obstacles to comedians like Clinton. Not unlike women in other traditionally male-dominated occupations (e.g., business executives, clergy, academicians), she has had to learn how to function successfully in a "man's world." Clinton has done this by learning the traditional tools of her trade well enough so that the public, who may be more accustomed to watching male performers, will recognize and affirm her as a legitimate stand-up comic. This negotiation against a male model is both implicit and explicit. Implicitly, Clinton uses elements of style that seem to be a compromise between stereotypical patterns of expression among women and men.[21] For example, her voice pitch is in middle range, neither extremely high (conventionally associated with the female) nor extremely low (conventionally associated with the male). Onstage her body language is fluid yet controlled, expressive (she uses occasional gestures and mimicry) without being too "flowery." Although she uses her hands to gesture while she talks, she does not flail them about. When she gestures, her fingers usually remain closed, thus creating an impression of strength and control of her immediate environment.

Explicitly, some of Clinton's material deals with the ways in which the experiences of women and men substantially differ in white, middle-class American culture and, moreover, how men often look foolish in the eyes of women. In so doing, she legitimizes her female identity and uses the contrast to strengthen her performance before an audience that is almost entirely composed of women: "How many of you think that if you were a guy . . . and you were going bald, that you probably *would* part your hair right here [gestures to the far right side of her head just above the ear]—and drag pieces of hair over your head? I know I would. Have you ever seen those guys come out of swimming? [She mimics long strands of hair hanging down the right side of her face down to her shoulder] Wow, lookin' good!" (1985). Similarly, in her 1987 performance, Clinton commented on the stifling conservatism and conformity that is endemic to the male-dominated business world, thereby ridiculing male standards of status: "Doesn't it feel like you live on the Planet of the Guys? I travel a lot, and when I'm in airports, I look around, and it's all guys. And they're all wearing those three-piece suits. What imaginative dressers! Whenever I'm at an airport, I always feel like going up to a guy and saying, 'Ooh, I love your outfit! Especially what you're doing with the pinstripes. It's just so—up and down!'" (1987).

Secondly, Clinton publicly describes herself as a feminist and is unusual in this way, even among women comedians. Her explicit identification with feminism is noteworthy since traditionally so much of both men's and women's humor has used women as its target. Although other, less-known women comics seem to be focusing less on humor that deprecates women, they often describe their approach not as feminist but as "enlightened, but still looking for a man" or as "gender-neutral."[22] In contrast, Clinton's jokes are decidedly pro-female, often revolving around the shared experiences of women, which she articulates, laughs about, and enjoins her audience to celebrate with their laughter:

> The thing that bugs me about the condom ads is, did you notice that when the problem with sex was just pregnancy, one million teenagers a year—mostly girls—when the problems with sex were just pregnancy or just some gay men with AIDS, there were no condom ads. But I'm telling you, when a couple of straight white guys get AIDS, then we've got ourselves some condom ads on TV. The other thing is, they're targeting women. Once again, we're in charge. What's the deal here? . . . See, I think that if we're supposed to carry condoms around for guys, that we should be able to go up to a guy in the street and say, "Oh, I just got my period. I'm kind of out of luck. May I borrow a tampon?" (1987)

Thirdly, Clinton introduces her act by making a reference to lesbianism: "Thank you all for *coming out*." Much of her humor, particularly her bawdy and sexual jokes, involves her experiences as a lesbian. Like her feminism, she talks about her lesbianism proudly, without apologies.[23] On the contrary, by poking fun at "straight" women, she offers a feminist critique of their compulsory heterosexual orientation: "Now, I went to a party once . . . and I was talking to this woman. And she was kinda neat. She came up to me and she said, 'You know, I really liked your show. Uh, I'm straight, but I liked your show.' I don't know, that tickles me, ya know? When I can get—it's powerful when you can make somebody, before you can start out, give you a heterosexual disclaimer: 'Loved your show, I'm heterosexual.' I say, 'Okay, but don't let it happen again!'" (1985) Sometimes Clinton becomes an advocate for lesbianism by using her humor to target public figures, wildly disrupting any conventional sense of propriety:

> I said I would go to this school in San Bernardino, I do all of these Gay Awareness weeks. I said, but do me a favor . . . I'm sick of the word *awareness. Gay awareness,* it's too passive: "I'm aware. I'm gay. It's okay." I said, "I want it to be more active, something like, oh, Gay Conversion Month." And its an easy thing. What you do is you select a hetero-sexual . . . you plan your strategy, and then you just go for it. Okay? I think that for me—I'm aiming high—I think that pound for pound Elizabeth Dole is the cutest Secretary of Transportation we've ever had, and I'm goin' for it! Can't you hear me say it: "Uh, Liz, come up to my room; I want to show you my underpass!" (1987)

Clinton performs in relationship to what Bauman calls "ground rules," either by conforming to them or by purposely disregarding them: "As a kind of speaking, performance will be subject to a range of community ground rules that regulate speaking in general."[24] In negotiating her performance, Clinton often chooses to use her skills as a stand-up comic to set herself over against traditional expectations.[25] While she observes certain conventions (e.g., standing on stage telling jokes, integrating material about the location in which she is performing, commenting on current events), Clinton purposely disregards others (by telling many bawdy jokes, being openly critical of men, and refusing to use disclaimers, apologies, or self-deprecation to legitimize her "intrusion" into a traditionally male-dominated arena of activity).[26] There is also "a set of ground rules specific to [the] performance itself."[27] Having attracted a female audience, predominantly feminist and lesbian, Clinton conforms to a particular set of expec-tations, addressing the experiences of women living within an androcentric and homophobic society. Accordingly, she avoids a style of communication that might be perceived as being too "male," stereotypically characterized by authoritarianism or emotional detachment. As a lesbian fem-inist performing in the public sphere, she is also under pressure to be "politically correct." One could hardly imagine, for example, that she would be accepted by her audience if she were to use humor to support anti-gay rights legislation, the policies of the Reagan and Bush administrations, or the anti-abortion movement.

Fourthly, Clinton's limited access to a particular form of verbal art is essential to the understanding of her humor as situated behavior. In Clinton's case, as a woman, and particularly as a lesbian feminist, her access to the public role of stand-up comedian is restricted and negotiated by cultural norms. Hence, within this traditionally male-dominated domain, she has to work very hard to find a forum for validation and public recognition. This affects her performance by putting increased pressure on her, as a woman performer, to measure up to conventional male-identified standards while simultaneously attempting to call them into question. Abby Stein, another female stand-up comedian, comments on the problems this poses for women: "What you're really trying to do is be imitative of a male comic because that's the only role model you have. What happened to me is what happens to all of us: we get into the business because we were naturally funny, because for years all our friends said we were the life of the party. Then we systematically try to destroy everything that made us funny to begin with."[28]

Clinton's performance also produces a feeling of incredulity for her audience. My reaction the first time I watched her was "I can't believe she's really up on stage doing this stuff!" Because of its lesbian feminist orientation, her performance was like nothing I had seen before from a stand-up comic. Clinton is able to create a sensation of increased and intensified enjoyment for her audience because she negotiates her unusual role successfully and offers them an unexpected surprise: humor resonant with their own life experiences. Because of her particular worldview, her audience is limited by each individual's ability to share, or at least sympathize with, her ideology. Restricted access to an expressive art form has encouraged Clinton to distill her material for a particular, non-mainstream audience that can accept and enjoy her art. This means that men and non-feminist or politically conservative women are not a large or visible segment of her audience.[29]

The Performer

As part of her style is dependent on self-disclosure, Clinton offers a considerable amount of personal information about herself during her performance. In so doing, she intimates that she plays social roles other than that of the entertainer.[30] Some of these roles are as follows: a member of a family (with parents, one sister and three brothers, aunts and uncles), ex-high school teacher, "recovering Catholic," lesbian lover, feminist critic in the community ("I keep up on these things"), political activist (working against the La Rouche Initiative), and everyday ordinary woman (who watches television, likes to eat, goes to a gynecologist, attends parties, and survived adolescence). The audience hears about these but does not see them. During the 1987 show, the audience was told her age (in November 1987, she turned forty) and that she is from upstate New York but recently moved to Los Angeles.

Since the audience does not actually see her in these capacities, her primary identity for them is still as a stand-up comedian. According to Bauman's theory, much of the verbal artist's success is determined on her ability to convince the audience of her eligibility as a legitimate performer.[31] As a performer, Clinton assumes responsibility to the audience for a display of communicative competence. Given the social setting, "this competence rests on the knowledge and ability to speak in socially appropriate ways."[32] For a stand-up comedian, establishing one's legitimacy usually entails special talent and training (practice, appearances in clubs, booking tours) and an arduous period of apprenticeship. I have already noted how Clinton is required to negotiate her performance against social expectations and how she uses that framework in her favor. Nonetheless, as a woman, feminist, and lesbian working in a traditionally male-dominated framework, the obstacles facing Clinton are formidable:

> Of all the avenues in humor women can pursue, stand-up comedy has got to be the toughest. The proving grounds are dingy clubs, often filled with audiences of persistent hecklers. The hours are long and late and require anxiously awaiting the nod to go on, which usually comes after the busboy has been given his chance. The pay is low or nonexistent, and the peer group of other women to turn to for support is minuscule. A look around at the number of women who have made successful careers in stand-up comedy confirms the grim prospects.
>
> Tremendous mettle is required for a woman to stand alone on a stage and attempt to capture the attention and amuse an assortment of skeptics who have paid hard cash for a good time. Most women don't consider the possibility. Many become discouraged and give up. A few make it.[33]

How does Clinton's humor compare with that of other contemporary women comedians? One similarity is the use of women's shared experiences as one of the primary subjects of her humor. As with Clinton, jokes about relationships, personal insights, adolescence, and women's appearance are common among comedians such as Joan Rivers, Phyllis Diller, Gilda Radner, and the new women comedians making their way into the comedy business on the East Coast (e.g., Abby Stein, Carole Montgomery, Carol Suskind, Phyllis Stickney). In a 1984 interview for *Ms.* magazine, for example, Joan Rivers mentions several personal experiences that Clinton also uses as a springboard for her humor, including learning to cope with the difficulties of being a woman comedian, having to pay the consequences for risk taking, and acknowledging the ways in which humor can be used as a mechanism to remind audiences about oppressive and painful situations. There are, however, aspects of Clinton's performance that, when taken collectively, distinguish her from other women comedians, or at least from those I have encountered. These include her attitude toward (1) self-deprecatory humor, (2) humor that demeans other women, (3) the use of comic characters or personas, and (4) public self-identification as a feminist.

First, although she satirizes difficult stages in her life (e.g., "coming out" to her family, teenage growing pains, being overweight as a kid), Clinton's humor is decidedly not self-deprecatory. Instead, she conveys self-confidence and celebrates her experiences through laughter. Recent interviews with younger, less-known women comedians suggest that self-deprecatory humor also plays a minimal role in their routines.[34] However, for older and well-known women comics, the tendency to make the audience laugh at the comedian's expense (usually at her stupidity, homeliness, or sexual inadequacy) was and is a common humor technique.[35] For example, journalist Lee Israel describes Joan Rivers's humor as "a comedy of tension and surprise, suspended uneasily between physical observation and vulgarity, between that which is about self-deprecation and that which is apologetic."[36] It is easy in hindsight to fault women comedians who first "made it" in show business for their self-denigrating style. Given the social climate of the day, however, these women may have had little choice if they wanted to succeed in a traditionally male-dominated profession.

Phyllis Diller noted: "People back then were not ready for a lady comic. They had no basis for acceptance. 'It's a *woman!* What's she trying to do?' 'She's got to be an ugly person.' 'She's got to be a butch person.' 'She's got to be a nasty woman.' Not true at all. No one is more feminine than I. I'm basically a mother and a wife and a grandmother and all those good things. But to make it on stage, I had to make fun of myself first . . . of course, I was accused of being self-deprecatory. I've got to be."[37]

In her discussion of women's consciousness-raising groups, Susan Kalcik cites the use of humor among group members as a support mechanism for group solidarity. Moreover, she notes the tendency of those women to turn "the humor in on themselves rather than on supposed oppressors."[38] Similarly, Rose Laub Coser, in her study of the uses of humor among hospital employees of varying rank and seniority, found that "a junior member can safely take the initiative to decrease social distance through humor if [s]he uses [herself/]himself as a target."[39] Given this trend of women's self-disparaging humor, it is noteworthy that Clinton makes a strong effort not to publicly devalue herself for the sake of a laugh.

There has also been a historical tendency among stand-up comedians—male and female—to use women as the targets of their humor.[40] In her article about the bawdy humor of Southern women, Rayna Green notes that "the media comediennes stand alone in their presentation of women as inventors and perpetuators of humor, but even there, few—beyond Moms Mabley and Lily Tomlin . . . have gone outside the boundaries of portraying women as humorous objects rather than as humorists."[41] This is not particularly surprising, since women in American society are frequently devalued and encouraged to compete with one another for favor and prestige. Among contemporary women media comedians, Joan Rivers has been particularly singled out for telling jokes that attack or degrade individual women:

> Increasingly, however, she is using real people in the comedy dynamic. I am bothered by that tendency. I can't help thinking that Elizabeth Taylor and Christina Onassis, in spite of their position and power, are still vulnerable human beings. It's one thing to say that the Emperor has no clothes, it's quite another to point to his double chin. That's not audacious, it's mean. While Joan may argue that it is necessary to shock in order to amuse, I'm sometimes hearing a different kind of laughter coming from her audiences—the kind that derives not from what is being said but from the

fact that it is being said at all. The laughter follows as a collective gasp and it is as much horrified as jollified.[42]

In fairness, it should be noted that Rivers degrades both women and men in her routines, and she contends that she drops out material if she believes (or is told by the "target" or the "target's" family) that it is hurting anyone. When asked why she does this kind of comedy, she replied, "I found myself saying to people: Don't you understand? It's *all* in fun. *All* in fun."[43]

Clinton is unusual because she publicly acknowledges her ideology about satirizing women: "Ali McGraw does something to me. It's not a good something. Ali McGraw, like, arouses my gag reflex. I mean, she is something. She is a woman who makes me regret that I ever vowed that I, as a feminist comedian, I would not make fun of other women. Because with Ali McGraw we are talking a major, major temptation!" (1985) In actuality, however, she does poke fun at a selected number of women, including (in her 1985 performance) women who speak to her after her shows and say silly things, Mary Lou Retton, Nancy Reagan ("she seems so lifelike"), her old Aunt Marjorie, her mother, and Ali McGraw. In 1987, she satirized the rock star Madonna ("a radical heterosexual separatist"), Mother Theresa ("she looks like the movie creature E.T. dressed up for Halloween"), Nancy Reagan, Fawn Hall, Vanna White, and Tammy Bakker ("I think about the days before the Lord appeared unto Tammy and told her about waterproof mascara"). Although Clinton contends that her humor does not make fun of women, in actuality she hedges somewhat on this principle. While her jokes about these women could rarely be considered cruel, they do represent a small portion of her material. Hence, there is a discrepancy between Clinton's ideology and her practice as a performer, one that goes unreconciled. It may be that Clinton's satiric characterization of certain women is a device for promoting group solidarity among members of her audience by defining them in opposition to other women of whom they disapprove (particularly those who are very rich, conservative, or naive).

In comparing Clinton with a range of other women stand-up comedians, I noticed that she makes little use of comedic characters or personas. In contrast, characters are central to the comedy of Lily Tomlin (e.g., Ernestine, the telephone operator; Edith Ann, the impertinent five-year-old girl: and Trudy, the bag lady), Gilda Radner (Roseanne Roseannadanna, the coarse East Coast woman; Judy Miller, the exuberant little girl with a vivid imagination; and Candy Slice, the punk rock star), and Whoopi Goldberg (who plays a crippled woman who loves to go disco dancing and wear a bikini; a poor Jamaican woman who is courted by a rich old man; and a junkie thief who has a Ph.D. in literature) come to mind as contemporary examples. These comedians seem to use personas to say things they cannot effectively communicate when they are "themselves." This technique was very common among women comedians of an earlier time (e.g., Elaine May, Phyllis Diller, Totie Fields) and may have been popular because through personas "they [the comedians] were all protected in some way by the kind of comedy they were doing, by their outside comedic *personas.* They were camouflaged, or, at least, accompanied."[44]

Finally, Clinton is unusual among women stand-up comedians because she publicly identifies herself as a feminist and talks about feminism, explicitly using that term in her routines. Other women comics, such as Joan Rivers, also consider themselves feminists: "Everyone forgets that I was the first lady ever to come on television and laugh about being single, laugh about all the nonsense and the first lady to bring Betty Friedan on television, on 'The Mike Douglas Show,' and deal with those issues. I always tell feminists that my life is a feminist life—just turn around, you idiots. I have done a movie—I cast it, got my own money, did my own editing—what do you want from me?"[45]

Lily Tomlin, in fact, is very articulate about her views on feminism, aptly describing gender inequalities by noting that

women are getting $1.57 an hour! I mean that the stretch
marks and $10,000 would not begin to cover it! (1987)

The Audience

Kate Clinton causes fun. Being in her audience reminds me
of the wild pleasure of being with slaphappy girlfriends. [52]

In that Kate Clinton's humor is directed to a particular
audience of women who can share, or at least sympathize
with, her worldview without being alienated or offended, her
jokes are gender-specific. Carol Mitchell, in her studies of
differences in joke telling between the sexes, confirms that the
gender of both the performer and the audience are crucial
factors in how they are appreciated: "In determining the
degree of appreciation of jokes, the sex of the performer and
the audience is probably as important as the content of the
joke itself. For instance, a joke that is primarily derogatory to
men is more likely to be appreciated by men when it is told
one man to other men, but it seems less funny to men if it is
told to them by a woman, and the reverse holds true of jokes
that are primarily derogatory to women."[53] The women in the
audience would not be amused upon hearing Clinton's
material delivered by a man. If this occurred, humor that she
now uses as celebratory of the female experience might be
taken as derogatory, alienating, or presumptuous.

Similarly, Clinton's performance would be affected if the
audience were composed of a substantial number of men,
attending either as individuals or as members of heterosexual
couples. The men who were a part of the audiences in Austin
were so few in number as to be virtually invisible, and Clinton
made no attempt to draw them in as participants in her
performances. In studying the differences between women's
and men's speech, Thorne and Henley have noted how "the
speech used in situations where both sexes are present may be
quite different from the speech of the single-sex occasions."[54]

This is evident both in the way Clinton speaks as though men are "out there somewhere," not present in the audience, and in the way she uses openly hostile jokes about men to create cohesion among women. As a member of the audience, I got the impression that Clinton's attempts focused not on demeaning or embarrassing specific men in the audience but rather on disregarding their presence altogether. This would correspond to Mitchell's findings that "women are still less likely than men to use jokes for the purpose of embarrassing the listener. And most of their openly hostile jokes will be saved for the all-female audience."[55]

Clinton's interaction with the audience is one of the keys to her success. Her approach is one of camaraderie between women, sisterhood in the feminist sense. She wants to convey the impression that she is "just one of the girls," confiding about her personal experiences, daily frustrations, and political views as though she were a close friend with the audience as a whole. This is not unlike Joan Rivers's hallmark phrase "Can we talk?" By creating the impression that she and the audience share a friendship, Rivers tries to win their sympathy and trust: "If you come on with a superior attitude, they [the audience] cannot relate to you. And you must relate in comedy, you must be friends or you have no chance at all."[56] But it is more than camaraderie that Clinton wants to engender. Since much of her material focuses on her experiences as a lesbian and a feminist living in a hostile society, she assumes that her audience has shared her experiences of alienation and marginalization. Clinton intentionally uses humor as a support mechanism for herself and the women she addresses.[57] In her study of the effects of humor on group dynamics, Coser observes that "by inviting the listeners to indicate through laughter that they share the awareness of the conflict, humor is both a means of self-protection and a means of providing the support of the collectivity. In both instances, the humorist may be said to play the informal role of an agent of socialization."[58] The following excerpt from Clinton's 1985 routine illustrates this dynamic:

> What you've gotta do is, whenever Reagan or any of his henchmen appear in your town—and I guess there is one living, isn't there? [George Bush comes from Texas.] What you've gotta do: you go by the house, maybe go by George's house, you know? And what you've gotta do is, you've gotta get all of your wildest lesbian-looking clothes out again, okay? Get 'em out. Some of you have been "femming" it up a little bit. I rolled a woman at the Inaugural Ball for this very outfit. . . . But what you've got to do is: you've got to get out your oldest lesbian-looking clothes, okay? You've got to get out your white painter pants again. You've gotta get out your flannel shirts again. You know, your rainbow suspenders out again; your purple tie-died underwear out again. You've gotta get your Birkenstocks out again, okay . . . ? And then your ten-pound, three-inch labyrises out again, okay, with blades so sharp as to make a Cuisinart seem dull, do you know what I'm saying? Get it all together now, and you take your wildest lesbian-looking friends out, okay? Amazonians at their very best. And then, whenever Reagan appears or any of his little buddies appear, you be there, okay? And you carry signs, and smile, that say: "LESBIANS FOR REAGAN!" (1985)

Clinton makes it a point to continuously interact with her audience. She does so by using set phrases ("You know?", "How many of you . . . ?"; "And did you notice . . . ?"; "Have you ever . . . ?"), asking for audience response ("I am interested in finding out more about my audiences"), and ending her act by walking offstage and up the theater aisle to the lobby, where she is available to autograph albums and talk with people who want to meet her. Several times during her routine, she tells the audience that an individual's requests and comments have later been incorporated into her routine ("I love it when people tell me stuff"). All of these devices work to strengthen her bond with the audience and to create an atmosphere of group participation.

Primary Subjects in Clinton's Humor

Clinton's routines address a range of topics. I have chosen four that are particularly characteristic of her worldview: (1) the Catholic church, (2) hostility toward men, (3) bawdy sexual humor, and (4) controversial political issues.[59]

Clinton calls herself "a recovering Catholic," often referring to her Catholic schooling (at "Our Lady of Psychological Warfare") and upbringing.[60] She sees herself as an iconoclast, making fun of the church and spurning the piety that seems to have caused her so much pain as a girl growing up under its influence. Through one-liners, run-on commentary, and wordplays, she lays waste all that is sacred (e.g., at one point in her 1985 performance she referred to the eucharistic wafer as "the deodorant pad of Christ"). Although they are couched in humor, one has the feeling that Clinton's criticisms of the church are deadly serious: "Now, you've probably read about the pope. The pope is very upset about these condom things. But just look what he's wearing on his head!" (1987). During her 1985 performance, Clinton asked four women from the audience who attended Catholic school when they were younger to come onstage to be her "backup band," which she named the "Vessels of Sin." In order to "qualify" for the band, they each had to answer one question about Catholic religious practice or doctrine. The questions she asks the first two women are "Are Gregorian notes square or round?" and "When you buy a pagan baby, do you buy it by the pound?" She turns to the last two women, who have attended Catholic school for a combined total of eight years, and instructs them: "Now, you two are going to work together on this one, okay? So, just get close now. [They wrap arms.] What you're going to do . . . I'm going to sing a song for you, and you have to tell me if this is an actual Catholic song—or the new Gay National S&M Anthem. All right, actual Catholic song or the new Gay National S&M Anthem? We've got eight years of experience on the line here. Are you ready? [Clinton begins to sing a litany.] 'Eat His body, drink His blood. Hallelu, hallelu, hallelu, hallelu . . . jah'" (1985).[61]

Clinton makes no apologies about her disgust concerning church dogma and church officials. She challenges what she sees as the superficiality of penance, hypocritical moral norms, and the pope himself:

> There's a guy who's been driving me crazy lately. I mean nuts . . . the pope. Pope John Paul George Ringo. Can you believe him? A grown man going all over the world kissing airports. [She motions towards the floor.] Get up! Get up! What are you looking at down there? He went to Canada. You know what he did in Canada? He made people up there nuts before he even got there. Women in Canada were crazed because before he went, he said, "I'm not going to go there. I will not perform any liturgical rituals there, because you use altar *girls*." And he said he only wanted altar *boys*. [Clinton hisses and encourages the audience to hiss.] I'll bet! And so what did he do for Canada? What he does to make it up to the women in Canada that he's offended, I guess: he raises to the level of sainthood a woman whose claim to fame is that she formed an order of housekeeping nuns! Don't do me any favors, Pops! Now, can't you see his new Encyclical on the Status of Women? [It will be called] "Spic-em and Span-em. Born to Clean." . . .
>
> I would like to talk to the pope, just for a sec. . . . I would say, "Your Largeness," or you could, "Your Extreme Roundheadness," [or] "Your Extreme Narrow-Mindedness." I would say to him, "Listen, if abortion is murder, why isn't fucking a felony?" I think it'd make a dynamite bumper sticker, don't you? And the trick of this bumper sticker is: you put it on *other* people's cars. (1985)

Clinton also uses her humor to criticize men. In fact, I was unable to detect a single instance in either the 1985 or the 1987 routine of her speaking positively about a man. Men are, at best, disregarded and, at worst, the targets for hostility and aggression. Clinton's humor about this subject is oppositional, satirizing men who are in positions of authority (such as governmental officials or the pope) or who simply appear ridiculous to her in trying to live up to a macho image.[62] The following is an assortment of her one-liners describing men:

> *On having a boyfriend as a teenager:*
> We're driving home in the car, and my mother says to me, "You'll never have a boyfriend if you're this heavy!" [Clinton's response was:] "Hey, there's a Kentucky Fried Chicken right over there!" (1985)
>
> *On women who have never "done it with a guy":*
> "Pure and proud" (1985).
>
> *On the first and only time she had intercourse with a man:*
> "He was about the size of a cocktail frank" (1985).
>
> *On men's valuation of large women:*
> "Guys don't like big women because they take up too much space" (1985)
>
> *On Ed McMahon:*
> "Doesn't it look like Ed McMahon probably ate his own children?" (1985)
>
> *On Phil Donahue:*
> "I can't really trust a man who has gray meringue for hair" (1987).
>
> *On various men in the Reagan administration:*
> "Have you noticed, too, that since Reagan has been in office there have been a lot more bran commercials?"
> *Donald Regan:* "The man has had a charisma bypass!";
> *Caspar Weinberger:* "What a slime!";
> *Oliver North:* "Based on a GI Joe Doll" (1987).

Clinton's jokes go beyond ridiculing the foolishness of men to the suggestion of open hostility and aggression against them.[63] In her survey of college students, Carol Mitchell detected two types of jokes about men that women particularly liked: (1) jokes whose theme is related to the female experiences, specifically jokes in which male sexual aggressiveness is ridiculed; and (2) jokes in which violence is done to a male by a female.[64] Clinton tells both kinds of jokes, making little attempt to disguise her intentions. In the following sequence of menstruation jokes, she comments on the "unspoken rule" that men are never supposed to actually see a sanitary napkin. She holds one up, waving it around, and notes: "They are *never* supposed to see these things, you know. . . ? And so, one of the fun things that I say to do at work, you know, they were never supposed to see these. You would think that if a guy saw one of these, it would kill him. So I say get 'em out! Having trouble with somebody at work? [She waves it around as if directed toward some particular man.] And it's so cheap, okay?" (1985)

Clinton delights in telling "bawdy" jokes, particularly those that make graphic reference to sexual activity. She excels in this area, breaking all the conventional rules about the "proper" topics of conversation for women in a public setting.[65] Clinton is not unique in including sexual humor in her comedy routines. Increasingly, mainstream women comedians such as Phyllis Diller and Joan Rivers use sex as a permissible humor topic. Rivers commented:

> sex is a good topic for everybody. Comedy is changing radically, thank goodness. We're all here because of Lenny Bruce—he broke the barrier. That means for the men as well as the women. Bruce said, "This is what I'm talking about and it's really true." So, obviously, sex comes out of that. But it has nothing to do with women and men. I talk about sex in my act about as far as I would talk about it in private with my friends. I don't know what the barriers are because I just pretend I'm in a livingroom. I guess you could talk more freely in the livingroom than you did ten years ago, but I'm not aware of it.[66]

In contrast to Joan Rivers, Clinton is unusual in that she uses sexual humor, although she does not make women the butt of her jokes. Folklorist Gershon Legman, well known for his work on sexual humor, apparently had not encountered material like Clinton's when he wrote that "one fact strikingly evident in any collection of modern sexual folklore . . . is that this material has all been created by men, and that there is no place in it for women except as the butt . . . the situations presented almost completely lack a protagonist position in which a woman can identify herself, *as a woman*, with any human gratification or pride."[67] Some of Clinton's bawdy sexual humor concerns the shared experiences of both lesbian and straight women, particularly menstruation rituals and taboos: "You think that's fun? One great thing to do . . . now, a woman told me about this. She said another great thing to do is to get out one of your tampons and just put it behind your ear. [She pauses and gestures as if she's doing so.] It is a riot! Put it behind your ear, and just walk around. Walk around. And then when somebody comes up to you and says, 'Uh, you've got a tampon behind your ear,' then you say, 'Oh my God, where *is* my pencil?'" (1985). Moreover, Clinton's use of bawdy humor is iconoclastic in that she also celebrates the lesbian sexual experience:

> The reason I gained thirty pounds the summer before my senior year was because that summer was the first summer I spent away from home—at summer camp. Do you hear what I'm saying? And I was a waitress, okay? And in about two days [I] immediately fell in love with another one of the waitresses I was working with, okay? And we wanted each other. It was "hot," you know? I mean it was "hot." But unfortunately, we were both good little Catholic girls. . . . So, instead of each other—we ate peach cobbler and chocolate pies, *whole* chocolate pies. Uh-huh. And we ate Schnecken. Do you know what Schnecken is? I'll tell you. It's this hot, sticky, swirly, caramel, cinnamony bun. [She pauses and then carefully enunciates with more sexual inference given to each word progressively.] Hot . . . sticky . . . swirly . . . cinnamon . . . buns. HOT . . . STICKY . . . SWIRLY . . . CINNAMON . . . BUNS. Do you hear where thirty pounds is happenin'? It was so beautiful and so delicious that you would want to kiss them before you even take a bite out of them, okay? Just like my girlfriend, yum! (1985)

Clinton also tackles controversial political issues with her incisive satirical commentary. Politics and current events are common subject matter for stand-up comedians; Clinton approaches these topics with feminist fervor.[68] In comparing the material in her two Austin performances, I noted a greater emphasis on overtly political issues in 1987. Clinton performs at political rallies and fund-raisers for the causes she supports. In her comedy routines, she is vehement in assailing right-wing legislators who work to restrict the rights of women or gays: "One of the things I did in the fall that was great was to do a benefit against the La Rouche Initiative. Now, the La Rouche Initiative—this was a guy, American Neanderthal—his idea, his idea was to quarantine people who had any kind of relation to the AIDS virus, alright? I mean, this man is clearly suffering from CRI, which those of you, yes, those of you in the health professions know that CRI is cranial rectal inversion. You like that? Know people at work who have it? Not a pretty thing to have, is it?" (1987)

In each of these four subject areas—jokes about the Catholic church, men, bawdy sexual humor, and politics—Clinton breaks the rules. The audience is incited to laughter because of repeated and unexpected shifting between the permitted and the taboo, the playful and the serious, fantasy and reality.[69] Clinton jokes about taboo subjects—or about socially acceptable subjects, but in a profane manner—in order to call dominant social structures and mainstream values into question. As I will attempt to demonstrate, this calling into question, or reversal, is the key to Clinton's unusual approach to stand-up comedy and to the way in which she uses her performances to do more than just entertain her audience.

Functional Aspects of Clinton's Humor, Particularly Humor as Subversion

Feminist humor is based on the perception that societies have generally been organized as systems of oppression and exploitation, and that the largest (but not the only) oppressed group has been the female. It is also based on the conviction that such oppression is undesirable and unnecessary. It is a humor based on visions of change. The persistent attitude that underlies feminist humor is the attitude of social revolution—that is, we are ridiculing a social system that can be, that must be changed. Female humor may ridicule a person or a system from an accepting point of view ("that's life"), while the non-acceptance of oppression characterizes feminist humor and satire.[70]

In her study of colleagues in the workplace, Coser outlines five functions of humor, noting that humor can serve as (1) entertainment, (2) a means of escape or release from a difficult situation, (3) self-validation for the humorist, (4) a mechanism to support or induce cohesion for a group or community of people, and (5) an expression of the desire to subvert established social orders or power structures.[71] These functions are all operative in Clinton's performances, and I will comment briefly on each. However, I give particular attention to the fifth function, since it is, I believe, the distinguishing mark of Clinton's humor.

First, certainly Clinton's routine is designed to entertain. There were times during both the 1985 and 1987 performances when the audiences were laughing so loudly and raucously that my tape recorder picked up little else. For a stand-up comedian, one of the nonnegotiable ground rules for a successful performance is the ability to amuse one's audience. I learned something from watching Clinton's performances, but most of all I had a great time.

Second, Clinton's humor also functions as a sort of pressure valve for herself and for her audience. As she puts it, "she who laughs, lasts" (1985). In performing against a mainstream societal background that stereotypes or devalues women in general, and is openly hostile to lesbians specifically, Clinton uses her humor as a survival mechanism. Clinton notes that "women laughing is a survival reflex."[72] However, instead of encouraging dissipation of rebellion by laughing at oppression, Clinton incites her audience to "talk back good."

Third, Clinton negotiates her performance in such a way that she is validated by the audience for her verbal skills and for her ability to make them laugh. During the performances I attended, she accomplished this with commendable results; in both instances, Clinton left her audience roaring with laughter and calling for an encore. As a performer using traditional and nontraditional tools of her trade, she must convince her audience of her competence as a stand-up comedian worthy of their time, attention, and financial support and her legitimacy in that role as a woman, a feminist, and a lesbian.

Fourth, I have already noted how Clinton encourages a sense of common identity and group cohesion with and among the audience. As such, her humor is a means of socialization, "of affirmation of common values, of teaching and learning, of asking for and giving support, of bridging differences."[73] Since much of Clinton's humor is adversarial, that is, descriptive of how she sees her role *over-against* what she considers to be oppressive social forces (i.e., the church, men, heterosexual bias, repressive political policy), she calls on the audience to accept—if only temporarily within the performance frame—a shared identity in order to perceive themselves in this adversarial position. She uses a number of techniques for engendering the notion that "we're all in this together," including rhetorical linguistic devices (e.g., "Ya'know?" or "Now, I know you'll understand this"), jokes that focus on the shared experiences of women (menstruation and rite-of-passage jokes), and audience participation ("Let's have a show of hands," or "How many of you have . . . ?").

Finally, and most importantly to this analysis, Clinton uses humor as a tool for subversion and transformation. Kaufman and Pabis argue that feminist humor, by virtue of its critique of male dominance, is inherently transformational: "Feminist humor is based on the observation that most modern societies are organized as systems of exploitation, and that the largest, but not the only oppressed group, has been women. It is also based on the idea that such systems can and must be changed, but it envisions positive changes."[74] Much like the bawdy Southern women described by Rayna Green, Clinton defies the rules by ridiculing and satirizing that which is supposedly sacred. Green states that Southern women's obscene tales are a form of counter-socialization, debunking and inverting social norms: "Women are not supposed to know or repeat such stuff. But they do and when they do, they speak ill of all that is sacred: men, the church, marriage, home, family, parents."[75]

In Clinton's performances, the tables are turned against those who would otherwise seek to victimize her. This stance of "nonacceptance" causes Clinton to use the frame of conventional performance (stand-up comedy) in an unconventional way. The setting, ground rules, audience, content, and style of Clinton's performance all contribute to its transformation into something more than an entertainment event. Through humor, Clinton confronts—and thereby calls into question—the status quo, to undermine authority, to exercise control, to refuse to play by the rules.[76] She encourages members of her audience to do likewise. This is the kind of threatening potential that Coser also noted in her study of humor, stating that women's humor "may be acceptable in some situations, but it is disapproved in those social situations in which there is danger of subverting implicit or explicit male authority. What is aggressive in humor is that it takes control temporarily out of the hands of those higher in the hierarchy."[77]

The transformation of a performance that is merely humorous into one that suggests subversion is potentially dangerous to those who support and maintain the social order. While still meeting some conventional expectations (e.g., the ability to make her audience laugh by standing before them telling jokes onstage), Clinton manipulates her craft in unexpected ways (by utilizing humor in exhorting the audience to take action against repressive social norms). Bauman describes phenomena such as this as the "emergent quality" of verbal performance:

> the participants are using the structured, conventional performance system itself as a resource for creative manipulation, as a base on which a range of communication transformations can be wrought. . . . The structured system stands available to them as a set of convenient expectations and associations, but these expectations and associations are further manipulated in innovative ways, by fashioning novel performances outside the conventional system, or working various transformational adaptations which turn performance into something else. [78]

Moreover, in deliberately violating cultural taboos, Clinton takes full advantage of the double-edged character of performance noted by Bauman: "[There is a] . . . documented tendency for performers to be both admired and feared—admired for their artistic skill and power and for their enhancement of experience they provide, feared because of the potential they represent for subverting and transforming the status quo. Here too may lie a reason for the equally persistent association between performers and marginality or deviance, for in the special emergent quality of performance the capacity for change may be highlighted and made manifest to the community."[79] Clinton sometimes uses her humor as a weapon, incorporating openly adversarial jokes about men, the church, and the social order. She contradicts two aspects of Mitchell's findings on gender differences in joke telling: (1) that women tell more jokes with women as the target of humor than men do, and (2) that "as a general rule, the aggressive and/or hostile jokes that women tell are less openly aggressive and hostile than the jokes men tell."[80]

Clinton's humor also provides a counter-example to Coser's findings about the way humor functions among people within societal contexts where power and prestige are distributed hierarchically.[81] Coser concludes that among hospital staff members humor functions in socially acceptable structures so as to *relax the distances between people, without seriously attempting to overturn the hierarchy.* In this way, the aggression of those lower in the hierarchy "is safely used only within the limits of social approval."[82] She notes, for example, that women staff members who told jokes in informal situations "hardly ever used their wit and their sense of humor" in more formal settings such as staff meetings.[83] When humor is used by "the less powerful" (in Coser's study, by junior members of the staff), it is socially acceptable only when presented "in the guise of an aggression upon a specifically mentioned and legitimate target."[84] Traditionally, in women's humor the "legitimate target" or scapegoat has often been themselves. Noting that in the majority of cases humor is used aggressively by the more powerful against the less powerful (she calls this "downward humor"), Coser states that "those who are 'on top' have more right to be aggressors; those who are low in the hierarchy are not as freely permitted this outlet, even if it appears under the disguise of humor."[85]

Clinton's performance differs with these conclusions in several aspects. First, while she works to establish a feeling of camaraderie with the audience, she also uses comedy to heighten the tensions, rather than relax the distances, between herself and other types of people. Her routines are full of examples of this, particularly in relationship to men. Second, in general Clinton uses neither herself nor other women as "primary targets" in her material. That is, her humor is neither self-denigrating nor misogynist, traits often found in the materials of popular women stand-up comedians in the past. Third, rather than functioning as a support mechanism for the social order, Clinton's humor works to subvert it. Using Coser's terminology, it is "upward humor," turning against the "more powerful" in an attempt to call them into question.

As I have suggested throughout this essay, Clinton intends to do more than entertain. She intimates this, for example, in one of the phrases she used several times in her 1987 performance: "You create the world; you invite the people in." By continually breaking the performance frame, she calls on the audience to participate in subversion. Clinton represents herself as a troublemaker, and, in asking the audience to identify with her, she implicates them in her rebellion:

> The gold glints in the hair are in honor of my new spirit guide for the '80s. Now, I know a lot of you have taken on a spirit guide. Do you have a spirit guide? No? Maybe you'd like mine. She's a multifaceted gal and she could, she's yours too? Okay now, the gold glints in the hair are because I've taken as my spirit guide—you're going to love this— Cruella Deville from the movie *101 Dalmatians*. Do you remember? Can you sing the theme song? [She gets someone in audience to sing it. The audience applauds.] But isn't that a perfect person to have as your spirit guide? A devil kind of gal! That's what we need. (1987)

Clinton moves beyond the confines of her performance by enjoining the audience to take their experience of the performance back into real-life situations.[86] In much the way that she uses a conventional genre—stand-up comedy—in an unconventional manner to call the status quo into question, she encourages her audience to reclaim their power to reject traditional social norms and create revolutionary ways of thinking and acting. Clinton makes little attempt to conceal her political purposes. Her description of feminist humor includes elements of critique, transcendence, and change:

> Feminist humor—as different from mainstream male and female humor—is active, based as it is on the possibility of change. . . . Feminist humor is not escapist. It is transformational. It transforms painful expression, and in transforming, it transcends them. It transcends the old dichotomy between serious and humorous—the one which says that serious is more real. Serious is truth. Humorous is less than real, trivial, trifling. Very often, I think, women try to "out-serious the boys." And we stay forever in painful, albeit comfortable, corners examining old wounds, old scars, old sufferings. Feminist humor moves us out of those

corners. Here is the reclamation of making light. We make light, light enough to move through our heavy issues. The power of this making light is measured only by the power of that old insult: "the women's movement lacks a sense of humor." Feminist humor is not absurdist; it is thoughtful, frontal, I call it "fish jerky humor"—it's good for the brain, and it gives you something to chew on. Feminist humor is a reclamation of the practical joke. It is *good* practice, an antidote against absurdity. Humor demands a physical, visible response. Unlike music and poetry readings, where women can look like they're involved, but be thinking about what they're going to eat after, humor demands a certain response. It demands a presence. It demands that women laugh, and in that laughing that women put their bodies on the line. I think that's very good practice. The whole world hates the happy women, and it does its best to keep us apart. Times when women are laughing together are times which suggest and give intimations of how we can be together in community, and I think that's what we're all thinking about. They suggest another dimension, where separations and divisions are bridged. I don't mean to suggest some otherworldly kind of karmic zone, some transcendent leap into a world that is "oh, so beautiful." It's a very real place where, because we are present to ourselves, we are absent to the world of men—where we are thus present and absent at the same time. It is a utopic dimension in the here and now, and it is predicated on the sharing of joy. Feminist humor is not a compendium of jokes or reversal; it is a radical analysis of our being in the world, based on our commitment to our right to be joyful. In the context of male humor, our humor has too often been used for female binding. We have told jokes on ourselves, we have trivialized our actions, we have not taken ourselves seriously as we have tried to keep each other in place. The difference between the female binding of male humor and the feminist bonding of fumerists is that we are encouraging each other to be all that we can be. Male penile humor—the ultimate in stand-up comedy—is based on the hierarchical power structure of the putdown. Fumerists are more "stand-with" comedians. Each of us is equal to the task of making light, shedding light on our experiences, encouraging each other to change and move. [87]

Using her role as performer, Clinton exhorts the audience to use the "power of the old double reverse" and to subvert the established social order in the interests of a feminist vision. This is a trademark of her performance, one that she makes explicit at the conclusion of her comedy routines:

> But we call [my second album] "Making Waves." This is another one of those warnings that we always get, generally when we've really started to rock the boat. And I think it's time that women, feminists, lesbians, all of us learn to take the power of the old "double reverse." And that's why we watch football sometimes, we take those insults that we always get—"Oh, you castrating, ballbusting bitch!"—as *invitations;* and those warnings—"Don't make waves!"—as *welcomes.* So I encourage you to keep taking the slide down "the great turquoise waterslide called life" to make waves. Big waves! Tsunamis! *Whatever* it takes to turn the tide. (conclusion of 1985 performance)
>
> Somebody once said to me, "Kate, when you get up in the morning, each one of us has to decide if we're going to save or savor the world." And when I came out, I told a friend of mine that I was a lesbian, and she said to me, among other things—this is an ex-friend—she said to me very scornfully, "Well, you've certainly made a commitment to joy in your life!" And I almost denied it, but she's right. As a lesbian, as gay people in this world, we have made a commitment to joy in our lives, and Joy is not an easy woman to please! And we know we have to work at it, we really do. And we know it's not a question of either/or: either save or savor the world. We know we have to do both: save *and* savor the world. And it's a world that would like to gentrify the wildness of our souls, and just lock us up completely. And we know that we can't do that, we know that we have to do both, save and savor the world. So here in Austin, as always, keep it up. Keep up the good fight, and be bold! Be very bold! But most of all, be *bad!* (conclusion of 1987 performance)

In affirming and supporting women, Clinton exhorts audience members to validate their own experiences and to develop a stance of non-acceptance. Moreover, she incites women to action, encouraging them not to be afraid to laugh about—and thereby to be critical of—social norms that privilege men and male dominance. Here Clinton moves beyond her role as comedian to become a social critic who is at the same time a political activist, using humor as her tool for subversion and transformation.

Notes

M. Jane Young, Richard Bauman, Kay Turner, Laura Lein, and Jim Foley were kind enough to comment on earlier drafts of this essay. I thank them for their suggestions and insights. Most of all, I thank Kate Clinton for her wicked and inspiring humor. She makes us laugh, and these days a good laugh can be hard to find.

1. Gloria Kaufman, "Introduction," in *Pulling Our Own Strings: Feminist Humor and Satire,* eds. Gloria Kaufman and Mary Kay Blakely (Bloomington: Indiana University Press, 1980), 16.

2. Quotes from Clinton's routines are followed by the year of the performance in which they occurred. Clinton's April 4, 1987, shows took place in a very different setting, demonstrating elevation in her status as a performer. Her performances at Ellington's—a private club with the atmosphere and accoutrements of a nightclub—seemed classier and less "funky." Ellington's has a cash bar; the audience is seated around cocktail tables. Bamboo plants, reed mats, and pink plastic flamingos were used to decorate the stage, supplementing the dark walls of the club. Rather than appearing alone, Clinton was preceded by an opening act, Ann Reed, who was introduced as a feminist folk singer. Clinton performed in two consecutive shows, in contrast to the single performance of 1985. As in 1985, the shows were sold out. In her 1987 Austin performances, Clinton included a "channeling" routine in which she mystically assumed the persona of a "forty-thousand-year-old lesbian named Mona." Mona told the audience something about her own past experiences and then asked, "Is this a sort of tribal meeting right now?"

3. Richard Bauman, "Verbal Art as Performance," *American Anthropologist* 77 (1975), 290–312. All citations are taken from the book form of this essay by Richard Bauman: "Verbal Art as Performance," in *Verbal Art as Performance* (Prospect Heights, Ill.: Waveland Press, 1984), 3–58.

4. For an introduction to the performance approach, see Américo Paredes and Richard Bauman, eds., *Toward New Perspectives in Folklore* (Austin: University of Texas Press, 1972).

5. See Mary Douglas, "The Social Control of Cognition: Some Factors in Joke Perception," *Man* 3 (1968), 361–76.

6. Bauman, "Verbal Art as Performance," 4.

7. For an analysis of various approaches to the study of humor from an anthropological perspective, see Mahadev L. Apte, *Humor and Laughter: An Anthropological Approach* (Ithaca and London: Cornell University Press, 1985).

8. See Joan B. Levine, "The Feminine Routine," *Journal of Communication* 26, no. 3 (1976), 173–75, for a statistical analysis of the material used by well-known male and female comedians.

9. Mary Kay Blakely, "Dear Gloria," in *Pulling Our Own Strings: Feminist Humor and Satire,* eds. Gloria Kaufman and Mary Kay Blakely (Bloomington: Indiana University Press, 1980), 10.

10. Clinton began her 1987 routine by commenting on her regret that the Lady Longhorns, the well-known women's basketball team at the University of Texas, lost the championship finals. She mentioned Austin's active lesbian community, and she satirized pseudo-spiritualism by soliciting audience response to her question "Do you like my aura? I just knew I could ask you that in Austin." These are devices for establishing rapport with the audience and creating a bond of similar interests that become a foundation for her humor.

11. Denise Collier and Kathleen Beckett, *Spare Ribs: Women in the Humor Biz* (New York: St. Martin's Press, 1980), xi–xii.

12. Joan Rivers, quoted in Lee Israel, "Joan Rivers and How She Got That Way," *Ms.*, October 1984, 110.

13. Bauman, "Verbal Art as Performance," 28.

14. Ibid., 27.

15. Some journalists have noted the recent increase in the number of women stand-up comics who are trying to establish themselves in the entertainment business. Suggesting that newer female comedians owe a debt of gratitude to Lily Tomlin, Joan Rivers, and Phyllis Diller for so visibly invading a male domain, McGuigan and Huck report that "today one hopeful in three is a woman. At the Comedy Store in Los Angeles . . . the ratio of female to male performers has jumped from 1 in 100 to 1 in 10." Cathleen McGuigan and Janel Huck, "The New Queens of Comedy: Women Comics Aren't Putting Themselves Down When They Do Stand-up," *Newsweek,* April 30, 1984, 58. See also Stewart Klein, "The Queens of Comedy," *Harper's Bazaar,* August 1983, 166.

16. I have intentionally chosen to use the word *comedian* to describe Clinton and all other women comics, since the term *comedienne* is itself a diminutive form.

17. David Zippin, "Sex Differences and the Sense of Humor," *Psychoanalytic Review* 53 (1966), 214. The notion that humor (particularly sexual humor) is alien to women has been popular with a range of authors. For other examples of male bias in this literature, see Gary Alan Fine, "Obscene Joking across Culture," *Journal of Communication* 26 (1976), 134–40; Sigmund Freud, *Jokes and Their Relation to the Unconscious,* trans. and ed. James Strachey (New York: Norton, 1960), 99–101; Martin Grotjahn, *Beyond Laughter* (New York: McGraw-Hill, 1957), 37; Gershon Legman, *Rationale of the Dirty Joke, An Analysis of Sexual Humor* (New York: Castle Books, 1968), 10, 12, 319–25; Naomi Weisstein, "Why We Aren't Laughing . . . Any More," *Ms.,* November 1973, 49–51, 88–90. For a summary and analysis of this trend, see Mary Jo Neitz, "Humor, Hierarchy, and the Changing Status of Women," *Psychiatry* 42 August 1980), 211–23.

18. Rose Laub Coser, "Laughter among Colleagues: A Study of the Social Functions of Humor among the Staff of a Mental Hospital," *Psychiatry* 23 (February 1960), 85. Unlike others (see above), Coser does not suggest that women have no sense of humor or do not tell jokes. Instead, she notes that in mixed gender staff meetings women rarely made jokes, although some of them demonstrated excellent senses of humor and made witty remarks in other settings.

19. Apte, *Humor and Laughter,* 81. Although Apte acknowledges (p. 76) that women's humor is not totally constrained, that the social constraints that do delimit women's humor are not universal, and that not all women conform to them, he nonetheless makes a number of generalizations about women's humor that Kate Clinton contradicts. These include the contentions that women's humor generally lacks the aggressive quality of men's humor: that it does not attempt to belittle others (p. 70); that images of women as tricksters or clowns are not found in the narrative of any culture (pp. 70–71); and that women do not engage in slapstick humor or "horseplay" (p. 71). Apte observes that some types of humor usually absent from women's expressive behavior in the public domain are present in the private domain, where there are all-women audiences (p. 76). I contend that Clinton blurs the conceptual boundaries between the public and private domains, since humorous treatment of women's "private" or personal experiences are the essence of her public performances.

20. Alice Sheppard, "From Kate Sanborn to Feminist Psychology: The Social Context of Women's Humor, 1885–1985," *Psychology of Women Quarterly* 10 (1986), 167. Sheppard notes that "although American history books and literary anthologies are generally silent on the topic of women's humor in the nineteenth century, popular women humorists existed, contributing to newspapers and magazines; writing short stories, children's books, and novels; and earning reputations as brilliant and witty conversationalists" (p. 159).

21. The differences, actual or imagined, between the expressive patterns of women and men have been the subject of some debate. Among scholars such as Lakoff, Phillips, O'Barr, and Thorne and Henley, there is disagreement about the degree to which women and men use distinctive forms of speech and gesture. Without going into the particulars in great detail, I am taken by O'Barr's argument that what had formerly been identified as "women's language" is, in fact, "powerless language." Relevant to my analysis is O'Barr's finding that "powerless language" is less convincing and less credible to the listener. My reference to "stereotypical patterns of expression among women and men" relies on just that: stereotypes rather than reality. Thorne and Henley enumerate these, and I have applied a few of them in my description of Clinton's performance style simply to illustrate the way in which she, as a woman, must negotiate her performance against a male standard. See Robin Lakoff, *Language and Women's Place* (New York: Octagon Books, 1976); William M. O'Barr, "Speech Styles in the Courtroom," in *Linguistic Evidence: Language, Power, and Strategy in the Courtroom* (New York: Academic Press), 61–91; Susan U. Phillips, "Sex Differences and Language," *Annual Review of Anthropology 9* (1980), 523–44; Barrie Thorne and Nancy Henley, "Difference and Dominance: An Overview of Language, Gender and Society," in *Language and Sex* (Rowley, Mass.: Newbury Publishers), 5–42.

22. McGuigan and Huck, "The New Queens of Comedy," 58. Shelley Levitt notes, in interviewing "four of the funniest women in America" (Rita Rudner, Beverly Mickins, Carol Suskind, and Carol Leifer), that while all of these comedians tell jokes about the shortcomings of men and the strengths of women, much of their material still focuses on bemoaning the difficulties of finding a "good man." Shelley Levitt, "Take My Boyfriend—Please!" *Mademoiselle* 92, no. 5 (1986), 170–73, 256.

23. Adrienne Rich has noted that "lesbian existence comprises both the breaking of a taboo and the rejection of a compulsory way of life." "Compulsory Heterosexuality and Lesbian Existence," *SIGNS:*

Journal of Women in Culture and Society 5, no. 4 (1980), 649. Certainly Clinton stresses both of these characteristics in her humor.

24. Bauman, "Verbal Art as Performance," 28.

25. There are several ways in which the characteristics of Clinton's humor are similar to those of a Texas "madam" described by Robbie Davis Johnson. Both women (1) use a tone of self-confidence that refuses to be self-denigrating, (2) tell profemale jokes that are triggered by men's antifemale sentiment, (3) enjoy bawdy sexual humor, and (4) take pride in their verbal skills. See Robbie Davis Johnson, "Folklore and Women: A Social International Analysis of the Folklore of a Texas Madam," *Journal of American Folklore* 86 (1973), 215.

26. For a complete list of what have been termed "women's language" traits, see Lakoff, *Language and Women's Place.*

27. Bauman, "Verbal Art as Performance," 29.

28. Abby Stein, quoted in Julia Klein, "The New Stand-Up Comics: Can You Be a Funny Woman without Making Fun of Women?" *Ms.*, October 1984, 124.

29. I have recently heard that Clinton has begun to perform before more mainstream, mixed-gender audiences. Her material will undoubtedly reflect this change.

30. Bauman, "Verbal Art as Performance," 31.

31. Ibid., 30.

32. Ibid., 11.

33. Collier and Beckett, *Spare Ribs,* 1.

34. McGuigan and Huck note that, in contrast to the routines of those who are more established in the professional comedy circuit, the material of many up-and-coming women comedians no longer focuses on self-deprecation. "The New Queens of Comedy," 58.

35. In comparing the recordings of comedy routines by four popular male comics (George Carlin, Robert Klein, Bill Cosby, and David Steinberg) and four female comics (Totie Fields, Moms Mabley, Phyllis Diller, and Lily Tomlin), Levine found that the women used self-deprecatory humor 63 percent of the time, while the male comics only did so in 12 percent of their material. See Levine, "The Feminine Routine," 174.

36. Israel, "Joan Rivers," 110.

37. Phyllis Diller, quoted in Collier and Beckett, *Spare Ribs,* 3.

38. Susan Kalcik, "Like Anne's Gynecologist or the Time I Was Almost Raped: Personal Narratives in Women's Rap Groups," *Journal of American Folklore* 88, no. 347 (1975), 5.

39. Coser, "Laughter among Colleagues," 87.

40. Cantor reported that controlled statistical studies in both 1970 and 1975 revealed it was still funnier to see a woman, rather than a man, as the butt of a joke. Her analysis provided evidence that in 1975 the antifemale bias still existed, and that it was the sex of the victim in the joke—rather than the sex of the dominator—that determined the effect. That is, more people believed it was funnier to watch a female be ridiculed than a male, whether the dominating agent was a male or a female and whether the subject (the reader of the joke) was a male or a female. For both males and females, the condition associated with the highest degree of humor was that of the male dominating the female. Joanne R. Cantor, "What Is Funny to Whom?: The Role of Gender," *Journal of Communication* 26, no. 3 (1976), 164–72. Neitz, however, argues that when a joke is a sexual joke, Cantor's generalizations appear to be less true. While several surveys reported that men enjoy sexual jokes more than women do, a study by Hassett and Houlihan qualified this. They found that men enjoyed sexual humor that was judged sexist by both men and women, but that they did not enjoy sexual humor when the status of men was threatened. In contrast, women did not enjoy misogynist sexual humor, but did enjoy sexual humor that was not sexist. Neitz, "Humor, Hierarchy," 219, citing J. Hassett and J. Houlihan, "Different Jokes for Different Folks," *Psychology Today* 12, no. 8 (1979), 64–71.

41. Rayna Green, "Magnolias Grow in Dirt," *Southern Folklore* 4, no. 4 (1977), 32–33.

42. Israel, "Joan Rivers and How She Got That Way," 114.

43. Joan Rivers, quoted in ibid., 110.

44. Ibid. In 1987, Clinton closed her act with a "channeling" routine in which she pretended to be going into a trance in order to become the mouthpiece for a forty-thousand-year-old lesbian named Mona. Mona—a self-described activist, tether ball champion, and bull dyke—took impromptu questions from the audience. This was the only attempt Clinton made during her Austin performances to use humorous personas or characters, and, in my estimation, it was not terribly effective.

45. Joan Rivers, quoted in Collier and Beckett, *Spare Ribs,* 10–11.

46. Lily Tomlin, quoted in Gloria Kaufman and Mary Kay Blakely, "Clicking," in *Pulling Our Own Strings: Feminist Humor and Satire,* eds. Gloria Kaufman and Mary Kay Blakely (Bloomington: Indiana University Press, 1980), 66.

47. Lily Tomlin, quoted in Diane Judge, "Talking with Lily Tomlin," *Redbook,* January 1981, 16.

48. Susan Dworkin, "Roseanne Barr: The Disgruntled Housewife as Stand-up Comedian," *Ms.,* July–August 1987, 106.

49. Ibid. Like Clinton's, Barr's humor is often sarcastic and aggressive. Commenting on women's self-deprecating humor, she proclaimed, "Hey, I will not be insulted anymore. I will not hate myself anymore. There is no way to beat me, because I am so pissed."

50. In fact, in the fall of 1988, Roseanne Barr first appeared in the leading role of the ABC television sitcom "Roseanne." Apparently television executives believed that her humor would be palatable enough to a mixed-gender audience to risk putting the show in a prime-time slot.

51. Joan Rivers, quoted in Collier and Beckett, *Spare Ribs,* 7. McGuigan and Huck suggest that many of the up-and-coming women stand-up comedians joke not only about sex but also about such topics as parents, cars, and politics. The authors argue that there is no longer anything called "women's comedy," because women comics are not just joking about feminine hygiene and blind dates anymore. They cite the example of Sandra Bernhard, who played in comedy clubs for eight years before she was offered a co-starring role in the film *The King of Comedy,* and who asserts: "Both men and women can relate to both the man and woman in me." McGuigan and Huck, "The New Queens of Comedy," 58–59.

52. Mary Kay Blakely, "Kate Clinton on the Feminist Comedy Circuit," *Ms.,* October 1984, 128.

53. Carol Mitchell, "The Sexual Perspective in the Appreciation and Interpretation of Jokes," *Western Folklore* 36 (1977), 305.

54. Thorne and Henley, "Difference and Dominance," 12.

55. Carol Mitchell, "Hostility and Aggression toward Males in Female Joke Telling," *Frontiers* 3, no. 3 (1978), 21.

56. Joan Rivers, quoted in Collier and Beckett, *Spare Ribs,* 10.

57. Neitz notes that "cohesion is also a result in situations in which a witty remark is ostensibly directed against a target but actually is intended to reaffirm the collectivity and the values held in common." Neitz, *Humor, Hierarchy,* 215. See also Stanley H. Brandes, *Metaphors of Masculinity: Sex and Status in Andalusian Folklore* (Philadelphia: University of Pennsylvania Press, 1980), 87–97; and Apte, *Humor and Laughter,* for insights on the use of humor in order to promote shared group identity.

58. Coser, "Laughter among Colleagues," 90.

59. In his comparative study of the anthropology of humor, Apte notes that common topics for humor in all-women gatherings include "men's physical appearance, their social behavior, their idiosyncrasies, their sexuality, their status-seeking activities, and their religious rites. These characteristics are generally presented in an exaggerated and mocking fashion." Apte, *Humor and Laughter,* 76.

Certainly Clinton makes light of all of these topics, although a great deal of her material focuses on women's existence apart from men, especially with the lesbian community.

60. In her observations about joke telling among the women at a brothel, Johnson (in "Folklore and Women") notes that there are two types of jokes "the girls" especially like to tell: antimale jokes and antireligious jokes. Clinton shares this passion.

61. For an interesting comparison, see Apte, *Humor and Laughter,* 78, for a description of how Kwakiutl women mock the religious ceremonies of men in their tribe.

62. Mitchell notes that the female college students she surveyed expressed their appreciation for "gross jokes" in which men were made to appear disgusting. This parallels Clinton's attempts to denigrate men in her material. Mitchell, "Hostility and Aggression," 317.

63. Kaufman and Pabis contend that feminist humor is more "pick-up" than it is "put-down" humor, while mainstream or nonfeminist humor is "attack humor," built on and continuing to build negative stereotypes. They argue that feminist humor does not attack people, although it may attack ideas. Gloria Kaufman and Madeleine Pabis, "The Politics of Humor: A Feminist View," videotape produced and directed by Gloria Kaufman. This simply does not hold true of Kate Clinton, who makes women laugh by pointing out the absurdity of particular men (often public figures) and of men in general.

64. Mitchell, "The Sexual Perspective," 306.

65. In much the same way, but in more private settings, the older Southern women in Green's study used "bawdy tales [to] debunk and defy rules." Green, "Magnolias Grow in Dirt," 33.

66. Joan Rivers, quoted in Collier and Beckett, *Spare Ribs,* 8.

67. Clinton, in performing her material as though she were close friends with the women in the audience, contradicts Legman's assertion that sexual jokes are actually "a disguised aggression or verbal assault directed against the listener, who is always really the butt." Gershon Legman, *Rationale of the Dirty Joke: An Analysis of Sexual Humor* (New York: Breaking Point, 1975), 20.

68. Kaufman and Pabis note that in her stand-up comedy Whoopi Goldberg also focuses on controversial political issues, including race relations and the exploitation of Third World Countries by the United States. Kaufman and Pablis, "The Politics of Humor."

69. See Maria Weigle, "Women as Verbal Artists," *Frontiers* 3, no. 3 (1978), 5–7, for her discussion of the prevalence of these tensions in women's verbal art.

70. Kaufman, "Introduction," 13.

71. Coser, "Laughter among Colleagues," 82.

72. Kate Clinton, "Making Waves!" recording, Wyscrack Records, 1984.

73. Coser, "Laughter among Colleagues," 83.

74. Kaufman and Pabis, "The Politics of Humor."

75. Green, "Magnolias Grow in Dirt," 33.

76. Emerson (1969) discusses the negotiation of humor usage as a means of providing a useful channel for covert communication on taboo topics. She argues that normal social rules about proper subjects for discussion can be suspended through negotiation between the joke teller and the audience: "When parties succeed in negotiating such agreements, they establish a presumption of trust. Not only can they trust each other in routine matters, but they share complicity for rule violations which potentially can be extended. Thus, the contradictory pressures of social settings may encourage the formation of subgroups where an independent culture, subversive to the general culture, flourishes." John P. Emerson, "Negotiating the Serious Import of Humor," *Sociometry* 32, no. 2 (1969), 180.

77. Coser, "Laughter among Colleagues," 86.

78. Bauman, "Verbal Art as Performance," 34–35.

79. Ibid., 22.

80. Mitchell, "Hostility and Aggression," 20. Neitz, on the other hand, notes that the jokes told among a group of radical feminists were more overtly hostile, and the mention of castration more direct, than in the data reported by Mitchell. She found that these more radical women refused to participate in anti-woman jokes when told by outsiders. Neitz, "Humor, Hierarchy," 221. I recognize the problems inherent in trying to make generalizations about the functions of humor in different contexts. Mitchell's research only involved joke telling among college students in an academic setting, whereas Clinton's humor occurs in the formal setting of a professional stand-up comedy routine. I compare the two only in the hopes of identifying performance "ground rules" that appear to be operative for Clinton and may be unusual to the ways in which women conventionally use humor.

81. Coser's study involved both female and male staff of a mental hospital. Her findings about how those with prestige use humor differently from those without prestige have interesting correlations to O'Barr's theory of "powerful" and "powerless language."

82. Coser, "Laughter among Colleagues," 95. Structuralist-functionalist explanations of humor abound, although they do not adequately account for the subversive intent of Clinton's comedy.

Douglas, for example, acknowledges the way that humor can point to the arbitrary nature of social norms, but she believes that humor is ultimately "frivolous in that it produces no real alternative, only an exhilarating sense of freedom from form in general." Douglas, "The Social Control of Cognition," 365. Similarly, Brandes argues that "political humor dissipates energy or deflects it away from direct political action." Stanley H. Brandes, "Peaceful Protest: Spanish Political Humor in a Time of Crisis," *Western Folklore* 346. However, Babcock-Abrahams notes that one of the pitfalls of the conventional structural-functionalist approach is that it tends toward teleological interpretations. Symbolic forms "are analyzed in terms of the function they play in maintaining the social system—as mechanisms of social control in the form of 'ritualized rebellion,' 'licensed aggression,' or some other steam valve." Barbara Babcock-Abrahams, "A Tolerated Margin of Mess: The Trickster and His Tales Reconsidered," *Journal of the Folklore Institute* 11, no. 3 (1975), 157. Apte observes that functional explanations focus on humor as the release of tension, avoidance of conflict, enforcement of social control, and thereby the reinforcement of social harmony and stability. This approach emphasizes the eventual reduction of hostility and the maintenance of social cohesion. Apte notes, however, that structural-functionalist assertions of this type are educated guesses at best. Because many functionalist explanations are merely hypotheses that cannot be tested, it is difficult to demonstrate that joking actually serves these functions. He concludes that humor can function either as a lubricant to smooth social interactions or as a way of expressing hostility and aggression. Apte, *Humor and Laughter,* 60–62, 261.

83. Coser, "Laughter among Colleagues," 84.

84. Ibid., 87.

85. Ibid., 85.

86. Compare this with Phyllis Diller's claim: "There's no reality whatsoever in my act. It's all for fun." Collier and Beckett, *Spare Ribs,* 4.

87. Kate Clinton, quoted in Kaufman and Pabis, "The Politics of Humor."

SELECTED BIBLIOGRAPHY

Historical Overviews of Women's Humor in America

Bruère, Martha B. and Mary R. Beard. *Laughing Their Way: Women's Humor in America*. New York: Macmillan, 1934.

Curry, Jane. "Women as Subjects and Writers of Nineteenth Century American Humor." Diss. University of Michigan, 1975.

Dresner, Zita. "Twentieth Century American Women Humorists." Diss. University of Maryland, 1982.

———. "Women's Humor." *Humor in America: A Research Guide to Genres and Topics*. Ed. Lawrence Mintz. Westport, CT: Greenwood Press, 1988.

Gale, Steven H., ed. *Encyclopedia of American Humorists*. New York: Garland, 1988.

Kaufman, Gloria and Mary K. Blakely. *Pulling Our Own Strings: Feminist Humor and Satire*. Bloomington: Indiana University Press, 1980.

Little, Judy. "Humoring the Sentence: Women's Dialogic Comedy." *Women's Comic Visions*. Ed. June Sochen. Detroit: Wayne State University Press, 1991. Pp. 19–32.

MacKethan, Lucinda H. "Mother Wit: Humor in Afro-American Women's Autobiography." *Studies in American Humor*, 4 (1985): 51–61.

Morris, Linda A. F. *Women Vernacular Humorists in Nineteenth-Century America: Ann Stephens, Frances Whitcher, and Marietta Holley*. New York: Garland, 1990.

Sanborn, Kate. *The Wit of Women.* New York: Funk & Wagnalls, 1886.

Sheppard, Alice. "From Kate Sanborn to Feminist Psychology: The Social Context of Women's Humor, 1885–1985." *Psychology of Women Quarterly,* 10 (1986): 155–69.

Toth, Emily. "A Laughter of Their Own: Women's Humor in the United States." *Critical Essays on American Humor.* Ed. William Bedford Clark and W. Craig Turner. Boston: G. K. Hall, 1984. Pp. 199–215.

Walker, Nancy. *A Very Serious Thing: Women's Humor and American Culture.* Minneapolis: University of Minnesota Press, 1988.

————. "Wit, Sentimentality, and the Image of Women in the Nineteenth Century." *American Studies,* 22.2 (Fall 1981): 5–22.

Walker, Nancy, and Zita Dresner. *Redressing the Balance: American Women's Literary Humor from Colonial Times to the 1980s.* Jackson: University Press of Mississippi, 1988.

Weisstein, Naomi. "Why We Aren't Laughing . . . Any More," *Ms.,* 2.2 (Nov. 1973): 49–51+.

Works on Individual Humorists

Kate Clinton

Pershing, Linda. "There's a Joker in the Menstrual Hut: A Performance Analysis of Comedian Kate Clinton." *Women's Comic Visions.* Ed. June Sochen. Detroit: Wayne State University Press, 1991. Pp. 193–236.

Fanny Fern

Greenwood, G. "Fanny Fern: Mrs. Sara Willis Parton; Birth Into Literary Life." *Legacy,* 5 (1988): 72.

Harris, Susan K. "Inscribing and Defining: The Many Voices of Fanny Fern's Ruth Hall." *Style*, 22 (1988): 612–27.

Warren, Joyce W. "Legacy Profile: Fanny Fern (1811–1872)." *Legacy*, 2 (1985): 54–60.

Wood, Ann Douglas. "The 'Scribbling Women' and Fanny Fern: Why Women Wrote." *American Quarterly*, 23 (Spring 1971): 3–24.

Marietta Holley

Curry, Jane. *Samantha Rastles the Woman Question.* Urbana: University of Illinois Press, 1983.

Graulich, Melody. "Wimmen is My Theme, and Also Josiah: The Forgotten Humor of Marietta Holley." *American Transcendental Quarterly*, 47–48 (1980): 187–98.

Morris, Linda A. F. "Marietta Holley." *Women Vernacular Humorists in Nineteenth-Century America.* New York: Garland, 1990.

Williams, Patricia. "The Crackerbox Philosopher as Feminist: The Novels of Marietta Holley." *American Humor*, 7 (1980): 16–21.

Winter, Kate. "Marietta Holley, 'Josiah Allen's Wife' (1836–1926)." *Legacy*, 2 (1985): 3–5.

———. *Marietta Holley: Life with "Josiah Allen's Wife."* Syracuse: Syracuse University Press, 1984.

Zora Neale Hurston

Lowe, John. "Hurston, Humor, and the Harlem Renaissance." *The Harlem Renaissance Re-examined.* Ed. Victor Kramer. New York: AMS Press, 1987. Pp. 283–313.

Sarah Kemble Knight

Thorpe, Peter. "Sarah Kemble Knight and the Picaresque Tradition." *CLA Journa*, 10 (December 1966): 114–21.

Stephens, Robert O. "The Odyssey of Sarah Kemble Knight." *CLA Journal*, 7 (1964): 247–55.

Alice Duer Miller

Dresner, Zita. "Heterodite Humor: Alice Duer Miller and Florence Guy Seabury." *Journal of American Culture*, 10.3 (1987): 33–38.

Schwarz, Judith. *Radical Feminists of Heterodoxy: Greenwich Village 1912–1940*. Lebanon: New Victoria Press, 1982.

Anna Cora Mowatt

Barnes, Eric Wollencott. *The Lady of Fashion*. New York: Scribner's, 1954.

Dorothy Parker

Bone, Martha. "Dorothy Parker and New Yorker Satire." *Dissertation Abstracts* (1986): 2689A.

Bunkers, Suzanne L. "'I am Outraged Womanhood': Dorothy Parker as Feminist and Social Critic." *Regionalism and the Female Imagination* (1978): 25–34.

Grant, Thomas. "Dorothy Parker." *American Humorists*. Ed. Stanley Trachtenberg. Pt. 2. Detroit: Gale, 1982. Pp. 370.

Toth, Emily. "Dorothy Parker, Erica Jong, and New Feminist Humor." *Regionalism and the Female Imagination* (1977–1978): 70–85.

Florence Guy Seabury

Grant, Thomas. "Feminist Humorist of the 1920s: The 'Little Insurrections' of Florence Guy Seabury." *New Perspectives on Women's Comedy*. Ed. Regina Barreca. New York: Gordon and Breach, 1992. Pp. 157–67.

Frances Miriam Whitcher

Morris, Linda A. "Frances Miriam Whitcher: Social Satire in the Age of Gentility." *Last Laughs: Perspectives on*

Women and Comedy. Ed. Regina Barreca. London: Gordon and Breach, 1988. Pp. 99–116,

Morris, Linda A. *Women's Humor in the Age of Gentility: The Life and Works of Frances Miriam Whitcher.* Syracuse: Syracuse University Press, 1992.

O'Donnell, Thomas F. "The Return of the Widow Bedott: Mrs. F. M. Whitcher of Whitesboro and Elmira." *New York History*, 55 (1974): 5–35.

INDEX

Recover